T0319604

Destructive Creation

AMERICAN BUSINESS,
POLITICS, AND SOCIETY

Series editors
Andrew Wender Cohen, Pamela Walker Laird,
Mark H. Rose, and Elizabeth Tandy Shermer

Books in the series American Business, Politics, and Society
explore the relationships over time between governmental
institutions and the creation and performance of markets,
firms, and industries large and small. The central theme of
this series is that politics, law, and public policy—understood
broadly to embrace not only lawmaking but also the
structuring presence of governmental institutions—have been
fundamental to the evolution of American business from
the colonial era to the present. The series aims to explore, in
particular, developments that have enduring consequences.

Destructive Creation

American Business
and the
Winning of World War II

Mark R. Wilson

PENN

UNIVERSITY OF PENNSYLVANIA PRESS

PHILADELPHIA

Published by
University of Pennsylvania Press
Philadelphia, Pennsylvania 191041-4112
www.upenn.edu/pennpress

Printed in the United States of America
on acid-free paper
1 3 5 7 9 10 8 6 4 2

A Cataloging-in-Publication record is available from the Library of Congress
ISBN 978-0-8122-4833-3

For Christine

Contents

Introduction

World War II was won not just by brave soldiers and sailors but also by mountains of matériel. This was true even in times and places where guts were at a premium, as during the Allied invasion of Normandy, in June 1944. On D-Day and in the days that followed, American GIs and their British and Canadian counterparts were sometimes disappointed (and killed) by their own machines, too many of which sank below the waves, missed their targets, or otherwise failed to work as advertised. Even so, the soldiers preparing to land on the Normandy beaches could not help but be overawed—and deafened—by the firepower assembled to support them. In the skies just ahead, they saw hundreds of military aircraft, which, on the morning of 6 June alone, dropped thousands of high-explosive bombs. Behind them in the English Channel floated more than a hundred hulking warships, their big guns close to overheating from their constant shelling of German positions on the shore. Along with the naval vessels, the soldiers could also see a fleet of hundreds of cargo ships and landing craft, stretching to the horizon. These vessels, by the end of the two weeks starting with D-Day, would deliver to the Normandy beaches nearly 94,000 vehicles and over 245,000 tons of equipment and supplies, along with nearly 620,000 men. Here was the beginning of the end for the German armies, which, in the weeks to come, would be overwhelmed by the speed and power of Allied forces.

D-Day was truly an Allied operation, in which Britain (and Canada) provided much of the equipment and manpower. Yet even in a battle that took place just a hundred miles from England, one of the world's great industrial nations, it was obvious how much the Allied war effort depended on the economic output of the United States. The skies above Normandy buzzed with the bombers of the Eighth Air Force and Ninth Air Force: B-17 Flying Fortresses, B-24 Liberators, and B-26 Marauders (among other aircraft), made in Seattle, San Diego, and Baltimore. Many of the GIs who struggled ashore at Omaha Beach owed their lives to the sailors manning the five-inch guns of a whole group of the U.S. Navy's *Gleaves*-class destroyers, sitting in shallow waters just behind them. Those destroyers had been built during the early months of the war, in places such as Norfolk, Newark, and Seattle. At Omaha Beach and elsewhere, soldiers went ashore in small landing craft, built largely in New Orleans. Once they landed, the Allied armies relied on thousands of Sherman tanks, two-and-a-half-ton trucks, and jeeps, most of which were made in Toledo and Detroit. These tanks and trucks were disgorged by the score at Normandy by a fleet of some 230 tank landing ships (LSTs), the biggest of the Allied landing vessels, most of which were constructed in Pittsburgh, Chicago, and southern Indiana. And most of the fuel for the Army vehicles, along with most of the high-octane gasoline guzzled by Allied aircraft, came from the United States, as did most of the aluminum and steel used to make the planes, ships, tanks, and trucks.[1]

Normandy was an exceptional military operation, but its reliance on American-made machines and matériel was part of a broader pattern of Allied war-fighting. During World War II, the United States helped vanquish the Axis powers by converting its enormous economic capacities into military power. By producing nearly two-thirds of all the munitions used by Allied forces—including huge numbers of aircraft, ships, tanks, trucks, rifles, artillery shells, and bombs—American industry became what President Franklin D. Roosevelt once called "the arsenal of democracy," providing the foundations for a decisive victory.[2]

So the U.S. military-industrial mobilization for World War II worked well, or at least well enough. But how exactly did it work? How were all those bombers, ships, and planes produced, in such short order, under the pressures of a war emergency? And how was the mobilization related to broader, longer-run political and economic developments? What lessons should we take from its history? Seven decades after the end of World War II, we still lack good answers to these questions.

Since the 1940s, most accounts of the U.S. industrial mobilization for World War II have emphasized one of two stories.[3] The first is a tale of the patriotic contributions of American business leaders and their companies. This account of the war contains a large element of truth. Private companies—including those led by remarkable wartime entrepreneurs such as the shipbuilder Henry Kaiser, as well as large manufacturing corporations like General Motors—did indeed shoulder the burden of munitions production. Many business leaders threw themselves into the work, with impressive results.[4]

The second account tells a far more critical story about American business leaders. Indeed, it claims that big industrial corporations exploited the war emergency, to regain political power and reap economic gains. This story emphasizes the activities of corporate executives who went to Washington to run the war economy, in special civilian mobilization agencies such as the Office of Production Management and its successor, the War Production Board. Using their new foothold, so the story goes, the big corporations allied themselves with a conservative military establishment to thwart smaller firms, New Dealers, consumers, workers, and other citizens. According to this account, big business enjoyed huge wartime profits, thanks to an abundance of no-risk, cost-plus military contracts, which evidently prefigured the Cold War–era "military-industrial complex."[5]

Despite their differences, these two accounts share a tendency to ignore, or disdain, the role of the public sector, including the work of the men and women who staffed powerful military and civilian governmental agencies. In the stories that celebrate the wartime achievements of American capitalism, the main characters are for-profit firms and their executives, some of whom took temporary jobs in government to help win the war. These same executives also figure prominently, albeit as villains, in the anticorporate version of events. That story is ultimately no less disparaging of civilian governmental and military authorities, because most of those public officials are presented as the handmaidens of big business.

This book shows that the military-industrial juggernaut of the early 1940s relied heavily on public investment, public management of industrial supply chains, and robust regulation. These powerful state actions shaped the dynamics of political struggle on the World War II home front. Wartime government-business relations were often antagonistic. Many business leaders regarded the wartime state as an annoyance: an imposing, overreaching regulator, as well as a threatening rival. They said so, openly, throughout the war. Their protests included aggressive, coordinated public-relations efforts, which played up the achievements of the private sector while dismissing the value of public contributions to the war economy. This pro-business framing effort was never uncontested, but it proved remarkably successful during World War II—and long after.[6]

This book builds on a third, loosely woven and overlooked set of studies, which have called attention to the importance of public finance, military administration, and government enterprise on the American home front.[7] Drawing on new research in a great deal of previously underused evidence, including the archival records of leading military contractors and U.S. military bureaus, this book calls our attention to important but poorly remembered actors. Like many previous studies, this one includes characters such as William Knudsen, Donald Nelson, Henry Kaiser, and the War Production Board.[8] But it also describes the work of less familiar individuals and agencies, such as the Army Air Forces' Materiel Command (based at Wright Field, in Ohio); military "price adjustment" boards; and plant seizure teams, led by career military officers such as Admiral Harold G. Bowen. It also considers a variety of important war contractors, including midsize and larger companies in several industries, along with some of the era's most politically active business executives. Many of the latter, including Frederick C. Crawford and J. Howard Pew, joined the ranks of top military contractors in the early 1940s, despite their deep distrust of the federal government.

Following the activities of this diverse cast of characters, this book weaves together two stories about "destructive creation." During the early part of World War II, the economist Joseph Schumpeter coined the phrase "creative destruction" to refer to the dynamism of capitalist economies, in which entrepreneurs created economic growth, even as they caused painful disruptions. Schumpeter did not use the phrase to refer specifically to the U.S. war mobilization, about which he knew little.[9] But he presented it at a moment in which the U.S. economy was being transformed into a generator of devastating military power. Here was what might be called a "destructive creation," in which a giant capitalist economy was harnessed for the purpose of annihilating its enemies.

Successful conversion of the U.S. economy into an agent of "destructive creation" owed as much to socialism as it did to capitalism. To be sure, the American war economy relied on private-sector capacities, allowed for profits, and involved some competition among private firms. But it was also a war economy full of state enterprise and ramped-up regulation. The government paid for, and owned, acres of new industrial plant; it managed complex supply chains. It collected huge amounts of information about its contractors' costs and business operations, which helped it to strictly control prices and profits. It even seized the facilities of several dozen companies, including those led by executives who flouted federal labor law.

Remembering this public management and regulation of the industrial mobilization for World War II illuminates the history of modern conservative politics.[10] Contrary to common belief, the war did not suspend politics as usual.[11] In fact, the business community continued the energetic public-relations effort begun in the 1930s to counter the New Deal. During World War II, business leaders expanded that antistatist political effort, adjusting it to take account of new circumstances. As more and more firms and executives experienced the heavy hand of wartime state regulation, the business community and its political allies gained solidarity and strength. Executives from "big business" and the leaders of midsize and smaller firms, across many industries, joined together to resist government encroachment during wartime and—perhaps more important—to create a postwar future in which state enterprise and regulation would play a smaller part. Business leaders' political energy and unity, far from weakened by the stresses of war or patriotic duty, seem to have been bolstered by their common encounter with a formidable wartime state. This hardly made them all-powerful in the political arena but did leave them well positioned, after 1945, to continue to reverse the setbacks that they had experienced in the 1930s.[12]

During and after the war, the business community was remarkably successful in framing the lessons of the military-industrial mobilization. According to business leaders, only for-profit enterprises made positive contributions to the production "miracle" of the early 1940s. This story, which was substantially destructive of the truth, contributed to a longer-running strain of American political discourse, which has disparaged governmental actors, condemned labor unions, and celebrated private enterprise. The history of the political struggles of the World War II era suggests the inadequacy of depictions of a static mid-twentieth-century liberal "consensus" or New Deal "order."[13] Conservative business leaders in the 1940s saw themselves as engaged in a long war against excessive government regulation. From their point of view, the battle to frame the political lessons of the nation's economic mobilization for the biggest war in history seemed like a significant one, even if it might not offer any sort of immediate, wholesale triumph in the larger war.

Transformations in the military-industrial sector shaped American political and economic development.[14] Starting in the 1940s, the American military economy swung toward privatization. By the mid-1960s, much of the government-controlled weapons production and design capacity, which had existed in the United States since the early nineteenth century, had been shed. This was no small achievement for the champions of free enterprise—especially during the early Cold War, when the military accounted for the majority of all national governmental expenditures. The oft-discussed rise of deregulation and privatization that occurred in the 1970s and 1980s was preceded, and then accompanied, by an equally significant shift in the military-industrial field.[15]

By the end of the twentieth century, many American leaders had accepted conservative myths about wartime industrial mobilization. Their own defense policies relied heavily on free markets and private contractors, while neglecting targeted public investment, state enterprise, and regulation of prices and profits. This policy orientation, which extended well beyond the defense sector, evidently allowed for plenty of technological innovation and economic growth. However, it is far from clear whether it has provided the United States, or the world, with optimal or even adequate solutions to many of the more pressing problems of the day. In the future, as some of those problems develop into more acute crises, there may be more interest in reviewing what we have learned from the history of the American response to the challenge of World War II. Such an exercise in lessons-learned history, should it be undertaken, may be unsettling, for it will be hard not to conclude that today's domestic and global political economy has been shaped by a misreading of the past.

Chapter 1

Shadows of the Great War

In late October 1940, Samuel Crowther was worried. The successful biographer of American business leaders had spent the last several years as a public-relations consultant to the mammoth U.S. Steel Corporation. As the war in Asia and Europe entered its second year and Franklin D. Roosevelt ran for an unprecedented third term as U.S. president, Crowther shared his feelings with two top U.S. Steel executives, Irving S. Olds and Edward Stettinius, Jr. Crowther complained that the Republican candidate for president, Wendell Willkie, was too liberal for his tastes. But above all, Crowther was concerned about the wartime expansion of public enterprise. "The trend which alarms me," Crowther wrote, "is the effort to put the Government more and more into business."

Crowther's worries about this trend were informed by his understanding of the past: not only the recent New Deal but also the events of World War I, over two decades earlier. New rumors that the federal government might join with organized labor to build a steel plant evoked Crowder's memory of 1917–18, when the administration of President Woodrow Wilson took over American railroads, "with disastrous consequences." In Crowther's mind, such initiatives were dangerous. "The last war proved that the more Government entered the picture, the less got done," Crowther asserted. "The railroads under McAdoo almost ceased to function." If current trends continued, Crowther warned, the United States would likely emerge from World War II with a national economy riddled with inefficient but entrenched government enterprises, in competition with the private sector. "The outstanding example of this sort of thing" in World War I, he reminded the U.S. Steel executives, "was Muscle Shoals, out of which we eventually got T.V.A. [the Tennessee Valley Authority]."[1]

Crowther's worries in 1940 suggest the inadequacies of popular understandings of business and war, which often assume that corporations favored military conflict and the large profits that accrued from it. Historians often suggest that industry and the armed forces held hands during World War I and into the 1920s and 1930s.[2] This was also the assumption of many contemporaries, in an era that saw widespread critiques of "merchants of death," along with plenty of support for isolationism in Congress, which passed Neutrality Acts designed to keep profiteers from dragging the nation into another overseas conflict.

Yet Crowther remembered correctly: a powerful regulatory state had operated during World War I. If many firms had profited from making munitions, they had also chafed under many of the wartime measures imposed by the Wilson administration and progressives in Congress, including new taxes, a government-assisted expansion of labor unions, and the growth of government enterprise. These developments were partially reversed in the 1920s, as Republicans regained power. But in the 1930s, President Roosevelt and congressional Democrats enacted a series of New Deal programs that revived, and expanded, the national government's regulatory activities. As another global military conflict started, many business leaders, like Crowther, feared that any potential benefits of a new American war mobilization would be overshadowed by its political costs.

Private and Public Enterprise in World War I

In 1917–18, the United States sent nearly two million soldiers to fight in Europe. Because it took months to set up new military production lines, the American Expeditionary Forces, led by General John J. Pershing, would end up using lots of French and British equipment. Nevertheless, the United States undertook a major industrial mobilization. During the nineteen months that the nation was at war, American factories delivered about two million rifles, three billion rounds of small arms ammunition, 375 million pounds of explosives, eighty thousand Army trucks, and twelve thousand airplanes. To carry the troops and their equipment across the Atlantic, nine hundred new cargo vessels were built in a crash effort by U.S. shipyards.[3] All this required major new initiatives in manufacturing and logistics across many different segments of the economy, from individual plants to the national and international levels.

Most histories of the American economic mobilization for World War I focus on the War Industries Board (WIB), an emergency, civilian-led agency. These histories tell the story of how business leaders came to Washington in wartime to solve big problems of economic coordination. The WIB was populated by "dollar-a-year" men, who could work without compensation from the government because they continued to receive salaries from the companies loaning them to Washington. These businessmen-mobilizers, working closely with trade associations and big corporations, capped prices to control inflation and used a system of priority ratings to distribute critical materials. Most historians have agreed that this was a business-friendly economic mobilization that relied heavily on private enterprise and voluntarism instead of on coercion.[4]

But if the Great War industrial mobilization was so business-friendly, how do we explain the negative memories of pro-business conservatives such as Crowther, as they looked back during the early months of World War II? Certainly, the Great War showed some business leaders that military conflict could bring opportunities for unprecedented profits, as well as new gains in power and efficiency via state-approved self-regulation. At least as important, however, was the lesson that wartime could enhance and nationalize populist and progressive initiatives for public enterprise, which before 1914 had been confined largely to the state and local levels.[5] As the great public entrepreneur David E. Lilienthal pointed out at the beginning of World War II, it was really the Great War crisis that caused "the entry on a major scale of the Federal Government in the conduct of business, as opposed to its regulation."[6]

The full story of the American mobilization in 1917–18 is not only about voluntarism and the leadership of corporate executives but also about military capacity, government enterprise, and heavy regulation.[7] Even the WIB, despite its evidently business-friendly staff, wielded the threat of coercion far too often for the taste of most executives. Bernard Baruch, the wealthy Wall Street investor who led the WIB, favored using personal contacts and appeals to patriotism to gain price concessions for military orders. He did this in March 1917 with copper producers, who agreed to sell to the United States at far below market prices. But when Baruch made less headway with the steel industry, he resorted to threats. In a heated discussion in September 1917, Baruch told Elbert H. Gary, the formidable chairman of U.S. Steel, that if the steelmakers could not agree to price reductions, the

WIB would use President Wilson's commandeering powers to take over their plants. When Gary protested that the government would have no clue how to operate U.S. Steel, Baruch reportedly replied, "Oh, we'll get a second lieutenant or somebody to run it." Soon after this, an agreement was reached. According to Baruch's colleague Robert S. Brookings, the WIB's chief price fixer, the steel case was not exceptional. "We threatened to commandeer concerns," Brookings recalled after the war, "unless they abided by our decisions as to prices."[8]

Even Herbert Hoover, the Food Administration chief known for his commitment to voluntarism, found himself considering the prospect of mandatory production orders and forced takeovers. This occurred when the nation's leading meatpacking companies refused to come to terms with Hoover on an agreement to limit wartime prices. Annoyed by this impasse, Hoover asked President Wilson to sign a mandatory price order, which the packers would be compelled to observe. Meanwhile, an even more coercive solution was drafted by the Federal Trade Commission (FTC), which proposed to nationalize one of the "big five" meatpacking companies. This would later be known as a "yardstick": a public enterprise that would give the government firsthand knowledge of production costs, to be used in price negotiations with private companies. This scheme was too much for Hoover, whose aversion to such practices would be demonstrated in the decades to come. But the fact that the FTC's seizure scheme was considered seriously by Wilson spoke to the depth of wartime tensions between government and business.[9]

Although threats were more numerous than actual seizures, plenty of real commandeering did occur. After the country entered the war in early 1917, the Navy Department seized goods from hundreds of warehouses and exporters; it also issued more than three thousand mandatory production orders, which required reluctant companies to sell it goods at a "reasonable profit" to be determined later. The assistant secretary of the Navy, Franklin D. Roosevelt, apparently considered the commandeering option but decided against it, before awarding a large torpedo contract in December 1917. But earlier that year, Roosevelt carried through on a threat to have the Navy seize two battleships built by Bethlehem Steel's Fore River Shipyard, after the company refused to release them to Argentina until payment was guaranteed. The coerced procurement of finished goods was also carried out by the War Department, which issued roughly a thousand compulsory orders of its own.[10]

Among the most remarkable instances of government coercion in the Great War industrial mobilization, which set important precedents for World War II, were the outright takeovers of privately owned enterprises. One of the most prominent of these involved the Smith & Wesson Company, which was filling large military contracts for revolvers. Like many other private employers on the home front, Smith & Wesson had been affected by a wartime surge in labor-union membership and activism, boosted by the Wilson administration's friendly relations with the American Federation of Labor (AFL).[11] In July 1918, Smith & Wesson fired eight workers at its Springfield, Massachusetts, plant for joining a union. These workers, like their counterparts across the country, were calling for measures such as a 25 percent raise to offset wartime inflation, a standard forty-eight-hour week with time and a half for overtime, and collective bargaining rights. On July 12, about five hundred of the 1,400 employees at the Springfield plant went out on strike. The company's president, Joseph H. Wesson, threatened to replace them. When the dispute dragged on, it was referred to the National War Labor Board (NWLB), the wartime agency charged with mediating such disputes.[12]

On August 22, the NWLB ruled that Smith & Wesson had to reinstate the fired workers and stop forcing its employees to sign "yellow-dog" contracts forbidding them to join unions. Wesson responded by saying that he would rather have the government seize the plant than obey the order, although he did agree to move to an eight-hour day. On September 13, the War Department seized the plant, which ended up being run by Ordnance Department officers through early 1919.[13] Meanwhile, President Wilson threatened to seize several war plants in Bridgeport, Connecticut. In this case, it was striking workers, not company leaders, who were failing to observe an NWLB decision. If the government did take over the Bridgeport plants, Wilson warned the workers, they would lose their draft exemptions. After this announcement, production resumed, without any seizures.[14]

Even more dramatic takeovers occurred on a national scale. Before the conflict ended in November 1918, various agencies of the United States government had taken formal control over the railroads; the telegraph and telephone industries; and the nascent radio industry. The national state was also in the midst of constructing its own massive fleet of merchant ships; and it owned hundreds of millions of dollars' worth of industrial facilities, including shipyards and explosives plants. For anyone interested in the present and future role of government in the American economy, these were significant developments. And they were not attributable simply to some kind of natural logic or necessity of modern war but also to political choices—most notably, those of the members of President Wilson's cabinet, who together demon-strated a great enthusiasm for expanding public enterprise.

At least four prominent members of Wilson's cabinet—Secretary of State William Jennings Bryan, Postmaster General Albert S. Burleson, Trea-sury Secretary William Gibbs McAdoo, and Navy Secretary Josephus Daniels—qualified as champions of public enterprise. Bryan, one of the era's best-known political figures, favored government ownership of the railroads and was friendly to organized labor.[15] Burleson, as chief of the postal system, ran a well-established enormous government enterprise; but he wanted more. After taking office, encouraged by a sympathetic Presi-dent Wilson, he called for public ownership of telecommunications—a measure that, during this era, had considerable public support. Burleson's goal was realized in the summer of 1918, when telegraph workers threat-ened to strike if the companies would not recognize their union. When Western Union executives refused (and fired several hundred union mem-bers), Wilson sided with the AFL and nationalized the telephone and tele-graph. Burleson ended up having formal control over telecommunications for one year, during which he managed to alienate workers and consumers, as well as corporate executives. Although this experiment in public opera-tion failed, it was part of a larger pattern of government intrusion into business, which alarmed the private sector.[16]

McAdoo, the energetic secretary of the Treasury (and Wilson's son-in-law), led two major wartime initiatives in what would soon be called "state capitalism." During Wilson's first term, McAdoo called for the creation of a large new American merchant fleet, managed by a government-controlled corporation. McAdoo, a former urban railroad executive, did not normally prefer government enterprise over private action, but he advocated for it in this case because of market failure. Merchant shipping, he contended, was one of those fields "where the intervention of the government is urgently demanded in the interest of the public welfare." At first, McAdoo's dream was thwarted by conservatives. The powerful banker J. P. Morgan, who con-trolled a private shipping company, paid him a visit to express his disapproval of the scheme. The Chamber of Commerce of the United States, the leading business association at the national level, called it "un-American." Elihu Root, a former secretary of war and secretary of state who was then serving as a Republican senator from New York, compared the plan to "state socialism."[17]

McAdoo was frustrated by this opposition, which he regarded as more ideological than rational. But after the country went to war in April 1917, McAdoo got his public enterprise. This was the Emergency Fleet Corporation, established under the auspices of the U.S. Shipping Board. These entities oversaw the construction of some 1,400 merchant ships, most of which were constructed in giant new government-owned, contractor-operated (GOCO) shipyards. The government spent a total of $270 million on dozens of new shipyards. The biggest of them all was "Hog Island," near Philadelphia. Hog Island, owned by the government but run by the American International Corporation, cost the government about $65 million to build. The world's largest shipbuilding complex, Hog Island was home to a workforce of thirty-four thousand people.[18]

After his merchant-shipping scheme was well under way, McAdoo became concerned with the railroads. Regulated by the Interstate Commerce Commission (ICC), which had the power to set freight rates, the American railroad industry was still composed of independent private companies. Their executives had been dismayed by the Adamson Act of 1916, in which Congress, backed by Wilson, had provided railroad workers with the eight-hour day. Indeed, this issue, along with the activities of McAdoo and other progressives in the cabinet, had persuaded much of the American business community to oppose Wilson in 1916.[19]

By late 1917, the strain of increased wartime demand for transport, combined with the lack of coordination among the various companies, had brought the railroad network to a breaking point. McAdoo urged Wilson to have the government take over the railroads. In December, Wilson gave the order; McAdoo, despite his other commitments, became chief of a new Railroad Administration. For the next two years, the federal government served as the nominal operator of the nation's railroads. Although the private railroad companies continued to manage most day-to-day operations, this nationalization was more than just a formality. McAdoo relieved four hundred managers working for the private lines, replacing them with U.S. government officials, who oversaw seven regional districts. In May 1918, he ordered a significant increase in workers' wages, paid for by a hike in shipping rates. The workers were now U.S. employees, whose paychecks bore McAdoo's signature.[20]

Whereas McAdoo claimed to support state enterprise only in cases of market failure, Navy Secretary Josephus Daniels often seemed to prefer it as the default option. Indeed, despite stiff competition, it was Daniels who emerged as the most energetic public entrepreneur of all the members of Wilson's cabinet. Like many of his fellow Southern Democrats, Daniels was both a booster of white supremacy and an advocate of progressive economic policies. A newspaperman from North Carolina, Daniels had long been a thorn in the side of the tobacco "monopoly."[21] At the Navy Department, his reflexive hostility to big business quickly embroiled him in clashes with some of the nation's biggest industrial concerns. This conflict in the mid-1910s revived older struggles. Since the 1890s, when the nation started to spend large sums on steel warships, several members of Congress had been accusing the Navy's leading contractors of collusion and profiteering.[22] Now, with Daniels at the helm in the Navy Department, these critics were in a position to shake up the system.

In 1913, soon after he took up his new post, Daniels began to investigate collusion among contractors for armor plate, which the Navy required for its new vessels. Daniels concluded that the steel companies had been cheating the government. So he worked with Senator Benjamin R. ("Ben") Tillman (D-SC) to urge Congress to fund a government-owned, government-operated (GOGO) armor-plate plant. In 1916, they fought a public-relations battle over the issue with Charles M. Schwab of the Bethlehem Steel Corporation, which, thanks to abundant European war orders, had become one of the world's largest military contractors. As Daniels saw it, this fight was a clear-cut contest "between those who stood for the big interests fattening on government favors and those who were hostile to seeing the taxpayers mulcted by profiteers."[23] In the short term, Daniels and Tillman prevailed. In August 1916, President Wilson signed the bill authorizing the GOGO armor-plate plant. Ironically, the growing American role in the war delayed the completion of the $22 million plant, as construction materials were diverted to more urgent projects.[24]

The armor-plate business was just one of many in which Daniels worked to expand the Navy's GOGO capacities. Here he was able to build on a strong foundation because the Navy had long operated its own network of shipyards, which dated back to the earliest days of the republic. Daniels believed that the GOGO yards should be expanded, so that they could provide the Navy with even more independent production capacity and more leverage to drive down contractors' prices. When he entered office in 1913, Daniels appeared at times to favor a full nationalization (that is, government takeover) of warship construction. During the Great War, Daniels told Congress that the Navy should use in-house facilities to produce between a third and two-thirds of its needs, depending on the prices offered by contractors.[25] At the end of the war, Daniels used his annual report to Congress to explain that he believed that the Navy should have enough in-house capacity to make it independent of private industry. "The Navy's policy," he stated in December 1918, "is that in its own plants it should be able to construct every type of ship and every character of munition required."[26]

During the Great War, under Daniels's leadership, the Navy relied on a combination of public and private yards. Many orders for new warships went to contractors, including Bethlehem Steel, New York Shipbuilding, Newport News, Bath Iron Works, and Electric Boat, which built the vessels in their own yards. In other cases, the Navy—like the Emergency Fleet Corporation and the War Department—paid for large new facilities ($71 million worth, in all) operated by contractors. The biggest of these GOCO warship facilities created during the Great War was an eighteen-acre destroyer yard in Squantum (Quincy), Massachusetts, run by the Fore River Shipbuilding Corporation, a division of Bethlehem Steel.[27]

The Navy's own yards also served as an important source of supply. Although they were occupied with the repair and refitting of older ships, the U.S. Navy yards also handled a considerable amount of new construction. Their share of this work had fallen in the 1890s, although the Brooklyn Navy Yard had built some of the new steel battleships. During Wilson's first term, before the United States entered the war, Daniels pushed to have more new shipbuilding done by the Navy yards.[28] He stepped up this effort in 1917–18, when the eight U.S. Navy yards were expanded significantly, with more than $70 million of new construction. At the Philadelphia Navy Yard, which employed fifteen thousand people by war's end, a $20 million expansion was used to allow the facility to build the largest warships, such as battle cruisers. The Navy used its own yards to build about half of the ninety-nine submarines that it ordered during the Great War, along with several destroyers and dozens of submarine chasers. By the end of 1918, the eight Navy yards employed about a hundred thousand people, four times what they had done in 1914.[29]

Even outside the Navy's core business of warship construction, Daniels championed a major expansion of government ownership and operation. He was well pleased with the Navy's takeover of the nation's infant radio industry.[30] Daniels expanded the Navy's own smokeless powder plant, so as to make the government less dependent on Du Pont. In 1917, he ordered the creation of the Naval Aircraft Factory, with which the Navy could design and build its own planes. Daniels approved the construction of a new GOGO torpedo-manufacturing plant at Alexandria, Virginia, which complemented the Navy's existing in-house torpedo works in Newport, Rhode Island. Daniels also laid the groundwork for the Naval Research Laboratory, which would open after the war. Throughout his time in the Wilson administration, Daniels supported the permanent nationalization of the railroads and telecommunication industries. After leaving office, he would continue to support these measures, along with government control of coal mining and hydroelectric power.[31]

The push for more public enterprise was somewhat more restrained at the War Department, led by Newton D. Baker. A few years before the Great War, as the mayor of Cleveland, Baker had supported municipally owned and operated streetcars and electric utilities. But he was more cautious than Daniels about bypassing the private sector.[32] One reason for this was Baker's greater (and growing) sympathies for capitalism. But it was also related to the different economics of Navy and Army procurement. In peacetime, much of the U.S. Army's demand for equipment and weapons was handled by its own GOGO arsenals, which included the rifle works at Springfield, Massachusetts; an ammunition plant in Philadelphia (the Frankford Arsenal); and artillery-making operations in Watervliet, New York, and Watertown, Massachusetts. These were modern, efficiently run operations, whose costs were competitive with those of contractors. But most War Department officers did not want these long-standing operations to be the sole source of supply, especially in wartime. In comparison with the Navy, the Army was responsible for outfitting a far larger number of men; it needed a wider range of goods, many of them in huge quantities.

Just before the United States entered the war, an internal War Department inquiry concluded that it would be foolish not to order military equipment from the private sector, especially given that it had already started to produce munitions for European customers. This report recommended a major GOGO expansion only at the Rock Island Arsenal, on the Illinois-Iowa border.[33] This was the policy blueprint that Baker's department followed during World War I. Rock Island, where the workforce rose from about 2,200 people in 1916 to about fifteen thousand by the end of the war, did become a major facility. Meanwhile, the operations of the U.S. Army's other GOGO arsenals also expanded, but only by a factor of two or three.[34] For most needs of the nation's nearly four million soldiers, the Army would turn to private contractors.

Still, Baker and many Army officers understood themselves as independent of private business leaders, whom they saw not just as friendly partners but as rivals.[35] This dynamic was illustrated by a conflict that broke out in late 1917 between the War Department and Du Pont, which had served for decades as the nation's leading supplier of military explosives. Although the Army and Navy each had small in-house gunpowder plants, most of the national production capacity was held by Du Pont. (The other top private suppliers were the Atlas Powder Company and the Hercules Powder Company, both spun off from Du Pont in 1912 as part of an antitrust settlement.) Before the United States entered the war, it was private companies, led by Du Pont, that met the demand of European customers. Between July 1914 and April 1917, Du Pont expanded output at its own three smokeless gunpowder plants from one million to 33 million pounds a month. By April 1917, Du Pont had already sold the Allies 400 million pounds of smokeless powder, along with 50 million pounds of TNT.[36]

When the United States entered the war, the jump in requirements for explosives overwhelmed even the greatly expanded capacities of Du Pont and private suppliers. So the Army's Ordnance Department started a major effort to build large new government-owned plants, most of which were GOCO facilities, designed and operated by the private companies. By the end of the war, the government had spent $350 million on a network of fifty-three explosives plants.[37]

The explosives-plant program created tensions between the Wilson administration and business executives, who wondered if the government would end up creating a public monopoly. The most serious controversy occurred at the end of 1917. In October of that year, the Ordnance Department negotiated a contract with Du Pont to have the company build and run an enormous new GOCO smokeless powder plant. According to the original contract, Du Pont would be paid a fee amounting to at least 7 percent of the expected $90 million in construction costs (over $6 million), plus fees for powder production that were likely to amount to at least 15 percent of the cost of the powder. The terms of this deal raised eyebrows at the WIB. One of its top price controllers, Robert Brookings, believed that the fees were at least twice as high as they should be. These criticisms convinced Baker, who ordered the Ordnance Department to cancel the deal.

Having alienated Du Pont, Baker engaged private engineering and construction firms to design and build a large government-owned powder works in Nitro, West Virginia. In May 1918, the War Department hired Hercules Powder to operate the Nitro plant. By the time of the armistice, six months later, this big GOCO powder facility had barely started production.[38]

In the meantime, Baker and Du Pont had a rapprochement. Because the Nitro plant would be large enough to supply only about half of the nation's projected additional demand, the War Department went back to Du Pont. In March, they agreed on a contract that would have Du Pont build and operate a new GOCO plant on a 4,700-acre site outside Nashville, Tennessee. Known as "Old Hickory," this huge complex included housing for thirty thousand people, along with its own fire department, hospital, and segregated schools. Designed to produce 900,000 pounds of smokeless powder a day, Old Hickory cost about $84 million to build. On this deal, the government managed far better terms than those contained in the canceled October 1917 contract.[39]

Despite the Old Hickory deal, the earlier clash with the government had alienated Pierre du Pont, president of the nation's leading explosives supplier. Proud of their expertise and their contributions to the war effort, Pierre du Pont and his peers regarded their critics as ignorant ingrates. And, as they watched the government build giant public-owned facilities in their own industries, they could not help but worry about the consequences of this potentially serious encroachment into the private sector. As we shall see, similar concerns would lead Pierre du Pont and other top American business leaders to inveigh against the New Deal in the mid-1930s. But as the case of Pierre du Pont suggests, many of those executives came into the 1930s with a political sensibility that had been shaped by their experiences during the Great War, under an administration led by President Wilson and his progressive lieutenants.

Pierre du Pont and his allies may have had some cause to complain of the public's under-appreciation of their expertise, but few ordinary Americans would shed them many tears, given the evidence of what came to be called wartime "profiteering." In April 1917, as he led the nation into war, President Wilson had warned American companies to avoid "unusual profits."[40] But it was already too late. Thanks to big orders from the Allies, many American companies, including Du Pont and Bethlehem Steel, were making record returns. Until the summer of 1916, Du Pont had been selling smokeless powder to the Allies for a dollar a pound, twice as much as it

charged the U.S. military. The big-margin powder sales helped Du Pont
earn $82 million in profits in 1916 alone—more than ten times its average
annual earnings before the war.[41]

As long as the United States remained neutral, objections to these windfall profits were limited, at least domestically. But in April 1917, this
changed. As hundreds of thousands of young men prepared to risk their
lives in the trenches, some Americans—including those who held the fast-
appreciating stock of the munitions makers—were amassing wealth. "War
brings prosperity to the stock gamblers on Wall Street," said Senator
George W. Norris (R-NE), an outspoken progressive. But their gains would
always be "soiled with the sweat of mothers' tears," as they cashed in "cou-
pons dyed in the lifeblood of their fellow man."[42]

Whether or not one agreed with Norris that war profits amounted to
blood money, it was impossible to deny that the Great War earnings of
many American companies were huge. Bethlehem Steel, the nation's leading shipbuilder, as well as a steelmaker, recorded $43.6 million in net earn-
ings in 1916, about seven times its 1914 profits. Bethlehem's president,
Eugene G. Grace, was paid about $3 million in wartime bonuses. At U.S.
Steel, the biggest of the steelmakers, profits for 1916 were $272 million—
nearly twelve times what they had been in 1914. Meanwhile, J. P. Morgan,
the leading Wall Street bank, had collected at least $30 million in fees for
serving as the Allies' main purchasing agent in North America. At Du Pont,
where executives and stockholders shared millions of dollars in dividends
and bonuses, there was enough left over for the company to buy a 25 percent share in the General Motors Corporation.[43]

To many business leaders, the growing chorus of criticism of Great War
"profiteering" failed to do enough to recognize the decline in corporate
earnings in 1917–18, the period when the United States was actually at war.
The biggest reason for this fall was taxes. The Sixteenth Amendment, which
authorized federal income taxes, had been ratified in 1913. At first, federal
tax rates were very low. But during the Great War, the Wilson administration and Congress relied on high income taxes, on corporations and individuals, to cover a large fraction of the cost of the war. (Initially, Treasury
Secretary McAdoo hoped that taxes would pay half the expense. In the end,
taxes covered only a quarter of war costs; most of the remainder was paid
for with bonds.)[44]

From 1916 to 1919, Congress passed a series of new tax measures, which
reined in corporate profits. High taxes on manufacturers were favored by

many Southern and Western members of Congress, most of whom represented rural districts. One of these men was House Ways and Means Committee chairman Claude Kitchin (D-NC), who joined forces with McAdoo to devise the new laws. The first step came in September 1916, before the United States entered the war, when Congress passed a new revenue law containing a special 12.5 percent "munitions tax." This would be paid mainly by Du Pont.

A much larger group of companies was affected by the revenue law enacted in October 1917, which—besides hiking the income tax for individuals—created a new "excess profits tax" (EPT). The EPT applied a progressive ladder of rates, ranging from 20 percent to 60 percent, on any earnings in excess of what had been a company's average rate of return on capital investment during the designated prewar base period of 1911–13. The individual income tax and EPT rates were raised slightly in the last wartime revenue bill, which was not enacted until February 1919, after the armistice. But that law also created an additional "war profits" tax, which allowed the government to take 80 percent of any profits above the base-period average, in dollar terms. This meant that for 1918, companies paid two major new taxes on "excessive" profits: one calculated on the basis of the ratio of earnings to invested capital; and the other by looking at the difference between actual dollar profits in the prewar and wartime periods. This was a complex system but amounted to a robust, progressive corporate income tax, which succeeded in trimming business profits sharply during the last year of the war.[45]

Certainly, it is possible to overstate the strength of the regulation of American business during the Great War. As the record of World War II would show, taxes could have been higher. The Wilson administration might have been more hostile to business. Even Daniels, who was driven by an intense antipathy toward big business, was far from being an enemy of all forms of private enterprise. This distinguished him from the era's true radicals, including the Bolsheviks who seized power in Russia in late 1917 and, closer to home, American communists, socialists, and members of groups such as the Industrial Workers of the World. Franklin Roosevelt —who, as assistant secretary of the Navy, was second-in-command to Daniels—was more circumspect than his boss about public capacities. In 1919, Roosevelt called for the quick liquidation of the government's merchant marine; he opposed government ownership of the infant aircraft industry. Such views about the need to limit regulation and government enterprise were shared by Baruch, the WIB chief, among other leading Democrats.[46]

Beyond this, many of the large new government-owned plants built during the Great War, including merchant shipyards and explosives factories, were constructed and operated not by the government but by private firms. Inside many of the wartime agencies, business conservatives took key leadership positions. Charles Schwab, the Bethlehem Steel executive who had previously fought bitterly with Daniels over armor plate, became head of the Emergency Fleet Corporation in 1918. Meanwhile, much of the day-to-day work of the Railroad Administration, nominally headed by McAdoo, was handled by his assistant, Walter D. Hines, chairman of the Santa Fe line.[47]

But even if some of the wartime expansions of regulation and public enterprise looked more radical on paper than in practice, pro-business conservatives had good reason to take them seriously. Not long after the war ended (with an armistice that took effect on 11 November 1918), McAdoo suggested that the government control the railroads for at least another five years. Meanwhile, Burleson asked Congress to allow the post office to control telecommunications indefinitely. For a short while, at least, President Wilson seemed open to these schemes.[48] For many business leaders, these facts—along with the behavior of Daniels at the Navy Department, the seizures and compulsory orders, the high corporate taxes, and other troubling wartime developments—showed that modern war was a threat to their power and to the country's prosperity. Although this danger diminished when the war ended, some legacies of war proved hard to erase.

From Reconversion to the TVA

By the time Warren G. Harding entered the White House, in early 1921, many of the Great War expansions of government regulation and control had been eliminated or greatly scaled back. President Wilson, who was focused on international issues in 1919, favored a quick dismantling of the WIB, among other wartime agencies.[49] Most of the wartime experiments in government enterprise now came to an end. The management of telecommunications by the post office, which brought rate increases but never diminished labor unrest, was widely seen as an abject failure; it ended in mid-1919. This reversal helped to erode congressional and popular support for continued government management of the railroads, which ended in 1920, over the objections of labor unions and other groups on the political left. McAdoo was dismayed by what he regarded as unfair partisan criticisms of government operation and inflated claims by the private roads for damages. Nonetheless, McAdoo—who had his eye on the White House—dropped his call for an extended period of control. He was well aware of the mood in Congress, where the midterm elections of 1918 (held just a few days before the end of the war) had created Republican majorities in both houses. In the railroad industry, Congress used the Transportation Act of 1920 to revive the prewar order: private railroads, subject to ICC regulation. The ICC's new regulatory powers were robust enough to make the railroad industry remain one of the most tightly controlled of all sectors in the American economy. For instance, the new law required the agency to confiscate half of any profits that any company managed to earn in excess of 6 percent of its invested capital, so that the money could be loaned out to struggling lines. But in practice, very little money was ever turned over to the government.[50] More important, champions of private enterprise could at least take heart that the nationalization had been temporary.

Meanwhile, to the dismay of Daniels, the radio industry was privatized, with some of the Navy's former assets taken over by a big new for-profit enterprise: the Radio Corporation of America (RCA).[51] Daniels's beloved GOGO armor-plate plant, whose completion had been delayed by the war effort, was abandoned not long after it started casting steel in 1921. To Daniels, the reason for all this reform was obvious. "Monopoly won," he explained, "when it put Harding in the White House."[52] The new president put it differently: "We want a period in America with less government in business," Harding reportedly said, "and more business in government."[53]

Most American business leaders welcomed the shift away from progressive governance, for many reasons. One key field was industrial relations. During the war, the Wilson administration's policies had favored the AFL. But this changed in 1919, when the president spent many weeks abroad and was focused squarely on international concerns. During the major wave of labor strikes across North America in 1919, the Wilson administration did little to assist unions. As the Bolsheviks attempted to consolidate power in Russia, observers of international affairs wondered whether communism might become an important force in the postwar world. In the United States, a series of domestic bombings contributed to an antilabor, anti-immigrant "Red Scare," which culminated, by the end of the year, in mass arrests and wholesale violations of civil liberties by the federal government and by many states. These developments worked in favor of business leaders, some of whom combined antiunion efforts within their own firms with broader, more coordinated public campaigns against domestic "Bolshevism." By early 1921, as Harding entered the White House, organized labor was very much on the defensive. Calvin Coolidge, the new vice president, had risen to prominence thanks in part to his role in crushing a strike by Boston policemen in 1919. With men such as Coolidge in Washington, business leaders were reassured that federal labor policy would improve.[54]

For most business leaders, organized labor was not the only political concern: they also hoped to rein in the recent excesses of government. In 1917–18, business groups and Republican politicians had complained about what they saw as incompetence and excessive bureaucracy in the Wilson administration's management of the war economy.[55] During the last year of the war, the Chamber of Commerce had criticized the "growing tendency for government control of industries." Immediately after the armistice, the Chamber called for an end of government operation of transport and telecommunications. In 1919 and throughout the interwar period, Chamber members passed resolutions calling for an end to government competition with private enterprise. The same was true of the National Association of Manufacturers (NAM), another leading business association. One NAM leader, Francis H. Sisson, echoed the Republican Party's calls for "a business government for business people." In 1920, NAM president James A. Emery warned against "the undue and improper influence of government" in the economy, which stifled innovation.[56]

From the point of view of the NAM and the Chamber, the departure of the Wilson administration was a blessing. As Daniels recognized, it was Republican control in Washington, and not just the coming of peace, that guaranteed the death—or at least the downsizing—of many wartime experiments in state enterprise and heightened regulation. Working with a Republican-majority Congress, the Treasury secretary, Andrew W. Mellon, lowered taxes. Income taxes did continue to generate a large fraction of federal revenue. However, top rates dropped dramatically (eventually all the way down to 20 percent), and the excess profits tax was killed off.[57] Meanwhile, Congress and the Harding and Coolidge administrations liquidated the government's considerable fleet of merchant ships, in which the government had invested $3.5 billion between 1917 and 1924. At the beginning of 1920, the U.S. Shipping Board owned and operated a fleet of 1,525 cargo ships and tankers. These vessels competed with privately owned ships, whose owners (along with the NAM) lobbied Washington to get rid of the government fleet. Republicans were happy to oblige. By the end of 1925, the government-owned merchant marine, which just a few years earlier had been world-class, consisted of only 276 aging vessels.[58]

Such moves in the direction of deregulation and privatization were in keeping with the development of the Republican Party, which emphasized the need for economic liberty. When President Coolidge proclaimed in December 1923 that "the business of America is business," he meant that the government's role should be to assist private enterprise—and get out of its way. Nationally, there were now fewer Republicans who embraced progressivism and more who saw state regulation as an evil that needed to be minimized.[59] Progressivism was not quite dead in the 1920s, however. The Republican-majority Congress did pass bills providing subsidies for farmers, which were defeated only by Coolidge's vetoes. And at the state and local levels, certainly, voters and politicians, as well as many business leaders, continued to support some new regulations and state enterprises.[60]

Despite the ascendance of pro-business Republicanism in the 1920s, some progressive experiments of the 1910s did not fade away so easily. This was true for a small network of Navy-owned petroleum reserves, which included some lands in California that had been set aside in 1912, as well as some in Wyoming, created three years later, dubbed "Teapot Dome." Josephus Daniels, naturally, had argued throughout his tenure as Navy secretary that the oil reserves must remain under public control. But not long after Daniels left office in 1921, President Harding transferred authority over the reserves from the Navy to the Interior Department. That agency was now headed by Albert B. Fall, a former U.S. senator from New Mexico who was known as a friend to mining and oil companies. In 1922, as Fall proceeded to negotiate leases with private interests, Daniels put critics of the plan in touch with sympathetic Navy officers; he also used his Raleigh, North Carolina, newspaper to call for congressional investigations.

To Daniels's delight, Congress did discover some remarkable improprieties connected with the privatization of the Navy oil fields, which have gone down in history under the name of the "Teapot Dome" scandal. Perhaps the most sensational finding was that Edward L. Doheny, with whom Fall had negotiated a lease on one of the California reserves, had engaged his son to give Fall a small black bag containing $100,000 in cash. Fall received similar "loans" from his friend Harry Sinclair, who had received the Teapot Dome leases. One of the men hurt most by the investigation, ironically, was William McAdoo, whose law firm had assisted with some of Doheny's business in Mexico. Although this connection had no direct relation to the Navy reserve leases, it may have helped prevent McAdoo from becoming the Democrats' candidate for president in 1924. Instead, the party chose the more business-friendly John W. Davis. This decision encouraged Robert M. La Follette, Jr. to run as a third-party candidate, under the banner of the Progressive Party. Both were crushed in 1924 by Coolidge, who had managed to prevent Teapot Dome from damaging his campaign.[61]

Although the Teapot Dome scandal offered sensational evidence of corruption practiced by a single government official, it should be understood as part of the wider struggle over the economic legacies of the Great War. Even before Fall's bribe-taking was revealed, Daniels and his progressive allies—including La Follette in the Senate and Gifford Pinchot, the conservationist governor of Pennsylvania—were attacking the leases as evidence of the excesses of postwar privatization under the new Republican administration. In most fields, the progressives in the early 1920s lacked the political power to prevent this reassertion of private authority in the American economy. But in this case, thanks in part to Fall's crimes, they prevailed: the reserves were returned to the Navy.

There was another closely watched struggle over postwar privatization in which progressives managed to wield surprising influence during the 1920s, even without a dramatic corruption scandal. This was the Muscle Shoals controversy, which, after many twists and turns, ended with the establishment of one of the most important public enterprises in American history, the Tennessee Valley Authority (TVA).

The Muscle Shoals dispute originated with the War Department's massive efforts in 1917–18 to ramp up the nation's capacity to produce explosives. In December 1917, the War Department contracted with the American Cyanamid Company to build and run a large GOCO nitrates plant at Muscle Shoals, Alabama. This complex, built at a cost of $68 million, was slated to produce forty thousand tons of nitrates a year, which would help free the United States from its dependence on Chilean nitrates. To provide electricity for the plant, the War Department started to build a large new dam, which would take advantage of the natural waterfalls at Muscle Shoals. The nitrates plant was finished in October 1918, too late to make a contribution to the war effort. Construction on the dam, which, at the time, represented the biggest hydropower project ever undertaken in the United States, was still far from complete.[62]

During the 1920s, the fate of the big GOCO explosives plant and hydroelectric power project at Muscle Shoals became the subject of intense public debate. At first, it seemed certain that the facility would be leased or sold to the private sector. The most prominent of the early bidders was Henry Ford, the auto industry titan, who suggested that he was interested in using Muscle Shoals as the foundation for a new Detroit—a major manufacturing center for the South. "The destiny of our country, agriculturally and industrially," Ford proclaimed in early 1922 as he discussed terms with Secretary of War John W. Weeks, "lies at Muscle Shoals."[63] Ford appeared to be the choice of President Coolidge, who recommended in a December 1923 speech that Muscle Shoals be sold.

Resistance to such a sale proved unexpectedly potent. The growing Teapot Dome scandal encouraged critics of the proposed deal with Ford. They were led in Congress by Senator Norris, a champion of public ownership of electric power. One of Norris's allies, Congressman Fiorello H. La Guardia (D-NY), warned in March 1924 that privatization of the costly Muscle Shoals facilities could become an even bigger Teapot Dome. Such opposition helped delay any action before the 1924 elections. Frustrated, Ford withdrew his offer in October of that year. Although the progressives still had not won over a majority in Congress, they had succeeded, by the time Wilson Dam was finished in 1925, in keeping Muscle Shoals in government hands.[64]

During the late 1920s, Norris and his allies gained even more ground, thanks to public concerns about the organization of the American electric-utility industry, dominated by large holding companies. These entities, most of which were controlled by the J. P. Morgan financial empire and Chicago utility titan Samuel Insull, were criticized by progressives as a monopolistic "power trust" that harmed the public interest. In 1928, a Federal Trade Commission investigation of the industry noted that the holding companies had been lobbying against the creation of a public utility at Muscle Shoals. Senator Norris, backed by the League of Women Voters and a variety of other groups, had been working on a bill that would make Muscle Shoals the center of a large utility and waterways management system in the South. Norris managed to get Congress to pass one such bill in 1928, but President Coolidge vetoed it. In 1931, President Hoover vetoed a similar bill.[65]

Hoover's opposition to public power at Muscle Shoals suggests how much he differed from his former colleagues in Wilson's cabinet and from the New Dealers who would soon set up shop in Washington. Hoover's work to promote government-business cooperation, which he pursued especially during his tenure as secretary of commerce in the 1920s, is sometimes described as "progressive" and distinct from the approach of traditional free-market business conservatives.[66] And as president, Hoover continued to favor some policies that would make government bigger, not smaller.[67] But on the Muscle Shoals question, Hoover had no interest in compromising with progressives. During the 1928 campaign, he dismissed the Norris scheme as "state socialism." In his 1931 veto message, Hoover explained that the Norris bill "raises one of the most important issues confronting our people." For Hoover, there was only one acceptable position to take on this critical question. "I am firmly opposed," he announced, "to the Government entering into any business the major purpose of which is competition with our citizens."[68]

Hoover's opponent in 1932, Franklin Roosevelt, was well acquainted with the concept of public enterprise from his days in the Navy Department. In 1929, as governor of New York, Roosevelt called for public power projects at Muscle Shoals, Boulder Dam, and along the Saint Lawrence River. During the 1932 campaign, in a major speech in Portland, Oregon, he added a Columbia River project to this list. As Roosevelt explained it in 1932, among the benefits of these public power projects was their function as yardsticks with which the public could evaluate the claims of private utility companies about costs and proper rates to the public. They also served as "birch rods"—evidence that government could, in effect, punish the private sector if it failed to work in the public interest, by entering directly into the industrial field.[69]

After Roosevelt won the election, Norris's dreams were realized. The TVA was launched in early 1933, along with the rest of the early New Deal. According to Roosevelt, this was "the widest experiment ever conducted by a government."[70] Using the dam at Muscle Shoals as its foundation, the TVA would create a major government-owned, government-operated electric power enterprise.

This experiment was not welcomed by the private utilities. Nor did it please the leading national business associations, which had spent the past fifteen years fighting to keep government out of industrial operations. The creation of the TVA, as one of its leading historians once put it, precipitated "a battle between government and business as intense as any in American history."[71]

To the dismay of many businessmen, the TVA empowered a new generation of enthusiasts for public enterprise, including David Lilienthal, who would lead the agency. Lilienthal and his allies were most worrisome to private electric-utility executives in the South, where the TVA promised to compete directly with for-profit utilities. Many of those were controlled by the Commonwealth & Southern Corporation, led by Wendell Willkie. In the mid-1930s, Willkie became a prominent spokesman against what he and others regarded as the unfair use of federal authority to subsidize public power. After federal courts refused to find the TVA unconstitutional, Willkie was forced to compromise. In August 1939, he agreed to sell the Tennessee Electric & Power Company, one of the largest pieces of Commonwealth & Southern, to the TVA (along with a group of municipal governments) for about $80 million. This meant that at the end of the 1930s, just as World War II broke out in Europe, the TVA had established itself not only as a big hydropower producer but also as a major distributor of electricity.[72] (During World War II, the TVA would provide about 10 percent of all the power consumed by the nation's war effort. This included most of the electricity consumed by the uranium enrichment complex in Oak Ridge, Tennessee, which fed the atomic bomb program, as well as a large fraction of the power used to create the aluminum for tens of thousands of military aircraft.)[73]

Although the TVA represented a significant threat, the bigger issue, for many American business leaders, was whether it might represent the beginning of an all-out nationalization of one of the country's biggest industries. Although Roosevelt did not end up pursuing this extreme solution, his suggestion in November 1934 that the TVA model should be replicated in other regions was regarded by the private utilities as most unwelcome. So, too, was the Wheeler-Rayburn bill, which occupied Congress for much of 1935. Designed to break up the large holding companies, Wheeler-Rayburn included a "death sentence" provision, which required the dissolution within five years of any such entity that failed to prove that its large size was an economic necessity.[74] The private utilities responded to this bill with one of the most expensive and aggressive public-relations efforts in American history up to that time. "Government in business has been a failure for 100 years," they declared in paid advertisements placed in newspapers across the country; if enacted, the bill would push the country "into the morasses of state Socialism and Communism."[75] This effort failed to sway the Democrat-controlled Congress, which, after passing a modified version of the bill, allowed Senator Hugo Black (D-AL) to pursue a major investigation of the sometimes sordid details of the utilities' lobbying campaign.[76]

As the controversy over the Wheeler-Rayburn bill suggested, the Muscle Shoals fight had become part of a massive national political struggle over public enterprise. In the 1930s, a decade and a half after the end of Great War, progressive Democrats in Washington—now under the banner of the New Deal—were again making major intrusions into private industry. There were all sorts of public works and construction projects, built by several of the new "alphabet soup" of agencies. The largest of these, including the Civil Works Administration (CWA), the Public Works Administration (PWA), and the Works Progress Administration (WPA), each spent several billion dollars on construction. The PWA, which mostly paid private contractors to do the work, financed many big projects, including giant hydroelectric dams on the Columbia River in the Pacific Northwest. These operations were not entirely offensive, from the point of view of some businessmen, because they relied on private contractors. But the New Deal building agencies, like TVA, could also act as threatening rivals. The PWA actually worked hand in hand with the public power movement, by funding municipally owned electric utilities, some of which would buy electricity from the TVA or other public authorities.[77] Even worse, from the point of view of private construction firms, was the use of "force account" projects, in which the government served as contractor and employer. This was the method often used by the CWA, and later by its successor, the WPA, which directly employed more than two million people at once. Both agencies were the subject of complaints about government competition, especially from private firms in the construction industry.[78]

The TVA, PWA, WPA, and other public enterprises were among the most powerful manifestations of the larger New Deal, which transformed the economic role of the national state. By the end of the 1930s, national government spending amounted to nearly 10 percent of GDP, almost triple what it had been in 1929. There were now one million civilian federal employees (leaving aside those employed temporarily by WPA), nearly double the number in 1930.[79] The crisis of the Great Depression had helped usher in a more powerful, and more entrepreneurial, national state.

For conservatives, the New Deal—and the rise of public enterprise, more specifically—qualified as an abomination. Among the first to recognize this were conservative Republican politicians. Congressman James M. Beck (R-PA), who had been criticizing the growth of federal "bureaucracy" even before Roosevelt entered the White House, was against the New Deal from the first. "We are marching toward Moscow," Beck said in 1933.[80] Additional early warnings were provided by ex-president Hoover. Before the end of 1934, Hoover had published a book-length critique, *The Challenge to Liberty*, which devoted chapters and sections to the problems of "National Regimentation" and "Government in Competitive Business." The early New Deal programs such as TVA, Hoover wrote, amounted to "blows pounding in the wedge of Socialism as part of regimenting the people into a bureaucracy."[81] In the community of conservative politicians, this rhetoric spread. Senator Arthur H. Vandenberg (R-MI), a leading figure in the Republican Party, complained in February 1934 that Americans were "living under political dictatorship"; two years later, he warned of "a vampire of bureaucracy in Washington."[82] Some conservative Democrats, including Albert C. Ritchie, governor of Maryland, agreed. In 1935, Ritchie claimed that American freedoms were being degraded "by a counter spirit of bureaucratic centralization and by a regimented and nationalized economy."[83]

Many American business leaders shared this reaction to the New Deal. Naturally, this generalization does not apply universally. A few executives, including Owen D. Young of General Electric and the department-store magnate Edward A. Filene, maintained positive relations with the New Dealers, as did some leaders of firms whose fortunes most benefited from the new regime, such as construction contractor Henry J. Kaiser. But these individuals were uncommon.[84] For the majority of business leaders, the honeymoon with Roosevelt, to the extent that there was any, lasted only about a year. In 1933–34, some executives had held out hope that the National Recovery Administration (NRA) might offer a business-friendly version of price and wage regulation, which might help the country out of its economic death spiral. Even some of the more politically conservative executives, such as Pierre du Pont, worked at least briefly on NRA committees. But by 1934–35, most of them had given up. They did so not just because the NRA was proving to be an unpopular mess but because of how the rest of the New Deal developed.

The business community's rapid alienation from the New Deal was evident in the experiences of the Du Pont brothers. After the Great War,

Pierre, Irénée, and Lammot du Pont, who led the long-standing family business that had become the nation's leading chemical company, were all multimillionaires. They were also politically active men who gave generously to business associations and conservative political groups, as well as to charitable causes.[85] Pierre and his brothers became disturbed by the New Deal's enthusiasm for public enterprise, which was already being practiced by agencies such as the PWA and TVA. In May 1934, Irénée complained to Pierre of the recent explosion of "governmental capitalism."[86]

Three months later, the Du Pont brothers helped to found the American Liberty League. This anti–New Deal group was financed by many of the nation's most prominent business leaders. Among them were several executives from Du Pont and GM, including John J. Raskob, Alfred D. Sloan, Jr., and William S. Knudsen. Other leading Liberty Leaguers included J. Howard Pew (president of the Sun Oil Company), Raoul E. Desvernine (Crucible Steel Company), and Sewell L. Avery (American Gypsum and Montgomery Ward). A year after its founding in August 1934, the American Liberty League had ten thousand contributing members. In a little over two years, the organization distributed 51 million pamphlets, which pointed out the many dangers of New Deal policies. The league itself spent half a million dollars on the 1936 presidential campaign, in what would turn out to be a totally unsuccessful attempt to unseat Roosevelt. Individual members of the league made major contributions to the GOP that went well beyond this, including more than $1 million donated by the Du Pont and Pew families alone.[87]

The Liberty League's hostility toward the New Deal may have been especially pointed, but it was shared by many other organizations of American business leaders. By December 1934, when the NAM and the Chamber of Commerce of the United States held a joint meeting, most of their members had decided that they could not support Roosevelt and the New Deal. This alienation only deepened in 1935, when the Roosevelt administration worked with Congress to roll out a second wave of major reforms and programs. This "second New Deal" included the WPA, as well as the Wagner Act, which provided far more government support for unions. During the 1936 presidential race, the vast majority of business associations and executives supported the Republican candidate, Alf Landon. Even in industries that seemed to be benefiting most from the New Deal, such as construction, many business leaders worked hard to roll back state enterprise and regulation. As one White House staffer concluded in 1936, it was safe to say that "85% of business and industrial men today are against the Boss."[88]

The Boss, calculating that he could win reelection without much business support and concerned about containing potential challenges from his political left, launched a vigorous public-relations effort of his own. In June 1934, Roosevelt used a radio address to dismiss the "selfish minority" of men who opposed him. Their cries against "regimentation" (which had been voiced by Hoover, among others) amounted to a wild mischaracterization of the New Deal, Roosevelt complained.[89] Over the following months, as business opposition deepened, the president's rhetoric became even more heated. In his State of the Union address in January 1936, Roosevelt boasted that "we have earned the hatred of entrenched greed." During the 1936 campaign, the president regularly portrayed his detractors as "economic autocrats" and "economic royalists." Because he was focused on improving the welfare of the vast majority of Americans, Roosevelt explained, he didn't mind so much if a few of the country's most fortunate citizens opposed him. On the contrary, he said, "I welcome their hatred."[90]

Such was the general state of national-level government-business relations on the eve of the 1936 elections, which Roosevelt would win in a landslide. The business community was concerned not only about the growth of regulation and government in general under the New Deal; many executives were also worried about the specific evil of government competition, which was starting to occur on a scale that had not been seen since the Great War (see Figure 1). One legacy of that conflict, the Muscle Shoals complex, was actually being used by the New Dealers as the basis for a major new public corporation. But this was not the only important connection between the mobilization of 1917–18 and the development of business-government relations in the 1930s. In the military-industrial sphere, too, the 1930s saw a new push for heightened regulation and public control.

A New Deal for the Defense Sector

In early March 1936, the infant public-opinion polling firm led by George H. Gallup surveyed more than a hundred thousand Americans to ascertain their opinions about the arms trade. Gallup asked, "Should the manufacture and sale of war munitions for private profit be prohibited?" In response, 82 percent of those interviewed—one of the largest majorities

NATION'S BUSINESS

GOV'T. COMPETITION

BUSINESS

September
1939

Taxpayers Get a Break • The Riddle of Seniority • Air Conditioning
Takes on More Jobs • A Community Revises Relief

Figure 1. "Government Competition," September 1939 cover of *Nation's Business* magazine, a publication of the Chamber of Commerce of the United States. This cover suggests the business community's concerns about the threat of direct competition from government enterprises on the eve of World War II. Courtesy of U.S. Chamber of Commerce and Hagley Museum and Library.

Gallup had yet recorded—replied yes. Gallup found no subgroup opposed to the proposition. The idea appealed to 79 percent of Republicans and 85 percent of Democrats, compared with 91 percent of Socialists. (The group least enthusiastic were residents of Delaware, home to the Du Pont company, where only 63 percent approved of the idea.) As some of the widespread press coverage of the poll results pointed out, Americans seemed to be slightly less committed to eliminating private armaments companies than their British counterparts, 93 percent of whom had called for it in a comparable survey the previous year.[91] Still, the result was remarkable. It suggested that an overwhelming majority of the American public favored the nationalization of the defense sector.

The results of the 1936 Gallup poll suggest the political significance of national (and international) debates over the interwar arms industry, which culminated in the well-publicized Nye Committee hearings in the Senate. Too often, these debates are remembered as little more than the product of a naïve isolationist approach to foreign policy, which would be discredited by the lessons of World War II.[92] But this view is seriously deficient. First, it fails to recognize that American critics of the munitions business were participating in a transnational, popular political effort to come to confront systemic problems that might cause another terrible war. In the mid-1930s, Senator Gerald P. Nye (R-ND) and his allies were in many ways less "isolationist" than they were cosmopolitan and internationalist.[93]

Second, the munitions debate of the 1930s should be understood as a central chapter in the history of economic policy during the New Deal years. Revolving around issues of the relative merits of government and private ownership in an industry that was, in fact, already semi-nationalized, it was closely related to the TVA fight and other interwar battles over public enterprise. As such, it was taken very seriously by the American business community. Indeed, the struggle over munitions was intertwined with the broader political offensive, launched by conservative business leaders in the mid-1930s, which was designed to combat President Roosevelt and the New Deal.

During and immediately after the Great War, hundreds of thousands of people all over the world voiced their concerns about the intermixture of capitalism and modern warfare. To many people, including soldiers, veterans, and their families, the sorts of profits that had been earned by companies like Du Pont and Bethlehem Steel seemed objectionable, if not obscene. Beyond this, some critics worried that the profitability of munitions manufacture created dangerous economic incentives. The admixture of capitalism and warfare appeared to give companies and individuals a vested interest in promoting military conflict. After the armistice, there was a global movement to solve these problems. In 1921, the new League of Nations resolved that "the manufacture by private enterprise of munitions and implements of war is open to grave objections."[94]

In the United States, which had not joined the league, there was a political consensus that in the event of a future conflict, the sacrifice must be shared more broadly. As President Harding put it, the next time around, there should be "no swollen fortunes." The two leading veterans' organizations, the American Legion and the Veterans of Foreign Wars (VFW), both called for increased control of profits in wartime, possibly via a coercive "draft" of capital that would match the conscription of soldiers. In 1924, the Republican and Democratic party platforms both promised that in the event of a future conflict, there would be something closer to a "universal mobilization." All this sober activity did not prevent readers from chuckling at Harold Gray's "Little Orphan Annie" comic, which in 1924 introduced a sympathetic character named Daddy Warbucks.[95] But to a large number of Americans, the record of the radically inegalitarian distribution of war bucks in the late 1910s was really no laughing matter.

After 1929, as the nation slid into the Great Depression, Congress and the White House began to consider more concrete proposals for profit control in a future war. During the tenure of the Hoover administration, the most important work in this field was done by a presidentially appointed War Policies Commission, which held hearings in 1931. In its final report, which was influenced by the continuing lobbying efforts of the American Legion, the commission recommended that profit control in a future war go well beyond what had been achieved during the Great War. It called for broad price controls, as well as a new EPT that would capture 95 percent of any profits above prewar averages. Although Congress did not act immediately to institute these recommendations, it was clear that there was a broad consensus that in the event of a future war, the nation should use stricter controls than the ones applied in 1917–18.[96]

As the Depression worsened, there was an upsurge all around the world in calls for stricter regulation of the munitions business. The economic crisis, which naturally led to more questioning of the beneficence of large-scale capitalist enterprises of all kinds, seems to have further heightened interest in the sins of arms suppliers, in particular.[97] In 1933–34, books and articles about the "merchants of death" abounded in Europe and the United States. The public attention led to new action by governments. In Britain, where the Labour Party was calling for more nationalization of arms production, a Royal Commission was appointed to investigate the issue. Its report, issued in 1936, came out against full nationalization, but it did call for more regulation of production and profits. In France, a partial nationalization did occur, following the electoral victories of the Popular Front, in 1936. Not surprisingly, this move led to clashes between the government and executives at French companies that had been serving as military suppliers, including Renault and Schneider.[98]

In the United States, the largest and best-publicized of the efforts at defense-sector reform in the mid-1930s was the Senate's munitions inquiry, chaired by Gerald Nye. A populist Republican from North Dakota, Senator Nye had done some work in the late 1920s in the later stages of the Teapot Dome investigations. His munitions investigation originated with the efforts of the Women's International League for Peace and Freedom, which in 1919—when it was still led by the celebrated American progressive and pacifist Jane Addams—had pushed for a global ban on the private production of munitions. In 1932, a new president of the Women's International League, Dorothy Detzer, pushed Congress to investigate the issue. At first, Detzer hoped that the investigation would be led by Senator George Norris, the patron of the TVA. In the end, Norris helped her to enlist Nye.[99]

From the beginning, Nye made it clear that he wanted to use the hearings to persuade Congress to enact strict controls on the defense sector. In August 1934, just before the hearings started, Nye gave well-publicized speeches, one at the World's Fair in Chicago, and one on the CBS radio network. In these talks, Nye called attention to the enormous profits that had been collected during the Great War by Du Pont, among other companies. He also suggested that Congress should consider imposing a "government monopoly" over munitions manufacture. Two months later, after the hearings had started, Nye went back on the radio with more specific proposals. In the event of war, he declared, any incomes over $10,000 should be taxed at a rate of 98 percent. In addition, Nye said, the United States should nationalize its peacetime defense sector, so that private contractors had no role in making munitions.[100] These proposals went beyond what the War Policies Commission had suggested three years earlier; they were also more radical than the reforms demanded by the American Legion, which was still calling for a 95 percent EPT.[101]

Although the Nye Committee criticized a wide range of arms traders and military contractors, it was especially hostile to Du Pont. Senator Nye's speeches portrayed the Du Pont brothers as the greatest of the Great War profiteers. In the early hearings, which focused on collusion and bribery in the international arms trade, the committee criticized Du Pont for its cozy relationship with its British counterpart, Imperial Chemical Industries (ICI). Later, Nye used the investigation to publicize the Du Ponts' generous political contributions to conservative groups, including the American Liberty League—which had been founded just as the Nye investigation got under way.[102]

For their part, the Du Pont brothers regarded the Nye Committee as the creation of irresponsible radicals who knew nothing about the economics of defense.[103] But they realized that the attacks threatened the company's reputation and its future. Certainly, Congress and the Justice Department might try to cancel Du Pont's recent acquisition of Remington, an important American manufacturer of rifles and ammunition. More broadly, the Nye Committee's assault seemed to require an energetic public-relations counteroffensive. Du Pont prepared one, with the help of Bruce Barton, a top consultant in the field. In August 1934, Barton assured Du Pont executives that "most of the reckless charges against munitions makers have originated not with the great body of unselfish peace-lovers but with muckraking journalists."[104] But Barton and Du Pont still needed to prepare a careful rebuttal to educate Congress and the public. They prepared talking points for the executives called before the Nye Committee. These stressed that although some economic regulation in wartime was necessary, the country also needed to remember that "the profit motive," as "one of the strongest incentives to endeavor," should be understood as "a powerful weapon" in its own right, "which should not be tossed away." And in an open letter to stockholders, the company stressed its great contributions to national security in the Great War, the overwhelmingly commercial character of its business since 1919, and its interest in promoting peace.[105]

As Nye and the Du Ponts battled over public relations, the Nye Committee worked on formal recommendations. These did not depart much from the suggestions that Nye had made in his early speeches. Even before the majority of the committee issued its final report, in 1936, Nye and his colleagues had urged Congress to create steep wartime price and profit controls. Many of these details were written up by John T. Flynn, a journalist and sometime congressional staffer who became an important part of

Nye's team. Flynn's plan went well beyond the recommendations of Bernard Baruch, the former WIB chief, who testified regularly in Washington about the need to impose heavy price controls in wartime. The Nye Committee also wanted strict price control but added to this the Flynn plan for ultrahigh wartime income taxes and EPT, which would impose rates of 98 percent or 100 percent. These proposals became part of several bills that circulated in Congress in 1935. Meanwhile, President Roosevelt, who angered veterans in May 1935 by vetoing a bill that would have paid them a cash bonus a few years ahead of schedule, promised in more vague terms that in any future conflict, there must be strict profit controls.[106]

The other element of the Nye Committee's call for radical reform in the defense sector was its recommendation that the national state monopolize peacetime—if not wartime—munitions production. A minority of the committee's members, who issued their own final report, disagreed. According to the minority, there should be "rigid and conclusive munitions control" but not "complete nationalization."[107]

The majority, however, called for an end to the government's peacetime use of private contractors to supply key military goods such as weapons, ammunition, explosives, and warships. In doing so, they combined emotionally charged rhetoric with colder economic calculations. Both were used by Senator Homer Bone (D-WA), a well-known champion of public utilities. When contractors testified that the private sector was always more efficient, Bone responded that the record of the power industry in the Pacific Northwest had taught him otherwise. But Bone also made more moralistic arguments. In 1917–18, he recalled, some American "boys were butchered in the war, and thousands of men made multimillionaires overnight." Given this record of such reprehensible inequalities, Bone asked, "Why should we blink at socialization?"[108]

Such suggestions were actually less radical than they might seem because peacetime munitions manufacture was already semi-nationalized. After 1918, the War Department's own arsenals had returned to their traditional role, which was to supply the Army with most of its needs for small arms, artillery, and ammunition. Meanwhile, the Navy was sending a large fraction of its modest orders for new warships to its own yards, which Secretary Daniels had worked so hard to expand. These GOGO munitions facilities were examined carefully by the Nye Committee, which determined that they were competitive with private sources. The committee also asked the ICC to estimate what it would cost to expand the GOGO operations enough to supply all the peacetime needs of the Army and Navy. According to the ICC, it would take only about $24 million in additional investment in the Navy shipyards to fully nationalize peacetime warship construction. For an additional $23 million, the ICC estimated, the Army and Navy could expand their GOGO operations enough to create a peacetime government monopoly in the manufacture of finished small arms, smokeless powder, and aircraft.[109]

As the results of the Gallup poll in March 1936 suggest, most Americans supported some kind of increased regulation of the arms industry, if not all the Nye Committee's specific proposals. Surveys of college students and church groups in 1935, when the committee's hearings were widely publicized in the national media, found that more than 80 percent of those surveyed favored heavier government controls over munitions. First Lady Eleanor Roosevelt supported the Nye Committee's recommendations, including the call for nationalization.[110]

Veterans, who had been calling for major reforms since 1918, continued their efforts. At VFW-sponsored dinners across the country in 1935, officers demanded a policy of "profit for none" in any future war. Two years later, the American Legion was still pushing Congress to pass powerful wartime profit controls, so as to avoid any repetition of the Great War, when "some twenty-two thousand individuals at home stepped from the shadows of financial obscurity into the millionaire class." Such language continued to prevail among veterans, well after the Nye Committee hearings came to an end. At a local VFW event in 1937, Louisiana state senator Ernest Clements roused the assembled veterans by recalling that twenty years earlier, the nation had suffered "a hundred thousand soldiers dead to make a bunch of skunks American millionaires." In any future war, Clements demanded, the government must "take over munitions plants." This call brought loud applause from the assembled VFW men.[111]

The real question in the mid-1930s was not whether the government should strictly regulate war profits and build weapons in its own facilities, but exactly how far this should go. Some government officials, including NRA chief Hugh S. Johnson, indicated that they could support a full nationalization of peacetime munitions production with the understanding that in wartime, the government would need to contract with the private sector.[112] This idea was supported by Ernest Angell, a New York lawyer and Great War veteran who published a lengthy magazine piece on the issue in 1935. Angell did not oppose some kind of extension of peacetime nationalization, but he pointed out that any such move would have to grapple with the technical question of "at what point in the stream of production a proposed government monopoly shall take over."[113] The Navy might not have much trouble taking over all the production of finished warships and guns, which it already knew how to make. But such a scheme would still presumably require lots of private suppliers, who would sell the Navy most of the elements it needed, such as steel products, turbines, boilers, valves, and cable.

In the end, most of the Nye Committee's recommendations were not enacted by Congress. The committee's investigations did contribute to the passage of the 1935 Neutrality Act, which banned munitions exports to nations at war. But Nye's efforts to ramp up domestic regulation of the defense sector failed, in the shorter run. The government would not impose comprehensive price and profit controls until after a new world war had begun. Nye's nationalization scheme was resisted by civilian leaders and military officers in the War and Navy Departments, who preferred to maintain their more flexible systems of mixed public and private production. The military was backed by President Roosevelt, who had close ties to the Navy and opted to distance himself from Nye's more populist approach to the issue.

Although Nye was thwarted in 1936, it would be a mistake to understand the defense sector of the 1930s as an area that was immune to the progressive push for more regulation and public enterprise. This was obvious in warship construction, which, as the Nye Committee noted, was already semi-nationalized.[114] Here there was already a difference from the years before the Great War, when about 80 percent of new warships had been built by private contractors. After the 1922 Washington Naval Treaty, which limited warship construction, it was unclear how much of the Navy's modest orders would go to its in-house shipyards and how much to the struggling private yards. The private shipbuilders lobbied for more work, but their efforts were countered by those members of Congress who had one of the eight Navy yards in their districts. In the late 1920s, Congress settled on a fifty-fifty policy, which called for half the ships to be built by contractors and half by the Navy yards.[115]

The policy of building half the warships in the Navy's in-house yards was solidified in March 1934, when Congress passed the Vinson-Trammell Act. One of the most important pieces of legislation passed during the interwar period, Vinson-Trammell authorized the Navy to begin a major new building effort that would provide it 1.2 million displacement tons of warships, the maximum allowed under the 1930 London Naval Treaty. Its passage represented a victory for the proponents of a big Navy, including President Roosevelt and Congressman Carl Vinson (D-GA). It was also a victory for public enterprise. According to the law, every other warship needed to be built in a U.S. Navy yard, "unless . . . inconsistent with the public interest." (The same level of public production was not required for aircraft, even though the Naval Aircraft Factory had been a major producer during the early 1920s. According to the new law, only 10 percent of Navy planes should come from in-house sources.) Vinson-Trammell also regulated profits, by capping contractors' earnings on Navy shipbuilding work at 10 percent of production costs.[116]

Thanks to the generous appropriations provided by Vinson-Trammell, along with tens of millions of dollars from New Deal agencies, the private shipyards became much healthier. At companies like the Bath Iron Works, in Maine, and Newport News Ship, in Virginia, this was a welcome end to what had been more than a decade of inactivity and financial struggles.[117] However, the private yards were none too pleased by the statute's requirement that production be semi-nationalized. This clause was protested by the National Council of American Shipbuilders, which soon found itself trying to contain an even bigger threat—the Nye Committee's call for all-out nationalization.[118]

Having dodged that bullet, the National Council of American Shipbuilders rededicated itself to lobbying against the semi-nationalization required under Vinson-Trammell. Some of the council's arguments, which stressed that the costs of the GOGO facilities appeared to be competitive only because they were never fully accounted for, were very similar to the ones used by the private electrical utilities in their battle with the TVA. "If navy yards are to be used as yardsticks," the private shipbuilders complained to Congress in 1937, "then the yardstick should be exactly 36 inches long." The council also pointed to the private yards' modest profits, which, since the mid-1910s, had averaged only 5.5 percent of sales, barely half the 10 percent limit imposed by Vinson-Trammell. According to the shipbuilders, they had the added burden of facing tough Navy officers who appeared to enjoy their ability to squeeze the private contractors by subjecting them to the competition of public yards. The council pointed to the example of Admiral Emory Scott ("Jerry") Land, who had claimed that the art of submarine construction had been improved by the competition between the Electric Boat Company and the Navy's own yard in Portsmouth. The council quoted Admiral Land as having referred to the private shipyards as "my arch enemy, so far as doing business is concerned, all the time."[119]

Like other business leaders, the executives who led the private shipyards were disturbed by the Roosevelt administration's willingness to use the "birch rod" of government competition. Tensions over this issue mounted in 1936–37, after Congress passed the Walsh-Healey Act, which required government contractors to pay their workers overtime rates after forty hours a week. Some shipbuilding and steel companies, which were already engaged in a major struggle to prevent the unionization of their plants, began to suggest that they might avoid Navy contracts in the future. President Roosevelt, coming off his landslide victory in November, was willing to play hardball. If the steel companies did not want to fill contracts for armor plate, the president suggested, the government could always reopen its GOGO facility in West Virginia. Then, in a January 1937 press conference, Roosevelt said that although he preferred to continue the fifty-fifty distribution of orders outlined in Vinson-Trammell, he could, if necessary, give an even larger fraction of the work to the Navy yards. Roosevelt then announced that both of the first two *North Carolina*–class battleships would be built by the Navy's own yards, in Brooklyn and Philadelphia. Roosevelt's decision outraged executives at the New York Shipbuilding Corporation, who had expected that the usual fifty-fifty policy would allow them to build one of the massive vessels. This dispute would ebb over the following months, when the private yards would once again receive about half the Navy's new orders. But for the contractors, the episode demonstrated again the power of government competition.[120]

On the War Department side, the situation was somewhat different because the political struggles over Army procurement were more concerned with a future war mobilization. In peacetime, the U.S. Army's own arsenals were supplying many of the finished weapons demanded by its small force. But as War Department officers knew from the record of the Great War, they would need to equip several million men, instead of a couple hundred thousand, in the event of another major conflict. To accomplish this, they would carry out another "industrial mobilization," as they called it, comparable with what had occurred in 1917–18. As European observers recognized, the United States was a leader in planning for industrial mobilization. One reason for this was the nation's unique strategic situation: protected from leading military powers by vast oceans, the United States still seemed to enjoy the luxury of maintaining a small army, until an emergency developed. The U.S. also boasted the world's biggest national industrial capacity, which American officers expected to tap in the event of war.[121]

According to the National Defense Act of 1920, industrial mobilization planning was overseen by the Office of the Assistant Secretary of War (OASW). During the 1920s, the OASW created the new Army Industrial College (AIC) where some mid-career military officers could spend a year or two studying the problems associated with economic mobilization. Between 1924 and 1940, nearly nine hundred officers graduated from the AIC. Of these, more than a hundred also received MBAs from Harvard Business School, under a new program created by Harvard and the War Department. Meanwhile, the Ordnance Department, operating through the regional procurement districts that it had set up during the Great War, continued to work with companies and business associations. During the 1920s, the Ordnance Districts conducted surveys of thousands of manufacturing plants that might be tapped for munitions production in a future war.[122]

Army officers attached to the OASW, including Major Dwight D. Eisenhower, also helped compose the official Industrial Mobilization Plan (IMP). First released in 1930, and revised several times before World War II, the IMP was shaped by the ideas of former WIB chief Bernard Baruch, who frequently advised the military. The plan called for WIB-style civilian coordinating agencies, which would allocate critical materials and impose price controls. According to Baruch, a future coordinating agency could combine strong "administrative control" with a voluntaristic approach to mobilization, in which industry could mostly organize itself. At least in its public statements, the War Department promised to rely heavily on voluntarism. According to the Army's chief of staff, General Douglas MacArthur, any future industrial mobilization would depend on "spontaneous cooperation," not coercion. "The least possible disturbance must be caused in the normal economic life of the country," MacArthur promised Congress in 1931. This attitude was written into the IMP, which stated that future mobilizers must avoid imposing "arbitrary and unnecessary regulations" on businesses and consumers. "No radical changes in normal economic relationships between individuals and between an individual and Government should be instituted," the IMP declared.[123]

The War Department, like the Navy Department, rejected the Nye Committee's calls for a full nationalization. This was not because Army officers had no interest in manufacturing weapons: by the mid-1930s, they were using their own arsenals to supply almost all the peacetime Army's needs for rifles, ammunition, artillery, projectiles, and gunpowder. But because they expected these GOGO facilities to supply only about 10 percent of their needs in a future all-out war, Ordnance Department officers wanted to cultivate relationships with private companies. Their counterparts in the Army Air Corps, who procured planes by ordering from a highly competitive private industry, also opposed nationalization. Just as their predecessors had done during the Great War, these interwar officers believed that it would be much cheaper and easier, economically and politically, to rely heavily on private capacity in a major emergency.[124]

On the eve of World War II, the War Department's civilian leaders and regular officers emphasized their friendliness to the private sector. As conditions in Europe deteriorated, Assistant Secretary of War Louis A. Johnson promised executives that the military officers who would participate in any future industrial mobilization "have no designs to take over your business." Rather, Johnson promised business leaders, "[w]e have predicated our whole industrial mobilization program on the maintenance of the established American way of getting things done."[125] Among the military officers charged with planning procurement, including those attached to the AIC, there was a similar doctrine. "We are attempting to solve our industrial mobilization problems not by regimentation," one AIC pamphlet of 1938 stated, "but in accordance with democratic American methods." In May 1940, as France fell, the college's commandant, Colonel F. H. Miles, promised the Buffalo Chamber of Commerce that the military's intention was "to disrupt industry as little as possible."[126]

Given the record of the War Department in the 1920s and the 1930s, it may be hard not to conclude that the U.S. Army, if not the Navy, was overwhelmingly deferential to the private sector. Yet the attitude of War Department officers was actually not quite as reassuring to pro-business conservatives as it might appear at first glance.[127]

For one thing, military officers maintained pride in their own competence. With good reason, many of them resented Baruch's self-promoting accounts of the Great War mobilization, which exaggerated the influence of the WIB while downplaying the major contributions of the War and Navy Departments and their supply bureaus. The AIC was not intended to simply put the military in a position to tap private expertise but also to develop in-house competencies in wartime economic management.

Assistant Secretary of War Dwight F. Davis made this point in 1924, as the AIC opened. "The theory so often advanced . . . that we can quickly settle our supply problems by calling in from the industrial world men of high standing, in my judgment, is not sound," Davis said. Instead, the military needed to "know more about its work than any body else." This attitude endured, despite the War Department's many public promises to defer to industry. As Lieutenant Colonel A. B. Quinton, Jr., an AIC instructor, put it in 1937, "we should not have any inferiority complex in dealing with" business leaders.[128] Such language was significant because it shaped the attitudes of men who would wield great economic power on the World War II home front. Quinton, for example, would serve as one of the nation's top managers of the American war economy, as chief of the Ordnance Department's biggest contracting office, in Detroit.

Quinton and his fellow officers believed that the contractors should be subject to special forms of economic regulation, which might include price and profit controls, as well as compulsory orders. As one AIC study group concluded in 1937, even if the War Department did not favor increased nationalization, it did agree with the widespread public calls for "rigid control of the private munitions industry." Top military procurement officers, like many other Americans, wanted to limit war profits but without completely abandoning the profit system. As Colonel Charles Harris told Congress, more than a little awkwardly, in 1937, "it is the idea to disturb the normal process as little as possible. . . . On the other hand, the War Department is strongly opposed to profiteering. . . . On the other hand, the War Department believes in a fair profit." Two years later, Colonel James H. Burns promised the Chamber of Commerce that the military wanted to minimize any economic "regimentation" in wartime. Echoing the rhetoric of Herbert Hoover and other conservatives, this was music to the ears of most business leaders. Somewhat less reassuring, perhaps, was Burns's added qualification: "if we permit unreasonable prices and profits we . . . ruin the morale of the country."[129]

Business leaders also had reason to be concerned about the military's reliance on Baruch's vision of industrial mobilization, which was less voluntaristic than it seemed. As Baruch reminded the cadets at the U.S. Military Academy at West Point in 1929, the wartime state would have the power to allocate critical materials. This was "the iron fist in the velvet glove" that the government could wield to encourage private firms to do its bidding.[130] This attitude worried business leaders, as did Baruch's notion that as a last resort, the government could always just commandeer private property. As Baruch reported to a friend in 1924, executives such as Elbert Gary of U.S. Steel had insisted that "the taking over of industries was a communistic scheme" that should not be allowed even in wartime.[131] On this question, military officers sided not with Gary but with Baruch. During the 1930s, top War Department officers often noted that the IMP and other emergency schemes would provide ample coercive powers. Some of them echoed Baruch's "iron hand in the velvet glove" rhetoric; others described a "big stick available for use on the recalcitrant if necessary." For the officers, the wartime state's coercive powers were "like a policeman's club— always in sight but little used."[132] From the point of view of many business leaders, this was disturbing. It remained unclear who might be using the club, for what purposes it might be used, and who might be on the receiving end.

*   *   *

In the late 1930s, as international skies darkened, many Americans grew pessimistic about the future of domestic politics. Progressives worried that war mobilization might lead to American fascism. In 1939, Interior Secretary Harold L. Ickes warned that conservatives might use the war emergency to "destroy both American democracy and the social reforms of the New Deal."[133] Such fears reflected the political defeats suffered by New Dealers over the previous two years. Despite an overwhelming victory in the 1936 elections, President Roosevelt had struggled to expand the New Deal.[134] His early 1937 effort to add justices to the Supreme Court bolstered conservative criticisms that he was an autocrat. Then, government spending cuts had caused an economic downturn. After the 1938 elections, the House contained eighty-five more Republicans, who thwarted Roosevelt's plans. Moreover, the business community's ongoing public-relations campaign bore fruit. By the eve of World War II, Americans polled by Gallup blamed the Roosevelt administration for the recent recession; they also favored a "more conservative" government, more friendly to the private sector.[135]

Business leaders, while encouraged by these favorable developments on the domestic political front, feared that American entry into World War II might revitalize the Left. Most U.S. companies in the mid-1930s were content with neutrality from a financial point of view because they were not producing arms for export. Even Du Pont, which had made military explosives for decades, had become much more interested in civilian markets. In 1937, the Du Pont corporate board, which worried about the company's "evil reputation" as an armaments maker, only barely turned down a motion that would have had the company stop munitions work entirely.[136] Even in 1938, as the Munich crisis took Europe to the brink of war, American companies feared the political costs of taking military work. Furthermore, they anticipated that such work might not be especially profitable, given that the defense sector was often the target of intense regulation.

Business leaders remembered the Wilson administration's war policies, the Nye Committee, and the origins of the TVA. Their memories made them especially wary of war. Charles R. Hook, the NAM chairman and president of the American Rolling Mill Company, explained it in mid-1939: "Business men are normal human beings," no less horrified by the prospect of mass killing than any of their peers. Beyond this, they stood against war because it would bring tax increases, along with a "government invasion of private rights." This had occurred on many occasions during World War I, Hook recalled, most obviously during the government takeover of the railroads. What the business community really wanted, Hook explained, was "to continue the democratic system which includes the system of private enterprise under which the nation has flourished during the last century."[137] War would make this more difficult.

Yet Hook and his fellow business leaders could not avoid war. Well before the Pearl Harbor attacks of December 1941, they began participating in a massive industrial mobilization. To the consternation of business leaders, the World War II mobilization would feature many of the same government policies that had occurred during World War I and the interwar period. Indeed, in many respects, Roosevelt went beyond Wilson. One critical area in which this was true concerned the way that the United States went about expanding its capacities to manufacture munitions. More than anyone had anticipated, this process relied on direct government ownership of industry.

Chapter 2

Building the Arsenal

When World War II began in Europe in September 1939, the United States had the potential to produce vast numbers of warships, planes, tanks, and other weapons for use in the defense of England, France, Poland, and other allies. The United States possessed the world's largest national economy, abundant natural resources, and world-class manufacturers. But Americans disagreed about how this potential should be realized. Progressives, recalling the record of corporate profits in World War I, hoped to avoid policies that would boost the fortunes of big business. They believed that the government should maintain tight controls over war production; some even wanted the government to make much of the matériel. By contrast, conservatives worried that the war might reenergize the New Deal. They believed that private industry should lead the production effort, with the government providing the cash to buy the arms but otherwise staying out of the way.

Popular legend holds that conservatives won this political battle. To make this point, historians often relate an anecdote about William S. Knudsen, who, at the start of World War II, was president of the General Motors Corporation (GM). A Danish immigrant and former production manager for Henry Ford, Knudsen left Detroit in mid-1940 for Washington, where he served as a top industrial mobilization official. Just after the Pearl Harbor attacks, in January 1942, Knudsen presided over a meeting of executives from leading American manufacturing companies, including his peers from the automobile industry. As the story goes, Knudsen used the meeting to conduct a sort of informal auction of war contracts. He read from a list of new military requirements, asking the executives to volunteer to convert their plants to make mountains of machine guns, artillery shells, and all sorts of other munitions.[1]

The Knudsen story confirms progressive as well as conservative myths about the American industrial mobilization. It describes a business community rolling up its sleeves to lead a patriotic effort to punish the Axis. The story also appears to demonstrate how war contracts were being handed out to big business leaders by their friends in Washington. Indeed, more than half of the aggregate value of all American war contracts, as we are often reminded, went to just two or three dozen big industrial corporations.[2] Together, the progressive and corporate legends tell how the automakers and other leading industrial corporations converted quickly from civilian to military production, as they secured even more economic and political power.

In fact, the American war economy was not a private affair. Public authorities—civilian and military—managed the work of industrial mobilization. These public officials included not only Knudsen and his peers at agencies such as the War Production Board (WPB) but also public financiers, including the governments of France and Britain, the War and Navy Departments, and the new Defense Plant Corporation (DPC). War and Navy Department officers placed and managed most of the war contracts; they also served as the top managers of wartime industrial supply chains. Military agencies acted as powerful general contractors, as they ordered thousands of components, from hundreds of smaller and midsize manufacturers (those with fewer than ten thousand employees) as well as big corporations, and directed their flow into finished aircraft, ships, tanks, trucks, and guns.[3] So, while it is true that American capitalism supplied the Allies with mountains of munitions, it did so with immense amounts of support, supervision, and guidance from the agencies and officers of the U.S. government.

In the end, America's remarkable war production represented the triumph of compromise. Much to the irritation of many business leaders, the U.S. government went well beyond simply buying munitions, by building acres of public-owned industrial plant and establishing an array of powerful regulatory agencies. Progressives complained that corporations profited too much from the war, but their warnings that the war would promote monopoly proved overblown. The mobilization relied heavily on the contributions of midsize manufacturers, which often dealt directly with the Navy and War Departments as prime contractors, besides serving as subcontractors to bigger corporations. All in all, the American military-industrial machine was something much more than the creation of American big business; it was led not just by corporate executives like Knudsen but by a diverse cast of private and public officers. It took the combined efforts of politicians, entrepreneurs, workers, soldiers and sailors, and bureaucrats to build the arsenal of democracy.

Phase 1: Rearmament, 1938–40

One of the most important battles of World War II occurred in June 1942, when the American and Japanese navies faced off near Midway Island, in the middle of the Pacific Ocean. At Midway, American forces managed to sink four Japanese aircraft carriers while losing only one of their own. By winning at Midway, the United States managed to turn the tide of the Pacific War. This victory occurred just six months after the disaster at Pearl Harbor and only weeks after Allied forces suffered humiliating defeats in Southeast Asia.

The results at Midway are difficult to reconcile with stories of American war mobilization that emphasize inaction before Pearl Harbor. Indeed, at Midway, the Americans relied on ships and aircraft that had all been built or developed in the 1930s. Two of the three American aircraft carriers at the battle, *Enterprise* and *Yorktown*, had been ordered from the Newport News Shipbuilding Corporation, a Virginia company, in 1934; they were launched in 1936. The third, the *Hornet*, was ordered in 1939 and—after a speedy construction effort by Newport News—launched in December 1940. These carriers were platforms for what would turn out to be the decisive weapon of the battle at Midway: the "Dauntless" SBD dive bomber, made in southern California by the Douglas Aircraft Company. The Navy ordered twelve dozen of these planes in April 1939, almost half a year before war started in Europe; it bought another large batch in June 1940.[4]

As the provenance of the key weapons used at Midway suggests, the winning American war effort in 1942–45 depended heavily on munitions that had been designed—and, in some cases, even procured—in the 1930s. In hindsight, of course, these early activities seemed inadequate. But during the two years before the German offensives of spring 1940, the United States accomplished a first phase of industrial mobilization. Thanks to American, French, and British orders in 1938 and 1939, the aircraft and naval shipbuilding industries started 1940 in excellent financial health, and in the midst of a major expansion.

This first phase of industrial mobilization took place in the context of very difficult political and economic circumstances, domestically and internationally. In early 1938, the U.S. economy was still in a serious recession, which had begun in the middle of the previous year. Many companies were losing money. Although a recovery started before the end of 1938, the Great Depression lingered. The national unemployment rate, which had been terribly high for the entire decade, would remain close to 16 percent until 1940.[5] Outside the United States, the Depression had generally been less severe, but the political situation was harrowing. By October 1937, when President Roosevelt offended American isolationists with his "quarantine speech," suggesting the need for more active efforts to contain international aggression, the Spanish Civil War was under way; Mussolini's Italy had invaded Ethiopia; and Japan had pushed into China. In March 1938, Germany, led by Adolf Hitler, annexed Austria. By summer 1938, it looked as if Europe was only days away from the unthinkable: another terrible war among the great powers.

The bleak international situation in 1938 made it possible for the American naval shipbuilding and aircraft industries to expand, even before the European war broke out in September 1939. They did so through a combination of domestic and foreign orders. In the case of warships, one key step was a new, $1.1 billion Fleet Expansion Act, passed by Congress in May 1938. This bill allowed the Navy to begin to order vessels that would make the U.S. fleet expand by 20 percent.[6]

By passing the naval expansion act in early 1938, Congress reaffirmed the strong support that it had provided the Navy since Roosevelt entered the White House in 1933. In that chaotic year, Roosevelt managed to use some of the first New Deal appropriations to pay for thirty-two new warships. But this step paled in comparison with the legislation passed by Congress the following year. Sponsored by Georgia Democrat Carl Vinson, the Navy's greatest friend in Washington, the Vinson-Trammell Act of 1934 allowed the Navy to expand the fleet to the maximum level allowed under the Washington and London naval treaties. This meant 102 additional combatant vessels, which were to be procured over the following eight years.[7] Navy spending in the later 1930s averaged over half a billion dollars a year. This was 50 percent more than it had been before 1934 and slightly above the annual naval expenditures of Great Britain.[8]

For the fragile naval shipbuilding industry, which had suffered from the end of World War I through the first part of the Depression, the 1934 act provided much-needed cash, as well more stability. In the private sector, only six companies were still making major combatant vessels, including battleships, cruisers, carriers, destroyers, and submarines. The surface vessels were made by Newport News (the builder of the carriers at Midway); the New York Shipbuilding Corporation; the shipyards of the Bethlehem Steel Corporation; the Bath Iron Works; and a U.S. Steel Corporation subsidiary called Federal Shipbuilding. The only private-sector supplier of submarines was the Electric Boat Company, located in Connecticut. Most of these yards had served as Navy contractors since the 1890s, when they had helped build the country's first world-class steel navy.

Because these for-profit naval shipbuilders managed to survive the doldrums of the interwar period, they stood to gain from new orders. However, they also contended with an unusual degree of direct competition from the public sector. This division of labor continued under Vinson-Trammell, which required that half of the new combatants be built in the public yards. The public-private mix prevailed also in the production of naval ordnance, just over half of which came from the Navy's own plants during the late 1930s. Certainly, the Navy acted as if it expected its own yards to function as state-of-the art production facilities, capable of competing with the best of the private sector. During the 1930s, the Navy spent $180 million to improve its own eight shipyards. By 1939, they employed 46,000 civilians, or over a third of all American shipyard workers. Like the private yards, the Navy's in-house facilities were often led by talented engineers, many of whom had advanced degrees in engineering or ship architecture from MIT.[9]

For the private and public shipyards alike, Vinson-Trammell meant steady business, if not an impetus for expansion. During the second half of the 1930s, Electric Boat and the Portsmouth Navy Yard were each able to build two or three submarines a year. Two new destroyers a year were turned out by at least four builders—Bath Iron Works, Bethlehem Steel's Fore River (Quincy, Massachusetts) yard, Federal Ship, and the Charlestown (Boston) Navy Yard. In October 1937, the Brooklyn Navy Yard laid the keel for the *North Carolina*, the first new American battleship to be built since the signing of the Washington Naval Treaty in 1922. Altogether, the congressional appropriations from 1933 to 1937 allowed the Navy to order two battleships, three aircraft carriers, three heavy cruisers, nine light cruisers, sixty-three destroyers, and twenty-six submarines.[10]

The builders of warships received another boost in May 1938, with the passage of the Fleet Expansion Act. When the war started in Europe in September 1939, American shipyards were in the midst of building two new aircraft carriers, eight battleships, five cruisers, and three dozen destroyers. Of the 1.3 million tons worth of warships available to the Navy in 1940, half had been added to the fleet since 1934.[11]

The new contracts went to the handful of public and private yards that had been serving the Navy throughout the interwar period. In early 1939, Newport News received the order for the new aircraft carrier *Hornet*, along with one of the four new 35,000-ton *South Dakota*–class battleships. The other three ships in this class, which would not enter service until after Pearl Harbor, went to New York Ship, Bethlehem–Fore River, and the U.S. Navy Yard at Norfolk, Virginia. In mid-1939, the Navy ordered two bigger battleships, of the new 45,000-ton *Iowa* class, to be built in its own yards in Philadelphia and Brooklyn. Among the smaller combatants ordered under the 1938 act were six light cruisers, sixteen destroyers, and fourteen submarines. For Bath Iron Works and the Electric Boat Company, which specialized in destroyers and submarines, respectively, the new orders pushed 1939 sales to $15 million, double what they had been two or three years earlier.[12]

Because warships ordinarily took two to three years to complete, the 1938 orders determined the size and shape of the U.S. Navy fleet that was available for service immediately after Pearl Harbor. None of these orders in the 1930s could fully prepare the Navy's top shipbuilders for the sort of expansion that they would undertake in wartime, when they would grow temporarily into truly big businesses. However, the 1930s contracts did allow a handful of expert shipyards to thrive. Bath Iron Works, where employment had fallen to fewer than three hundred workers in 1932, boasted nearly two thousand on the payroll by 1938. Newport News saw its workforce grow from about 7,300 in 1937 to 11,500 by 1940.[13]

Besides enlivening individual yards, the rise of warship orders in the 1930s also strengthened the small network of public and private organizations that constituted the naval shipbuilding industry. This network went beyond the half-dozen private-sector shipbuilders and the eight U.S. Navy yards. Besides these shipbuilders, key players included the Navy's Bureau of Construction and Repair and its Bureau of Engineering, well-informed customers that helped determine the specifications for the vessels. Also critical were private ship architects, the most important of which was Gibbs &

Cox, based in New York City. Together with designers at the private shipbuilders and the Navy yards, Gibbs & Cox helped draft new hull designs that could be integrated with improved steam turbine power plants, using high pressures and high temperatures. The builders of these turbines, including General Electric (GE) and Westinghouse, ranked among the most important members of the naval-industrial complex. Thanks to the Navy orders of the 1930s, this tight network—comprising shipyards, designers, engine makers, and Navy procurement bureaus—started World War II able to draw upon several years of collaboration and familiarity.[14]

Besides naval shipbuilding, the other major World War II industry most stimulated by orders in the 1930s was the one that made aircraft. Here again, an expansion of orders in the late 1930s was critical for the disposition of forces that would be available by the time of Pearl Harbor. Planes and their engines could be produced somewhat faster than the large warships, but it still usually took at least two years to move from design to quantity production.[15] This lag meant that procurement of most of the planes available to the Navy and the AAF by early 1942 had occurred before summer 1940, when the United States truly ramped up its mobilization efforts.

The aircraft expansion was shaped by a new factor, which had not been significant in the case of warships. This was the role of foreign demand—most notably, in the form of large purchases and capital investments by France and Britain. By spring 1939, when the U.S. Congress authorized expenditures for aircraft expansion comparable with the funds that it had provided previously for warships, the British and French orders had already provided the American aircraft industry with a major stimulus.

The aircraft industry, like shipbuilding, had suffered from the end of military orders after World War I. But it was a less mature industry, with dreams of a future in which air travel would become commonplace. By the mid-1930s, after a wave of consolidation was reversed by antitrust action, the adolescent aircraft industry remained highly competitive. Across the country, at least a dozen viable airframe manufacturers had military contracting experience. With just 36,000 workers in 1938, the aircraft industry was still quite small. Dependent on military sales and exports, it was also fragile. Among the leading aircraft manufacturers, only Douglas—maker of the DC-2 and DC-3—enjoyed much success as a supplier of civilian airliners. From 1935 to 1937, modest orders from the Air Corps and the Navy, most of which offered low profit margins, accounted for 40 percent of the industry's sales. Another third or so of the industry's output was absorbed by more profitable export sales, many of them to Latin American nations and China.[16]

Exports became far more important from 1938 to 1941, when large orders from France and Britain transformed the American aircraft industry. The British and French purchases, along with smaller orders by a few other foreign customers, amounted to over $1 billion—nearly half of the industry's sales during those years.[17] By February 1939, before Congress increased funds for U.S. military aircraft procurement, the British and French governments had already ordered more than 1,200 planes from American companies. France alone spent over $300 million on American aircraft and engines in 1938 and 1939—about twice the amount spent by the U.S. military. By April 1940, Britain and France together had ordered nearly six thousand planes and more than fourteen thousand engines, at a cost of $573 million.[18]

For individual firms, the British and French aircraft purchases of 1938–40 were electrifying. The buying spree started in summer 1938, a few weeks after a British delegation toured aircraft plants in California. In June, Britain ordered two hundred of Lockheed Aircraft's two-engine "Hudson" bombers, which would not begin flight tests until year's end. Eventually, the British would order 1,100 more. But for Lockheed, a small company with two thousand employees, even the first order seemed enormous. With the Hudsons priced at $85,000 each, the initial order promised $17 million in revenue over the next couple of years—far more than the $2–$3 million in annual sales that the company had been recording in the mid-1930s. During the six months after the first Hudson order, Lockheed doubled its workforce and added a second eight-hour shift. Thanks to the British order, Lockheed was able to move more quickly into production of its fast two-engine P-38 fighter, which it started to deliver to the Air Corps in 1939.[19]

While Lockheed's change in fortunes was extreme, many other American airframe makers also grew rapidly. France and Britain ordered dozens of new planes from Douglas, North American Aviation, the Glenn L. Martin Company, and the Curtiss-Wright Corporation. From 1938 to early 1940, these companies and others across the industry tripled their workforces.[20]

For the airframe makers and aero engine manufacturers, foreign governments were important sources of capital. Britain, as part of its first Hudson bomber order, provided Lockheed with a cash advance of $360,000.

This helped tide Lockheed over until early 1939, when the company was able to raise $3 million by issuing more stock. Meanwhile, France provided Martin with $2.4 million to expand the company's main plant in Baltimore, in order to help Martin fill an order for Model 167 bombers. Foreign capital was even more critical for the early expansion of the two largest engine manufacturers, Pratt & Whitney (part of the United Aircraft Corporation) and the Wright Aeronautical Corporation, the engine-making division of Curtiss-Wright. By the time the European war started in September 1939, Pratt & Whitney had already received $85 million worth of engine orders from France. Then, just after the war began, France agreed to pay $7.5 million to build a whole new facility at Pratt & Whitney's works in Connecticut. Known as the "French wing," this doubled the company's plant space. Soon after, the British paid for their own $8 million "British wing." Together with a $14 million investment in new plant from the United States, the French and British outlays allowed Pratt & Whitney to increase its plant by a million square feet of factory space, all before January 1941. Something comparable was achieved at Wright Aeronautical's main plant in Paterson, New Jersey, which used a $5 million direct investment by France to triple its floor space between 1938 and 1941. By mid-1940, France and Britain had provided $72 million worth of direct investment in U.S. aircraft industry plant, nearly 50 percent more than the private investment in plant made by the companies themselves.[21]

Domestic military demand for aircraft also jumped in 1939. Before then, even experienced and talented manufacturers had been struggling to survive. A case in point was the Seattle-based Boeing Aircraft Company, designer of an innovative heavy bomber, the B-17. Enjoying enthusiastic support from Air Corps officers, Boeing received a small contract for thirteen B-17s, which it delivered in 1937. However, the penny-pinching secretary of war, Harry H. Woodring, decided to stop buying B-17, in favor of the cheaper Douglas B-18. This nearly destroyed Boeing, which had been struggling financially throughout the decade. In 1939, Boeing recorded a loss of $3.3 million; the company found itself compelled to take out a $4.7 million loan from the federal government's Reconstruction Finance Corporation (RFC).[22]

A dramatic shift in U.S. military demand for aircraft would not manifest itself until 1939. But it had its roots in the European diplomatic crisis of September 1938, when it appeared that Hitler's demands for control over territory in Czechoslovakia would throw Europe immediately into a major war. Although that outcome was delayed by the "appeasement" of Hitler via the Munich agreement, President Roosevelt responded to the crisis by asking his advisers to plan for a bigger air force. The planning was led by Harry Hopkins, the veteran New Dealer and top Roosevelt adviser, along with Assistant Secretary of War Louis Johnson, a champion of military-industrial preparedness. During the fall of 1938, Hopkins, Johnson, and Roosevelt discussed the possibility of having New Deal public works agencies build as many as sixteen new government-owned aircraft plants. They started to select sites for these new plants all around the country, from Utah to Alabama. Roosevelt unveiled his plans at a meeting at the White House on 14 November. There, he stunned members of his cabinet and top military officers by saying that he wanted the United States to build a ten-thousand-plane Air Corps (more than quadruple its current size), along with the industrial capacity to be able to build twenty thousand planes in one year.[23] (Over the weeks that followed, as the White House faced the problem of persuading Congress to pay for such a program in peacetime, these ambitious goals were scaled back.)[24]

During this early planning for a major expansion of U.S. aircraft output, private airframe company executives worked hard to ensure that the growth would be handled entirely by themselves and not by firms from other industries or the government. To airframe and aero engine makers, the threat of competition from the government seemed very serious. Might the Air Corps end up running the new government-owned plants, thereby setting up a mix of public and private operation such as the one that already existed in naval shipbuilding? This question worried the airframe manufacturers, who lobbied hard to prevent such a possibility. As one Air Corps officer put it, after a meeting with company leaders in early 1938, "all manufacturers interviewed were unfavorable to any scheme whereby the Government would own and operate aircraft facilities."[25]

The airframe manufacturers also objected to any scheme that would give large prime contracts for planes to firms in other industries, such as the big automakers. If these firms were to participate in an expansion, the aircraft industry representatives insisted, their role should be limited to that of subcontractors who would make parts, not finished planes. Here the industry was trying to prevent the United States from adopting the British model of "shadow factories"—reserve airframe plants operated by automakers or other outside firms. Throughout 1938 and 1939, aircraft industry leaders, including Glenn L. Martin and Donald W. Douglas, told military procurement officials that they objected strongly to "the shadow factory idea," as well as to any government-owned plants.[26]

In these struggles of 1938–39, the aircraft companies mostly got their way. On 3 April 1939, Congress passed the Air Corps Expansion Act, which called for a six-thousand-plane Air Corps, nearly triple its current size. Over the next few weeks, between April and August, the industry was flooded with over $100 million worth of new U.S. military orders.[27] Among the other companies receiving contracts for at least $7 million worth of planes or engines in 1939 were Boeing, Consolidated, Curtiss-Wright, Douglas, Lockheed, North American, Pratt & Whitney, Wright Aeronautical, and GM's Allison Division. This big order jump-started the production of most of the American bombers that would be flown in large numbers in World War II, including the B-17, the Consolidated B-24, North American's B-25, and the Martin B-26.[28]

Thanks to the time lag between initial orders and the delivery of finished planes, all the contracting in 1938 and 1939 failed to create impressive results before the German offensives of spring 1940. Unfortunately for France, only a third of the $300 million worth of American planes and engines it had ordered since 1938 had been delivered by then. The U.S. Army Air Corps still had only 2,665 planes, barely a tenth of the size of the fleet operated by the Luftwaffe. But this situation was changing fast, even before Congress provided huge new military appropriations in the summer of 1940. Of all the American military aircraft that would be deployed in significant numbers during World War II, all but four (the Boeing B-29 heavy bomber and the Republic P-47, Grumman F6F, and Chance-Vought F4U fighters) were flying before Pearl Harbor.[29]

The big new foreign and domestic purchases were reflected in the airframe makers' financial performance in 1939, which, for most of them, was a banner year. At North American Aviation, net income after taxes jumped to $7 million, about 25 percent of the company's gross sales for that year. Lockheed's earnings for 1939 were $3.1 million, on about $35 million in sales. Compared with Lockheed's performance in the mid-1930s, which averaged only about $150,000 in annual profits and $3 million in annual sales, the 1939 numbers were astonishing. Most other airframe makers were not quite so successful in 1939, but with the notable exception of Boeing, they enjoyed high earnings.[30]

Thanks to the domestic and foreign orders of 1938–39, the United States started 1940 with its existing naval shipyards and aircraft plants running at full blast. During the first weeks of 1940, with the war in Europe apparently stalled, the future of this military-industrial activity was far from clear. As Americans looked ahead to a presidential election in November, which would see President Roosevelt run for an unprecedented third term, there was plenty of uncertainty on the domestic front to go along with the global chaos.[31] The situation was soon clarified. During the summer of 1940, the United States would begin an enormous new mobilization push. Unlike the procurement efforts of the late 1930s, which relied on the military's own plants and midsize specialty contractors in the private sector, this new effort would involve many of the nation's largest industrial corporations. It also brought a cascade of U.S. government investment in manufacturing plant.

Phase 2: Creating a GOCO Arsenal

Coming after a quiet winter, the news from Europe in May and June 1940 stunned Americans. On 10 May, German forces had begun to smash into Belgium, Holland, and Luxembourg; they soon crossed into France. In late May and early June, Britain barely managed to evacuate more than 300,000 British and French troops from the beaches at Dunkirk. In mid-June came the greatest shock of all: the Germans had rolled into Paris, and France had surrendered. Britain quickly prepared itself for bombings and invasion. For Americans, this news was grim. By the end of May, the U.S. military was already conducting serious discussions of its "Rainbow 4" war plan, which had the United States fighting alone—following a defeat of Britain and France—against the combined forces of Germany, Italy, and Japan.[32]

On 16 May, responding to what he called the "swift and shocking" developments in Europe, President Roosevelt presented Congress with a shock of his own. Seemingly pulling numbers out of thin air, Roosevelt demanded that the country quickly create the capacity to build "at least 50,000 planes a year." Although the aircraft industry had grown significantly in previous months, this target would require another quadrupling of its output. Nonetheless, Congress responded quickly to the president's call. By mid-July, it had appropriated funds for 24,000 more planes for the Air Corps and Navy.[33]

Roosevelt's call for fifty thousand planes a year was merely the most spectacular piece of what quickly became a massive crash rearmament program. "Had we not done what we did in the eighteen months before" Pearl

Harbor, Undersecretary of War Robert P. Patterson would later explain, "there would have been no D-Day in 1944, nor any V-J Day in 1945." During the summer of 1940 alone, Congress authorized over $6.5 billion in military spending. Total military appropriations for July 1940–June 1941 (the government's fiscal year 1941) were $12 billion—ten times their level at the end of the 1930s. This money would be used to outfit an expanded American army. Even before the Selective Service Act of 1940, which started a new draft, the War Department started to order equipment for an army of two million soldiers. Because the U.S. Army still had a little more than 200,000 men in the spring of 1940, this two-million-man short-term target would force the War Department to scramble over the next few months to buy nearly $4 billion worth of new goods.[34]

The expanded mobilization effort of 1940–41 coincided with improvements in the health of the American economy. Starting in early 1940, the unemployment rate dropped dramatically. By mid-1941, it was down to about 4 percent.[35] By that time, many American businesses were starting to see profit levels that they had not experienced since the 1920s. Certainly, military spending was an important contributor to this change. But once the economic recovery was under way, it actually threatened to make rearmament more difficult. Military and civilian demand now started to compete for scarce resources; individual firms making good money on civilian orders could become more reluctant to consider military contracting.

The growing potential for conflict between the civilian and military economies gave rise to new initiatives and organizations. Among them were economic mobilization boards, starting with the National Defense Advisory Commission (NDAC). As the months went by, NDAC was succeeded by new bodies, including the Office of Production Management (OPM), established in January 1941, and the Supply Priorities and Allocations Board (SPAB), established in August 1941. These organizations shared a similar cast of top officials, including William Knudsen of GM; Sidney Hillman, a top labor leader; and Donald M. Nelson, formerly of Sears, Roebuck, the giant retailer. Although they left contracting in the hands of the Navy and War Departments, the civilian boards helped to locate new war plants and emerged as the chief regulators of the distribution of key materials, such as steel and aluminum.[36]

The prospect of business executives running the war economy, which had caused some vocal protests back in 1939, now became even more worrisome to critics on the left. In the eyes of progressives, President Roosevelt seemed far too willing to defer to pro-business conservatives. To fill the position of new civilian chief for the Navy Department, Roosevelt tapped Frank Knox, the Republican newspaper editor who had run as his party's vice-presidential candidate in 1936. Knox's top lieutenant was the new Navy Department undersecretary, James Forrestal, a onetime navy pilot who had spent the interwar years as a Wall Street investment banker. For secretary of war, Roosevelt nominated Henry L. Stimson, a seventy-two-year-old Republican who had held several cabinet positions over the previous three decades. The new undersecretary of war was Robert P. Patterson, a World War I veteran and federal judge. Together, these appointments suggested that Roosevelt was willing to allow enemies of the New Deal to run the most powerful offices in the wartime federal government.

Meanwhile, foreign orders were finally outpaced by domestic appropriations. The change occurred well before the end of December 1940, when the president, in a fireside chat, announced that the United States "must become the great arsenal of democracy." These words paved the way for the Lend-Lease Act, which Congress passed in March 1941. Lend-Lease paid for $7 billion worth of additional ships, planes, tanks, and other munitions, much of which the United States would effectively donate to Britain. After July 1941, when Germany invaded the Soviet Union, Lend-Lease authorities began to plan for shipments to the Soviet Union as well. By September 1941, the military had already prepared a "Victory Program" plan for a nine-million-man army, which came very close to anticipating the ultimate size of the U.S. armed forces. According to one estimate, between June 1940 and December 1941, $64 billion was spent and promised for defense production. This was a third of the total amount that would be spent by 1945.[37]

The so-called defense period of 1940–41 also saw the U.S. government displace Britain and France as the leading public investors in war plant. In 1938 and 1939, British and French capital had served as the most important source of funds for the American aircraft industry's expansion. But now, suddenly, the U.S. government became the world's most important investor in manufacturing capacity. Between June and December 1940, U.S. government agencies spent at least $1.4 billion on manufacturing facility projects, compared with about $1.0 billion invested in them by the private sector. The government spent another $1 billion to build new Army camps, where recruits could be housed and trained.[38]

These public outlays in 1940 were just the beginning of a flood of public investment in manufacturing plant. During all of World War II, the U.S.

Table 1. U.S. Government Investment in War Plant, by Industry, 1940–45

Industry	U.S. Investment	Capacity Owned by U.S., 1944–45
Enriched uranium and plutonium	$1.38 billion	100%
Shell and bomb loading	$1.25 billion	100%
Synthetic rubber	$0.70 billion	97%
Aircraft	$3.43 billion	89%
Ships	$2.19 billion	87%
Guns and ammunition	$1.60 billion	87%
Nonferrous metals (aluminum, magnesium, etc.)	$1.72 billion	58%
Chemicals and explosives	$2.26 billion	43%
Aviation gasoline	$0.25 billion	33%
Machine tools	$0.15 billion	26%
Combat and motor vehicles	$0.60 billion	23%
Iron and steel products	$1.20 billion	14%

Sources: WPB, "Selling the Surplus Plant," *War Progress Report* 256 (11 Aug. 1945), in folder War Progress Reports, box 208, entry 118, RG 80, NARA; atomic weapons plant cost data from Richard G. Hewlett and Oscar E. Anderson, Jr., *A History of the United States Atomic Energy Commission*, vol. 1, *The New World, 1939/46* (University Park: Pennsylvania State University Press, 1962), 723.

government would spend close to $20 billion on manufacturing facilities and machinery, more than double the amount invested by the private sector. Public capital had financed only about 10 percent of American war plant during World War I; during World War II, it financed over two-thirds of new plant. The construction of new government-owned plant was so widespread that by 1945, the United States would own most of the manufacturing capacity in the aircraft, shipbuilding, synthetic rubber, and aluminum industries, as well as in ordnance production (see Table 1). This massive investment in war plant transformed the shape of the broader American economy: by war's end, the federal government would own close to a quarter of the nominal value of all the nation's factories.[39]

Although the public investment in new war plant would not peak until early 1942, it took shape during the second half of 1940. During those months, the U.S. government started to build a huge new war economy based largely on the form of the government-owned, contractor-operated (GOCO) plant. The GOCO scheme had been used during World War I in the merchant shipbuilding and explosives industries but became much more important during World War II. There were several varieties of GOCO plant arrangements. Most commonly, the government would pay for a large new plant, which was built, leased, and managed by a private contractor. The contractor was paid for his trouble with fees, normally set as a small fraction of anticipated costs.

The GOCO plants financed by the DPC and the military were not the only important form of wartime investment in manufacturing. Government-owned and operated plant, such as the U.S. Navy yards and the Ordnance Department arsenals and armories, received nearly $2 billion in new investment. Private companies (mostly in the steel, oil, rail transport, and electric utility industries),taking advantage of new tax incentives, paid for about $8 billion worth of new plant in 1940–45.[40] Besides all this new plant, plenty of older private facilities ended up being used to make munitions.

But it was the GOCO plant that constituted the largest part of the wartime investment in manufacturing capacity.[41] All the largest new plants built especially for the war were paid for entirely with public funds. And of all plants, including those that predated the war, that turned out the most finished munitions (by dollar value), all but a handful were entirely government financed, or had been renovated with millions of dollars of new public investment (see Table 2 and Table 3).

Nearly half of the government investment in the new GOCO plant came directly from the War and Navy Departments. The other half flowed through the Defense Plant Corporation (DPC). Created in summer 1940, the DPC was a new subsidiary of the Reconstruction Finance Corporation (RFC), which had been serving since 1932 as the federal government's biggest bailout machine, infrastructure bank, and multipurpose source of loans and credit.[42] The DPC became especially important as a financier of new plant in the aircraft and aluminum industries.

As military expenditures ballooned and as the GOCO model took off in 1940 and 1941, the shape of the American industrial mobilization shifted. During the late 1930s, it had been confined mostly to transactions between experienced, midsize contractors and the Navy and War Departments (along with foreign purchasing commissions). Starting in 1940, military procurement began to rely more heavily on larger industrial corporations, many of which started to serve as builders and managers of large GOCO plants. It was at this point, during the months before Pearl Harbor, that critics of the mobilization were perhaps most justified in claiming that the

Table 2. The 25 Most Expensive Plants Built in the U.S. for World War II, by New Investment in Buildings and Equipment, 1940–45 (in millions of dollars)

			Investment in Plant	
Location	Operator	Main Product(s)	Public	Private
Oak Ridge, TN	Union Carbide	Enriched uranium	$458.3	$0
Hanford, WA	Du Pont	Plutonium	$339.7	$0
Oak Ridge, TN	Eastman Kodak	Enriched uranium	$300.6	$0
Geneva, UT	U.S. Steel	Steel	$187.6	$0
Eudora, KS	Hercules Powder	Smokeless powder, TNT	$186.7	$0
Chicago, IL	Chrysler	Aircraft engines	$182.5	$0
Brooklyn, NY	U.S. Navy	Warships	$180.4	$0
Charlestown, IN	Du Pont	Smokeless powder	$179.5	$0
St. Louis, MO	Western Cartridge	Small arms ammunition	$147.6	$0
St. Paul, MN	Du Pont	Smokeless powder	$141.4	$0
Lockland, OH	Wright Aeronautical	Aircraft engines	$141.2	$0
Tonawanda, NY	General Motors	Aircraft engines	$136.1	$0
Merrimac, WI	Hercules Powder	Smokeless powder	$126.8	$0
Las Vegas, NV	Basic Magnesium	Magnesium metal	$126.2	$0
Melrose Park, IL	General Motors	Aircraft engines	$125.6	$0
Sylacauga, AL	Du Pont	Smokeless powder, TNT	$119.6	$0
Indianapolis, IN	General Motors	Aircraft engines	$101.3	$14.9
Mare Island, CA	U.S. Navy	Warships	$114.8	$0
Kingsport, TN	Eastman Kodak	Explosives (RDX, comp. B)	$108.5	$0
Dearborn, MI	Ford Motor	Aircraft engines	$89.9	$10.6
Fontana, CA	Henry J. Kaiser	Steel	$96.6*	$1.6*
Radford, VA	Hercules Powder	Smokeless powder, TNT	$96.3	$0
Philadelphia, PA	U.S. Navy	Warships	$95.0	$0
Ypsilanti, MI	Ford Motor	Heavy bombers (B-24)	$94.9	$0
Warren, MI	Chrysler	Medium tanks (M3, M4)	$94.9	$0

Sources: Non–Manhattan Project data from CPA-*Facilities*; atomic weapons program cost data from Richard G. Hewlett and Oscar E. Anderson, Jr., *A History of the United States Atomic Energy Commission*, vol. 1, *The New World, 1939/46* (University Park: Pennsylvania State University Press, 1962), 723.

*The public investment at the Kaiser steelworks at Fontana, California, came in the form of a long-term RFC loan, which Kaiser would need to repay out of future profits; so in this one case, the figures may overstate the degree to which the investment was fully "public."

war was serving as an engine of economic concentration. By July 1941, of the $9 billion in current munitions orders, a third of the dollar volume was in prime contracts handled by just six corporations.[43] Three of these—Bethlehem Steel, New York Ship, and Newport News Ship—were among the handful of experienced warship builders that had been expanding since the mid-1930s. Another, Curtiss-Wright, was a leading producer of planes and aero engines. But the other two, GM and Du Pont, had not held any significant military orders during the 1920s and 1930s. Their appearance in the top ranks of contractors in mid-1941 indicated the rise of new patterns of government-business interaction. During this second phase of the American industrial mobilization, from June 1940 to December 1941, "big business" became an important player. And its most important role was as builder and manager of the giant new network of GOCO plants.

Even in the major war industry that made the least use of GOCO arrangements (naval shipbuilding), public-owned facilities were essential. In the summer of 1940, Congress authorized the Navy to spend about $5 billion on more than two hundred new combatant vessels, enough to double the size of its fleet. Most of the new warships were built by a beefed-up version of the same network of Navy-run and private shipyards that had done the job in the 1930s. The Navy spent half a billion dollars to expand the capacity of its own shipyards, which continued to serve as top producers of warships. Of the one million Americans working in the naval shipbuilding industry by the middle of the war, a third worked in the Navy's own facilities. But the Navy also invested heavily to increase the capacities of its established contractors. In Groton, Connecticut, the Navy paid over $9 million to build a whole new GOCO submarine works. It was operated by Electric Boat, whose own facilities were located next door. The Navy also began to invest large sums at the works of the established warship builders, including the main yards of New York Ship, Newport News, and Bethlehem. By war's end, each of these facilities had been expanded and improved by about $20 million, using funds provided by the Navy's Bureau of Ships. Across the industry, the Navy investments in plant typically exceeded the established contractors' own private investments by a factor of five or ten.[44]

In the merchant shipbuilding industry, GOCO arrangements were even more important. The cargo ship program was overseen by an independent government authority, the U.S. Maritime Commission (USMC), which dated from 1936. By the time the U.S. mobilization effort began in earnest in summer 1940, an expanded USMC program was in place; America's small merchant shipbuilding industry was already busy. However, it still was nowhere close to having the capacity that would be required for the United States to send large ground forces abroad. (By the end of World War II, the USMC would build 5,700 vessels, at a cost of $13 billion, nearly as much as the $18 billion spent on warships by the Navy.)[45]

Table 3. Leading Privately Managed Plant Sites, by Value of Prime Contracts for Finished Munitions, with Amounts of Wartime Public Investment, 1940–45 (in millions of dollars)

Contractor	Plant(s) Location	Main Products	Prime Contracts	Public Investment, 1940–45
Ford	Dearborn, MI	Aero engines, tanks, trucks	$2,928	$154.6
Chrysler	Detroit, MI	Tanks, trucks	$2,696	$112.5
Lockheed	Burbank, CA	Airplanes (P-38, B-17, A-29, etc.)	$2,526	$23.6
United Aircraft	East Hartford, CT	Aero engines	$2,363	$27.6
GM-GMC Truck	Pontiac, MI	Trucks	$2,018	$0.0
Convair	San Diego, CA	Airplanes (B-24, B-32)	$1,887	$25.9
Wright Aero	Lockland, OH	Aero engines	$1,785	$141.1
Wright Aero	Paterson, NJ	Aero engines	$1,724	$39.8
Packard	Detroit, MI	Aero engines, marine engines	$1,723	$35.9
Martin	Baltimore, MD	Airplanes (B-26, A-30, etc.)	$1,587	$41.6
GM-Allison Div.	Indianapolis, IN	Aero engines	$1,463	$103.9
Western Electric	Kearny, NJ	Radar and radio equipment	$1,412	$0.1
Gen'l Elec. (GE)	Schenectady, NY	Radio equipment, ship turbines, etc.	$1,391	$17.3
GM-Chevrolet	Tonawanda, NY	Aero engines	$1,364	$134.1
Grumman	Bethpage, NY	Airplanes (F4F, F6F, etc.)	$1,343	$24.1
Ford	Ypsilanti, MI	Airplanes (B-24) and subassemblies	$1,285	$94.9
Studebaker	South Bend, IN	Aero engines, trucks	$1,281	$50.1
Douglas	Long Beach, CA	Airplanes (B-17, C-47)	$1,239	$29.6
GM-Clev. Diesel	Cleveland, OH	Marine engines, etc.	$1,176	$11.4
Curtiss-Wright	Buffalo, NY	Airplanes (P-40, C-36, P-47)	$1,169	$49.6
Boeing	Seattle, WA	Airplanes (B-17, A-20, B-29)	$1,162	$19.0
GM-Fisher Body	Flint, MI	Tanks	$1,083	$51.3
Western Electric	Chicago, IL	Radar and radio equipment	$1,013	$1.3
Bethlehem Steel	Quincy, MA	Warships (CV, CA, DD, DE, LST)	$965	$21.2
GM-Buick Div.	Melrose Park, IL	Aero engines	$962	$125.6
Kaiser-Permanente	Richmond, CA	Cargo ships, etc.	$925	$28.1
Convair	Fort Worth, TX	Airplanes (B-24, B-32, C-87)	$918	$58.7
Boeing	Wichita, KS	Airplanes (B-29, PT-17)	$843	$33.3
Douglas	Santa Monica, CA	Airplanes (A-20, C-54, P-70)	$818	$0.7
US Steel–Fed Ship	Kearny, NJ	Warships (DD, CL, etc.)	$814	$10.3
North Am. Aviat.	Inglewood, CA	Airplanes (P-51, B-25, etc.)	$804	$10.4
Newport News	Newp't News, VA	Warships (CV, CA, LSD, etc.)	$789	$21.6
North Am. Aviat.	Kansas City, KS	Airplanes (B-25, etc.)	$770	$34.3
Sperry	Brooklyn, NY	Gun directors, automatic pilots, etc.	$757	$5.9

Table 3 (continued)

Contractor	Plant(s) Location	Main Products	Prime Contracts	Public Investment, 1940–45
New York Ship	Camden, NJ	Warships (CV, CB, CL, etc.)	$723	$21.4
Kaiser-OR Ship	Portland, OR	Cargo ships, landing craft, etc.	$722	$41.2
Bell Aircraft	Buffalo, NY	Airplanes (P-39, P-63)	$704	$0.0
Republic Aviation	Farmingdale, NY	Airplanes (P-47, P-43, etc.)	$703	$18.8

Sources: Calculated from CPA-*Contracts* and CPA-*Facilities*. In a few cases, the published figures combine multiple sites operated by the contractor in the same metropolitan area. The largest government-operated Navy yards, such as Brooklyn and Philadelphia, likely produced ships worth more than those made by largest private yards, such as Newport News and Federal Ship, but they are not represented in the contracts data.

The big order that changed the American merchant shipbuilding field followed a visit by a British delegation in October 1940. Working with the USMC, British officials decided to order sixty new merchant ships. These were to be "Ocean"-type vessels—slower, cheaper ships than the "C" types ordered previously by the USMC. One "Ocean" might be built for about $1.5 million, about 40 percent less than the cost of a "C"; each new ship might be completed in just six months, instead of a full year.[46]

The British order of late 1940 would be filled by just two as-yet-unbuilt shipyards, which would be paid for in full by the British. The contracts for the ships would be of the cost-plus fixed-fee (CPFF) variety, with the contractors to be paid a flat fee of $160,000 for each ship, or about 10 percent of its estimated total cost. This meant that each of the two yards selected stood to earn about $5 million, with all costs reimbursed by the British government.[47] These terms appeared to be favorable. But because the United States had few competent merchant shipbuilders, and even fewer who were not already swamped with USMC business, there was no obvious candidate to take the British order.

The winner of the British contract was a consortium of East and West Coast shipbuilding and construction companies, led by Henry Kaiser. Half of the sixty ships would be built in South Portland, Maine, where the British spent nearly $10 million on a new seven-shipway yard, to be co-managed by Todd Shipbuilding and the Bath Iron Works. The other thirty ships would be built at a new yard in Richmond, California, near San Francisco, where the British invested another $7 million for seven Kaiser-run shipways.[48]

The British order of late 1940 became a model for the giant Liberty ship program, which would account for nearly half of all the vessels built for the USMC. The Liberty ship project started in January 1941, after President Roosevelt announced that the United States needed to build two hundred additional merchant vessels. Like the British "Ocean" types, the Liberties, initially priced at about $2 million apiece, were meant to be relatively cheap, slow ships.[49]

In order to get the two hundred Liberties built, the USMC paid for seven large new GOCO shipyards. Built mostly in the South and the West, these seven new yards were to be operated mostly by companies with some previous experience. The biggest of the new yards, a $35 million facility in Fairfield, Maryland, outside Baltimore, was run by Bethlehem Steel Corporation, a major builder of commercial and naval vessels. In Wilmington, North Carolina, the USMC paid for a $20 million yard run by Newport News, the Navy's top builder of aircraft carriers. On the West Coast, the USMC spent about $25 million apiece to build big new yards in Los Angeles and Portland.[50]

The nine large new merchant shipyards created to handle the British and American orders of the winter of 1940–41 served as the core of the U.S. cargo ship program throughout World War II. Kaiser's yards in Richmond and Portland would end up building 821 Liberties. With a total of 197,000 employees at their peak, the various Kaiser yards on the Pacific Coast worked on nearly $4 billion worth of ships, or about a quarter of the value of all USMC construction. On the East Coast, the giant Bethlehem-Fairfield yard in Maryland finished 312 Liberties; Newport News Ship's Wilmington yard built 126. In Maine, Todd-Bath had serious production problems, especially with a new Liberty shipyard that was built in 1941 alongside the original British-financed facility. However, despite the setbacks, the two South Portland yards together built 244 Liberties.[51]

The Liberty shipbuilders, including Kaiser, have been justly celebrated for their innovative use of welding and modern assembly techniques, which allowed them to produce the vessels with astonishing speed. But the miracle of American wartime shipbuilding should also be credited to public actors, who paid for everything and coordinated the larger program. The hard-driving leaders of the USMC, Admirals Jerry Land and Howard L. Vickery, were both graduates of the U.S. Naval Academy. Both were experienced builders of ships, thanks to their service at the Navy's in-house warship yards. Land and Vickery were instrumental in the Liberty program, by coordinating it at the national level and advising the private builders, including Kaiser.[52]

Above all, the British and USMC contracts and investments of 1940–41 created enormous new capacities. This was difficult to see in the production record of 1941, when the USMC took deliveries of just twenty-one Liberties, a third of the number originally scheduled. Until mid-1942, Germany's U-boats succeeded in sinking more tonnage of cargo shipping than the Allies were producing. However, even before Pearl Harbor, the USMC was already planning to build five million deadweight tons of new shipping—about five hundred vessels—in 1942, and another seven million tons in 1943.[53] These impressive targets were conceivable only because of the network of large, GOCO merchant shipyards that the British and American governments had built in 1941.

New GOCO plants were also the central mechanism for several other military-industrial expansions. One of the most important of these was in the explosives industry, which produced the smokeless gunpowder and TNT needed for ammunition and bombs. During World War II, American explosives plants made over two million tons of TNT and nearly two million tons of smokeless powder. This immense destructive power was manufactured almost entirely by new GOCO plants, representing a government investment of about $3 billion.[54] These plants were among the largest and most expensive of all the facilities built for the war effort. Even if the so-called Manhattan Project is left out, the GOCO explosives facilities accounted for seven of the twenty most expensive new American war plants. Their operators, including Du Pont and the Hercules Powder Company, ranked among the most important of all the nation's military contractors (see Table 2).

At the heart of the explosives program was the relationship between Du Pont and the U.S. Army's Ordnance Department, which had been business partners for decades. In early September 1939, the Ordnance Department chief, General Charles M. Wesson, approached Du Pont to ask if the company would be willing to manage a large new GOCO smokeless powder plant with the capacity to produce 100,000 pounds a day. This level of output would triple the nation's existing manufacturing capacity. Wesson's proposal was approved quickly by Du Pont's executive committee, even though several company officials worried that taking munitions contracts might generate more of the controversy over war profiteering that had bedeviled the company since the Great War.[55]

Meanwhile, Du Pont was negotiating with British authorities over big powder contracts and the financing of new plants. In a deal finalized after the crisis of May 1940, the British government paid for a large new powder plant, which Du Pont would build in Tennessee. This $26 million smokeless powder plant started producing at full capacity in February 1941. (A month later, the American government took it over from the British. Renamed the Chickasaw Ordnance Works, it became part of the Ordnance Department's growing network of GOCO explosives plants.)[56]

On the heels of the British deal came a bigger one, with the War Department. In late June 1940, Du Pont agreed to build and run a smokeless powder facility on a five-thousand-acre site in Indiana, near the Ohio River. This was the very first big new American GOCO facility contract to be signed in World War II. The Du Pont project in Indiana was a model for the many large greenfield facilities that would spring up all over the country over the coming months. By the spring of 1941, when powder production began, more than 27,000 people were working to finish the construction of the sprawling Indiana plant. After several expansions, the facility would end up costing the U.S. government nearly $180 million. By the second half of 1942, when the plant employed about 9,400 workers, it was making smokeless powder at a rate of nearly a million pounds per day.[57]

These early smokeless powder plant projects, which made Du Pont the leader of the explosives program, were only the first of many similar wartime projects for the company. Indeed, by the time of Pearl Harbor, Du Pont, together with its Remington subsidiary, had become the military's leading GOCO plant manager. It built and operated huge new explosives plants in Illinois, Alabama, and Oklahoma. Similar GOCO facilities in Kansas, Wisconsin, Virginia, and Tennessee were run by Hercules and Atlas.[58] All in all, the Ordnance Department's explosives and ammunition program encompassed seventy-three GOCO plants, which, at their peak, employed about 400,000 people. By the time of Pearl Harbor, seventeen of these facilities were already up and running; another thirty-two were already under way or planned.[59]

The War Department also relied on new GOCO plants for tanks. Here, the lead contractor was the Chrysler Corporation, the highly profitable, younger competitor of GM and Ford. Chrysler's participation was arranged by Knudsen, the OPM chief, not long after he left GM for Washington. In

Figure 2. Photo of M-3 "Grant" medium tank production at the big U.S.-owned, Chrysler-operated tank arsenal outside Detroit, Michigan, ca. 1941. This plant was one of the first, and one of the most important, of the dozens of large new government-owned, contractor-operated (GOCO) factories built for World War II. FSA/OWI collection, Prints & Photographs Division, Library of Congress, LC-DIG-fsa-8b00695.

early June 1940, Knudsen persuaded Chrysler president K. T. Keller to take the tank job. Keller then took a team of engineers to the Army's Rock Island Arsenal, which provided Chrysler with 168 pounds of old blueprints. By August, Chrysler was breaking ground on a 690,000-square-foot GOCO tank plant on farmland in Warren, Michigan. Like most other operators of big GOCO plants, Chrysler worked under CPFF contracts, in which the government reimbursed all authorized production costs and allowed for profit in the form of a fixed fee.[60]

The GOCO plant managed by Chrysler became known as the Detroit Tank Arsenal (see Figure 2). It ended up manufacturing twenty thousand medium tanks (including M3 "Grant" and M4 "Sherman" models), more than a quarter of total American production. The second-biggest tank builder was another new GOCO facility, built in 1941–42 in Flint, Michigan, and operated by GM. (Another important source of tanks was the long-suffering locomotive and railcar industry, which used British and American tank contracts and direct capital investments to help return to profitability).[61]

The big automakers also became major players in the aircraft industry, starting in 1940, as contractors for aero engines, subassemblies, and finished planes. Meanwhile, the established aircraft industry firms, which had been handling the rearmament orders of the last two years, grew into truly big businesses. As in other parts of the growing war economy, this was mostly a GOCO affair: public capital paid for the new plant, which was run by private companies to fill military contracts.

In the aircraft industry, the government paid for nearly all the wartime expansion. One important piece of the effort was the so-called Knudsen Plan, which took shape in the final weeks of 1940, after Knudsen met with executives from the automobile and aircraft industries. The Knudsen Plan provided for four large new GOCO bomber plants to be built in the Midwest—far from the reach of enemy forces. These plants, located in Fort Worth, Tulsa, Kansas City, and Omaha, were paid for by the Army's Air Corps and built under the direction of the Army Corps of Engineers. They were operated by experienced airframe manufacturers: Consolidated, Douglas, North American, and Martin. The big automakers also joined the effort, as suppliers of large subassemblies, including wing and tail sections.[62]

Most of the subsequent expansion of the aircraft industry was financed with funds that ran through a civilian entity: the Defense Plant Corporation (DPC). A new subsidiary of the RFC, the DPC was established in early August 1940. It was born amid negotiations between the RFC and the Wright Aeronautical Corporation over the terms of a deal to finance the construction of a giant new aircraft engine plant. This became the first major DPC contract. In October 1940, Wright executives agreed to a deal that had the DPC pay for a 1.7 million-square-foot plant at Lockland, Ohio. The facility would remain government-owned, with the company leasing it for the nominal sum of $1 a year. Dozens of similar $1-a-year lease arrangements were made in the following months by the DPC, especially as it paid for large new plants in the aircraft industry.[63]

By early 1941, the DPC lease arrangements had almost entirely displaced an alternative, the Emergency Plant Facilities (EPF) contract. Because that scheme required contractors to find private financing for new war plants that would be acquired by the government over a five-year period, it was much less effective than the simpler DPC method of direct government ownership. The EPF contracts were used in the aircraft industry to begin eleven major projects in 1940–41, including an expansion at Boeing's Seattle plant, to enable it to make more B-17s.[64] But most of the EPF deals were converted into DPC contracts. Few private bankers were interested in serving as financiers for war facilities, especially those that would eventually be owned by the government. As one aircraft industry executive explained a few weeks before Pearl Harbor, "the average banker's opinion of a government contract is not favorable."[65]

Bypassing private banks, the DPC, along with the Navy and War Departments and the USMC, became a giant financier and owner of industrial plant. This was not inevitable. The DPC plant leases, as historian Gerald T. White explained long ago, reflected the efforts of progressive New Deal lawyers to limit the potential gains of war contractors. These mid-level government lawyers, led by Clifford J. Durr and Hans A. Klagsbrunn, saw themselves as protecting the public interest from the excessively pro-business inclinations of their superiors. The latter included Knudsen, the OPM chief, as well as Jesse Jones, the wealthy Houston businessman who had become chair of the RFC back in 1933. (During World War II, Jones continued to oversee the RFC—and its subsidiaries, including DPC—as the federal loan administrator. Beginning in September 1940, Jones also served as secretary of commerce.)[66]

In 1940–41, the DPC paid for several large new airframe plants, similar to the ones being financed directly by the War Department under the Knudsen Plan. The DPC-owned bomber plants included one run by Boeing in Wichita, where that company already had a small subsidiary. In Dallas, where North American had already started to build a small plant to manufacture trainer aircraft, the DPC paid for a $34 million, million-square-foot bomber plant. Completed in April 1941, the Dallas plant ranked at the time as the biggest fully air-conditioned, artificially lit building in the world.[67] The DPC eventually became the owner of an even bigger bomber factory: Willow Run. This was the Ford-run plant, built near Ypsilanti, Michigan, which, under the Knudsen plan, had been designated as the main supplier of subassemblies for the new B-24 plants in Fort Worth and Tulsa. In mid-1941, as the bomber program expanded, Ford officials received the green light to make complete B-24s. By that time, thousands of construction workers were at work on the massive Willow Run complex, which would end with 3.5 million square feet of factory space, built with 38,000 tons of steel and over 1.5 million square yards of concrete.[68]

Despite Willow Run, the automakers' most important contributions to the aircraft program were their management of DPC plants that made not airframes but engines. Here they served as licensees of the nation's top two aero engine manufacturers, Pratt & Whitney (a division of United Aircraft) and Wright Aeronautical (part of the Curtiss-Wright Corporation). In August 1940, a team from the Ford Motor Company, led by Edsel Ford and Charles E. Sorensen, toured Pratt & Whitney's facilities in Connecticut. That visit led directly to Ford's effort to mass-produce Pratt & Whitney's powerful eighteen-cylinder R-2800 engines under a wartime licensing agreement that had Ford pay a fee of $1 for every engine it made. Ford built the engines at a plant within its giant River Rouge campus, built with $10 million of its own money, along with an investment by the DPC that would eventually come to $90 million.[69]

The Ford–Pratt & Whitney agreement served as the model for the American aero engine expansion program. In October 1940, GM's Buick division became the second big Pratt & Whitney licensee, as an operator of a new $30 million DPC plant in Chicago. After the expansion of the bomber program in May 1941, the DPC authorized the building of two huge new engine plants. On a site in Tonawanda, New York, GM's Chevrolet division would make Pratt & Whitney–designed engines used in the B-24. At this point, Wright, which had been far more reluctant to license the manufacture of its engines, now gave in to Air Corps pressure. To supplement Wright's production of engines for the B-17, Studebaker would run a new DPC plant in South Bend, Indiana. In the end, the DPC plants run by the auto companies, acting as licensees of Pratt & Whitney and Wright, made half of all the aircraft engines produced in the United States during World War II.[70]

The dramatic expansion of the U.S. aircraft industry required lots of aluminum. At the beginning of World War II, aluminum accounted for about 70 percent of the weight of a military airframe. A single B-17 bomber required about ten tons of it.[71] Without enough aluminum, the new airframe plants would be useless.

In the case of aluminum, as in so many other major war industries, expansion was accomplished primarily by building new GOCO plants. Here the story was complicated because of the prewar domestic monopoly held by the Aluminum Company of America (Alcoa). A federal antitrust action against Alcoa was already under way. The outbreak of war, with its huge new demands for aluminum, threatened to turn Alcoa from a midsize monopoly into an immense one. How would mobilization officials deal with this political problem?

The solution, forged in 1940–41, was an awkward compromise. The government nominally broke Alcoa's monopoly, by arranging large RFC loans and military orders that helped Richard S. Reynolds, Sr., leader of the foil-making Reynolds Metals Company of Richmond, Virginia, to integrate backward into the production of aluminum ingot. Reynolds used the government loans to build new aluminum plants in Alabama and Washington, where cheap electricity was available from public utilities.[72] However, the government depended heavily on Alcoa, both as a private supplier and as a GOCO plant manager. Alcoa responded to the war emergency by tripling its own privately owned production capacities, using the "accelerated amortization" tax breaks provided by Congress in the October 1940 revenue act.[73] But Alcoa was also enlisted by RFC chief Jesse Jones as the operator of two dozen new DPC plants, in which the government invested half a billion dollars.[74] (According to the deal struck with Jones, Alcoa would immediately reduce its prices, from seventeen cents a pound to fifteen cents. It would also handle the construction of the plants on a cost basis, with no additional fees. Alcoa would keep 15 percent of any profits on metal produced at the government-owned plants; the remainder would go to the DPC.)[75] So Alcoa, which served during the war as something like a giant semipublic entity in its own right, continued to dominate the industry.

For the critics of Alcoa, including Richard Reynolds, Interior Secretary Ickes, and other New Dealers, the DPC contracts authorized by Jones were a major disappointment. Their profit provisions seemed too generous; more important, they put the for-profit monopolist in charge of a giant public investment. Thanks to the complaints of Ickes and others, the DPC contracts did not offer Alcoa an option to acquire the plants after the war. So Reynolds and other aspiring aluminum makers would have the chance to acquire some of the GOCO plant at war's end.[76] However, Washington's reliance on Alcoa was remarkable, even in the context of the government's general practice of turning to big business to manage GOCO facilities across the war economy. In magnesium metal production, where the Dow Chemical Company had held a prewar monopoly similar to Alcoa's (and in which Henry Kaiser occupied a position almost identical to Reynolds's), the new GOCO plant was managed by many companies.[77] Even in the explosives and ammunition sector, where Du Pont was so important, the government had engaged several firms to manage public plants. Of all the large war industries, aluminum remained by far the most monopolistic, even with the participation of Reynolds.

Alcoa's dominant role in aluminum production made it an unusual case in the larger universe of American military-industrial arrangements. However, it was perhaps not entirely unrepresentative of the broader pattern of economic mobilization that took place during the eighteen months before Pearl Harbor. During that period, "big business" entered the defense effort in force, mostly as the builders and managers of large new GOCO plants. This development broke sharply with the economics of the rearmament of 1938–40, when most of the expansion was handled by midsize, experienced military contractors. Those companies, which continued to grow, still stood at the center of the war economy. However, they had been joined there, in 1940–41, by industrial giants like Du Pont, GM, Ford, Chrysler, and Alcoa.

Together, the big industrial corporations, along with the specialty military contractors and the War and Navy Departments, had begun, before Pearl Harbor, to oversee an impressive arsenal. Because many of the new GOCO plants were still under construction in late 1941, figures of actual munitions output before Pearl Harbor failed to suggest how much had been done. However, even that output was considerable. From the summer of 1940 through the end of 1941, the United States manufactured 269,000 displacement tons worth of warships, 136 cargo ships, 4,200 tanks, and 23,000 aircraft. Aluminum output had nearly doubled, to about sixty million pounds a month. The U.S. Army's Ordnance Department, which had calculated back in April 1941 that the new plants under construction would allow it to supply an army of four million men, was already beginning to take delivery of huge amounts of ammunition.[78] In 1942, the new GOCO plants coming on line would make the United States into the world's greatest producer of munitions. Most elements for a massive military-industrial mobilization were already in place, even before Japanese planes closed in on their targets in Hawaii.

Phase 3: All-Out Industrial Mobilization

Despite the considerable work that had been done over the previous months, military-industrial planners—like all Americans—were stunned by the Pearl Harbor attacks. Before 7 December 1941, the United States had acted as a giant supplier of munitions to the Allies. Now it became an all-out participant, which needed enough military-industrial capacity to fight a two-theater war. The War and Navy Departments immediately called on many existing war plants to add night shifts, so that they could operate round the clock.[79] Beyond this, clearly, new plants would be needed. But how large was the production gap, and how would the United States manage to close it?

How big a difference did Pearl Harbor make to the trajectory of American military-industrial mobilization? Across the war economy as a whole, the continuities with what had already been done in 1938–41 seem at least as important as any innovations. On 6 January 1942, President Roosevelt used an address to Congress to announce bold new targets: 60,000 planes and 45,000 tanks produced in 1942, and another 125,000 planes in 1943. Roosevelt's new targets demanded about $50 billion in war spending for 1942, roughly double the amount planned before Pearl Harbor. This was an aggregate figure but still described the experiences of many industries and firms. Immediately after Pearl Harbor, the bomber program was doubled. At the Sperry Gyroscope Company, the nation's premier designer of complex targeting equipment, executives started 1942 with the task of doubling its production of sights for the .50-caliber machine guns that would be installed in the bombers. Sperry's output of automatic pilots would need to be tripled. Similar expansions were contemplated by executives in dozens of companies across the country and by the military officers responsible for acquiring the goods.[80]

The task of doubling aggregate munitions output was formidable, but much of it was handled by the same kinds of government-business interactions that had been used to expand the arsenal over the previous months. Procurement officials continued to rely heavily on GOCO arrangements; private investment in new war plant became even less important. Three of the most remarkable post–Pearl Harbor military-industrial efforts—the synthetic rubber program, the B-29 bomber program, and the atomic bomb project—were managed almost entirely with the GOCO method, using experienced military contractors and big industrial firms. Thanks to all the newly authorized GOCO plants, in addition to the ones that had broken ground late in 1941, the months immediately after Pearl Harbor marked the peak of wartime building. Of all war spending in 1942, about a third went to construction. Three-fourths of this plant building and tooling was paid for by government agencies.[81]

Despite these continuities, the third phase of arsenal building did bring some changes in the shape of the military economy. One was more genuine conversion of manufacturing, from civilian to military production. Conversion had been much less common during the months before Pearl Harbor, when the civilian economy had been humming. In 1941, the auto industry had sold 4.6 million passenger cars, nearly as many as it had managed back in the banner year of 1929. Now, in early 1942, automakers and other companies were forced to stop much of their production for civilian markets. Managing conversion in 1942 was one of the essential tasks of the War Production Board (WPB), created on 16 January to succeed OPM. In its very first meeting, the WPB agreed that the automobile industry would need to cease its production of civilian passenger vehicles by mid-February. By April, the WPB had issued several orders that prohibited or drastically limited the manufacture of many civilian consumer durables, such as furniture and refrigerators.[82] Companies formerly producing these goods would now be expected to make goods for the military; indeed, many of them would need to do so, if they wanted to stay in business. So one of the biggest changes in the shape of the war economy in 1942 was the way in which it broadened, to encompass hundreds of firms and plants that had stayed out of the first two phases of industrial mobilization.

As the nation transitioned into an all-out mobilization, hundreds of smaller firms became involved in the war economy, along with the biggest industrial corporations. Major prime contractors, such as Boeing and Chrysler, actually sent about half of their contract dollars to their subcontractors, which provided hundreds of small parts and larger components. Meanwhile, the War and Navy Departments, encouraged by the White House, Congress, and the WPB, used their large, decentralized procurement bureaus to push war orders even wider. By the middle of the war, most American manufacturers had some direct experience with military subcontracting, if not prime contracts. Even the producers of smaller components might become major prime contractors, because the War and Navy Departments provided the assemblers of large weapons systems with a great deal of "government-furnished equipment" (GFE). Ranging from entire

Table 4. From Peacetime to Wartime Production: Expansion Orders of Magnitude, by Industry, 1939–45

Product	Prewar Baseline Output	Wartime Peak Output	Peak/ Baseline
Synthetic rubber	3,200 long tons (1940)	922,000 long tons (1945)	288.1
Aviation gasoline	4,000 barrels/day (June 1940)	520,000 barrels/day (March 1945)	130.0
Merchant ships	0.3 million dw tons (1939)	18 million dw tons (1943)	60.0
TNT	100,000 lbs./day (June 1940)	4 million lbs./day (Dec. 1942)	40.0
Airframes	20.3 million lbs. (1940)	797.1 million lbs. (1944)	39.3
Magnesium	12 million lbs. (1940)	368 million lbs. (1943)	30.7
Aluminum	327 million lbs./year (1939)	2.3 billion lbs./year (late 1943)	7.0
Electric power	28 million kilowatts (1940)	44 million kilowatts (April 1944)	1.6
Steel	82 million net tons (1940)	96 million net tons (1945)	1.2

Sources: WPB *Minutes*, 39; "Administration of Cost-Plus-a-Fixed Fee Contracts, for the Operation of Government-Owned, Contractor-Operated Ammunition Plants" (Washington, DC: Office of the Chief of Ordnance, Mar. 1945), copy in folder General Files–General Correspondence (1 of 3), box 4, DPED; Patterson, *Arming the Nation for War*, 173; Gilbert, "Expansion of Shipbuilding," 158; Turrell, *Rubber Policies*, 23; Lane, *Ships for Victory*, 398; Holley, *Buying Aircraft*, 548; Koistinen, *Arsenal of World War II*, 136–49.

aircraft engines to small components such as valves, the GFE often amounted to a quarter or more of the total value of finished weapons, such as aircraft. Indeed, the ubiquity of GFE in the U.S. war economy suggests how heavily it was coordinated by military officers, and not just by civilian officials and prime contractors.

One of the biggest mobilization projects of 1942–43 was the creation of a huge new GOCO synthetic rubber industry. After Japan moved quickly after Pearl Harbor to dominate Southeast Asia, it controlled about 95 percent of the world's natural rubber supply. Suddenly, the Allies faced the real prospect of running out of rubber.[83] This was an ugly problem that exposed some corporations' early unwillingness to relinquish patent rights, as well as poor decisions in 1940–41 by Jesse Jones and President Roosevelt.[84] Of all major American war industries (outside the atomic bomb project), rubber was the one that required the most extreme expansion of prewar capacities. By war's end, the United States was making nearly three hundred times as much synthetic rubber as it had done in 1940 (see Table 4).

The big synthetic rubber expansion of 1942–43 was handled almost entirely by the GOCO method. In the opening weeks of 1942, the DPC financed the construction of eleven Buna-S synthetic rubber plants, each at least three times bigger than the four 10,000-ton plants that Jones and Roosevelt had authorized in 1941. The DPC would end up spending $700 million on the synthetic rubber program, which included three dozen facilities. The plants, many of which were located in Texas and Louisiana, were operated by big rubber, oil, and chemical companies, including Goodyear, B. F. Goodrich, Union Carbide, and the Standard Oil Company of New Jersey. (The DPC leased the plants for $1 a year to operators that received management fees that ran from about $6 to $15 a ton, depending on the volume of output.)[85] While the plants were under construction in 1942–43, anxieties about rubber supply remained high. But once they began to produce, tensions eased. Between June and December 1943, synthetic rubber output nearly quadrupled, to a rate of 36,000 long tons a month. By the winter of 1943–44, the synthetic rubber program was over the hump. Although rising military demand continued to absorb available supply through 1945, Allied military campaigns would not be crippled by a lack of rubber, after all.[86]

In most other major war industries, munitions output was already high in 1942, thanks in large part to the big public investments in GOCO plant before Pearl Harbor. In merchant shipbuilding, Admirals Land and Vickery at the USMC were called on to roughly double their production targets. They paid for a few new shipyards, but most of their orders were met by GOCO facilities and contractors they had helped put into business in 1941, including Henry Kaiser.[87] Like the USMC, the War Department continued to rely on its established GOCO plant operators. For smokeless powder production, the Army's Ordnance Department relied almost entirely on eleven GOCO plants, managed by Du Pont and Hercules Powder. In TNT production, the GOCO plants were managed by the big explosives producers—Du Pont, Hercules, Atlas Powder and Trojan Powder—which were now joined by a few other big industrial corporations: Monsanto, American Cyanamid, and U.S. Rubber.[88]

Even the revolutionary new explosive materials used in atomic weapons were produced with GOCO arrangements similar to those already used in many sectors of the war economy. In late 1942, when the Manhattan District of the Army Corps of Engineers faced the problem of how to manage the giant new facilities that it would need to generate atomic bomb fuel, it decided to use experienced GOCO plant operators. One of these was Du Pont, which agreed in November 1942 to take the lead on a plutonium plant—an immense, $330 million complex built in Hanford, Washington.

(Under the terms of the deal, Du Pont would be reimbursed for costs, without any additional fees or profits.)[89] Two more giant atomic fuel production facilities, which would make enriched uranium using different processes, were located in Oak Ridge, Tennessee. One uranium plant, designated K-25, would be run by Union Carbide, the big chemical company that was already the lead contractor on the essential alcohol-to-butadiene portion of the synthetic rubber program. The other, known as the Y-12 plant, was run by Tennessee Eastman, a division of Eastman Kodak, the well-known manufacturer of photographic film. Tennessee Eastman was considered a good candidate for the job because it had recently started work as the operator of a high-explosives GOCO plant in Tennessee.[90]

In the aircraft industry, of all the new projects that took off after Pearl Harbor, the most important was the effort to make the new B-29 bomber. This was the plane that the AAF would use in 1945 to drop the high-explosive bombs and firebombs (and, finally, two nuclear devices) that would destroy large portions of many Japanese cities. By war's end, the B-29 program turned out about 3,900 planes at a cost about $3 billion— about 50 percent more than the cost of the whole atomic weapons program. Actually, the Army's Air Corps had ordered 250 of Boeing's planned super-bombers back in 1941. Wright Aeronautical had been engaged to supply its massive R-3350 "Cyclone" engines, which it planned to make in a new $70 million GOCO plant in New Jersey. After Pearl Harbor, however, the AAF worked with Boeing to create a much larger B-29 program. Boeing itself would build many of the planes, at DPC plants in Wichita and in Renton, Washington. But the War Department also paid for a big new $50 million GOCO plant, outside Atlanta, to be operated by Bell Aircraft, a smaller company based in upstate New York. Later, the Martin-managed GOCO bomber plant in Omaha joined the B-29 program, by switching over from B-25 production.[91] The expansion of the B-29 program in early 1942 also created the very biggest of all the new factories built during World War II. This was a $175 million, Chrysler-Dodge-operated plant in Chicago, which manufactured the Wright-designed Cyclone engines. Paid for by the DPC, the Dodge-Chicago plant included 3.5 million square feet of factory space in the main assembly building alone, which stood beside the world's biggest parking lot, serving the plant's 30,000 employees.[92]

The last piece of the puzzle for the aircraft program, which worried mobilization officials all the way through the last months of the war, was to create an adequate supply of aviation gasoline. A standard four-engine bomber like the B-24 could use over three hundred gallons of 100-octane gasoline for each hour it flew; the big B-29s might use as much as ten thousand gallons on one long mission. So by early 1945, when AAF commanders started to use dozens of these planes at a time in raids over Japan, a single operation might require over a million gallons of 100-octane.[93]

In the high-octane gasoline program, Washington paid for some GOCO plants but also relied heavily on the expertise and investments of the for-profit oil companies. Like their counterparts in the steel industry, the oil companies anticipated that they would be able to find uses for new plant after the war, so they decided to take advantage of the favorable tax amortization rules. Financing new private plant projects was easier for oil companies than for many other firms because they continued to enjoy plenty of civilian business after Pearl Harbor, in addition to their war orders. Even in 1944, when their participation in the war economy peaked, the oil companies—including Standard–New Jersey, Shell Oil, Texas Company, Cities Service, Sun Oil, and others—sent only about a third of their output to the military. And their military sales came mostly from plants they built and owned, or "scrambled" facilities in which public-owned equipment and private plant sat side by side. From 1942 to 1944, as the United States added about 350,000 gallons a day to its 100-octane production capacity, about a hundred new plants were built, at a cost of nearly $800 million.[94] Only about a third of the funding came from the government (see Table 1).

The big oil companies' leading role in the growing aviation gasoline program, together with Washington's reliance on the GOCO model, made it easy for critics of the industrial mobilization to describe it as dominated by big business. The critics cited statistics such as those provided by an OPM study of mid-1941 that found that just fifty-six companies held three-quarters of the aggregate dollar value of prime war contracts.[95] Armed with such data, congressional champions of small business, including Senator Harry S. Truman (D-MO), cried foul. So, too, did many other populists and progressives, from farmers in the heartland to leftist journalists in New York. In June 1942, after a torrent of complaints, Congress created the Smaller War Plants Corporation, intended to help distribute war orders to deserving smaller enterprises. After a year of work, this body would complain to Congress that no matter how much it tried, it was never able to do enough to break through the military–big business alliance that was preventing full participation by small business.[96]

Much of this criticism was misleading. Part of it should be attributed to sour grapes: some members of Congress, as well as officials at the state and local levels, were frustrated by their inability to influence the distribution of contracts and new plant sites.[97] States and localities, along with their representatives in Congress, worked hard in 1940–41 to attract war plants and jobs. Many states set up their first formal Washington lobbying offices at this time, in an effort to attract more plants and contracts.[98] In Washington, mobilization officials contended with constant entreaties from politicians such as Congressman Karl Stefan of Nebraska, who reported in November 1941 that he was badgering OPM and the Navy and War Departments "almost daily" to ask for more war plants in his state.[99]

Stefan, Truman, and many of their peers remained dissatisfied and critical of the distribution of war work because their own influence was limited. The location of new plants was influenced less by the pull of congressmen and governors than by the calculations of military and civilian officials in the executive branch. Those officials often did favor the South and West because they endorsed a policy of decentralization, for strategic as well as political reasons.[100] However, even this spreading of the work failed to placate many congressmen because, in most cases, it was the military and its contractors who selected sites, using calculations of available transport, power, water, and local labor supply. Internal Navy correspondence from early 1941 shows that the Navy believed that it, and not Congress or even civilian mobilization officials, controlled the choice of plant sites. Under these conditions, even the most powerful congressmen might be stymied. This was true of Senator Walter F. George (D-GA), who fought in late 1940 to have one of the big new GOCO ammunition plants located in Georgia. When Remington (the prospective operator) said it preferred Denver and the Army's Ordnance Department agreed, Senator George was denied.[101]

Leaving aside the question of the location of new plant sites, critics of the distribution of war work decried the evident concentration of orders in the hands of big business. But this problem was also exaggerated. For one thing, the prime contracting numbers obscured the participation of smaller firms via subcontracting. As one Harvard Business School professor observed at the time, it was "politic to champion publicly the cause of small business," but, in fact, the widespread use of subcontracting meant that smaller enterprises were heavily involved in the defense program, from the beginning. To be sure, some subcontracts—such as those for aluminum, steel plate, or large bomber subassemblies—went to other big businesses.

But the leading prime contractors also needed millions of dollars' worth of smaller items, including nuts and bolts, welding equipment, pumps, and valves. A typical World War II bomber comprised more than 165,000 parts, as well as 150,000 rivets; each of its engines comprised more than 1,400 distinct parts.[102] To acquire many of these goods, prime contractors purchased from smaller manufacturers.

The placement of contracts (prime and sub) with smaller companies was promoted by civilian and military officials in Washington. Well aware that this was favored by Congress, they also regarded it as a way to achieve production goals faster, by reducing the burdens on the overloaded plants of prime contractors. Starting in 1940–41, Undersecretary of War Patterson used strongly worded memos to order the procurement services to do more to spread the work. In February 1941, OPM created a new Defense Contract Service (succeeded later that year by a Division of Contract Distribution), charged with boosting the participation of smaller companies. These efforts by civilian and military officials were redoubled in 1942, before and after Congress passed the Small Business Act, which set up the Smaller War Plants Corporation.[103]

Washington's policy of enlisting smaller firms was so vigorous that it created opposition among military procurement officers who believed that the initiatives sometimes went too far. In August 1941, General Levin H. Campbell, Jr., then assistant chief of the Army's Ordnance Department, complained privately that OPM seemed to be pursuing "the objective of having every Tom, Dick and Harry make [armor piercing] cores." To Campbell, it seemed that trying to get several companies in the auto industry to make the cores might create some jobs but "will be much more costly than it would be were we to build our own plant for this production." There were similar sentiments in the Navy Department, where some officials tried to push back against subcontracting policies that they believed detracted from efficiency.[104]

Subcontracting became even more prevalent after Pearl Harbor, when existing prime contractors were deluged with new orders. Leading airframe makers such as Lockheed and Grumman, whose limited plant space made them eager to find outside vendors, used subcontractors to supply half the total value of the finished airframes. Across the airframe industry as a whole, over a third of the total value of military orders was being subcontracted by 1944. Sperry Gyroscope, the nation's leading manufacturer of complex avionics and gun directing systems, subcontracted half the value of its orders. Chrysler, a pioneer in subcontracting in the prewar auto industry, claimed that the GOCO tank arsenal that it operated added only about a quarter of the total value of finished tanks. The rest was provided by more than six hundred subcontractors and providers of government-furnished equipment, located in twenty states.[105]

For many midsize manufacturers, which did not typically act as managers of giant new GOCO plants, World War II required industrial conversion. At a few companies, this transition from civilian to military work started well before Pearl Harbor. One early bird was the A. O. Smith Corporation of Milwaukee, a successful independent manufacturer of automobile frames and pipe that had been a major manufacturer of bombs during World War I. In the late 1930s, A. O. Smith executives were already communicating with the Ordnance Department about future bomb production; before Pearl Harbor, they already had $7 million worth of bomb contracts.[106] Other early converters included the Armstrong Cork Company and the York Safe & Lock Company, both located in south central Pennsylvania. Both began to solicit military orders in the late 1930s; both became important World War II prime contractors, as major suppliers of shells, cartridge cases, and gun mounts.[107]

For the hundreds of midsize manufacturers that did not undertake any significant conversion until after Pearl Harbor, the transition was not always associated with expansion or prosperity. Forced to stop their normal business by government, these companies sometimes found the war years difficult. In Bristol, Connecticut, for instance, the E. Ingraham Company, a midsize family-owned manufacturer of clocks and watches, had to stop making those goods in early 1942. The company converted entirely to the production of parts for time fuses for antiaircraft shells, along with bullet cores and other war products. It did so using its existing factory space, which, after its normal business ceased, was more than ample. The number of workers at the company actually decreased during the war; revenues would not recover until the later 1940s, after it reconverted to its normal business.[108]

Many important conversions and expansions were accomplished by turning manufacturers of civilian goods into licensee military contractors. Such arrangements had been used in 1940–41 to bring the automakers into the war program. But they also involved independent firms that were merely large, as well as those that were truly modest in size. In 1941, the AAF told the Sperry Corporation that it would need to license the manufacture of its .50 caliber machine-gun turrets, used in B-17 and B-24 bombers. The first of the Sperry licensees was the Briggs Manufacturing Company, a leading auto-body manufacturer in Detroit, which would make the turrets in a new $9 million DPC plant. The second was a smaller firm, the Emerson Electric Company, a manufacturer of small motors, fans, and welding equipment in St. Louis, which already had some small Navy orders.[109]

After Pearl Harbor, licensing arrangements continued to bring new companies into the war economy. By the end of the war, two dozen companies were manufacturing complex Sperry-designed products—including gun directors, gyrocompasses, autopilots, bomb sights, and turrets—to fill substantial prime contracts with the military.[110] Some of the licensees, including GM, Chrysler, and Ford, were giant corporations, far larger than Sperry itself. But many were midsize corporations whose prewar revenues of between $25 million and $75 million a year made them less than a tenth the size of the giant automakers. Such was the scale of Toledo's Electric Auto-Lite Company, a supplier of auto parts; it was also the size of many companies in the office equipment industry, including National Cash Register, International Business Machines (IBM), Burroughs Adding Machine Company, and Victor Adding Machine Company. All these companies became licensees of either Sperry or Norden, the other top designer of bombsights.[111]

Besides the several midsize manufacturers that converted to war production as licensees, several dozen firms were transformed by war demand into sizable enterprises. Concentrated in the aircraft industry, many of these "war babies" were suppliers of components for planes. One of these was the Elastic Stop Nut Corporation, founded as a small enterprise in the late 1930s, which became the leading manufacturer of the self-locking nuts used by the millions of airframe manufacturers. (A single bomber required 40,000 of the nuts.) By 1943, Elastic Stop Nut was running two $5 million plants, in New Jersey and Nebraska, which had been paid for by a combination of DPC and private funds; its annual sales had reached $40 million.[112] In San Diego, the Solar Aircraft Company specialized in the manufacture of stainless-steel exhaust manifolds for aircraft. During the year ended April 1939, its gross sales were only about $0.5 million. Four years later, Solar Aircraft's sales were $22.4 million, most of which came in the form of subcontracts with the airframe makers.[113]

A more prominent war baby was Jack & Heintz, Inc., a manufacturer of aircraft starters, founded in 1940. Before the end of 1941, this infant independent company had over $22 million worth of military orders. By 1944, Jack & Heintz had eight thousand employees, who worked in several Cleveland-area plants that together amounted to a million square feet of factory space. Financed by a combination of private and DPC funds, the $20 million worth of new war plant managed by Jack & Heintz produced thousands of airplane starters, as well as Sperry-designed autopilots. By war's end, Jack & Heintz would fill $421 million worth of prime contracts. This made it one of the nation's top hundred prime contractors.[114]

As the case of Jack & Heintz suggests, the participation of smaller companies in military contracting is easier to see if we consider the local level. Naturally, if we consider only the very largest plants and contractors at the national level, we cannot help but emphasize the role of big businesses— which by 1942 included the major airframe and aero engine makers, along with established industrial giants. However, by examining the local (micro) level, it is possible to appreciate the very considerable involvement of smaller enterprises as prime contractors and operators of publicly financed plant. The Cleveland area, where Jack & Heintz had its plants, is a case in point. Cleveland was home to two large GM facilities, as well as plants owned by other large corporations, including GE, Kennecott Copper, Republic Steel, and Standard Oil of Ohio. But forty other companies in the Cleveland area held at least $10 million worth of prime contracts. And there were forty-three plants in Cleveland that saw at least $1 million in new investment in buildings and equipment during the war years. Several midsize independent companies in Cleveland, including Jack & Heintz, Thompson Products, Cleveland Pneumatic Tool, Ohio Crankshaft, and Cleveland Graphite Bronze, were important suppliers of aircraft components. These items included engine valves, crankshafts, bearings, and cylinder heads, as well as landing gear struts. Each company ran plants built or overhauled with $8 million to $32 million of government money.[115]

The situation in Cleveland was somewhat unusual because that city was home to a large number of midsize independent manufacturers. However, there were comparable patterns in other localities, including Chicago, Milwaukee, and Los Angeles. Especially in these places, but also across the nation, the war economy had expanded enough by 1942–43 to directly engage all sorts of manufacturers, large and small. Hundreds of smaller, privately held firms held significant prime contracts and ran plants built with large sums of government money. Thousands more participated as subcontractors. Far from being monopolized by the largest corporations, the business of war was distributed broadly and deeply.

The local-level data from places like Cleveland merit close attention because they suggest something important about the organization of the American war economy. As the government's micro-level records of prime military contracts demonstrate, many components that went into the larger finished weapons, such as ships and planes, were supplied directly by the military bureaus, as "government-furnished equipment" (GFE). The War and Navy Departments contracted directly with the manufacturers of many key components, including aircraft parts, avionics instruments, landing gear, fire control systems for shipboard guns, and hundreds of other items. In many cases, these goods were made in plants paid for directly by the military or the DPC.

All this public involvement reduced the responsibilities of the contractors. GFE, ordered by the military and delivered to the prime contractors' plants, accounted for about a third of the dollar value of World War II aircraft, including the B-29.[116] To be sure, the prime contractors were extraordinarily busy with their own production and subcontracting; they were also responsible for installing much of the GFE. However, a war economy in which so much GFE was used was necessarily one in which the War and Navy Departments had a great deal of responsibility over project management. It required military agencies to deal directly with hundreds of smaller firms, as plant financier and buyer. They also used their power and knowledge of national supply networks to help contractors troubleshoot bottlenecks and other production problems.[117] So despite the large orders that they placed with the biggest prime contractors and GOCO plant operators, the War and Navy Departments were far from content to sit back and let a handful of big businesses meet their needs. Instead, they developed huge procurement organizations that dealt face-to-face with thousands of suppliers, large and small.

As the record of prime contracting and the extensive use of GFE suggests, military officers served during World War II as the national managers of weapons production projects. Some of them were based at the AAF's Materiel Command, at Wright Field in Ohio. Thanks to New Deal public works outlays, Wright Field at the end of the 1930s was already a significant research and testing facility, boasting the world's largest wind tunnel and its most sophisticated propeller-testing equipment.[118] During World War

II, Wright Field expanded into an immense engineering and procurement organization. (The AAF's Materiel Command, like the Army's Ordnance Department, had tens of thousands of employees, which made them far larger than the WPB.) Wright Field's Production Division, led by Major (later General) Kenneth B. Wolfe, became well known among aircraft industry contractors for its aggressive demands for quick design changes and faster output.[119] Wright Field served as the primary public authority over contracting, design specifications, testing, and inspection. It also interfaced with contractors to facilitate group projects. Early in the war, for instance, Wolfe and his team coordinated the expanded B-17 bomber program, which required Douglas and Vega-Lockheed to rearrange their California plants to make thousands of the Boeing-designed planes.[120]

*   *   *

As the record of U.S. industrial mobilization from 1938 to 1944 suggests, the American war economy was complicated enough to provide plenty of evidence for any number of stories about its workings. Probably the most common shorthand account, at the time and afterward, emphasized the role of the nation's leading industrial corporations, such as GM and GE. Because executives from several of the big corporations became top mobilization officials in Washington, they invited close scrutiny. However, the focus on the biggest businesses and their leaders has made it difficult to generate an accurate picture of the whole American war economy.

The largest industrial corporations were indeed important, but not until the middle phase of the mobilization, in 1940–42, when the government commissioned dozens of new GOCO plants. That new capacity was built atop an already substantial military-industrial base, which had been created in 1938–40, when increased Allied orders and direct plant investments boosted the operations of warship and aircraft manufacturers. Although those military contractors would become giant enterprises in wartime, before 1940 most of them qualified as midsize specialty manufacturers in competitive fields.

Even after Pearl Harbor, there was not much of the so-called monopoly capitalism that progressive critics of the U.S. war economy have long decried. In most of the major war industries, including airframes, ships, tanks, trucks, ordnance, and electronics, there were at least a dozen major prime contractors. And as the record of the expanded war economy of

1942–44 suggests, plenty of formerly small or midsize companies—not just the largest corporations—became important subcontractors and prime contractors.

A close look at the workings of the arsenal of democracy also suggests the complexity of government-business relations. As we might expect, given the structure of the American economy, the wartime state was extraordinarily dependent on the managerial and manufacturing expertise of private firms. Only in warship construction, in which the Navy itself managed large production facilities, did the public sector obviously hold the capacity to make a large fraction of the weapons required in wartime. (Even there, the critical job of building the propulsion systems was handled by private firms, including GE and Westinghouse.) Otherwise, even when the government built giant new facilities that it owned completely, it turned to for-profit companies to manage production and personnel. In theory, the Navy and War Departments and the USMC might have drafted enough engineers and prospective managers to staff most of the new government-owned plants with public employees. In practice, military and civilian officials chose an easier path, which was to give private firms the job of managing most of the war economy.

Despite its obvious dependence on private expertise, the American industrial mobilization also relied heavily on energetic public entities. The public contribution was perhaps most obvious in plant finance. Even during the rearmament phase of 1938–40, British and French government orders and direct investments, along with some from the United States, underwrote the expansion of the aircraft industry. The predominance of GOCO plant, paid for with public dollars via the DPC and the War and Navy Departments, was an even more obvious manifestation of the critical role of government. The work of civilian-led coordinating boards such as the WPB (see Chapter 4) helped the war economy avoid devolving into a chaotic scramble for scarce materials. Less obvious, but no less critical, was the economic work of the War and Navy Departments. The military bureaus contributed a great deal to weapons design. Perhaps most important, they were the top awarders and managers of contracts. They also helped build and coordinate supply chains, promoted the sharing of information among suppliers, and provided many prime contractors with huge amounts of GFE. Because the military and the public understood the military's core mission as fighting in combat theaters, its work on the home front was seldom fully appreciated. But the military's business divisions, together with a variety of civilian authorities, made the war economy work.

It may seem too obvious to point out that the dynamics of the American war economy were too complex to sum up in a few words. But we need to appreciate its complexity in order to evaluate the business community's efforts to influence public understanding of the subject. During World War II, these efforts took the form of a multimedia public-relations campaign, designed to highlight the private sector's leadership of an awesome war production achievement. There was more than a little truth to this claim. But it was also a selective account, which ignored important dimensions of the real industrial mobilization that played out in the late 1930s and early 1940s. This selectivity was to be expected, because the business community had already decided what lessons Americans should learn from industrial mobilization, even before the arsenal was up and running.

Chapter 3

War Stories

As American companies produced munitions to defeat the Axis, their executives worked to take advantage of what they saw as an important political opportunity. "The defense production job is the greatest news story of our generation," J. Howard Pew, the Sun Oil Company president, explained to his fellow industrialists in early 1941. "All the citizenry is watching. With a vigorous public relations program, competitive enterprise can dramatize its strength more successfully today than its enemies have ever been able to dramatize its occasional temporary mistakes."[1]

For Pew and many of his fellow business leaders, the stakes in this public-relations struggle seemed sky-high. Success would mean convincing Americans that victory in World War II should be attributed to the accomplishments of private enterprise. Failing to do so might result in challenges to the private sector that could go well beyond those that had emerged during the Great War and the New Deal. "Whether the free enterprise system prevails in America after the war," explained the public-relations department of the Automotive Council for War Production (ACWP) in early 1942, "may depend on the extent to which the American people associate this system with industry's wartime record."[2]

Although many American business leaders worked long hours during the war making weapons, they also gave careful consideration to politics and public relations. By 1940, energetic conservatives in the business community had already spent years decrying the evils of big government. During World War II, they flooded the public sphere with descriptions of the mobilization effort in which for-profit companies figured as the heroic engineers of a production "miracle." As business leaders explained it, World War II served as a natural experiment in comparative political economy, in which free American enterprise was pitted against the supposedly more planned regimes of the Axis. In this pro-business story, government was given no credit for success—or else characterized as an actual hindrance. If the American economy succeeded in delivering the goods, Pew and his fellow executives claimed, it would be only private enterprise that deserved the credit.

This business story about the war economy was at once self-evident and audacious. It was true that in most sectors of the war economy, private firms managed the production of munitions. The wartime American state relied heavily on the production and management expertise of for-profit firms. This was the case in the dozens of large new government-owned, contractor-operated (GOCO) plants, as well as in older facilities that converted to war production. Business leaders also occupied many of the top offices in emergency mobilization organizations, including the War Production Board (WPB) and its predecessors. But for all the truths it captured, the business story also engaged in serious distortions. It had no room for the substantial contributions of public actors, such as the Defense Plant Corporation and the military's technical bureaus. The role of public finance, as well as governmental coordination, was almost entirely absent from the business story.

No less bold than these omissions was the message's tone, which portrayed businessmen as underappreciated, beleaguered victims of tyrannical state regulation. Executives and their organizations worked hard during the war to promote the idea that the private business sector, continually abused by government, stood as the nation's only viable defender against the growing threat to liberty. Their success in managing war production despite the problems created by labor unions and the government, business leaders argued, showed that they were qualified to lead the country into a postwar period of greater prosperity and freedom.

Business propaganda distorted the realities of mobilization, concealing the substantial contributions of public actors. But its portrayal of the American war economy proved remarkably influential. Naturally, it contended with rival narratives, some of which assigned greater credit to ordinary workers, or even to the government. But these rivals were outflanked. By 1943, business leaders were satisfied that the American public had come to accept the idea that private enterprise—and not organized labor or the wartime government—deserved the lion's share of the credit for what some were calling a war production miracle. No less important, the pro-business story about the war economy was increasingly taken up by politically moderate public officials and legislators, including some prominent New Dealers. This was merely one successful battle in a broader political war that would last for decades; but it was a significant victory, which would influence the direction of future campaigns.

Free Enterprise Versus the Axis

Starting in 1940, conservative business leaders launched a coordinated public-relations effort designed to persuade audiences to associate the successes of American war production with free-market capitalism. Although this campaign built on anti–New Deal public-relations work of the 1930s, it tackled an important new problem. The World War II crisis brought with it the potential for new developments in domestic politics, including the rise of a new wave of regulation and public enterprise that might go well beyond anything that was accomplished by the New Deal. For business leaders, it was critical that the public—and, more specifically, legislators and policymakers—learn the correct political lessons from the record of the nation's massive military-industrial mobilization. This meant, above all, that dramatic successes in munitions output needed to be attributed to the special creativity and efficiency of for-profit enterprise.

After they failed to unseat Roosevelt in 1936, conservative business leaders continued to broadcast their message to the public. The National Association of Manufacturers (NAM) and the Chamber of Commerce of the United States, the two biggest national business associations, spent hundreds of thousands of dollars a year on public relations. By the late 1930s, the NAM and the Chamber were running campaigns that connected "free enterprise" with traditional American liberties such as political democracy and religious liberty. These business associations, along with individual companies like Du Pont and General Motors, used print advertising, film, and radio programming to emphasize an American past dominated by self-reliant pioneers and entrepreneurs, as well as a present in which social harmony should be the rule. Business associations, companies, and executives also sponsored conservative newspaper columnists and radio commentators.[3]

During World War II, one thing that conservative business leaders did in the field of public relations was simply to reiterate old messages. "Let us tell the story of free enterprise anywhere and wherever we can," General

Electric chairman Philip D. Reed urged his fellow executives in 1940, "and let us oppose any project or program that will weaken or destroy it." Throughout the war, this basic task of educating the public about the virtues of private enterprise continued to be a priority for many of the more politically active leaders of the business community, including H. W. Prentis, Jr., of the Armstrong Cork Company, and Frederick C. Crawford, of the Thompson Products Company.[4]

Prentis and Crawford both served as top officers in the NAM, which functioned during the war years—as it had in the late 1930s—as one of the business community's most important national-level organizations. By 1944, the NAM had eleven thousand members, about 50 percent more than it had had at the start of the war. By war's end, NAM annual budgets were approaching $4 million a year, more than double what they had been in the later 1930s. Within the NAM, the National Industrial Information Committee—a dedicated public-relations division that used print, film, and radio—saw its annual budget rise to an average of $1.5 million for 1943–45; its staff grew to nearly two hundred people.[5]

The NAM was hardly the only organization that expanded its activities in wartime. The family of J. Howard Pew, the Sun Oil president, continued to invest in conservative initiatives. The American Economic Foundation, which Pew helped launch in 1939, continued during the war to work on its mission of "changing public opinion toward business," via a radio program broadcast on the NBC network. Meanwhile, the Pew family expanded its ownership of magazines aimed at rural America; they also helped underwrite the wartime rise of George S. Benson, a conservative columnist and radio commentator (and college president) based in Arkansas.[6] Other conservative groups that expanded their efforts during World War II included the National Committee to Uphold Constitutional Government and the American Enterprise Association. Meanwhile, the Los Angeles Chamber of Commerce stepped up its efforts to promote "free competitive enterprise," by offering economic education for business executives and promoting the work of antistatist intellectuals such as Ludwig von Mises, Ayn Rand, and Rose Wilder Lane.[7]

Although there were plenty of continuities in the business community's public-relations efforts from the 1930s through the Cold War, the World War II emergency brought new challenges and opportunities. Clearly, a massive war mobilization might alter government-business relations and the public understanding of them, perhaps for the worse. However, many business leaders hoped that the war mobilization could offer them a chance to cast off much of the negative public opinion about business that had accumulated over the course of the previous decade.

To some extent, the task of boosting the reputation of business in wartime was simply a matter of sustaining the momentum of the late 1930s. By the time World War II broke out in Europe in autumn 1939, the American business community had already been enjoying a revival of its political fortunes. On the eve of the 1938 midterm elections, B. C. Forbes, the veteran business magazine editor, already sensed that that a new day for business's public image was dawning. "Torrents of abuse of business leaders, perpetual bespattering of men of affairs with mud mixed with vitriol," Forbes wrote, "are ceasing to win nationwide applause."[8] The election results in November 1938 seemed to confirm Forbes's assessment. As Roosevelt headed into the second half of his second term, the New Deal had stalled, as had much of the recent expansion of the organized labor movement.

When military conflict did break out in Europe, the American business community emphasized that it was not eager for war. This attitude was driven by careful economic calculation, as well as memories of the "merchants of death" accusations of the mid-1930s. Some business leaders were devoted isolationists, whose disagreements with President Roosevelt over foreign policy matched their disdain for his domestic programs. But even those more sympathetic to intervention claimed that business wanted to avoid war, which inevitably brought disruptions to markets, high taxes, increased regulation, inflation, the overexpansion of capacity, and the likelihood of postwar recessions. As we have seen in Chapter 1, many executives believed that the Roosevelt administration's hostility to business made the prospect of converting to war work even less appealing than it might otherwise have been.[9]

Despite these looming dangers, the business community took great satisfaction from one aspect of the early war mobilization: the transformation of the businessman from villain into national savior. Immediately after the start of war in Europe, NAM-sponsored speakers were telling audiences across the country, "American business is getting out of the dog-house."[10] At once aspirational and descriptive, this theme was reinforced by the president's moves in mid-1940 to bring William Knudsen, Edward Stettinius, Jr., and other business executives to Washington to help direct the war economy. As a writer for the journal *Sales Management* noted, there seemed now to be "a universal trend towards putting faith and reliance in private enterprise."[11]

For the business community, this revival of faith was a transformation to be savored. "For ten years our business system and business men have been under attack," the Chamber of Commerce's official magazine, *Nation's Business*, reminded readers in the summer of 1940. But as soon as the nation faced a real security threat, "business leaders were whistled out of the doghouse and put in charge. What irony!"[12] Alfred P. Sloan, Jr., the GM chairman, had a similar message for the convention of political scientists he addressed in November 1940. "Ironically the very individuals, the very industrial organizations, which, during the past few years, have been under political attack and held up to public scorn as enemies of the public interest," Sloan observed, "have now become vital instrumentalities of national defense."[13]

But if business's public image was already improving in 1940, this did not mean that it had overcome the political-economic crisis created by the rise of the overbearing New Deal state. On the contrary, business leaders argued, the outbreak of war actually threatened to worsen the situation, by allowing New Dealers to use the emergency to install an even more oppressive national state. There was a real danger, they insisted, of the United States falling into totalitarianism, even as it raised armies to defeat totalitarian powers abroad.

This nightmare vision of an all-powerful wartime state was evoked by business leaders and their allies even before America entered the war. Throughout 1939, several steel company executives, including Ernest Weir, Raoul Desvernine, and Tom Girdler, issued warnings about the likelihood of "dictatorship," novel "totalitarian instruments" of economic regulation, and a thoroughgoing "regimentation and control," if the country were to enter the war. Their concerns were echoed by leading conservative politicians, such as Senator Robert A. Taft (R-OH). "While the people's attention is diverted, and using the war itself as an excuse," Taft predicted in late 1939, "we will doubtless see the inner circle of the New Deal proposing more government dictation of business and individuals."[14]

Once the American industrial mobilization was under way, business conservatives and their allies continued to complain that the Roosevelt administration was using the crisis as a pretext for extending state control. Desvernine, the politically active president of the Crucible Steel Company, warned in September 1940 that the nation seemed to be slipping into a pattern of "governmental socialization of private industry," rather than the sort of reliance on voluntary measures and the "free enterprise system" that had been used to such good effect by the Wilson administration during the Great War. The broader community of business leaders seems to have shared these concerns. Three-quarters of the executives who participated in a *Fortune* magazine poll in autumn 1941 agreed with the notion that "[w]henever possible the Administration is using the national emergency as a pretext for pushing still further the more radical social and economic aims of the New Deal."[15]

Connecting their worries about wartime domestic reform with the broader geopolitical conflict, the authors of the pro-business narrative warned that the United States must not imitate the Axis. "Must We Hitlerize to Fight Hitlerism?" the editors of *Nation's Business* asked rhetorically in October 1940. "The road upon which we are galloping," they warned, "heads to complete subordination of the Man to the State."[16] A similar question was posed by Walter D. Fuller, leader of Curtis Publishing, who served in 1941 as NAM president. "What does it gain us to destroy totalitarianism in the world," Fuller asked audiences in his 1941 speeches, "if we cultivate totalitarianism at home?"[17]

According to the conservative business narrative, World War II was not only a struggle between the armed forces of the Allies and the Axis but a war waged by domestic and foreign enemies against the traditional American economic system. As Sloan, the GM chairman, explained in a speech delivered in late May 1940, as France was falling, the American "enterprise system may be regarded as engaged in a life and death struggle. It is under attack both from within and without." This was also the vision of Sloan's fellow GM executive Donaldson Brown, who, in a December 1941 luncheon address, explained to a group of New York statisticians that World War II was really a clash between "the system of free enterprise" and "the dictator system threatening the world."[18]

One part of the business community's developing narrative of the American mobilization described a domestic struggle between private industry and an aggressive New Deal state that threatened to impose increasingly totalitarian controls. But that narrative also settled on a vision of World War II in which the U.S. economy remained free enough to serve as the basis for a natural experiment that could test the merits of democracy and capitalism. As the conservative economist Alfred Haake told a meeting of oil industry executives in November 1941, "perhaps the most serious charge against democracy and competitive enterprise is that they are not efficient in war." Now the United States would have the opportunity to demonstrate, in the performance of its war economy, whether "our free enterprise system" could outperform the Axis nations, which relied on "government domination of all enterprise."[19]

In the two years before Pearl Harbor, business leaders had launched a narrative that would associate a successful munitions production record with the unique genius of American private enterprise. This public-relations strategy was not without risks. If war production foundered, the business community would have trouble escaping blame. As Edward Stettinius, Jr., the U.S. Steel executive–turned–mobilization chief, admitted to Arthur Krock of the *New York Times* in late 1940, there was no guarantee that the industrial mobilization would succeed. "The whole relationship of business with Government is on trial," Stettinius told Krock. Similar concerns troubled Bernard Baruch, the veteran Wall Street investor, Democratic Party donor, and Great War mobilization czar. "If this war is lost," Baruch reminded Navy undersecretary James Forrestal in early 1941, "or even if it is won and great profits or incompetence is shown, it will be a terrific blow at the capitalistic system."[20]

Although these risks were real, the business community enjoyed favorable odds. Despite the ravages of the Great Depression, the United States still ranked easily as the world's largest, most productive national economy. Thanks to the several billion dollars of new private and public investment in war plant in 1938–41, munitions output was expanding fast. It was likely that the nation would succeed in producing huge numbers of spectacular weapons, including warships, tanks, and bomber aircraft. Certainly, the odds seemed good to the NAM, which a year before Pearl Harbor had devised a public-relations plan that would involve "publicizing and encouraging industry to publicize its opposition to war, and at the same time publicize industry's fullest contribution to physical defense. This symbol of public interest," the NAM public-relations staff believed, "is too great to overlook its cultivation."[21]

Having taken the calculated risk to stake its reputation on the results of the defense production effort, the business community proceeded in 1941–42 to develop a multimedia campaign to highlight the contributions of private industry. Sometimes blunt, sometimes subtle, this campaign educated the public about increasing production at the country's most important defense plants. Because much of that production was truly impressive, the campaign had little trouble finding evidence to support its claims. Occasionally, it acknowledged the contributions of ordinary workers, or the military. But it generally obscured the giant role of public capital and government management in the American war economy, while associating production achievements with the names of private companies and the broader free-enterprise system.

One of the business community's primary outlets for its narrative about the war economy was radio. In 1941, American radio listeners began to hear a variety of programs describing the growing defense industries.[22] The NAM took the lead in these efforts by sponsoring two similar documentary-style programs designed to introduce the public to business's munitions-making accomplishments. The first of these, a half-hour program called *Defense for America*, ran on one of NBC's two national networks from February through October 1941, in the desirable time slot of 7 PM on Saturdays. It guided listeners into the plants of some fifty defense contractors, where workers and managers talked about their recent accomplishments. The NAM sponsored a second, related program, *Your Defense Reporter*, which was broadcast on Thursday evenings on the Mutual network. Hosted by the well-known conservative radio commentator Fulton Lewis, Jr., that program ran from May 1941 through June 1942.[23] After Pearl Harbor, the major business associations continued to sponsor similar nationally broadcast programs, such as the Chamber of Commerce's *Action on the Home Front*, the NAM's *This Nation at War*, and *War of Enterprise*, cosponsored by the Chamber and the ACWP.[24]

These business-sponsored radio programs offered straight reporting on war industries, inflected with a political message about the success and superiority of private enterprise. *Defense for America* presented technical details about some of the big machines used to hammer out munitions, along with simple patriotic messages, including regular incantations of the Pledge of Allegiance. For its special sixth-month anniversary show, in August 1941, *Defense for America* reviewed the record of the defense industry to date and found "the most astounding increases in defense production that anyone could hope for." But the programs also relayed more subtle messages, suggesting that defense output was a creation of for-profit business enterprise, without any significant government role. In a *Defense for America* program broadcast in late March 1941, for instance, listeners learned about the impressive shipbuilding feats of leading private yards, including those run by Bethlehem Steel, New York Ship, Federal Ship, Sun Ship, and Newport News Shipbuilding. Thanks to "the ships that American free enterprise is creating," the program explained, the country would soon be more secure.[25] Unmentioned were the massive government investments in these shipyards, as well as the fact that the Navy's own public-run yards were building a large fraction of the new warships.

The *Defense for America* radio program became the basis for one of NAM's original short feature films. Produced by Paramount Pictures, the *Defense for America* film was released in summer 1941. Like other NAM films, it was marketed to schools, clubs, and community centers, as well as some commercial theaters. The film emphasized the business community's narrative of World War II as a test of America's free, capitalist economy. Promotional posters for the film used banner headlines such as "Can America Out-Perform the Dictators?" and "Free Men Versus Regimented Slaves." The film opened with images of the Statue of Liberty, the U.S. Capitol building, wheat fields, houses, factories, and storefronts. These were set against shots of saluting crowds at Nazi rallies. "In Europe today, men are regimented," the film explained. It then presented an array of images from American war plants, turning out thousands of guns, shells, trucks, tanks, and warships. All this war production, the film declared, "is a graphic, living demonstration of the superiority of free men and free industry." Taking up a traditional NAM theme, the film also emphasized that free enterprise was intertwined with other basic American liberties, including freedom of religion and speech, as well as the right to vote. It closed with a shot of a fluttering American flag.[26]

The business associations' publicity of munitions production continued after Pearl Harbor. Immediately following the shock of that event, there appears to have been a brief pause in the public-relations offensive. Just after the attacks, GM's Sloan reportedly recommended that the business community tone down its free-enterprise rhetoric for a time, until the nation's nerves were calmer.[27] By spring 1942, however, the campaign was again running strong. The NAM created a new pamphlet, "Industry's War Production," detailing the impressive output of various American war industries. By the end of the year, it had published more than 107,000 copies of the pamphlet, which it circulated to Congress, schools, YMCAs, women's clubs, and churches.[28]

Spring 1942 also saw the start of a new public-relations initiative by the ACWP, the Detroit-based wartime auto industry association formed a few days after Pearl Harbor. It was led by George W. Romney, who would go on after the war to become an auto industry executive and then governor of Michigan. Working under Romney's direction, the ACWP's public-relations staff planned a campaign that would highlight "evidence of sheer production competence" by private industry, which would counter recent public criticism of defense production delays caused by cartel arrangements or other allegedly unpatriotic business behavior. They created a new magazine, *Automotive War Production*, devoted to "showing how the industry's peacetime operations—under a free-enterprise system—were responsible for developing the facilities which are now helping to win the 'BATTLE OF PRODUCTION.'" The organization also issued a report to the public, "The Job Is Being Done," explaining how the auto industry had rapidly converted to defense output. The ACWP report was taken up by the mainstream media, including *Newsweek* magazine, which informed readers that the "motor magicians" had succeeded in creating "mass production for mass destruction."[29]

One of the NAM's major public-relations projects for 1942, which built upon its efforts in radio and print media, was its "Production for Victory" tour, designed to show that "industry is making the utmost contribution toward victory."[30] Starting the first week in May, the NAM paid for twenty newspaper reporters to take a twenty-four-day, fifteen-state trip, during which they visited sixty-four major defense plants run by fifty-eight private companies. For most of May, newspapers across the country ran daily articles related to the tour, written by the papers' own reporters or by one of the wire services. The articles' headlines included "Army Gets Rubber Thanks to Akron," "General Motors Plants Turning Out Huge Volume of War Goods," "Baldwin Ups Tank Output," and "American Industry Overcomes a Start of 7 Years by Axis." Readers of the stories learned that the nation's war plants were ahead of schedule, thanks to the agile conversion and production efforts of manufacturers. "Everywhere," *Newsweek* explained in an overview of the stories filed by the reporters on the NAM tour, "the story was monotonously but encouragingly the same: production ahead of schedule and mounting rapidly."[31]

Like the business-sponsored radio reports, the articles generated by NAM's "Production for Victory" tour taught the public about the achievements of private enterprise, while obscuring public contributions. As Monsanto chairman Edgar M. Queeny noted with satisfaction, the tour had helped inspire stories like the one filed by Ray Sprigle of the *Pittsburgh Post-Gazette*: in his dispatches from the tour, Sprigle assured readers that "under a system of free enterprise," which was now "saving the nation," the United

States was already making the munitions that it would use to defeat Germany. Comparable stories were filed by the *New York Times* reporter on the tour, Sidney M. Shalett. Describing a visit to the large Pratt & Whitney aero engine works in Connecticut, Shalett praised the United Aircraft Corporation's "risky gambles in expanding its facilities" during the months before Pearl Harbor. Unmentioned in Shalett's piece were the millions in French, British, and United States public funds that went into the company's new plants. After a visit to a phosphorous plant near Nashville, Shalett wrote that "the Monsanto achievement symbolizes the native ingenuity of American manufacturers, who are the brigadier generals on the production front." These press reports differed little from the official line promoted by the NAM, which assured its members that the tour had generated "detailed accounts of production miracles." Together, these articles told "a story to warm the hearts of all Americans. It was the story of how U.S. Industry had won the Battle of Production."[32]

Coverage of the NAM tour was part of a flood of messages, starting in mid-1942, assuring Americans that the country was starting to win the war of industrial production. This optimism followed many anxious months, when news from the war fronts seemed grim and the whole country was on edge. Together with the reports of recent naval victories in the battles of Coral Sea and Midway, the news of success in the war of economies offered Americans some of their first good reasons to believe that the Allies would prevail. In May 1942, WPB chief Donald Nelson announced that American munitions output was already at a pace of $41 billion a year, and climbing fast. "We are over the hump on war production," Nelson said.[33] There were now frequent press reports and claims in corporate advertisements of striking increases in the output of merchant ships, tanks, planes, and other weapons (see Figure 3). Many newspapers and magazines now began to refer casually to "the miracles achieved by industry."[34]

Promoted by major business associations, the public-relations push to educate Americans about war production was also carried out by hundreds of individual companies. GM's fifteen-minute radio show about the feats of its plants and workers, *Victory Is Their Business*, was broadcast on the CBS network. The company also paid to saturate national magazines with its advertisements, which in 1942 emphasized the theme "Good News from the Production Front."[35] Many other manufacturers sponsored at least occasional radio pieces. These included the July 1942 program sponsored by the Electric Boat Company, which arranged to have the 127 stations in

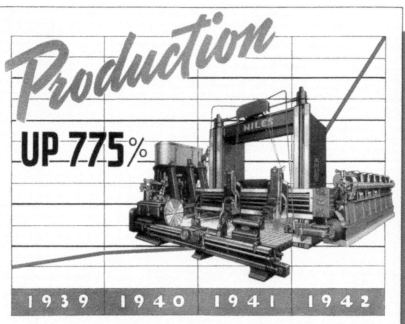

Figure 3. "Production Up 775%," advertisement by the General Machinery Corporation, 1942. This ad, from an important supplier of ship engines, machine tools, and rocket motors, appeared in the May 1942 issue of *Fortune* magazine, among other publications. It is representative of the business community's emphasis, starting in the late spring of 1942, on growing production figures as a measure of the success of free enterprise. Courtesy Atkins Library, University of North Carolina at Charlotte.

NBC's Blue Network broadcast the sounds of the keel-laying of the first submarine to be produced in its new Victory Yard.[36] Many companies, such as Curtiss-Wright, produced simple two-reel documentary films highlighting their plants' output.[37] A few companies created short dramatic features. For instance, U.S. Steel produced *To Each Other* (1943), a film that dramatized an exchange of letters between an American soldier abroad and a steel manufacturer at home, who educated each other about their important contributions to the war effort.[38]

Most contractors touted their munitions output in print advertisements, which became ubiquitous in newspapers and magazines. In May 1942, the Treasury Department ruled that "ordinary and necessary" advertising would be tax-deductible; the WPB, following the Treasury's lead, decided that some advertising in trade journals would be treated as an allowable cost under cost-plus-fixed-fee contracts.[39] Such policies—in an environment of very high tax rates—boosted business spending on ads. At Boeing, for example, the board of directors decided to spend nearly a million dollars a year on print advertising in 1943–45, nearly as much as it had set aside for research and development.[40] In their ads, contractors boasted of their roles in the war effort. Philco, a leading supplier of radar and radar equipment, ran a series of magazine ads in 1942 on the theme "All-Out U.S. Production." Featuring vivid drawings by the well-known cartoonist Rube Goldberg, the Philco ads showed the burgeoning American munitions output overwhelming stunned leaders of the Axis.[41] GM created a series of full-page ads in major magazines for 1943, headlined "Production, Production, and More Production." Each ad was accompanied by the tag (also the title of a company-made film) "General Motors—Victory Is Our Business."[42]

Besides pointing to high output overall, the ads educated the public about the provenance of specific weapons. Readers of popular American magazines came to know that the P-38 "Lightning" fighter plane was a product of the Lockheed Corporation.[43] This weapon, along with dozens of others used by the American armed forces, was, in effect, branded by the prime contractor.[44] This sort of presentation offered readers a detailed portrait of the organization of the American war economy. By explaining that nearly every weapon was made in a plant managed by a specific private company, these communications worked together to generate a view of the industrial mobilization that was mostly accurate. But they, like the NAM tour and other business-friendly presentations, also served to erase the essential role of public actors.[45]

Despite their success in spreading so much publicity, business leaders worried that the credit for the growing output of munitions might not be properly attributed. One potential public-relations problem, business leaders came to realize, came from the lack of specificity in the ubiquitous references to an American war production "miracle." This term was circulating as early as April 1941, when the insurance executive James Kemper told an audience at the Chamber of Commerce's national meeting that businessmen "have performed miracles in the way of preparation, expansion of plant capacity, and in actual production" for defense.[46] As output rose, the term was embraced by more members of the business community and the press. In April 1942, Eugene E. Wilson, president of United Aircraft, told a meeting of newspaper editors that "the aircraft industry has performed a production miracle." A few weeks later, Ford Motor ran ads announcing that its plants had achieved "the greatest miracle of mass production the world has ever known." In his State of the Union address in January 1943, President Roosevelt presented data on the nation's impressive munitions output, calling it "a miracle of production."[47] By that time, the term had become a cliché.

From the point of view of business leaders, the "miracle of production" rhetoric had the virtue of reinforcing a story of astonishing successes in munitions output. However, by implying that the production was magical, it failed to do enough to ascribe the success to the genius of free enterprise. So some business leaders began to explain to one another, and to the public, that the American industrial mobilization was decidedly not miraculous. At the NAM's annual meeting in December 1943, which drew hundreds of business leaders to the Waldorf-Astoria Hotel in New York, the organization's leaders stressed the no-miracle theme. NAM president Frederick C. Crawford reminded his colleagues that, in fact, management "know how" was the key to "the production record now termed 'a miracle.'" The war output might seem magical, as the president and others had implied, "but industry knows that there was nothing miraculous about it. One hundred and fifty years of free enterprise in this country," Crawford reminded his audience, "created the greatest productive machine that the world has ever known." This was also the message of Tom Girdler, the top executive at Republic Steel and Consolidated-Vultee Aircraft, who, in his own NAM conference speech, emphasized "a story of stupendous feats of plant expansion and production." These achievements came not from "miracles," Girdler insisted, but rather were "the natural outcome of America's creative enterprise."[48]

The business community's story of the war mobilization went beyond merely omitting references to public actors. Rather, it often engaged in a bold denigration of government, which was presented as not just an ineffective actor but as a real hindrance. As GM executive Donaldson Brown explained to NAM president William P. Witherow in July 1942, now that the evidence of a "miracle of production" was accumulating, the business community needed to ensure that the right parties were given the credit. It was essential that the war production record not be attributed to any form of "centralized planning and administration," Brown wrote, so that an "unenlightened public" would not learn the wrong political lessons from the war. As Brown's friend J. Howard Pew put it in a talk at a NAM-sponsored meeting in October 1943, the record of war production was impressive but needed to be properly interpreted for average citizens. "Now we must undertake to get the American people to understand," Pew told his fellow business leaders, "that industry was able to do this job only because individual initiative in this country remained unchained . . . despite the schemes of bureaucrats and economic planners."[49]

This language was spread by conservative journalists who also emphasized a story of patriotic entrepreneurs accomplishing great production feats despite the many obstacles thrown up by naïve New Dealers in Washington. "When the pinch came," B. C. Forbes of *Forbes* magazine boasted in 1942, "'Brain Trusters' had to be relegated to the background, theorists gave place to practical, experienced industrial and other executives." The same story was related by Samuel Crowther, the veteran business journalist, biographer, and public-relations consultant who published a book in 1942 that claimed that wartime economic controls had created a "full-slave" economy in the United States. "The enormous amount of war work that is actually being done throughout the country," Crowther declared, "is getting done in spite of and not because of the centralized controls. It is getting done because the spirit of free enterprise remains with us."[50]

This was the story that businessmen told one another in speeches to luncheon and dinner meetings across the country. In November 1942, for instance, public-relations specialist James P. Selvage told a group of Massachusetts advertising men that their industry had failed to do enough to publicize the record of "the most magnificent job of production in the history of the world." If they could only do more to expose the deceptions of a "small group of radicals, parlor pinks, and intellectual crackpots," Selvage said, "the people would today be rearing up and demanding that business be turned loose by the politicians to win the war." The need to unleash business was also stressed by George Romney, director of the ACWP. The "paper blizzard" emanating from U.S. government officials, Romney told an audience of Detroit bankers, smacked of "Hitler's methods," which held back the German war economy. What the United States really needed to do, Romney explained, was to tell contractors that "it's your ship," stand back, and let the private sector go to work. Crawford, during his term as NAM president in 1943, voiced the same idea. "We must make certain that production is not stunted," he told businessmen across the country in 1943, "by the whimsical restrictions of bureaucrats burdened with the blueprints and designs of economic planners."[51]

Encouraged by what they were hearing from their peers, their associations, and the press, business leaders proved willing, as the war went on, to speak of the public sector with contempt. As one executive of a Wichita manufacturing company told a Chicago business group in May 1944, he was no longer going to bite his tongue when he heard the usual criticisms of business. The next time someone did so, he promised, "I'm just going to ask him, very sharply, who was it that America turned to in her hour of danger and distress? Was it the crack-pots—the social planners—the something-for-nothing boys—the economists—the reliefers—the dreamers? Or was it to American factories, built and managed under our system of private enterprise?" A succinct version of the same message was offered by James F. Lincoln, the outspoken president of the nation's leading independent manufacturer of welding equipment. "It is not because of, but in spite of, bureaucracy," Lincoln explained in an early 1945 speech to a group of sales executives in New York City, "that we are the arsenal of democracy."[52]

Rival Narratives—and Their Limits

Throughout World War II, much of the American business community propagated and internalized a narrative that portrayed the private sector as the sole contributor to the nation's remarkable munitions production effort. Ordinary workers were largely absent from this narrative, while organized labor and, especially, government were portrayed as hindrances. Given the obvious importance of labor, as well as the somewhat more hidden but enormous role of public entities in financing and coordinating the industrial mobilization, the business community's campaign qualified as a bold piece of politics. It competed in the public sphere with alternative narratives, some of which challenged the distortions of the business story. However, these counternarratives seem to have been rather ineffective—and surprisingly so, given that the war years were a time of a major expansion of labor unions and a time when the executive branch continued to be run by New Deal Democrats. Despite these apparent advantages on the side of political progressives, they do not seem to have allowed the political Left to create a narrative that would overwhelm the one crafted by business elites. How can this be explained?

Before turning to the counternarratives, we might ask whether the business community itself generated any challenges to the conservative emphasis on the evils of government and superiority of free enterprise. Certainly, the American "business community" would seem to be far too large and diverse, politically as well as economically, to support sweeping generalizations about its behavior. Nevertheless, the record of the early 1940s suggests that even the most politically progressive business leaders did little to contradict the mainstream conservative story about the dynamics of the war economy. On the contrary, they often helped propagate it.

Certainly, few American business leaders were as vocal as the leaders of the NAM about the evils of government and the superiority of free enterprise, even if they endorsed those views in private. During the World War II emergency, hundreds of business leaders—perhaps even something approaching a silent majority—focused their energies on meeting military production requirements. This attitude was especially common during the anxious weeks that followed Pearl Harbor, when many business leaders earnestly embraced the notion that profits and public relations needed to take a backseat to helping the American armed forces prevail. Norman Lewis, president of Ridgway Company, a St. Louis advertising agency, expressed this attitude in a short piece published in *Forbes* magazine in April 1942. "I will ditch politics for the duration," Lewis promised.[53]

As the wartime actions of most business associations and many individual executives demonstrate, a large number of Lewis's peers proved unwilling to "ditch politics," especially after an Allied victory began to look more assured. Some executives, however, at least gestured toward a politics that allowed for more business-government cooperation than the more conservative free-enterprise camp would allow. For example, John L. Collyer, president of B. F. Goodrich, one of the "big four" rubber companies, suggested to his peers in mid-1944 that although tax cuts would obviously be necessary, some significant public spending might be desirable in the postwar era. Some of this public expenditure, by promoting industrial research, promised to benefit the private sector, suggested Collyer.[54]

Dozens of other top executives were willing to endorse this sort of vague commitment to a pro-business variant of Keynesian economics, in which adjustments in government spending could help stabilize the economy without challenging the autonomy of private companies. Some of these relatively progressive executives, led by Studebaker president Paul Hoffman, congregated in the Committee for Economic Development (CED), a small organization formed in 1942. Another business progressive was William L. Batt, head of SKF Industries, a leading manufacturer of ball bearings, who went to Washington in 1940 to work on industrial mobilization. Unlike his more conservative colleagues, Batt rejected the notion that business should try to re-create the "good old days" of the pre–New Deal era. Instead, as Batt argued in a 1942 speech, industry needed to move "forward to greater production and better distribution, forward to new products and new markets, forward to a greater industrial and social democracy and to greater economic stability."[55] Although this statement placed Batt on the left fringe of the progressive business community, Hoffman and others in the CED agreed that industry needed to pursue some kind of realistic accommodation with the New Deal state, rather than its utter destruction. Meanwhile, the much larger Chamber of Commerce began to move at least slightly away from the NAM, by doing more to suggest the need for engagement with labor unions and some kind of cooperation with government that would help create a high-employment postwar economy.[56]

The CED and the Chamber did present real alternatives to the traditional conservative view of political economy, which could have very significant implications for the shape of industrial relations and macroeconomic policy. They did not, however, produce anything resembling a coherent counternarrative about the lessons of the war mobilization. This was evident from the speeches and writings of Eric A. Johnston, the relatively progressive young executive who became the Chamber's new president in spring 1942. A charismatic ex-Marine, Johnston had succeeded in building a group of electric-appliance businesses in the Pacific Northwest. In his new job as head of the Chamber, Johnston worked quickly to build bridges with union leaders and the Roosevelt administration. In numerous speeches and publications, he promoted himself and the Chamber as capable of leading the country toward the elusive "middle way" between "ultraconservatives" and "clamorous collectivists."[57]

Johnston and his more conservative peers may have disagreed on questions of labor relations and the government's role in the postwar era; but on the matter of the lessons of the war mobilization, they spoke with one voice. This was clear from "America Unlimited," the speech that Johnston delivered to the Chamber in April 1943, which became the basis for his book of the same title, published the following year. "Everyone speaks of the miracle of American war production," Johnston said in the speech, but "not everyone remembers that it is a miracle made possible by individual initiative, using the mechanisms and the driving force generated by capitalism." In his book, Johnston went even further, claiming that the synthetic rubber program, "perhaps the most spectacular exemplification of the American productive system," was one in which "private industry did the job." Given that the nation's synthetic rubber industry had been paid for entirely by the government, this was a rather bold claim. But it reflected Johnston's agreement with the conservative business narrative about the war economy. "Any attempt to interpret war production as a triumph for state operation," Johnston argued in his book, "must miscarry, since it is easy to show that private capitalism carried out the assignment *despite* the handicaps of many government policies curtailing freedom of action, and *despite* myriad bureaucratic controls."[58] This rhetoric, of course, echoed that of the "ultraconservatives" whom Johnston claimed to disown.

Similar language was used by Henry Kaiser, the most celebrated of all American business leaders during World War II. Because of his willingness to take on the big corporations and his relatively friendly relations with the Roosevelt administration and labor unions, Kaiser was seen as an unusually progressive captain of industry. During World War II, when his efforts in merchant shipbuilding and other fields were portrayed by *Time* magazine as "fabulous," Kaiser became a hero of the home front.[59] Regarded by many of his peers as an overrated darling of the New Dealers and the press, Kaiser, by most measures, ranked as a politically progressive business leader. In May 1943, he attacked "the remnants of monopoly and vested interests," which hurt themselves and the nation by being "selfish, short-sighted, [and] anti-social." And in a January 1945 speech in New York, broadcast nationally on one of the NBC radio networks, Kaiser criticized his conservative peers for failing to see the need to build a postwar economy that would achieve "both social justice and economic progress."[60]

Despite these statements, Kaiser's rhetoric about the war economy never posed any significant challenge to his more conservative peers. Much of the content of Kaiser's wartime speeches was drafted by Paul F. Cadman, an economist attached to the American Bankers' Association. Just after the 1942 midterm elections, Cadman advised Kaiser that he should break with the New Dealers' "utopian" notions about the abilities of government to "deliver abundance." The American public, Cadman told Kaiser, was "already weary of super-states, the burden of bureaucracy, and the cultivated philosophy of discontent." This advice quickly found its way into Kaiser's wartime speeches, which emphasized "the freedom to produce" and the desire of Americans to "enjoy independence and freedom from bureaucracy."[61]

As Kaiser's incoming mail suggests, most of those who listened to his wartime utterances understood him not as a pro-labor New Dealer but as a champion of competitive capitalism. His speeches drew praise from those listeners, including ordinary workers and members of Congress, who believed in more autonomy for the private sector and less government.[62] On the other hand, listeners more concerned with the plight of ordinary people were disappointed by Kaiser's wartime talk. "To millions of us," as one of Kaiser's correspondents put it, "the 'paternalistic' concern of the 'social politicians' upon whom you cast such scorn represent the only place where our interests are even considered."[63]

Although it was accepted by moderate and conservative business leaders alike, the free-enterprise story about the American war economy did have to vie with rivals. Two counternarratives were particularly important. One told a story of the machinations of profiteering, monopolistic big businesses that were placing their private interests above the public good. (Among Americans on the political left, this anticorporate narrative has remained influential to this day.) A second counter-narrative, which celebrated the contributions of ordinary workers and other "soldiers of production," was less critical of big business. But it, no less than the anticorporate story, challenged the free-enterprise account of a war effort that owed all its success to capitalists.

The anticorporate story about the American economy was broadcast by three influential sets of actors: progressive journalists, congressional investigators, and the organized labor movement. The first of these groups, the journalists, published their work in a handful of left-leaning magazines and newspapers. These included the long-running magazines *New Republic* and the *Nation*, which in 1940 were joined by *PM*, a new daily tabloid published in New York. These publications were not popular.[64] But they circulated widely enough among elite and rank-and-file progressives to influence national political conversations, including the one about the development of the war economy.

During World War II, progressive publications continued to support a liberal welfare state, albeit while retreating from some of the most confrontational antibusiness political positions that they had taken in the 1930s.[65] When it came to the subject of the early military-industrial mobilization, they had few reservations about attacking big business. Of all the investigative journalists writing on this subject, the leader was I. F. Stone, who wrote regularly for the *Nation* and *PM*. In August 1940, Stone informed his readers that the aircraft industry, holding out for more favorable tax rules and contract prices, had been engaged in a "sitdown strike." Over the following months, Stone and his colleagues kept up the offensive. They portrayed the top civilian mobilization agencies in Washington as dominated by dollar-a-year men, on loan from the big corporations, who were more interested in protecting private interests than protecting the country. They emphasized the cartel arrangements between Standard Oil of New Jersey and I. G. Farben, the German chemical giant, that had allegedly delayed the American effort to make synthetic rubber. Other large companies, such as GM and Alcoa, they reported, were resisting expansion for national defense purposes because they wanted to maximize profits. But the government was handing these industrial giants generous defense contracts, to the detriment of smaller, more patriotic companies.[66]

Especially during the early months of the conflict, in 1940–42, the progressive journalists' anticorporate message became an important part of mainstream political debates. Millions of newspaper readers encountered suggestive bits about cartels and profiteering in Drew Pearson's popular "Washington Merry-Go-Round" syndicated column, among other sources.[67] In Congress, a special committee chaired by Senator Harry S. Truman (D-MO), which became the legislative branch's most important investigator of the war economy, began its work by criticizing big business. In its first reports, issued in 1941–42, the Truman Committee faulted the military for its alleged failure to give more orders to small business and attacked large corporations such as Alcoa and Standard Oil of New Jersey for impeding the defense program.[68] Similar accusations were made by Thurman Arnold, the energetic chief of the Justice Department's antitrust division. In 1941–42, Arnold used a series of speeches and articles to claim that the defense program was being damaged by the anticompetitive practices of the nation's leading industrial corporations, including GE, Dow, and Alcoa.[69]

Another important proponent of the anticorporate frame was organized labor. By the time of World War II, the American labor movement, led at the national level by the American Federation of Labor (AFL) and the Congress of Industrial Organizations (CIO), was a powerful, growing political force. Even the AFL, the older and more conservative of the two national umbrella organizations, accused business of unpatriotic behavior. Especially before Pearl Harbor, AFL leaders and publications blamed corporations for mobilizing too slowly and for taking excessive profits.[70] Even during the latter part of the war, the AFL occasionally issued pointed attacks on the business community's story of the mobilization. In early 1943, for instance, the AFL's monthly newspaper published a letter to the editor, signed by Janet Kleinsmid of Memphis, who rejected business claims that salary limits or other controls would harm war production. "The executives don't have to display any initiative these days," argued Kleinsmid. "Not a bit of it. Our government is throwing billion-dollar contracts at them all the time. The government tells them what to make and how to make it. The government takes all they do make, and that's all there is to it. So all this stuff about 'destroying incentive' is just a lot of baloney." A year later, a similar argument was voiced by George Meany, a top AFL official. "How much enterprise is a manufacturer called upon to manifest to keep his plant humming," Meany asked in 1944, "when the customer, the government, obligingly comes to him and shoves a mass of million-dollar contracts at him?"[71]

Within the CIO, and in more radical labor circles, attacks on alleged corporate profiteering were more widespread. Before Pearl Harbor, top CIO leaders, including Philip Murray and Walter Reuther, joined New Dealer all-outers in calling for faster conversion to war production. They wanted to do so by creating new tripartite industrial organizations, in which labor would share power with business and government. After these proposals were dismissed out of hand by corporate executives and many government officials, the CIO was in a good position to argue, after Pearl Harbor, that it had been more prescient than business leaders about the need for more defense production. In 1942, CIO leaders emphasized an "Equality of Sacrifice" campaign that demanded that business submit to tight price and profit controls. They succeeded in having President Roose-velt endorse a cap of $25,000 on after-tax executive salaries—a measure that Congress would reject in early 1943.[72]

Especially at the local level, CIO-affiliated unions and other left-labor groups offered strong challenges to the business community's story of the war economy. On the far Left, socialist publications such as *Labor Action* overflowed with cartoons and articles about the government-guaranteed profit-taking of fat-cat executives.[73] Similar images and stories were broad-cast by many CIO unions, including the United Autoworkers.[74] At the grassroots level, unions and companies struggled bitterly over how much profit was being taken and how much was legitimate. (This was not just a matter of principle but also a pragmatic issue for unions, many of which were trying to convince government officials that profits were high enough to justify adjustments to the wartime wage freeze.) The high tensions over alleged profiteering were suggested in developments in early 1944 at Pullman-Standard, the railcar manufacturer that had become one of the nation's leading producers of tanks. After Pullman-Standard ran national advertisements boasting that its pretax profit margin was below 2 percent, the United Steelworkers local representing some of the company's workers in Chicago used its own newspaper to question the company's claims. The company promptly sued the union for libel.[75]

As such disputes suggested, business leaders were sensitive to union discourse at the local level, where organized labor stood as an important political and ideological opponent. However, at the national level, labor's ability to broadcast a compelling counternarrative about the war mobiliza-tion was less effective. For the CIO and its allies, responding to business claims about who was winning the war of production was just one small job among many. Led by Sidney Hillman, the veteran garment industry organizer who became a top defense mobilization official, the CIO did suc-ceed in launching a national political action committee, which may have helped President Roosevelt win a fourth term, in the November 1944 elec-tions. But the CIO's new political action committee (CIO-PAC), which endorsed a "People's Program" that included calls for full employment, more public works and public housing, health care, social security, and racial equality, was mainly interested in postwar policy.[76] On the whole, the AFL and CIO, despite their impressive membership numbers and sizable coffers, found it impossible to match the public-relations efforts of the business community. Their biggest wartime public-relations efforts, such as the CIO's $100,000 advertising campaign against strict wage caps, were considerably less well funded than those of the NAM and other business groups. The unions did generate hundreds of local periodicals, along with partisan films, pamphlets, and radio programs. But these were never as numerous, or as well funded, as those created by companies and their media allies. Most labor leaders seem to have been too busy dealing with practical issues, such as maintaining membership and containing potential strikes, to focus on crafting political messages for national audiences.[77]

Anticorporate narratives about the industrial mobilization faded after 1942, especially at the national level. However, the business community had to contend with another important challenger: a "soldiers of production" story that described ordinary workers as essential contributors to the war effort. This was a potentially powerful message that surely encouraged some Americans to revise their notions about their own political status and their relationship with the national state.[78] However, as a rival to the business-conservative narrative about the war economy, it proved surprisingly weak. One reason for this was that its proponents in Washington, including President Roosevelt, presented the "soldiers of production" narrative in a way that allowed it and the conservative business line to coexist.

From their posts in the big emergency civilian agencies in Washington, business leaders-turned-mobilizers emphasized the role of ordinary workers in the production war. They often did so, however, in ways that complemented the pro-business frame. Certainly, this was true of William Knudsen, the former GM president, who served in 1940–41 as the most important of the nation's civilian industrial mobilizers. Addressing the NAM's annual meeting in December 1940, Knudsen called for "the spirit of sacrifice from everybody." But in May 1941, when he addressed a small NAM gathering in Chicago, Knudsen made it clear that he embraced the business perspective. World War II represented "a struggle between centralized and de-centralized society," he explained. Management and labor would need to cooperate, Knudsen explained, but not in any way that should threaten NAM members. "Let's do it in a way that will help individual initiative and free enterprise," said Knudsen.[79]

The pro-business line was also embraced by Secretary of Commerce Jesse Jones, who, as overseer of the Reconstruction Finance Corporation and its subsidiaries (including the Defense Plant Corporation), ranked as one of the most powerful of all industrial mobilization officials. Although

Jones may have qualified as a progressive Democrat in the circles of the business elite of Houston, where he had made his fortune in real estate, he had long ranked among the most conservative members of the Roosevelt administration. Under the circumstances, the American business community of the early 1940s could hardly have asked for a more sympathetic overseer of the government's multibillion-dollar investment in war plant. In his postwar memoir, Jones would reserve his highest compliments for the wartime work of Knudsen and the big industrial corporations, including Du Pont, Alcoa, and U.S. Steel.[80] To be sure, Jones did talk some during the war about how the production "miracles" were made possible by "business and government working together, hand in hand, in the greatest effort the world has ever known." But Jones made it clear that he saw this partnership as a temporary, somewhat distasteful, expedient that would need to be dismantled at war's end. As he told members of the CED and the New York Board of Trade in 1943, he believed that the government needed to liquidate its position in war plant as soon as possible. This process, he hinted, might become part of a broader effort to roll back some of the New Deal's intrusions into the private sector. "Certainly there will be an opportunity for private initiative and private capital to replace government in business" after the war, Jones told his fellow businessmen in 1943. "It is your responsibility to see that this opportunity is not missed."[81]

In comparison with Jones and Knudsen, Donald Nelson, the former Sears executive who led the WPB, was understood to be something close to a New Dealer. In his wartime pronouncements, Nelson often balanced praise for management with celebrations of the nation's "soldiers of production."[82] But many of Nelson's statements echoed the ideas and rhetoric of the business narrative. In his widely broadcast national radio addresses in March 1942, for instance, Nelson presented the war as a test of the ability of a "free economy" to outdo a system based on "the way of the totalitarian state," which relied on slavery. The American "production offensive" required the cooperation of "management and labor," the WPB chief declared. By helping soldiers and sailors win the war, Nelson explained, Americans would preserve their liberties, not least of which was "freedom of enterprise." Nelson went even further after the war, when he recalled that government's greatest accomplishment in the mobilization was getting out of the way of the private sector. "America's reliance on democracy and on its tradition of free, unfettered enterprise," Nelson claimed, "never justified itself so brilliantly as it did in the war."[83]

Labor leaders, naturally, emphasized the contributions of ordinary workers. Especially among the more progressive captains of the CIO, this praise for workers was accompanied by calls for economic and social reform. In late 1942, for instance, Walter Reuther encouraged Americans to understand the conflict as a "people's war" that had demonstrated the loyalty and "creative and technical knowledge" of workers, who had shown themselves to be deserving of more power.[84] Another version of the story, somewhat more compatible with the business community's messages, was related by AFL leaders. In his 1942 Labor Day message, William Green boasted that "the workers of America, a mighty army of production soldiers, have now proved to Hitler's discomfiture that free labor will outproduce slave labor." Throughout the war, Green and other AFL leaders stressed the "teamwork" of business, labor, and the military.[85]

The military establishment, which in 1942 was just starting to move into its offices in the new Pentagon building, became one of the most important promoters of the "soldiers of production" narrative. The military's top civilian mobilization officials, including Robert Patterson and James Forrestal, along with regular military officers, praised the efforts of the nation's "production army," while urging workers to produce even more.[86] At times, these officials and officers embraced the pro-business story. In late 1942, for instance, General Levin H. Campbell, Jr., the Ordnance Department chief, reassured businessmen that the Army believed that "the best way to get production results is to turn business men loose, whenever possible, on the job they know how to do best."[87] But the military officials, who prized high output and stable industrial relations, sometimes clashed with the right wing of the pro-business movement. This happened in early 1942, for instance, when Patterson and Forrestal joined with Nelson and Labor Secretary Frances Perkins to close ranks with organized labor. After a group of congressmen, business leaders, and radio and print columnists attacked unions for allowing too many strikes, the Pentagon joined union leaders in condemning conservatives for exaggerating the problem and harming national unity.[88]

The War and Navy Departments were the architects of some of the most important ritual enactments of the "soldiers of production" narrative at the local level. These were the Army-Navy "E" award ceremonies, held at more than four thousand plants across the nation during the war years.[89] At these events, crowds witnessed the celebration of a tripartite wartime political economy in which ordinary workers and their unions stood shoulder to shoulder with business and the military as the heroic winners of the war on the home front. In the context of a wartime discursive environment in which pro-business rhetoric was so ubiquitous, the "E" award ceremonies represented a potent alternative—at least at the local level.

The Army-Navy "E" awards, created by the mid-1942 merger of separate War and Navy Department programs, were designed by the military to encourage efficient production.[90] By the latter part of 1942, after the Navy and War Department created the joint award, the ceremonies were becoming standardized. To open and close the proceedings, a company or military band led the audience in the singing of patriotic anthems. Before the crowd, up on a bunting-draped stage, sat a group of company executives, military officers, employees, and—in many cases—leaders of the union local. Sometimes, mayors, governors, or other public officials would offer a few words. War or Navy Department officials, often from nearby installations, praised the employees for their work as production soldiers. The military men would then present the "E" pennant, which was normally accepted by a company executive or plant manager. The officers also presented pins—in the shape of miniature pennants—to a handful of workers. These employees represented their peers, sometimes thousands of them, all of whom were presented later with their own pins.[91]

The Army-Navy "E" award ceremonies, some of which were broadcast on local radio stations, were taken seriously by company officials and workers alike.[92] Far more than most other statements about the workings of the war economy, these events presented the nation's production achievements as the product of a fruitful alliance between the military, business, and labor. In many of these military-directed events, labor unions, which were mostly written out of the conservative business narrative, enjoyed a prominent role. In the December 1942 award ceremony at the U.S. Rubber Corporation–operated ammunition plant in Des Moines, for instance, organizers planned a major role for Fred Knight, president of the CIO-affiliated local. Knight, along with U.S. Rubber vice president Thomas Needham and Commander Lewis Strauss of the Navy's Bureau of Ordnance, sat at center stage, listening as the Women's Auxiliary Corps band played the "Star-Spangled Banner" and "Praise the Lord and Pass the Ammunition." Like the top representatives of the company and the Navy, Knight addressed the crowd, praising the workers for their excellence.[93]

Especially when they gave unions such recognition, the story of the war economy suggested by the Army-Navy "E" award ceremonies could clash with the one being told by the business community. Taking note of this problem, the NAM offered companies and local chambers of commerce its own version, which it called "Soldiers of Production" rallies. The first was held at a Du Pont plant in July 1943; over the year that followed, 135 of them took place. Scripted by the NAM's public-relations staff, each of these events began with a thirty-minute pep rally, during which a live band would play the national anthem. Then the assembled employees would hear a talk from one of the motivational speakers on the NAM payroll, who offered employees a more directly pro-business version of what they might have experienced at an Army-Navy "E" event. According to the NAM public-relations staffers who organized them, these rallies were successful. Collectively, however, they could not do much to crowd out the official Army-Navy "E" events, ten of which were staged for every "Soldiers of Production" rally.[94] Even for the NAM, competing directly with the wartime Pentagon was a difficult task.

Fortunately for business conservatives, the Pentagon and other elements of the wartime state rarely challenged them head-on. Instead, most military and civilian officials emphasized the need for national unity, secrecy, high munitions output, bond-buying, and compliance with government edicts. Such were the priorities of the wartime state's most prolific producers of propaganda, including the Treasury Department and the Office of War Information (OWI). These agencies ran multimillion-dollar public-relations campaigns that dwarfed anything created by any single actor in the private sector. Before it was downsized by Congress in 1943, the OWI alone had as many as nine thousand employees. The OWI and the Treasury engaged the services of Hollywood studios, radio stations, and many of the country's most popular artists and entertainers, such as Norman Rockwell, Kate Smith, and Bob Hope. The power of these government public-relations units disturbed conservatives, some of whom believed that the propaganda was designed to garner votes for the Roosevelt administration.[95] Certainly, the government-produced messages were intended to boost civilians' support for the war effort. The wartime state told them to buy more bonds, comply with rationing and price controls, and embrace their neighbors and coworkers as fellow Americans and fellow soldiers of production.[96] By valorizing ordinary workers and citizens, the government communications told a different story from the one pushed by the business community. But because the government demonstrated little interest in celebrating its own substantial role in the military production, its storytelling did little to compete directly with the business narrative.

Nor did the business story confront any serious challenge in the nation's movie houses, where millions of Americans every week watched newsreels, documentary shorts, and Hollywood feature films. Much of the nonfiction cinema content, including the films in the *Why We Fight* series (1942–45), directed by Frank Capra, were produced or sponsored directly by the OWI. Like that agency's output in other media, these films stressed production and national unity. So, too, did most of the Hollywood features, which were influenced, to varying degrees, by the OWI, the military, and other public agencies. A few of these films, including the sabotage thriller *Joe Smith, American* (1942), celebrated the courage of ordinary workers. Female soldiers of production were hailed by Hollywood in several features, including *Tender Comrade* (1943), *Swing Shift Masie* (1943), *Rosie the Riveter* (1944), and *Since You Went Away* (1944). For the most part, however, Hollywood and its audiences focused on the troops. In the typical war film, ethnically diverse groups of soldiers or sailors overcame their ethnic and regional differences, apathy, or fears, in time to confront the enemy as a team. Many war films, including *Sahara* (1943), *Bombardier* (1943), *Destination Tokyo* (1943), *Thirty Seconds over Tokyo* (1944), and *They Were Expendable* (1945), also highlighted impressive weapons technologies, including modern tanks, bomber aircraft, submarines, and torpedo boats. In the movies, these weapons were not so clearly branded by their corporate producers as they were in so many of the ads that filled popular magazines. But the messages sent by Hollywood, like those of the OWI, inspired few questions about the business community's narrative about how the production war was being won.[97]

Of all the narrators of the "soldiers of production" story, one of the most influential was President Roosevelt himself. It seems conceivable that the president could have articulated a sharply progressive version of that story, which might have served as the foundation for a leftist rejoinder to the business narrative. Certainly, Roosevelt does not seem to have been naïve about conservative efforts to make political gains in wartime. In a fireside chat delivered in late May 1940, Roosevelt promised the American people that he would not allow the coming war mobilization to create any "breakdown or cancellation of any of the great social gains we have made in these past years."[98] Given these concerns, and given Roosevelt's record of conflict with the business community, it might seem that the White House might have worked throughout the war to develop a strong, coherent counternarrative about the lessons of the industrial mobilization.

As it turned out, Roosevelt's articulation of the "soldiers of production" story proved remarkably unthreatening to conservatives. Like other public officials, the president emphasized the need for shared sacrifice, unity, and high munitions "production." All Americans shared responsibility for the production war, Roosevelt told the country.[99] As the president explained in an October 1944 speech before a huge crowd in Chicago, the country's munitions production "has been due to the efforts of American business, American labor and American farmers, working together as a patriotic team." While "private enterprise" did need to be kept healthy, Roosevelt explained, its health was tied to "the well-being of the worker and the farmer. It works both ways."[100] But even this sort of subtle jab against free-enterprise rhetoric was absent from many of the president's messages on the subject. In May 1941, in his declaration of unlimited national emergency, Roosevelt suggested that Americans needed to buckle down and help win the war, "to the end that a system of government that makes private enterprise possible may survive."[101] In 1943, in a speech to the national Chamber of Commerce meeting, the president praised the business leaders. The United States, he explained, "based . . . on a system of free enterprise, is meeting successfully the challenges of the totalitarian Governments."[102]

The White House's failure to mount any serious challenge to the business community's framing project was most obvious during the president's national tour of American war plants, in September 1942. During the second half of that month, Roosevelt's train car covered nearly nine thousand miles, as he visited industrial plants and military installations across the country.[103] One of the first stops was Detroit, where the president and Eleanor Roosevelt visited the Chrysler-operated Detroit Tank Arsenal, as well as the Ford-operated Willow Run bomber plant. On the West Coast, Roosevelt visited Kaiser's remarkable merchant shipbuilding operations in Oregon; the U.S. Navy yards in Washington and California; and the giant Consolidated Aircraft plant in San Diego. On the way back to the East Coast, the tour stopped at the Consolidated-operated bomber plant in Fort Worth, as well as the New Orleans shipyards of Higgins Industries, the nation's premier builder of smaller landing craft.[104] This group of mostly GOCO facilities included many of the country's most productive war plants, most of which were built entirely with government money. Potentially, the president's tour, which occurred just four months after the NAM's "Production for Victory" tour, might have served as a platform to explain the government's major contributions to the successful military-industrial mobilization.

This did not happen. Instead, the president's plant tour, designed to generate a burst of good press in advance of the midterm elections, became something close to a public-relations fiasco. One reason for this was that Roosevelt insisted that only three wire-service reporters be permitted to accompany him on the trip and that even they be banned from reporting on it until it was over, and after he had been able to review their work. Predictably, this alienated much of the press corps.[105] Then, at the first press conference held upon his return to Washington, in front of an audience of already-irritated reporters, Roosevelt turned in a dismal performance. It consisted of little more than a listing of his stops, with no coherent message other than that most of the war plants seemed to be in good shape. "And well," Roosevelt ended awkwardly, "here we are!"[106] In a fireside chat a few days later, Roosevelt went a bit further: thanks to the efforts of war workers, he explained, "we are getting ahead of our enemies in the battle of production."[107] Given that the president had devoted two full weeks to the national plant tour, this halfhearted recitation of the "soldiers of production" message did remarkably little to advance any progressive political agenda. The tour's failure seems to have been widely understood in Washington, even by the president. In typical fashion, however, he tried to minimize the problem. Any negative press didn't really matter, Roosevelt told Interior Secretary Harold Ickes, because "the people didn't believe the newspapers."[108] Coming from a man who had already won three presidential elections despite the opposition of the majority of papers, this remark was perhaps not entirely unjustified. However, it also suggested why the White House was failing to match the far more coherent, disciplined, and energetic public-relations campaign being carried out by the business community.

Indeed, the unimpressive results of Roosevelt's September 1942 plant tour, together with the rest of his wartime communications on the subject of the war economy, suggest that the White House may never have fully appreciated the importance of the political struggle to define the lessons of the industrial mobilization. To be sure, the president was focused on war strategy and international affairs, which, understandably, absorbed much of his finite energies. Famously, Roosevelt admitted as much in a December 1943 press conference, when he explained that "Dr. Win the War" had taken over for "Dr. New Deal," at least for the duration of the global emergency.[109] This transition can be traced back to 1939, when Roosevelt had already started to lose interest in new domestic reform initiatives.[110]

Nevertheless, even once these factors are given their due, the White House's wartime domestic public-relations efforts seem incompetent. Ickes, the interior secretary, pointed to this problem in March 1942, in a letter he sent to Freda Kirchwey, editor and publisher of the *Nation*, the left-wing political affairs magazine. "[T]here is a very powerful group in this country that is taking advantage of this situation to try to 'get' the President, break labor, and destroy the New Deal," Ickes wrote. Even in the wake of the Pearl Harbor attacks, Ickes believed, business conservatives and their allies in Congress were gaining political ground. "As usual, we are taking this lying down," the interior secretary complained. "The President doesn't seem to understand yet that ideas are as important, and sometimes more so, than actual arms."[111]

Although the White House did little to directly refute the business community's denigration of government's role in the industrial mobilization, some other Americans did so, at least occasionally. As we have seen, some strains of the anticorporate and "soldiers of production" narratives challenged the business story. So, too, did individuals within progressive circles, some of whom issued very explicit critiques of the pro-business narrative. One of the most cogent of these came from Julius Hochman, a veteran garment workers' union officer. In early 1943, Hochman used an article in the AFL's monthly newspaper to call attention to the NAM's sophisticated, well-funded public-relations campaign. Together, Hochman estimated, American companies were spending close to half a billion dollars a year on advertising that portrayed business as the winner of the war: "'*We* Make the Planes,' '*We* Make the Guns,' '*We* Make the Tanks'; and by Implication, 'We Win the War.'"[112] The business public-relations offensive was also condemned by Robert S. Lynd, the prominent Columbia University sociologist, who argued that it was "preventing us from learning the lessons of this war."[113] For Lynd, left-leaning economists, and other progressives, the real lessons pointed to the need for a robust postwar public works program and other government interventions.

Even among political moderates, there were occasional outbursts of impatience with the pro-business story of the war economy. James F. Byrnes, the former congressman from South Carolina and top Roosevelt adviser who left the Supreme Court to become head of the Office of War

Mobilization, generally had little interest in challenging the prerogatives of private enterprise. But Byrnes, like other Washington officials, came to tire of the constant barrage of complaints about the alleged evils of "bureaucracy." Byrnes expressed his frustrations in an early 1943 address to a group of newspaper editors. "The total organization for total war is a complicated business," he explained. "It cannot be made simple. Scold the bureaucrats and brass hats [top military officials] as we do, we need them. Without bureaucrats and brass hats we cannot win a total war." Many of the "bureaucrats," Byrnes pointed out, were actually business executives who had come to Washington to assist with the mobilization effort.[114]

A similar reminder came from Raymond Clapper, the politically moderate syndicated newspaper columnist. In late 1942, Clapper informed his readers that rising munitions output was not simply the product of private initiative. "Willow Run is not Ford's," wrote Clapper. "It belongs to the Defense Plant Corporation. The big Detroit tank arsenal is not Chrysler's. It is the Government's, built and operated by Chrysler for the Government." Many of the nation's largest war plants, in other words, were fully financed—and, in many cases, remained fully owned—by the national state. "So," Clapper concluded, "when you look back on industry's miracle of war production, and look ahead to the greater volume that is to come, just tuck away somewhere in the back of your mind the thought that it could not have come without Government extravagance."[115] Clapper's matter-of-fact discussion of the contributions of government was far from radical, but it did challenge the business community's story. If most Americans ended up subscribing to Clapper's view—or to the other available counternarratives—the business community's efforts would have been in vain.

Measures of Success

How successful was the business community effort to win the wartime contest of rival narrative frames? Measuring success or failure is difficult, especially if we consider that the struggle may have continued to influence Americans' ideas and debates for many years after 1945. However, there can be little doubt that business leaders enjoyed more success than failure when it came to the contest of stories about the war economy. Business leaders, who were far from satisfied about the progress of their broader political struggle against progressives, concluded that they did quite well in this particular battle over public opinion. Equally important, the pro-business story also came to be embraced by people who had formerly ranked among the most prominent critics of business's wartime behavior.

Within the business community, most expert observers were happy with the results of their framing efforts. This assessment came early. By the end of 1941, B. C. Forbes, the magazine publisher, was already satisfied with the record of recent months. "Every sounding of public opinion," he informed readers, "has revealed that far more people have developed admiration for industry's 'emergency' record than for the record of either Washington or organized labor."[116] This was not just wishful thinking. Forbes, no doubt, followed the results of Gallup polls, which showed consistently that most respondents blamed unions and government, and not business, for delays in munitions output. This attitude was of great concern to White House staffers who believed that President Roosevelt was unfairly blamed for alleged war production shortfalls in 1941, while his critics, led by Senator Harry F. Byrd (D-VA), won public approval.[117] The following year, as war production started to soar, business was given even more credit, by the general public and by top mobilization officials such as Donald Nelson. By mid-1942, Forbes reported happily that "Washington is now daily lauding industry's amazing production achievements."[118]

Another sign of success, from the point of view of business leaders and conservative politicians, was the result of the midterm elections of 1942. In that contest, the Republican Party gained nine seats in the U.S. Senate and forty-seven in the House. As professional pollsters concluded, the most important factor in this outcome seems to have been low turnout among Democratic voters, rather than any major shift in the public's political sensibilities.[119] But the election did have major consequences. According to *Life* magazine, it represented "the biggest shift of political power since Franklin Roosevelt was elected the first time, in 1932." Across the country, allies of Roosevelt were replaced by conservative, pro-business Republicans. Many of the new congressmen, reported *Fortune* magazine's political correspondent Eliot Janeway, believed that "they have a mandate to repeal all New Deal reforms." Because there were so many conservative Democrats, Janeway wrote, "Republicans will of course have working control of Congress," even without a technical majority.[120]

With some reason, then, business leaders interpreted the results of the 1942 elections as validation of the arguments that they had been making about the war economy for more than two years. One cause of the results at the polls, as they understood it, was public discontent with Washington's overuse of bureaucratic controls. Many Americans seemed to be upset with the implementation of price controls and rationing, handled by one of the most powerful agencies on the home front, the Office of Price Administration (OPA). Thanks to the rationing of goods such as sugar and gasoline, along with the General Maximum Price Regulation of April 1942, which froze most prices, the OPA extended its reach into the daily transactions of millions of retailers and households.[121] Although much of the public favored wartime controls (and helped enforce them), the rules also generated resistance from ordinary citizens as well as businesses. As Edgar Queeny, the Monsanto president, put it in a 1943 book, the elections showed that "war was not being waged in a businesslike way! The people disliked rationing—'being pushed around,' they called it!"[122] The White House's response to the elections may have actually encouraged this interpretation. In December 1942, conservatives were cheered by the resignation of Leon Henderson, the progressive economist who had headed the OPA. This news was merely the "first victory," the NAM reported confidently to its members, in what promised to be a powerful "Congressional rebellion against bureaucratic control."[123]

In the wake of the 1942 elections, congressional conservatives and their allies stepped up their attacks on excessive state power. As the House began its work in early January 1943, Charles L. Gifford, a long-serving Republican from Massachusetts, announced that it was time to "win the war from the New Deal."[124] One part of that war was simply to begin killing off many of the New Deal agencies, something that Congress did accomplish in 1943–44, even though moderates continued to be influential.[125] But the struggle also entailed an expansion of the rhetorical assault on big government.

By mid-1943, millions of middlebrow readers of *Reader's Digest*, among other publications, were being offered a steady diet of politicians' complaints about the expanded national state. Senator Byrd joined Ohio governor John W. Bricker in lamenting the fact that there were 90,000 employees of the federal government in Ohio, compared with 25,000 state employees. In fact, the vast majority of these federal employees were working directly for the military establishment (roughly a third of them worked at the AAF's huge procurement and testing center at Wright Field). But for Byrd, the figures showed that the New Dealers were out of control. "Bureaucracy, rabbit-wise, is self-multiplying," he observed. "I believe that only a great upsurge of national indignation against this Frankenstein monster," he declared, could save the nation from ruin. The protests of Senator Byrd, who had long ranked among the most vocal congressional critics of the Roosevelt administration, were not new; nor were the protests assembled by journalist Lawrence Sullivan in his *Bureaucracy Runs Amuck* (1944), an updating of Sullivan's own 1940 treatise, *The Dead Hand of Bureaucracy*. In the new book, Sullivan decried the "bureaucratic lawlessness" of the OPA and other wartime agencies. Full of quotations from conservative Southern Democratic members of Congress, including Byrd, Millard E. Tydings, Eugene Cox, Howard W. Smith, and Martin Dies, Jr., the book warned Americans against "an infection of alien socialist bureaucracy."[126]

It was not only strident conservatives who joined the fray. By December 1942, Congressman Lyndon B. Johnson (D-TX), a solid New Dealer, was giving speeches complaining of "over-stuffed government" and "red tape."[127] More prominent in the national media were the complaints of another pro–New Deal Democrat, Senator Joseph C. O'Mahoney of Wyoming. In August 1943, O'Mahoney, who had been upset by a federal order that enlarged the boundaries of Grand Teton National Park, placed an essay in *Forbes* magazine and *Reader's Digest*, in which he railed against the offenses of "the bureaucrats" who were violating the sovereignty of the common people. On the eve of World War II, when he had overseen a giant federal inquiry into monopolistic business practices, O'Mahoney had seemed to stand solidly within the Western populist-progressive, antitrust tradition.[128] But by 1943, O'Mahoney had become more concerned about the evils of excessive state power. Echoing many of the Roosevelt administration's critics on the right, he suggested that the president, who had issued four thousand executive orders in a decade, was at the center of a dangerous dictatorship. Warning that the nation was in danger of falling into "totalitarianism," O'Mahoney cautioned Americans that they must act to keep America from traveling further down the "road to national socialism."[129]

This sort of antistatist rhetoric, coming from influential policymakers in the middle of the political spectrum, encouraged conservatives to believe that their point of view was prevailing. More specifically, many business leaders were satisfied that they were winning the battle to define the political lessons of the industrial mobilization. A month after the 1942 elections, NAM members had been given an encouraging report by Walter B. Weisenburger, the organization's executive vice president and public-relations chief. According to Weisenburger, the NAM's public-relations division "kept the record straight that industry did not start this war for profit. . . . It has kept the war production record of industry before the public. . . . It has sold the public the private enterprise system." The campaign had been so forceful and effective, Weisenburger said, that the main danger now might be offending members of the armed forces by claiming too much of the credit for victory. Therefore, he suggested, "let's not harp too blatantly on how industry is winning the war by production." Instead, the business community might do even better at this stage by adopting a more moderate tone, so as to "keep it on the 'we helped' basis."[130]

As Weisenburger suggested, by the beginning of 1943, the business community's leading public-relations departments were satisfied that American political culture generally, and Americans' views of the war economy in particular, had shifted in their favor. "Particularly since the elections," the public-relations division of the ACWP noted in early 1943, "but basically as a result of the production record, the Washington political climate towards industry has changed so that the type of attack which flourished in the thirties is not particularly feared."[131] Similar ideas circulated among the NAM's public-relations experts, who concluded "that the American people already have recrystallized their faith in certain attributes of free enterprise." There were two reasons for this, the NAM men believed: the actual production record of private industry; and their own efforts to publicize and frame it. "Both the job itself and the way it has been dramatized have had a profound impact on public opinion," they believed. With this victory in hand, the NAM believed, it was now (in early 1943) already time to focus on influencing postwar policies.[132]

Like their public-relations staffs, many individual business leaders were confident that the public had learned the correct lessons from the record of the industrial mobilization. According to Crawford, NAM president and head of Thompson Products, "private enterprise has proved for all time that the free American way is the best way to produce." Better yet, the public understood this. "The American people," Crawford told NAM members in late 1943, "have a profound respect for the war production of industry. . . . The greatest opportunity in years now confronts industrial management, because the public is turning with confidence again to business leaders." Meanwhile, they were turning against government, "fed up with promises, bureaucracy and bungling, and red tape."[133] Many of Crawford's peers, including Chamber of Commerce president Eric Johnston and

B. F. Goodrich president John L. Collyer, expressed similar sentiments about the public's newfound faith in business. Another satisfied business titan was Sloan, the GM chairman, who in mid-1944 told the New Jersey Chamber of Commerce that the New Deal had been discredited. "We think the attitude of the American public is completely changed with respect to industry and industry's problem," Sloan explained, "as the result of their experience in the war."[134]

To be sure, the business community's efforts were never a total success. Thousands of Americans embraced alternate narratives about the war economy, in which business appeared less than heroic. Some of the mainstream media coverage of the industrial mobilization, such as a *Life* magazine piece in August 1942 that emphasized labor-management conflict and racial tensions in Detroit, annoyed business leaders and their public-relations teams.[135] Because the success of the business narrative depended on high munitions output, any serious production setbacks might be damaging. When the giant Willow Run bomber plant ran behind schedule in 1943, NAM president Crawford took it upon himself to tell Ford executives that "what is imperative in my judgment, is that we keep up the effort, particularly with the public, to show the elements of production delay beyond your control."[136] Another bothersome trend was the American public's continued support for government-provided social security. Many conservatives were disappointed by poll results showing that much of the public seemed to approve of President Roosevelt's January 1944 call for an "economic bill of rights," including, even, the right to a job.[137] Disappointing, too, was Roosevelt's reelection in November 1944, along with a small increase in the Democratic majority in the House, just a year after conservatives had been encouraged by victories in a handful of governor's races and other off-year elections.[138] Clearly, the larger war against the New Deal was far from over; conservatives would continue to fight it for many years to come.

But the failure of conservatives to completely vanquish their opponents during World War II did not mean that they made no progress. For business leaders, one of the brightest spots was the success of the narrative about the war economy. This was evident to those standing outside business circles, as well. It struck David Lilienthal, a prominent New Dealer whose leadership of the TVA made him an important player in the war economy. Writing in his diary in December 1942, Lilienthal noted that the popularity of the pro-business narrative was rather stunning. "The campaign against 'bureaucracy' has been successful," Lilienthal wrote, "beyond the dreams of the smart boys who have been pushing it so long. The 'sacrifices' we talked about at first now are simply and always the crazy mistakes or overbearing works of the 'bureaucrats.' So successful has this line of attack been that many people at the heart of things in the Government believe it themselves." There was "beautiful irony" in all this, Lilienthal believed, because it was actually businessmen—installed in posts at the WPB and other mobilization agencies—who were doing much of the regulating.[139] Lilienthal was not the only one who noticed the wartime shift toward celebrating business and blaming government. Joseph Dodge was a politically moderate Detroit banker who served during the war as one of the War Department's top officials overseeing the renegotiation of military contracts. In January 1944, Dodge noted in a memo that "the general trend in Congress and in the country as a whole appears to be strongly in favor of re-establishing so-called 'free enterprise' and the elimination of 'bureaucracy and bureaucratic control.'"[140]

The success of the pro-business story of the military economy is perhaps best illustrated by its endorsement by influential policymakers who seemed to be, at the outset of the war, among its most dangerous critics. One of these was Senator Truman, who chaired the most important of the congressional committees investigating the war economy. The Truman Committee in 1941–42 ranked among the most important proponents of an anticorporate narrative about the war economy. Truman, who saw himself as a champion of small businesses and average citizens, condemned what he saw as the "selfish" behavior of big businesses like Alcoa, which, like some labor union leaders, were trying to use the defense emergency to gain at the expense of "the general run of the American people."[141]

As time passed, Truman and his committee moved away from the anticorporate message. The shift was evident in 1943–44, as the American war economy reached full tilt. In early 1943, the Truman Committee was still targeting big business. In February, its report on the steel situation blamed the industry for its early reluctance to expand capacity.[142] In March and April, the Truman Committee held hearings and submitted reports on two potentially serious cases of wartime corporate fraud. One of these involved the Carnegie-Illinois Steel Company, the huge subsidiary of U.S. Steel. At one plant, Carnegie-Illinois employees had forged inspection reports on certain batches of steel plate. There were similar problems at the huge Wright Aero engine plant in Lockland, Ohio, where company workers and on-site Army Air Forces employees had both participated in fraudulent inspections. Scandals like these had the potential to do serious damage to the business community's public-relations project. However, the damage was contained. Juries found that there was not enough evidence of deliberate fraud, or enough serious damage to military equipment, to convict the companies. And the Truman Committee, after publicizing these potentially explosive cases, chose in the end not to harp on them.[143] One reason for this was that its investigations showed that the cases were somewhat less egregious than they had seemed at first. But another reason was that Truman and his colleagues were already starting to abandon the anticorporate talk that they had embraced early in the war, while moving toward something far more agreeable to American business.

Well before the summer of 1944, when Truman emerged as a candidate for the vice presidency, he and his fellow committee members had abandoned their earlier attacks on corporate America. Like many other observers of the war economy, Truman and his colleagues were impressed by the private sector's ability to deliver huge quantities of munitions. Their change in tune was also likely influenced by their reading of the political winds, which suggested that the public's worries about malfeasance in the private sector was becoming overshadowed by its concerns about the wartime state. For Truman, whose ideas about economic policy were shaped by his personal struggles as a small businessman and farmer, the switch to criticizing big government—along with big business and big labor—was no stretch. In November 1942, he had published a magazine article in which he criticized excessive "red tape" in wartime Washington.[144] But even Truman was probably surprised by the extent to which this theme, even more than attacks on big business, resonated with the public. By the middle of the war, Truman's mailbags suggested that Americans seemed to be more upset about the evils of government than they were about the sort of private-sector abuses that his committee had described earlier. "I want to congratulate you," one Los Angeles resident told Truman in December 1942, "on the good work you are doing to get rid of the bureau 'rats.'" A few months later, a Baltimore businessman suggested that Truman's work should now focus on the public sector. "There seems to be lots of bureaus and bureaucrats in Washington who should be investigated," wrote Frank J. McQuade, "and I hope you will crack down on them." Even stronger terms were used by H. D. Kissenger, a

Kansas City lawyer who wrote Truman to encourage him to rein in John L. Lewis, leader of the coal miners' union. But Kissenger had broader political concerns: "I believe that the Nudeal Burocracy [sic] is as far removed from real Americanism as the Kremlin," he informed Truman, "yes, I believe that the Nudeal Burocracy and the American Republic cannot exist side by side."[145]

Evidently impressed with the receding interest among their colleagues and constituents in hearing bad news about business, members of the Truman Committee adjusted their message. The shift was discernible in the language of the committee's December 1943 report on transportation, which suggested that the American industrial mobilization had "proved the superiority of cooperation and freedom over regulation imposed from above through force and fear."[146] But the committee's transformation became most obvious in the language of its third annual report, released in March 1944. The U.S. war economy's "astounding performance," Truman and his colleagues now declared, "exceeds anything of its kind ever achieved in the history of the world." Some of the wartime government controls may have been necessary during the height of the war emergency, the committee explained; but even then, they were undesirable expedients. "Experience has taught us that our country will flourish best when least hampered by Government control," the committee concluded. As for profiteering, it was true that some companies may have enjoyed some excessive gains. But on the whole, this was not a serious issue; indeed, "a great many of these corporations are entitled to the gratitude of the people for doing an efficient and economical job in war production."[147]

At least as remarkable as the Truman Committee's shift was the wartime behavior of Harold Ickes, the self-described "curmudgeon" who ranked among the longest-serving members of the Roosevelt administration. During the 1930s, Ickes—who was head of the giant Public Works Administration as well as secretary of the interior—had attacked the alleged monopolistic behavior of big business, as well as what he described as conservatives' stranglehold on the media. At the beginning of World War II, Ickes urged the president to prevent another appearance of "a large number of war millionaires" (as in the Great War) and to fight against wartime strengthening of "monopolies." He urged Roosevelt to criticize the "sit-down strikes" of companies like Ford, which seemed, to Ickes, to be too slow to convert to defense production. Meanwhile, Ickes pushed for tougher terms in war-plant financing agreements with Alcoa and other companies and for less generous corporate tax policies.[148] Throughout the war, Ickes understood himself as part of a small circle of clearheaded public servants dedicated to protecting the people from the special interests. At the end of 1943, when President Roosevelt told the press about the displacement of "Dr. New Deal" by "Dr. Win the War," Ickes agreed with budget director Harold Smith that this was a foolish move—a "full retreat in the face of the enemy." And in July 1944, Ickes told vice president Henry Wallace that they were the only real liberals left in Washington, the only ones left to resist the growing power of conservatives.[149]

In fact, Ickes's political attitudes during World War II were far from stable. Although he never abandoned progressive causes, the interior secretary dropped much of his hostility toward business. Appointed by Roosevelt as chief of the Petroleum Administration for War (PAW), the top civilian authority over the wartime oil and gasoline programs, Ickes surprised company executives with his friendliness. The change in his attitude was clear to the press and to his peers, many of whom were evidently baffled by it. Chester Bowles, the successful advertising executive and liberal Democrat who served as chief of the OPA for part of the war, could never understand why Ickes "became the most vigorous spokesman for the big oil companies during the war."[150] This was an interesting puzzle: How did a leading New Dealer who was critical of the Roosevelt administration's failure to respond to the business community's public-relations offensive end up offering effusive praise for the private sector?

This question, which speaks to the broader issue of why the business community's wartime political efforts were so successful, is at least partially answerable because Ickes left detailed diaries. In Ickes's case, it appears, two factors were especially important. First, because Ickes happened to oversee an especially diverse and competitive industry, in which public financing of war plant was less widespread than it was in most other sectors, it was difficult for him to dismiss its leaders as monopolists. Like many other Americans with expert knowledge of the developing war economy, Ickes knew that the crude anticorporate narrative about the monopoly profits in the war economy was not accurate. Second, Ickes was genuinely impressed with the patriotism and the capabilities of oil industry executives. His deepest affections were reserved for Ralph K. Davies, a former Standard Oil of California vice president who became Ickes's top lieutenant at the PAW. But Ickes also came to admire other leaders of the private oil companies who worked with the PAW to deliver the aviation gasoline and other goods that the nation required to win the war. Remarkably, the executive who impressed Ickes the most was Sun Oil chief J. Howard Pew, who ranked among the nation's most energetic proponents of pro-business conservatism.

Struck by the competitiveness, technical proficiency, and patriotism of the American oil industry, Ickes proceeded, in his role as the PAW chief, to act as an ally of the oil companies. Convinced by the oilmen that strict price controls threatened them with losses, Ickes pressed the OPA to allow the industry to charge higher prices. Ickes's experience at the PAW made him less sympathetic to the views of I. F. Stone, who occasionally visited Ickes to conduct interviews. In September 1943, after Stone published a new piece on the oil industry in *PM*, Ickes noted in his diary that Stone's work was "a tissue of lies." Ickes also took offense at a related *PM* investigation that was gathering information about the PAW's practice of allowing the employees it recruited from industry to have their federal salaries supplemented by payments from their companies, so that their total compensation matched the level that they had received before coming to Washington. "This made me pretty sore because we can't do our petroleum job without these experts," Ickes complained. Ickes was especially bothered by Stone's assumption that Davies, his valuable assistant, was a just a tool of big oil. "He just cannot get it through his head," Ickes wrote of Stone just after the war, "that Davies, because he is an oil man, is also an honest and capable public servant."[151]

Ickes also thought highly of oilmen who remained in the private sector, such as the leaders of Sun Oil, J. Howard Pew and his brother, Joseph N. Pew, Jr. Ickes's affection for the Pews dated to a meeting with them in August 1942. On this occasion, Ickes wrote in his diary, "I was astounded," by the Pews' deep erudition, as well as their willingness to place the goal of winning the war above any concern with short-run profits. Despite the Pews' well-known record as conservative Republicans, Ickes concluded, he could not help but admire their "high patriotism." Ickes carried this feeling into the meetings of the Petroleum Industry War Council, an emergency oil industry association that worked closely with the PAW. At one council meeting in early October, Ickes rose to deliver an impromptu speech praising the patriotism of the whole industry, and the Pews in particular. The assembled oilmen responded by giving Ickes a standing ovation. The same friendliness informed Ickes's 1943 book, *Fightin' Oil*, in which he described the many accomplishments of a harmonious wartime relationship between government and industry. In the opening of the book, Ickes explained that "in spite of contrary opinions here and there, I believe in the American system of free enterprise. It is also the fact that I believe that business can best do its part—in peace as in war—with the least possible direction, and with the least interference, by the Government."[152]

Ickes found that good relations with the oilmen came with attractive benefits. In late 1942, Eliot Janeway of *Fortune* magazine hinted that if Ickes were to leave the Roosevelt administration, the Pews might back Ickes as a Republican candidate for office. (Because Ickes had been a progressive Republican before joining the New Deal, it was not the party identity but the possibility of support from arch-conservatives that was the most remarkable element of this flattering suggestion.) In January 1944, J. Howard Pew stopped by Ickes's office to say that he agreed that the nation's coal miners deserved the raise that Ickes had recently helped negotiate. Pew then presented Ickes with a sizable marble inkstand, adorned with gold plates. As Ickes noted in his diary, he could not bring himself to refuse this gift, which he believed was worth at least $500 (over $5,000 in 2016 dollars) and was undoubtedly "in excellent taste." There were other benefits: by war's end, when Ickes took his family for their summer vacation in Bar Harbor, Maine, they were able to travel in the private plane of the Texas Company, courtesy of the company's chairman, W. S. S. Rodgers.[153]

Ickes was apparently seduced by the wealth and power of the oilmen, in addition to being won over by their patriotism and efficiency. But what is most striking about Ickes's wartime relationship with the business community is not a government official's acceptance of a few favors but rather the willingness of a politically savvy veteran New Dealer to overlook the one-sidedness of their ideological exchange. Throughout the war, Ickes praised the oil industry and voiced pro-business rhetoric, in public and in private. This support was not just personal but institutional. In July 1945, for instance, the PAW agreed to help the oilmen of the Petroleum Industry War Council with their new $300,000 multimedia public-relations campaign. As Davies told them, praise from Ickes's agency might prove useful because "the government agency can say things about the industry that the industry can't say about itself."[154]

For the oilmen, this public-relations assistance from the government was welcome. But it was hardly reciprocated. For the Pews and many of their colleagues, close cooperation with the government during the war mobilization was not cause for rethinking their long-standing commitment to antistatist politics. On the contrary, at the end of long workdays, following their friendly meetings with Ickes, they devoted huge amounts of time and energy to destroying the New Deal order. Ickes's relationship with the oilmen was unique but spoke to broader patterns in wartime politics. The Pews, like many of their peers in American business community, were committed to holding their political ground, no matter what might transpire during the war mobilization. For these disciplined conservatives, the central political goals and messages remained remarkably constant over time. This was far less true of their ostensible political opponents.

*   *   *

Business leaders worked hard throughout the war to convince their fellow Americans that the record of the nation's giant industrial mobilization demonstrated the superior competence and agility of the private sector. This narrative was being broadcast long in advance of Pearl Harbor, well before most businesses, or other Americans, had much direct knowledge of the workings of the developing war economy. In many ways, therefore, the business community's public-relations campaign, which stressed the same themes throughout the war, seems to have been remarkably impervious to actual experience.

It seems unlikely that the wartime success of the business community's narrative could have come entirely from its broadcasters' inflexible, disciplined repetition of the free-enterprise theme. Even among the population of business owners, actual experience might have altered some attitudes about the political and economic lessons of World War II. For instance, it seems possible that the experience of military contracting, which is often thought to have involved easy profit-taking, via contracts administered by the most conservative elements within the national state, might have relaxed some business leaders' enthusiasm for strident antigovernment rhetoric. Yet the evident public-relations success of conservatives suggests that business leaders' lived experience of the war mobilization did remarkably little to discredit the pro-business, antistatist narrative. How could this have been?

One reason for the growing appeal of the conservative story about the war economy was that the wartime encounter between American business and the national state worked to make the narrative more resonant, rather than less. Even the military establishment, which was ostensibly far more business-friendly than New Dealer–run civilian agencies such as the OPA, proved to be a source of much consternation. Together, various wartime agencies generated demands for paperwork that many business leaders found insufferable. Military demand, while sometimes allowing for something resembling mass production of munitions, often turned out to be surprisingly irregular. Profits on military contracts could indeed sometimes be impressive, especially for companies that were transformed by the war into big businesses, but often they ended up smaller than executives had anticipated, or thought that they deserved. Especially for smaller and mid-size businesses, in other words, the wartime encounter with the national state was something of a shock, and not one that inspired reverence for government. However, the dismay felt by business leaders during this encounter came not only from the obvious instances of bureaucratic incompetence, about which the conservative public-relations message had so thoroughly warned them. They were also shaken by a very different problem: the wartime state's growing economic knowledge and regulatory agility. Although the business community's political storytelling rarely acknowledged it, the government's competence could prove at least as annoying to companies as its bungling. During World War II, hundreds of military contractors came to realize these facts.

Chapter 4

One Tough Customer

In November 1944, the Aviation Interim Committee, a body established by the California state legislature, distributed surveys to hundreds of midsize and smaller companies, inquiring about their experiences filling military contracts and subcontracts. The survey asked company managers about what they liked and disliked about war work and how things might be improved. The responses to this survey were telling. War work, the survey results suggest, was not understood by business as an easy ticket to generous profits, or necessarily as a patriotic enterprise undertaken cheerfully. On the contrary, many manufacturers claimed that military contracting and subcontracting were more of a burden than a boon.

As they responded to the survey in the winter of 1944–45, the California manufacturers vented their many frustrations with war work. Particularly telling were answers to a question about what they liked best about doing business with the government. A few respondents managed to list some advantages, including relatively low risks, prompt payments, some large production runs, and assistance with financing. But twenty of the fifty responders to this question rejected its premise outright, explaining that they worked on government orders only out of patriotism, or because in wartime they had no other choice. Some observed that there were more opportunities for profit in civilian markets, where, as one respondent explained, "we are not bothered by government agencies regarding re-negotiation, re-pricing, and other limitations." When asked to list some of the disadvantages of war work, survey respondents replied energetically. Among the seventy-seven specific replies to this question, the most commonly cited evils included excessive regulations; "enormous amounts of paper work," including "interminable surveys, reports and interviews," which absorbed much of the energy of executives and office staff; frequent changes in specifications; and sudden contract cancellations. When asked about how to improve the situation, the business leaders called for cuts in government regulation. As one respondent put it, the answer was simply "Less Red Tape." Another replied, more bluntly, "Suggest hanging some bureaucrats."[1]

More than a few business leaders went into World War II with fiercely antistatist convictions. Many of these ideas changed very little over the course of the conflict, despite the massive economic transformations that accompanied the war effort. But businesses' actual experiences with wartime government also mattered; and they seem to have reinforced the claims of conservatives. Many businessmen who participated in the war economy came out of the experience more ready than ever to criticize government and fight regulation. The most obvious reason for this, and the one that fit most neatly with conservatives' own convictions, was that some aspects of the war mobilization helped demonstrate the incompetence of giant bureaucracies.[2] But equally disturbing to business leaders, if less readily acknowledged, was a different problem: the government's growing economic knowledge and its regulatory flexibility and capability. Far from being a blind behemoth or price-insensitive pushover, the wartime state often acted as a tough customer.

The Annoyances of Red Tape

Among the many sins of the wartime state, according to business leaders, were the inefficiencies of its bloated bureaucracies, which produced little more than red tape. As the newspaper columnist William F. McDermott explained to his readers in late 1943, the country was seeing "a wartime revulsion against bureaucracy, paternalism, red tape, governmental muddling and meddling." Mountains of paperwork, which were familiar to big business, had begun to bury smaller enterprises and average citizens. "Businessmen are irritated by the number of governmental questionnaires they have to answer, by the additional bookkeeping thrust upon them," wrote McDermott, "and by the morass of red tape they must wade through in getting business done. . . . The uneasiness is reaching down now to the small shopkeepers and the mass of people who have to fill out ration cards and income tax blanks."[3]

The flood of paperwork generated by wartime agencies started before Pearl Harbor, when it was noticed first by leading military contractors. "We are subject to the rules and regulations of the Priorities Board, the Office of Production Management, the Army, the Navy, the Civil Aeronautics Authority, the Securities and Exchange Commission [(SEC)] and the Treasury," Robert E. Gross, the Lockheed president, noted in March 1941. Gross claimed that half of the time of Lockheed executives was absorbed by their dealings with government agencies. The early wartime rise of red tape was even bothersome to larger companies, which were already accustomed to supplying information to the SEC and other New Deal agencies. At International Harvester, the big agricultural equipment manufacturer, executives were already complaining in 1941 of excessive new burdens of paperwork.[4]

By the beginning of 1942, as the nation transitioned to an all-out war economy, few military contractors or other large corporations remained untouched. Protests abounded, even among the military's favorite contractors. One of these, Sperry Gyroscope, made its case to federal authorities in the form of a formal report, issued in February 1942. Sperry explained that various U.S. agencies were already requiring firms to submit periodically at least fifty major questionnaires and forms, many of them asking for the same information. Sperry's requirements for metals, for instance, were being surveyed simultaneously by the Bureau of Mines, the Office of Price Administration (OPA), the War and Navy Departments, and the War Production Board (WPB).[5]

Although the business community often directed its sharpest attacks against the OPA, the powerful price-controlling authority, many companies were bothered by the overlapping demands of multiple agencies. In 1942, when the National Association of Manufacturers (NAM) created a special committee on excessive government paperwork, the top concern seems to have been OPA forms that required businesses to detail recent profits and losses.[6] But the problem was exacerbated by government agencies ostensibly more friendly to business, including the WPB and the military bureaus. In late 1942, when the Chamber of Commerce's monthly magazine reported on the problem, it noted that while the WPB had done a bit to trim its requests, it still required companies to complete 360 different forms. These were among the 6,500 different forms and questionnaires that the wartime state had sent to companies.[7] A similar story was reported in 1943 by *Forbes* magazine, which reported that, thanks to the aggregate demands of the War Labor Board, the SEC, the OPA, and the WPB, "[b]ureaucratic regulation is being pushed towards strangulation. . . . Red tape is the nation's number one output."[8]

The costs of the wartime state's heavy paperwork requirements were evident at the micro level, in the offices of individual companies. By autumn 1942, Chrysler was using a clerical staff of four dozen people to complete WPB paperwork, including the elaborate forms that the agency was trying to use to compute requirements for metals and other critical materials. By the middle of the war, several corporations, including East-man Kodak, reported that government-required paperwork absorbed over 100,000 person-hours, costing them $100,000 to $200,000 a year. The paperwork problem was frustrating enough to one executive from Parke, Davis & Company, the pharmaceutical manufacturer, that he told a Senate committee that "we can go no further."[9]

Smaller and midsize firms found the wartime state's paperwork demands to be especially difficult. Unlike the larger corporations, they entered the war without large clerical staffs and often without much hands-on experience with federal agencies. "We believe the unnecessary three-fourths of all government reports and report forms should be eliminated immediately," resolved a group of Nebraska manufacturers in October 1942. In Houston, E. M. Briggers, owner of Briggers Printing, compiled a list of 2,241 wartime "bureaus," and then printed 200,000 copies of the document for distribution. "I am convinced the people in America are awakening to the dangers involved in these damnable Bureaus," Briggers told his congressional representatives in 1943. The Briggers list made its way into the hands of the president of a small Cleveland company who used the 2,241 "bureaus" figure in a speech to a local Shriners club. "[A]s one of thousands of small businessmen," L. M. Evans told the Shriners in 1944, "I have felt the constantly increasing pressure of bureaucratic controls that have proven almost unbearable." Only by standing up to the growing "regimentation" demanded by the wartime state, Evans argued, could Americans issue a much-needed rebuke to "the long-haired boys in Wash-ington so eager to remake the world."[10]

It was not only "the long-haired boys" who were producing reams of red tape and other regulatory burdens that so troubled wartime business leaders. The unwanted regulation came not just from the New Dealers at the OPA but also the corporate executives-turned-mobilizers at the WPB. For many military contractors, one of the most troubling manifestations of excessive government oversight was the WPB's early, ill-fated attempt to collect data that would allow it to properly allocate critical materials: the Production Requirements Plan (PRP). Imposed at the same moment as many of the OPA's price controls and rationing requirements, the ill-designed, short-lived PRP added significantly to the business community's growing frustrations with wartime red tape.

The PRP, introduced on a partial, voluntary basis in early December 1941, was expanded after Pearl Harbor. By February 1942, about three thousand manufacturers were participating in it. Starting in July, the WPB imposed the PRP across the entire war economy. At least thirty thousand companies were now required to complete detailed forms describing their inventories and anticipated future requirements of various forms of steel, aluminum, brass, bronze, copper, lead, magnesium, nickel, tin, and zinc. The main PRP quarterly questionnaire, "Form PD-25A," was long and complex enough that the WPB had it tabulated by computer at the Census Bureau. The PRP complemented the existing priority-rating system, which mobilization planners (imitating their Great War predecessors) had been using since 1940. As recalibrated in May 1942, the system used the AAA label for the programs deemed most important, followed by AA-1, AA-2, and so forth. In theory, the WPB staff could use these ratings, together with data generated by the PRP, to allocate critical materials to contractors, expertly and smoothly.[11]

In practice, the PRP proved a failure, not least because it required companies and the government to manage overwhelming volumes of paperwork. Many companies discovered that they had not been collecting the data required by the PRP questionnaires, so a huge amount of work was required even before they could start filling out what looked to be an endless flood of forms. In Washington, the WPB discovered, once the PRP was mandated for all contractors and subcontractors starting July 1942, that it was drowning in data.[12] By early September, just two months after the PRP had been applied universally, the WPB Planning Committee jumped at the chance to implement a simpler system.

The new system was the Controlled Materials Plan (CMP). It was designed by Ferdinand Eberstadt, a veteran Wall Street investment banker and friend of James Forrestal, the Navy undersecretary. Eberstadt had come to Washington to take an executive position at the Army-Navy Munitions Board, where he helped devise priority ratings. Starting in early 1942, Eberstadt worked on an alternative to the PRP, which he regarded as too complex and top-heavy. His alternative, the CMP, would track and allocate just three critical metals: steel, copper, and aluminum. Equally important, Eberstadt's plan would reduce the number of firms dealing directly with the WPB, by relying more heavily on the prime contractors. Under the CMP, the prime contractors collected "bills of materials" (estimates of needs for the next eighteen months) from their subcontractors and added these requirements to their own, before submitting the totals to the War Department, Navy Department, or other government "claimant agencies." Once the military and the White House decided upon how much to give to which weapons programs, the claimant agencies allocated the rights to metals to their prime contractors, which became responsible for distributing the warrants among their subcontractors.[13]

Eberstadt's CMP has been described as a brilliant example of the virtues of managerial decentralization, critical to the success of the American war effort. This view exaggerates its importance, not least because CMP arrived so late—in 1943, as munitions production was already peaking.[14] Certainly, the CMP, among its other virtues, did help limit paperwork. But it could not address the problem of even more direct intrusions into the business operations of contractors, many of which were perpetrated not by the WPB but by the military establishment.

As its work on priorities and materials allocations suggests, the WPB was a powerful mobilization agency. However, it was a body that mostly acted from on high, as a prodigious information-gatherer and economic coordinator at the national level. From the point of view of some War and Navy Department officers, the people who actually made and supervised the war contracts, the WPB did not seem to be all that useful. In one report to Washington in the summer of 1942, the chief of the Army's Rochester (New York) Ordnance District explained that his office rarely interacted with the WPB's local and national offices. What little contact there was convinced him that WPB representatives had "not been very helpful." Even worse, the WPB men, despite their "general lack of production experience," had manifested an "apparent anxiety to obtain entire credit for work accomplished," even though the military was doing most of it. These views were echoed by other Ordnance District chiefs around the country who reported that the WPB suffered from "mediocrity" and did little to aid their procurement efforts.[15]

The officers' skepticism about the value of the WPB reflected their experience of military-industrial relations on the ground. The military's procurement organizations, which (along with the USMC) handled nearly all contracting, were the most important public players in the American war economy. The War Department alone contained three giant procurement entities—the Ordnance Department, the AAF Materiel Command (based at Wright Field, in Ohio), and the Army Service Forces. Each of these three entities employed nearly 50,000 people, in comparison with the roughly 25,000 working for the WPB.[16] These organizations were substantially decentralized, which meant that contractors dealt frequently with regional-level military offices. Under the leadership of General Charles E. Branshaw, the AAF's Materiel Command brought itself into even closer contact with its suppliers, by expanding its regional procurement districts. By the end of 1943, there were still nearly 16,000 people working at Wright Field, but another 27,000 were employed in the Materiel Command's regional offices. The AAF's Western Procurement District in Los Angeles, for example, employed more than 4,500 civilians, who worked on contracting, inspections, and a variety of other jobs.[17]

No less decentralized were the War Department's two other main procurement bureaus, the Ordnance Department and the Quartermaster Corps. By the end of the war, the Ordnance Department had 35,000 personnel in its thirteen district offices, each of which employed 2,000 to 5,000 people. The Ordnance Department also created a whole second headquarters, first known as the "Tank Automotive Center" and later as the "Office of the Chief of Ordnance—Detroit," which allowed the Army to do more high-level business with the auto industry without having to call constantly upon Washington.[18]

It was not just paperwork that drove business leaders to distraction. The War and Navy Departments also made a variety of regulatory demands, some of which were far more intrusive than requests for more information. As the conservative journalist John T. Flynn (the ex-progressive who, in the mid-1930s, designed excess profits tax policies for the Nye Committee) noted in a 1942 piece published for the mass audience of *Reader's Digest*, the agencies of the wartime state often seemed to retard war production because they "constantly deluge the producer with questionnaires, inspections, changes in design, and the like."[19] What Flynn did not make explicit was that most of this work—especially when it came to inspections, design changes, and other aspects of the administration of war contracts—was handled by the War and Navy Departments.

For business leaders, among the most striking manifestations of the War and Navy Departments' power were the public inspectors and auditors who worked in their plants. These civilian employees of the military bureaus were charged with double-checking the quality of goods—already being inspected by inspectors employed by the contractors—before they were accepted by the government. The War and Navy Departments stationed inspectors at nearly all the plants managed by its prime contractors as well as in some facilities of subcontractors. By late 1941, about half of the Chicago Ordnance District's 1,400 civilian employees were inspectors. By that time, two of the nation's most important producers of Sherman tanks, Pressed Steel Car and Pullman Standard, each had three dozen Army inspectors working in their Chicago-area plants. By late 1942, when the Chicago Ordnance District reached its peak size, it employed nearly 3,000 inspectors. Inspection was also a big part of the work of the AAF Materiel Command. By the middle of the war, the Materiel Command employed about 14,000 inspectors across the country. In the larger airframe and aero engine plants, the AAF maintained large on-site offices, each of which employed dozens of inspectors—in some cases, as many as two hundred. The Navy Department, which employed about 28,000 inspectors by 1944, also actively supervised the output of its suppliers.[20]

In the plants of many leading contractors, the inspectors were joined by teams of resident government auditors. Military and civilian agencies both dispatched on-site auditors to the plants of companies holding large cost-plus-fixed-fee (CPFF) contracts—arrangements under which the government reimbursed the contractor for all costs, plus a fixed amount that represented a sort of negotiated profit. Especially during the early part of the conflict, CPFF agreements were in force in most of the nation's largest war plants. In order to better monitor reimbursable costs, the War and Navy Departments and the General Accounting Office (GAO) stationed auditors on site in the plants. In some cases, as in the big airframe plants and the shipyards of the USMC's leading contractors, including the Kaiser companies, the resident government auditing staffs might consist of as many as sixty people at a single plant.[21]

For the executives and managers of individual companies, the many demands of the military bureaus and other state agencies could seem difficult to bear. Ford Motor executives and managers, when they looked back on the war years, would recall how difficult it was to adjust to the intrusions of the military. Charles E. Sorensen, a top company executive, explained that by mid-1941, Ford was already "a government subsidiary. . . . Army and Air Force officers were in the plant constantly." One Ford manager, Anthony Harff, remembered: "The captains, lieutenants and majors . . . were in our hair all the time, particularly out at the bomber plant." According to one of the company's own accountants, "several hundred government auditors," from the Ordnance Department, the AAF, and the GAO, were working on-site in offices at Ford plants, where they frequently dug into the company's books. This physical presence at the local level, on top of the demands that came from the military and civilian agencies elsewhere, could be imposing. As one Ford manager put it in June 1944, there was "terrific pressure placed upon us" by the AAF Materiel Command, which alone used sixteen separate departments and offices to interact with the contractor.[22]

The Unevenness of Military Demand

For all the challenges they created, the wartime state's paperwork demands and on-site inspection efforts were understandable because they seemed to relate directly to the larger mobilization effort. More puzzling and alienating, for some business leaders and their workers, were government mandates that seemed to clash with the broader national experience of all-out mobilization: mid-war contract cutbacks. These micro-level disruptions are easy to forget today, when we remember a booming national war economy that kept every factory busy and ended the unemployment troubles of the Great Depression. However, the cutbacks were widespread in 1942–44. They were an important aspect of the wartime experiences of business firms and their employees, who discovered that military demand could be quite unsteady. Indeed, from the point of view of many companies, the war orders coming from their single giant customer seemed to produce swings in demand at least as violent as those that had been generated by civilian markets during the Depression.

One reason for the mid-war contract cutbacks was that even the United States, which enjoyed such tremendous economic advantages in comparison with other combatant nations, had limited resources. This problem of the nation's finite—if uncertain—aggregate capacity was of great interest to government economists. They insisted, as the country started its all-out industrial mobilization in 1942, that the munitions program be reduced, so as to protect the civilian economy. This was disputed by some military officials who wanted to protect their munitions production schedules. Such were the foundations of the so-called feasibility dispute, which reached a climax in October 1942.

The feasibility dispute grew out of the ambitious production targets set by President Roosevelt. In his State of the Union address in January 1942, Roosevelt had called for 60,000 airplanes in 1942 and another 125,000 in 1943; he wanted 45,000 tanks in 1942, along with 75,000 more in 1943. Responding to Roosevelt's challenge, the War Department created new projections that had the country spending $63 billion on munitions and war plant in 1942 and $110 billion in 1943. This was well above the upper limit of feasible all-out war expenditures that had been calculated before Pearl Harbor by Stacy May and Robert Nathan, economists attached to the Office of Production Management (OPM). Given that the entire U.S. gross national product in 1940 had been only about $100 billion, the military's projections seemed unrealistically high, even after taking into account the considerable ongoing expansion of GDP. Such was the conclusion of Simon Kuznets, a professor at the University of Pennsylvania and the leading authority on national income accounting. In March 1942, after he joined the WPB's Planning Committee, Kuznets drafted a memo suggesting that without drastic cuts to the civilian economy, the military's recent projections of munitions output for 1942 and 1943 could not help but fall short by about 20 percent. These arguments seemed compelling to Donald Nelson, head of the WPB. In April, Nelson told the military to make plans to reduce aggregate munitions spending to $45 billion for 1942 and $75 billion for 1943. The War and Navy Departments responded by cutting their programs by several billion dollars. However, backed by President Roosevelt, they held off from making the full reductions demanded by the WPB.[23]

The feasibility dispute continued into the second half of 1942, as the military continued to make minor cutbacks. For some in the Pentagon, including Undersecretary of War Robert Patterson and General Brehon B. Somervell, head of the Army Service Forces, the calls to make do with fewer munitions and troops seemed wrongheaded. The clash between the military men and the civilian economists came to a head at an intense three-hour WPB meeting in early October, when Nathan again insisted that maximum annual war spending should be no more than $75 billion. After Somervell objected that this figure was far too low, he found himself on the receiving end of a tirade by Leon Henderson, head of the OPA. Surprisingly, perhaps, the economists got the better of the argument. In November, the military and the WPB settled on a plan for $80 billion in munitions spending for 1943. The Navy would need to cut $3 billion from its most recent plans for 1943; the War Department, $9 billion.[24]

The early cuts to the munitions program affected many industries and firms. Before Pearl Harbor, industrial mobilization officials had sought an eleven-million-kilowatt expansion of the nation's capacity to generate electricity. In summer 1942, this was scaled back to seven million kilowatts, despite the heavy electricity consumption of many key war industries, such as aluminum.[25] The growing awareness of finite resources also contributed to one of the largest contract cancellations of 1942. Earlier in the year, the USMC had asked Andrew Jackson Higgins, the New Orleans–based manufacturer of landing craft, to join the Liberty ship program. The irrepressible Higgins quickly drew up plans to construct what would likely be the world's largest shipyard. In March, the USMC told Higgins that he would have a contract for two hundred Liberties. But then, as the steel shortage became more serious (and as the Liberty yards run by Kaiser and other established contractors started to speed up their deliveries), the USMC had second thoughts. In July, it canceled the Higgins contract outright. Higgins responded by denouncing the USMC for its "incompetency, obstructive bureaucracy and confusion." The cancellation, he said, was completely "heartless and indecent."[26]

The early cutbacks involved not only big individual contracts but entire weapons programs. In 1942–43, the most important of the major programs to see serious cuts was the one that made Army tanks. Across the tank program in 1942–43, leading prime contractors were told to scale back output—in some cases, only months after they started production.

The record of the tank program in 1942–43 shows that the Army's Ordnance Department retreated quickly from the targets that the president had set after Pearl Harbor. In February 1942, the War Department drew up a schedule calling for the production of 105,000 medium tanks (in a projected three years of war). This program would have come close to meeting the president's targets but did not last very long. In April, after the WPB's first order to cut back the overall munitions program, the wartime total figure was lowered to 95,000; the goal for 1942 was reduced to just 14,000 medium tanks. Although the revised target amounted to ten times the number that had been delivered in 1941, it was far below Roosevelt's stated goal for 1942 of 25,000. In September, the targeted wartime total was reduced again, to 80,000; by November, after the cuts that came with the settlement of the feasibility dispute, it stood at 62,000. So in the nine months leading up to the U.S. landings in North Africa, the size of the Ordnance Department's planned medium tank program had been reduced by about 40 percent.[27] Faced with limited resources, the WPB and the Joint Chiefs had decided that they were willing to get by with fewer tanks, to avoid giving up large numbers of planes and ships.[28]

The tank cutbacks were felt deeply by individual contractors and their workers. The rapid scaling back of the program in 1942–43 contrasted markedly to the contractors' recent experiences, when the War Department had recruited them so aggressively. From June 1940 through November 1941, American and British orders had created a large group of tank contractors. Led by Chrysler, operator of the largest GOCO tank arsenal, the group also included several locomotive and railcar manufacturers, as well as Ford and GM. By early 1942, most of these contractors were getting ready to produce some version of the Army's new M4 "Sherman" medium tank. Contractors began to deliver the first Shermans around April 1942, just as Washington was starting to cut back the total munitions program.

The first serious cutback in the program occurred in April 1942, when the War Department completely withdrew its $7 million order for 670 tank engines from Guiberson Diesel Engine, a smaller manufacturer with plants in Texas and Illinois. At the time, the Guiberson-made engine, which performed poorly in early testing, was one of five power plants already being developed for use in the Sherman tank.[29] The Guiberson affair forced the War Department to figure out how to handle its first multimillion-dollar contract cancellation, which it decided to manage with an innovative negotiated settlement, using rapid spot-checking of accounts, rather than a slow, comprehensive audit.[30]

Tank contractors began to notice major changes immediately after mid-October 1942, the climax of the feasibility dispute. One of the affected companies was the Pullman-Standard, whose plant in Hammond, Indiana, near Chicago, had become one of the biggest producers of Sherman tanks. Suddenly, the Ordnance Department asked Pullman-Standard to cut production by more than half, from a target of four hundred tanks a month to under two hundred. Company executives protested the change, which would require them to lay off as many as 1,200 workers. They told Ordnance Department officers that this put the company "in an unfair position in the tank program," especially relative to Chrysler, which had not been asked to cut back as much. The War Department's sudden change "has created situations which just cannot be explained to our 5,000 employees," they wrote, "and the people in this town who want to know, 'What is the matter?' "[31]

The disorder continued into 1943, when many other tank contractors were hit with cutbacks. In March and April, as Pullman-Standard managers continued to complain, they were joined by executives from GM's Fisher Body Division, which was compelled to lay off 850 people.[32] One of the most serious cutbacks involved the Berwick, Pennsylvania, plant of American Car & Foundry (ACF), a railcar manufacturer that had served since the beginning of the war as the nation's primary producer of light tanks. In early 1943, the War Department informed ACF that it would want only 2,500 of the M3 tanks, instead of the 12,000 originally ordered; the company was expected to focus on a planned five-month transition to making a newer light tank model, the M5. This news upset company executives, who faced the prospect of dismissing nearly a third of the plant's workforce of 9,500 people. They relayed their concerns to top mobilization officials in Washington, who worked to keep more work in Berwick by shifting more cuts to contractors in Detroit, where there was a labor shortage.[33]

ACF's need for more work, together with the reports of the combat ineffectiveness of smaller tanks, contributed to the largest of all the early military contract cancellations: the termination of a $217 million order of light tanks from International Harvester (IH), the giant manufacturer of agricultural equipment. Signed in January 1942, the IH contract had originally called for two thousand units of the new twenty-ton T7 tank, which was bigger than existing light tanks but much smaller than the thirty-four-ton Sherman. In order to get the T7s made, the War Department paid over $16 million to build a new IH-operated "Quad Cities Tank Arsenal," in Bettendorf, Iowa. By early 1943, as IH prepared to launch production, it had developed a network of 438 subcontractors, located in twenty states; at the Bettendorf plant, it had assembled a workforce of nearly two thousand. But in mid-March, the Ordnance Department told IH to end tank production immediately. Only twenty-eight T7s were ever built. This cancellation did little to harm the fortunes of IH, which was in the midst of filling nearly $1 billion worth of other military orders, along with its civilian business. (After settling the tank contract with the government for $25 million, IH proceeded to use the Bettendorf plant to make hundreds of "prime mover" tractors that could be used to haul heavy artillery.)[34] But the big-tank contract cancellation of 1943 demonstrated to business leaders that they could not necessarily regard a major war order as guaranteed, even in the short run, before the end of the war was in sight.

"What happened to International Harvester," newspaper columnist Karl Keyerleber explained, "was a manifestation of the thing they call fluidity in this global war." According to Keyerleber, writing in May 1944, "war contract cancellation has become our No. 1 home front problem."[35] Many of his peers agreed: as one member of the Washington press corps noted in his diary in February 1944, "the Army goes on cancelling contracts right and left, throwing thousands abruptly out of work."[36] Certainly, in the tank program, where production peaked in 1943, cutbacks and cancellations had become widespread. In July 1943, the Ordnance Department estimated that it could meet its Sherman tank requirements with just three producers: the Chrysler-run Detroit Tank Arsenal, GM's Fisher division, and Pressed Steel Car, in South Chicago.[37] By the end of the year, four other manufacturers of Sherman tanks—Pullman-Standard, Ford, Lima Locomotive, and Pacific Car & Foundry (PC&F)—left the program for good. They were followed in 1944 by other formerly important tank suppliers, including Baldwin Locomotive and GM.[38]

Although the cutbacks were disruptive, they were not always unwelcome. As early as January 1942, Ordnance Department officials noted that some other locomotive manufacturers complained that GM's Electromotive Division (already the leading producer of diesel locomotives) had been given "a preferred position because they [GM] weren't making any" tanks.[39] So when the cuts came, some companies figured that it might actually be helpful to return early to civilian production. In July 1943, Ordnance Department officials asked Paul Pigott, president of PC&F, if his company would be willing to retire from the tank program. Pigott reasoned that if he could not get a large order for tanks, the company would be better off making tractors for the Army, along with railcars for civilian customers. So he and the Ordnance Department agreed that PC&F would end production by December. The PC&F cancellation had the benefit of freeing up nearly a thousand workers, who were desperately needed in other jobs in Seattle's very tight labor market.[40] There was a similar labor shortage in Detroit, where Ford was struggling to find enough workers for its giant B-24 bomber and aero engine programs. Under these conditions in 1943, Ford executives agreed with Ordnance officers that the company should make fewer than half of the 4,050 Sherman tanks that it had been originally scheduled to produce.[41]

"I was talking with a high-ranking member of the automobile industry the other day," a newspaper reporter mentioned to war mobilization czar

James Byrnes at a press conference in June 1943, "and he says they are having a devil of a time now, where they shut down in the making of one war product and want to put them into production on something else."[42] Such protests came from many suppliers in the tank program, and not just the prime contractors for finished vehicles. In March 1943, the Ordnance Department told its suppliers that the Army would keep using rubber tank tracks after all, despite the Ordnance Department's announcement seven months earlier that rubber shortages would require everyone to switch to steel tracks. For the track suppliers, as Ordnance officers themselves noted, the sudden changes caused "much confusion, unnecessary commitments, and financial loss." Indeed, the officers noted, contractors were complaining, not without some justification, that "[n]o business would be operated by industry in the manner that Ordnance expects business to operate for them."[43]

The irregularities of military demand also affected shipbuilders, who worked on the Navy side of the munitions program. For the experienced yards that supplied the bulk of the major combatant vessels—battleships, aircraft carriers, cruisers, destroyers, and submarines—the fluctuations were relatively minor. However, the Navy oversaw two other giant shipbuilding programs in which the changes were far more violent. In 1942–44, the emergency initiatives that built hundreds of destroyer escorts (DEs) and thousands of landing craft were ramped up and down very quickly. This was hard on the private yards that built these vessels, many of which were smaller firms without much experience doing business with the Navy.

The DE and landing craft programs ranked among the largest of all the post–Pearl Harbor initiatives in the American mobilization effort. Indeed, the DEs cost the United States slightly more than the $2 billion atomic bomb program; the landing craft, which cost a combined $5 billion, were far more expensive. But unlike those other programs, which peaked very late, the DE and landing craft efforts were ones in which production rose and fell fast, in the middle of the war. This made them among the most difficult of all the wartime munitions efforts to manage, from the point of view of contractors, as well as the Navy's.

The DEs were small combatant ships, built in 289-foot and 306-foot versions. Priced initially at about $3 million apiece (and eventually at $2 million), they cost only half as much as regular destroyers and could be built quicker. The DEs were intended to help solve the Allies' terrible problems with U-Boats, early in World War II, by providing merchant convoys with real firepower. The Navy awarded its first contracts for DEs in November 1941. The first deliveries were scheduled for early 1943. After Pearl Harbor, the DE program was expanded. By early June 1942, the DEs (along with landing craft) had jumped to the very top of the Navy's list of priorities. Seventeen shipyards, public and private, were brought into the program, which was supposed to deliver 1,005 DEs. However, as the Allies began to prevail in the battle of the Atlantic, the DEs became less important. In autumn 1943, the Navy canceled its most recent orders. First, it dropped the schedule to eight hundred vessels; then down to seven hundred; and then to just six hundred.[44] A once-giant munitions program had been cut nearly in half; by the beginning of 1944, DE construction was halted completely.

No less dramatic were the swings in the production program that produced landing craft. These vessels, which ranged in size from small boats to sizable vessels like the 328-foot LSTs ("landing ship, tank"), were essential for a variety of Allied operations, from the landings of U.S. forces in North Africa in late 1942, to island-to-island fighting in the Pacific, to the D-Day invasion of France in 1944. In April 1942, after President Roosevelt and his military advisers discussed the prospect of getting ground troops to Europe, the landing craft program jumped to the very top of the priorities list. By the end of June 1942, the Navy had placed orders for landing craft with five of its own yards, as well as seventy-four private facilities, including twenty-one smaller shipyards on the Great Lakes. For the next two years, landing craft remained at or near the top of the list of the nation's "must" munitions programs. A second big push for production started in August 1943, as the Allies settled on plans for landings in northern France. After D-Day, however, this giant war program faded into insignificance.[45]

The sudden rise of the DE and landing craft programs disturbed Navy officials, accustomed to concentrating on the major combatant ships. In July 1942, Admiral S. M. Robinson, chief of the Navy's Office of Procurement and Material, reported "almost continuous turmoil" and "great confusion" in Navy shipbuilding. In the spring, the steel shortage had forced the Navy to cancel four cruisers, along with more than a hundred smaller vessels. The DE and landing craft programs, which compelled several yards to stop production on other vessels already under way, had added to the chaos. Robinson's concerns were shared by Navy Undersecretary Forrestal, who told the WPB that the assignment of a top priority rating to the larger landing craft in mid-1942 had had "disastrous consequences." For the remainder of the year, Forrestal reported, there had been "a condition almost of production anarchy in plants, shipways, etc.," which had caused serious delays in the DE program, among others.[46]

The disorder in shipbuilding returned in the autumn of 1943, as the Navy canceled dozens of DEs, including 119 that it had only just ordered. The giant new Bethlehem-Hingham yard in Massachusetts, built especially for DE production, had its orders reduced by eighty-one ships. This $165 million cancellation did little to affect the overall fortunes of Bethlehem Steel, one of the nation's largest prime contractors. But for the smaller midwestern companies that had worked as Navy suppliers for only a few months, the cutbacks were dramatic. Defoe Shipbuilding of Bay City, Michigan, a smaller company, was told to cut fifteen DEs, worth $33 million. The Dravo Corporation, based in Pittsburgh, had its aggregate DE orders drop by more than half, from fifty-eight to twenty-seven ships.[47]

Because the DE cancellations of 1943 were followed by a second big push for landing craft, some shipyards found themselves attempting to quickly change over from one program to the other. Landing craft had been a top priority in June–November 1942, until the landings in North Africa. During that period, several private and public shipyards—including some of the USMC's top suppliers of Liberty ships—had stopped work on other vessels, in order to make LSTs and other landing vessels. From October 1943 through the landings in France in June 1944, when landing craft again ranked as an ultrahigh-priority munitions program, the violent swings were repeated. At Dravo, the big DE cutbacks coincided with even bigger increases in Navy orders for landing ships. Between the fall of 1943 and the spring of 1944, Dravo's managers and employees worked furiously on orders for ninety-two additional LSTs, as well as sixty-five medium landing ships (LSMs).[48]

Although the experienced producers of the larger combatant vessels enjoyed smoother demand curves, the Navy's aggressive, early expansion efforts also required some major warship cutbacks. In mid-1943, the Navy aborted its entire *Montana*-class battleship program, which at one time contemplated the building of five huge (58,000-ton) combatants; it had already been suspended in 1942 for lack of steel, amid questions about the value of battleships in a new age of carrier warfare. Another serious cutback occurred in late July 1944, when it was decided that the Navy could do without more than a hundred submarines. For the private shipyards in the submarine program (Electric Boat, Manitowac, and Cramp), this meant cancellations of sixty-eight vessels.[49]

Of all the major munitions sectors, the one that saw the most dramatic swings in demand was the small arms ammunition program. Overseen by the Army's Ordnance Department, this sector consisted almost entirely of large GOCO plants built in 1940–42. Most of them were operated by Remington, a Du Pont subsidiary, or by one of the divisions of Western Cartridge, led by the Olin family.[50] By mid-1943, a dozen GOCO ammunition plants were producing 1.5 billion rounds a month. But these facilities and their workers did not enjoy steady employment. As early as the summer of 1942, the giant St. Louis plant (operated by U.S. Cartridge, a Western Cartridge subsidiary) dismissed hundreds of workers. Meanwhile, the War Department canceled the construction of an additional small arms ammunition plant, planned for Kenosha, Wisconsin. This step annoyed the leaders of Simmons, the mattress-making firm that had been scheduled to run the plant.[51]

These early disruptions in the small arms ammunition program were nothing compared with the events of 1943–45, which saw truly violent swings. In late 1943, after the War Department determined that there was a surplus, it shut down six of the GOCO plants. By summer 1944, only five remained in operation; national production levels dropped to just half of what they had been in 1943.[52] Even at the plants that remained open, such as the St. Louis facility, several thousand workers lost their jobs. The layoffs brought protests from unions, which complained that the government was botching the manpower mobilization.[53]

But in November 1944, the ammunition situation changed again. In Europe, General Eisenhower and his staff discovered that the troops were using ammunition much faster than anticipated. So the WPB and the War Department ordered a re-expansion of the small arms ammunition program, which was suddenly asked to raise aggregate employment from 53,400 to 115,600 workers. (This occurred even before the surprising German counteroffensive of December 1944, the Battle of the Bulge. In response to that setback, the military and the WPB increased overall munitions schedules for 1945 by about 15 percent.)[54] In the ammunition plants, the results were dramatic. In St. Louis, the payrolls shot up to 31,000 workers, from 14,000. At the Twin Cities facility, the number of workers would rise quickly, from 8,200 to 21,000. In Utah, where the GOCO ammunition plant had been shut down entirely, Remington rehired nearly 6,000 people. By early 1945, the production of small arms ammunition, which had declined sharply the previous year, reached an all-time high.[55]

Even in the aircraft industry, where aggregate output did not peak until 1944, some individual plants and their workers saw significant cutbacks. As time passed, certain planes became obsolete, or were determined to be inadequate. The production of Curtiss-Wright's P-40 fighters, which had been so important in 1940, peaked very early, in 1942. The following year saw peak production of the P-39 Airacobra fighter and Martin's B-26 Marauder medium bomber.[56] Among the most spectacular of the canceled aircraft programs was a joint effort, between Henry Kaiser and Howard Hughes, to make enormous, seventy-ton cargo planes. In February 1944, after over a year of problems, the WPB cut off funding for the behemoth plane; fed up with the eccentric Hughes, Kaiser abandoned the project.[57] Another well-publicized cancellation occurred in May 1944, when the Navy ended its relationship with Brewster Aeronautical, a troubled manufacturer of fighter planes.[58]

Aircraft cutbacks also victimized Andrew Jackson Higgins, the top producer of smaller landing craft, who had been hit with a huge Liberty ship contract cancellation back in 1942. Later that year, Higgins had arranged to build 1,200 units of the C-76, a plywood transport plane designed by Curtiss-Wright. In August 1943, as the aluminum situation improved, the AAF canceled the C-76 program. Higgins was placated with an AAF order for five hundred units of the C-46, another Curtiss-Wright aircraft. But in August 1944, just as production was starting up at the Higgins C-46 plant in Louisiana, that contract was canceled, as well. The victim of three major contract cancellations in three years, Higgins could be forgiven at least some of the anger that he directed toward the procurement authorities.[59]

The cancellation of the Higgins planes was part of a larger rearrangement of AAF production schedules that the War Department announced in August 1944. As the B-29 bomber program was given top priority, other programs were selected for downsizing. One victim was the B-24 Liberator bomber. This was bad news for the North American Aviation–run plant in Dallas, which, in August 1944, absorbed the brunt of the B-24 cutbacks. In Dallas, about 4,000 workers were laid off immediately, along with several thousand more by year's end. To alleviate the shock, the AAF gave the Dallas plant an additional order for C-82 cargo planes. But employment decreased steadily, as did the morale of employees, hundreds of whom quit even before they were asked to do so. By the end of September, total employment at the Dallas plant had already dropped to 26,000, nearly 10,000 below what it had been a year earlier.[60]

For business leaders, the variability of military demand made it difficult to manage current operations and to plan for the future. This was true even for elite contractors with the closest relationships with the military, such as Sperry Gyroscope. In September 1944, Sperry executives forecast that sales throughout the next year would remain in a narrow range, $21–$25 million a month. But by November, as the Allies made progress in Europe, the company widened this estimate, to an estimated range of $15–$26 million a month; it also predicted that by early 1946, monthly sales would drop off sharply, to just $7 million. However, in February 1945, Sperry officials projected that monthly sales would reach $27 million in early 1946, before the end of the Pacific War caused a sharp decline. As it turned out, the older forecasts were more accurate.[61]

Sperry's planning difficulties were caused not just by general uncertainties about the timing of the war's end but by the military's changing orders. The record of Sperry's K-13 gun sight, an improved aiming mechanism for the .50-caliber machine guns mounted on American bombers, is suggestive. Sperry received its first order for the K-13 sights in April 1944, when the AAF asked it to produce 20,100 units, with deliveries to begin in October. Under this original schedule, production was supposed to peak at 3,300 units per month. In July, the AAF announced that it planned to buy 33,124 units; peak production would be nearly doubled, to 6,000 units a month. But in late September, the AAF retracted this increase. In early October, it told Sperry that peak production would need to be only 2,500 units a month. At the end of November, soon after the K-13 sights were first used in combat, the AAF told Sperry that it actually wanted 3,000 units a month. Sperry evidently was able to use this production target for the next several months. Then, on V-E Day (8 May 1945), the AAF terminated the contract.[62]

All these examples of the irregularity of military demand—in the tank program, in shipbuilding, in ammunition production, and even in the aircraft industry—help us understand why some company executives and their employees found war contracting to be something less than a dream come true. Across the country, many plant managers and their workers grappled with the consequences of dramatic shifts in military requirements; in some cases, they found themselves shutting down production lines, even as the war economy as a whole was beginning to peak. Often, the War and Navy Departments seemed to be excessively demanding customers, if not tyrannical ones.

The irregularity and uncertainty were balanced, in most cases, by valuable protections. Most laid-off workers, if they were willing to relocate, had little trouble finding new jobs on the home front. For company executives, even the most severe contract cutbacks rarely caused permanent damage. In many cases, manufacturers were able to find new orders to at least partially replace their lost ones. Because the government generally reimbursed contractors for their costs (in one way or another), even on partially completed munitions, it was unusual for wartime businesses to sustain any serious financial losses. Given these facts, and given what we know about how World War II pulled the American economy far out of the Depression, it is easy to assume that companies experienced the war years as a profit-taking bonanza. But this was not how American business leaders interpreted their wartime experiences. To understand why, we need to explore the details of the many ways in which the wartime state worked to regulate prices and profits.

Profit and Price Control

Many discussions of business profits in World War II quote Henry L. Stimson, the venerable lawyer and public servant who was tapped by President Roosevelt to be secretary of war. "If you are going to try to go to war, or to prepare for war, in a capitalist country," wrote Stimson, "you have got to let business make money out of the process or business won't work, and there are a great many people in Congress who think that they can tax business out of all proportion and still have businessmen work diligently and quickly. This is not human nature."[63] At the moment when he recorded these words in his diary, in August 1940, Stimson was thinking of the pending tax bill, which would provide the accelerated amortization incentives that the new secretary of war hoped would encourage private investment in war plant. But his comments suggest broader questions. Was it true that high taxes and other strict controls, by depressing incentives, would prevent the American capitalist economy from winning the war of industrial production? The answer is no. The wartime American state did not eliminate profits but did regulate them powerfully. From the point of view of business leaders, wartime price and profit control turned out to be among the most intrusive and disturbing aspects of wartime government-business relations.

As Stimson's diary entry suggests, one of the most important issues in Washington during the early months of the war was the shape of tax policy. There was actually a good deal of consensus about the need for high wartime tax rates. Even before Pearl Harbor, when Congress, the president, and the general public were already demanding major tax increases, business leaders rarely challenged the idea. And in 1942, as Congress and the Treasury Department drafted the highest tax rates in American history, business leaders did little to oppose them directly.[64] Despite Stimson's comments in his diary and despite the commitment of many business leaders to continue their political battle against the New Dealers, sky-high tax rates were widely understood as a given. One of the most important reasons for this sensibility was that Americans entered World War II determined to prevent the sort of improper "profiteering" that they remembered from the Great War.

The widespread commitment after the Great War to limit profits on military orders helped inspire the Vinson-Trammell Act of 1934, which capped Navy contract profits at 10 percent of costs. In April 1939, Congress revised Vinson-Trammell, setting shipbuilding profits at 8 percent and capping profits on Army and Navy aircraft contracts at 12 percent. In June 1940, the 8 percent limit was applied to aircraft, as well as ships.[65]

In September 1940, Congress suspended Vinson-Trammell, in order to replace it with different profit-control mechanisms. The most powerful of these, in terms of dollars recovered, was a new excess profits tax (EPT). The EPT was part of the revenue act passed by Congress in autumn 1940. Before the new tax law was drafted, President Roosevelt and his advisers made it clear that they expected Congress to prevent profiteering. In his fireside chat of 26 May 1940, Roosevelt assured Americans that he would not permit the creation of a "new group of war millionaires," comparable with the one that allegedly sprang up during the Great War. No one supported "the idea of any American citizen growing rich and fat in an emergency of blood and slaughter and human suffering," the president declared in his radio address.[66] Similar language was used by Treasury Department officials, who, in August 1940, told Congress that "we want to avoid the millionaire class that was created in the previous war."[67]

This antiprofiteering language came naturally enough to New Dealers. But it was also taken up by the business community. As World War II began, business representatives vowed that they, too, wanted to prevent unjust profit-taking. During the tax-bill hearings of the late summer of

1940, NAM and Chamber of Commerce witnesses agreed that there must be no "creation of war millionaires," no "unjust enrichment as a result of the national defense program," and "no profiteering."[68]

Business leaders were eager to avoid any association with alleged profiteering. Executives at Automatic Electric in Chicago, a midsize manufacturer of telephone equipment, calculated during the summer of 1940 that military contracts would probably not be highly profitable because the savings provided by relatively big production runs would be mostly offset by increased costs of new plant, changing military specifications, and other factors. However, as Automatic Electric's P. W. Conrad explained in a confidential letter to the dean of Harvard Business School, his company worried that if it quoted high prices to the War Department, "we are apt to incur government ill-will on the suspicion of profiteering."[69] Such concerns were shared by business leaders across the country. "We don't want to be known as profiteers," C. S. Guggenheimer of the Tennessee Copper Company explained to the Army's Ordnance Department in October 1941. "A fair profit is all we want."[70]

In the Second Revenue Act of 1940, Congress began to use the tax law to define what would be considered a "fair profit" for companies in wartime. (This was the same act that created the accelerated amortization provision, which encouraged private investment in war plant by allowing companies to write it off over the course of just five years, instead of the usual twenty.) The new EPT of 1940 reproduced elements of the war taxes on corporations that Congress had created back in 1917–18. It allowed corporations to choose one of two ways to calculate their "excess profits." The first of these defined excess profits as those in excess of 8 percent of a company's invested capital. The second, known as the "annual earnings method," was based on the corporation's returns during the prewar, four-year "base period" of 1936–39. Under this method, any wartime profits above 95 percent of the average annual base period net income were defined as excessive, and therefore subject to the EPT. Once the amount of excess profits was determined, it was taxed at rates between 25 percent and 50 percent, with larger amounts subject to higher rates.[71]

In 1942, as the United States shifted into an all-out mobilization, Congress worked on a new revenue bill that redefined "excess profits." From 1940 to 1941, thanks in part to war orders, corporate profits had risen by about 20 percent. Now, as the nation became fully engaged in the war, most Americans agreed that wartime gains needed to be sharply limited. During this phase of the war, as surveys of letters to Congress and "man on the street" interviews showed, popular concerns about Great War–style "war profiteering" ran very high.[72] As one resident of North Carolina put it to his congressman, in February 1942, "a new crop of war millionaires out of dead sons is not going to sit so well with the American people."[73] Again, this apparently populist sentiment was endorsed even by pro-business conservatives. "No business should make a profit from the war," proclaimed Senator Robert Taft of Ohio, in a February 1942 talk to a group of Young Republicans in Tennessee.[74] As Congress started to work on the new revenue bill, the NAM announced that it would support raising top EPT rates to as high as 90 percent.[75] Such a policy would put the United States in the league of Britain and Canada, which had already combined a 100 percent EPT with a promise of a 20 percent postwar refund (creating an effective EPT rate of 80 percent).

In the end, Congress did create a much stronger EPT, which became a major source of war revenue and an important constraint on wartime profits. The revised EPT was part of the massive Revenue Act of 1942, which also required many average Americans to pay individual income taxes for the first time. After extended hearings and discussions, which lasted from March through August, Congress settled on a new EPT rate of 90 percent. To be sure, there were measures in the new legislation, many of them the result of lobbying by the business community, which made the EPT less severe. Ten percent of EPT payments were set aside for a postwar refund, which, in effect, lowered the top EPT rate to 81 percent. Congress set the "normal" corporate rate—which was applied to the profits exempted from the EPT—at 40 percent, far lower than the 55 percent level requested by the Treasury. And the 1942 law introduced other measures of relief, including new carryback provisions, which created additional postwar refunds for many leading contractors. Nevertheless, the 90 percent EPT remained a very powerful measure. During World War II, the EPT alone raised $35 billion in revenue, a quarter of all wartime Treasury receipts. As a source of dollars to pay for the U.S. war effort, the EPT was second only to the vastly expanded individual income tax. And for individual companies, the EPT—which Congress would raise to 95 percent in 1944—had very serious implications. It drove the effective wartime tax rates paid by all American corporations to over 50 percent, on average. Some companies, including many top military contractors, paid effective rates closer to 70 percent.[76]

Because the 90 percent EPT enacted in 1942 took such a large bite out of earnings, business leaders were especially sensitive to what some of them perceived as its serious inequities. This issue divided the national business community, despite its continued support of the principle of a high EPT. The complaints came mostly from those firms that discovered that neither of the methods of calculating their EPT exemption allowed them to shelter wartime profits. The capital-investment exemption method was most helpful to those firms that already had low ratios of profit to investment, such as the railroads and steel companies. And the average-earnings option helped those companies that had enjoyed high profits during the 1936–39 "base period"—a group that included industrial superstars such as GM, Chrysler, and Du Pont. For example, GM had performed so well in the late 1930s that its first $180 million in profits would be exempt from the EPT.

In contrast, companies that had neither giant private investment in plant nor high prewar earnings had no way to avoid having the EPT applied to nearly all their wartime profits. This group included many newer, fast-growing companies. At the congressional hearings on the 1940 and 1942 tax bills, representatives of many of these companies—including members of the Aircraft Parts Manufacturers' Association, Pepsi-Cola bottlers, and Universal Pictures, protested the EPT formula.[77] One of those most deeply concerned was the treasurer of Boeing, the nation's premier designer and builder of heavy bombers. Because Boeing had failed to make profits in the late 1930s, its treasurer, H. E. Bowman, explained in August 1942, the revised EPT might leave his company with an effective wartime tax rate of nearly 90 percent. Such a policy, Bowman complained, "will probably effectively end [Boeing's] existence."[78]

The worst fears of Boeing's executives never came to pass, thanks in part to the relief provisions that Congress inserted into the bill before its passage. But their concerns highlight the importance of EPT rules, which certainly did favor some industries and firms over others. Indeed, it was the tax policies created by Congress—and not the contracting practices of military procurement officials—that qualified as the public policies that did the most to help the largest, best-established industrial corporations. Conversely, the EPT did more to limit the wartime profit-taking of newer, faster-growing enterprises, including most firms in the aircraft industry. Industrial giants like GM and Du Pont managed to pay the 40 percent "normal" rate on a large portion of their wartime profits, thanks to the large exemptions provided them by the tax rules; but hundreds of smaller companies saw the 90 to 95 percent EPT applied to nearly all their 1942–45 earnings. From their perspective, the wartime state was an aggressive tax collector and an unfair one, to boot.

Despite the consensus about the need for high wartime taxes, there were plenty of struggles between companies and the commissioner of internal revenue. Hundreds of midsize firms went to federal court over disputes about how much they would be allowed to deduct for executive compensation, employee benefits, and other items.[79] In some cases, high taxes seem to have energized the antistatist political commitments of business leaders. Such was the case for Vivien Kellems, head of a company that manufactured cable grips, who was recognized as one of the most prominent female manufacturing executives of the day. In 1944, Kellems became involved in a well-publicized battle with the Roosevelt administration, after she announced that she had not paid her most recent income-tax bill because it left her with too little money to prepare her company for reconversion. For Kellems, who would spend the next several decades leading antitax organizations, the experience of the powerfully regulated war economy—and high wartime taxes, in particular—seems to have inspired a lifetime of conservative political activism.[80]

Although some business leaders griped about wartime taxes, they usually directed their loudest complaints toward other, even more intrusive, measures of price and profit control. For retailers, the most important among these were the regulations issued by the OPA, which attempted to dictate the prices (and, in some cases, also the design) of thousands of consumer products. OPA prices were strictly monitored and enforced at the local level by thousands of volunteers, along with paid administrators working out of district offices. This vast administrative apparatus impinged directly upon the autonomy of hundreds of firms, including independent, mom-and-pop grocery stores and other small shops, as well as the big chains. Although some of these companies had grappled with some national regulation during the New Deal, even that experience could not prepare them fully for the shock of the OPA's far more comprehensive controls.[81]

For military contractors, the most intrusive regulation of prices and profits did not come from the OPA, which in autumn 1942 abandoned its piecemeal efforts to regulate the prices of finished munitions.[82] Instead, contractors dealt most directly with the War and Navy Departments, which acted as powerful price and profit regulators in their own right.

In comparison with the OPA, which some business leaders attacked as being led by naïve New Dealers, the military establishment seemed in some ways to be a more sympathetic regulator. As World War II started, it was the stated policy of the War Department to pursue cooperation with private firms, rather than conflict. "The plans as being formulated by the War Department," General Charles T. Harris, Jr. explained at a gathering of Ordnance Department officers in October 1939, "are based upon this being a capitalistic nation and that fair profits shall be made and that losses shall be guarded against. Fair profits mean, of course, fair profits."[83] Although Harris's guidance was comically vague, his words made it clear that the War Department preferred a cooperative approach. This conciliatory attitude persisted through the war, as War Department contracting officers were frequently told that their goal should be to negotiate "fair and reasonable prices." According to Army Service Forces doctrine, procurement officers were supposed to work toward a "meeting of minds" between industry and army.[84]

This meeting of the minds was made easier by the fact that some of the top men in the military's wartime procurement offices were recent recruits from the private sector, comparable with the "dollar-a-year men" who populated the WPB. One of these was A. R. Glancy, an experienced businessman who had worked for GM in the 1920s as a leading developer of its Pontiac brand. In 1942, Glancy became chief of the Detroit Ordnance District, one of the most important of all the military's regional procurement districts. Glancy, who took pride in the fact that contractors greeted him with a friendly "Hi-ya, Al," was one top supply officer whose sympathies seemed obviously to lie with business.[85]

But Glancy, who lasted only a few months in Detroit, was not a typical military procurement chief. More representative of the cohort of top Army supply officers in World War II were the professionals who worked alongside Glancy. One of these was Colonel (later General) John Kay Christmas. A leading force behind the development of the Sherman tank, Christmas had served as an artillery officer in France during the Great War, just after graduating from Lafayette College with a degree in mechanical engineering. During the interwar years, Christmas pursued graduate studies in engineering at MIT; he interned at the Westinghouse Corporation, as well as at the Army's own Watertown Arsenal. In the late 1930s, before heading to Detroit, he led the Army's automotive testing division at Aberdeen Proving Ground, in Maryland.[86] The other top officer at the wartime Detroit

Ordnance District was Colonel (later General) A. B. Quinton, Jr., who had studied engineering at Cornell and MIT and had served as an Army Ordnance officer during the Great War. During the interwar years, Quinton completed the Harvard MBA program established for military officers; he also studied and taught at the Army Industrial College, where officers completed courses in industrial mobilization planning.

Christmas's and Quinton's counterparts in the Air Corps (later AAF), who spent much of the war at the Materiel Command at Wright Field, had similar backgrounds. Nearly all these men, who included Colonels (later Generals) K. B. Wolfe, Oliver P. Echols, George H. Brett, and Philip Schneeberger, had been born between 1885 and 1900, which meant that by the time of World War II, they were in their forties and fifties. Most had served during the Great War, and most had stayed in the military during the interwar years. Echols and Schneeberger, like Quinton, were graduates of the Army Industrial College. These were seasoned, smart officers, many of whom had theoretical and practical knowledge of engineering and manufacturing.[87] Most of them, along with their Navy counterparts, had great respect for what they regarded as innovative, well-run companies, such as Boeing, Grumman, Westinghouse, GE, and GM. But they were not the kind of men who would simply defer to contractors, some of which they regarded as inadequate.

Before Pearl Harbor, top Air Corps procurement officers observed that some of the Army's leading contractors seemed more competent—and more patriotic—than others. As Colonel Schneeberger explained to a fellow officer in July 1941, some of the new GOCO plants were being "uneconomically handled" by the private companies that ran them. These contractors had not only run the plants with excessively "high costs and seeming disregard of Government funds," Schneeberger believed, but had displayed "selfishness and grasping tactics." Among the companies with bad performance and bad attitudes, he warned his colleagues, were two of the nation's leading airframe manufacturers—Martin and Douglas—as well as Dow, the leading producer of magnesium. Schneeberger was also disappointed with other important Air Corps contractors and subcontractors, including Republic Aviation, Goodyear Aircraft, Cleveland Pneumatic Tool, and Hughes Tool.[88]

Even when they dealt with the contractors they liked best, procurement officers used their monopsony power—the influence that came from their status as the only available customer—to push for lower prices. One high-performing contractor pressed by the military to reduce prices was Boeing, the designer and manufacturer of the B-17 heavy bomber. By March 1939, top Air Corps officers such as Colonel Brett and General Henry H. ("Hap") Arnold were already discussing how they might use Consolidated Aircraft's forthcoming B-24 bomber, expected to be about 25 percent cheaper than the B-17, to pressure Boeing to lower its prices. For Boeing, which had already invested nearly $1 million in developing the B-17 and had recently suffered a $3 million annual loss, a big Air Corps order was essential. In September 1939, Boeing signed a contract to deliver thirty-eight B-17Cs, for $8.1 million, or about $213,000 per plane. Boeing expected to lose money at this price but hoped to make it up on future orders, as its per-unit production costs declined.[89]

The Air Corps continued to apply pressure. In March 1940, Air Corps officials met with Boeing executives to discuss their interest in ordering forty-two more B-17s, which, together with the September order, would make eighty planes. Boeing explained that it could supply the additional planes for $196,000 per unit, which would bring the average per-unit cost for the eighty-plane order to $208,000. To Boeing's dismay, General Arnold, the Air Corps chief, responded by demanding a per-unit price of $198,000 for the entire order of eighty planes. If Boeing could not meet this price, Arnold suggested, future Air Corps orders would favor the Consolidated B-24.[90] Boeing president Philip G. Johnson complained to his fellow executives that this price was "entirely too low" and would likely cause Boeing to lose money. However, Johnson essentially met the Air Corps demands by agreeing to a price of $199,000 per unit. As he left his March 1940 meeting with Air Corps officers, a shaken Johnson wondered if the Air Corps might never again order heavy bombers from Boeing.[91]

Boeing did not end up being shut out of the heavy bomber business. After the fall of France, and again after Pearl Harbor, its orders increased to levels that had been unimaginable during the tense contract talks of March 1940. Boeing sold nearly seven thousand of its B-17s; by the second half of the war, when it led the B-29 bomber program, it had become the AAF's star contractor. But Boeing found that military procurement authorities demanded that its cost savings from large production runs be accompanied by price reductions. The AAF told Boeing that it would need to accept lower fees on its cost-plus-fixed-fee (CPFF) contracts, which, starting in June 1941, covered all new orders for B-17s and B-29s. Originally set at 6 percent of the projected costs of a given order, Boeing's fixed fees for heavy bombers were reduced to 5 percent in early 1942, and again in

December of that year, down to 4 percent.[92] Combined with the company's very high effective tax rate under the EPT rules, this arrangement ensured that Boeing's profit margin on sales during World War II was only about 1 percent.

Some contractors resisted the fee reductions. When the AAF informed Douglas Aircraft in 1942 that its CPFF contracts would need to have fixed fees of 5 percent, instead of 6 percent, the company's executives balked. Indeed, Donald Douglas and his colleagues protested so strenuously, before eventually giving in, that the AAF considered issuing a mandatory production order.[93] Another executive who disliked the cuts in fees was W. Stuart Symington, Jr., future secretary of the Air Force. In 1940–41, as head of Emerson Electric in St. Louis, Symington helped the firm win large contracts for bomber gun turrets. Just after Pearl Harbor, Symington boasted to AAF procurement officers at Wright Field that his company would take any type of additional contract, "so long as I don't lose money on it." But in September 1942, when the AAF announced that Emerson Electric's CPFF contract fees would drop to 4 percent, Symington claimed that this would prevent the company from accumulating enough cash to pay taxes and prepare for reconversion. In 1944, after some AAF officers suggested to him that even a 4 percent pretax margin on sales might still be "excessive," Symington could not contain his frustration. "The matter is out of hand," he told authorities at Wright Field.[94]

Another contractor that faced steady War Department pressure on prices was Du Pont, the leading operator of the new GOCO explosives plants. Under the terms of the initial agreement for the big new smokeless powder facility in Indiana, the War Department agreed to pay Du Pont half a million dollars to oversee its design and construction; the company would also receive a fee of 1.75 cents per pound of smokeless powder produced, which amounted to 5 percent of projected production costs.[95] This initial deal was considerably less generous than the one negotiated for the Tennessee plant by the British government, which paid Du Pont nearly $5 million in fees by the end of September 1941.[96] As the war progressed, the War Department pushed Du Pont to accept lower fees. In spring 1942, Du Pont agreed to reduce its Indiana Ordnance Works operating fee from 1.75 cents to 1.5 cents per pound, and then to 1.25 cents per pound. It negotiated similar reductions in fees at the other larger GOCO explosives plants that it operated, including the Tennessee plant (which had since been taken over from the British by the United States) and a newer facility in Alabama.[97]

As the Ordnance Department's leading supplier of explosives, Du Pont had a working relationship with military authorities that was generally good. But their close ties did not prevent the two sides from squabbling over fees. They did so repeatedly in 1941, in the initial negotiations over the new Alabama plant and over the size of overhead fees at the Indiana plant. The pressure from military officers annoyed Du Pont executives, who would calculate that they were actually taking small losses on GOCO plant overhead in 1942. Tensions continued into the last part of the war, even after Du Pont agreed to serve as the lead contractor for the giant plutonium plant in Hanford, Washington, on a zero-fee basis. In March 1944, the Ordnance Department informed Du Pont that it planned to pay the company $6.5 million in fees for the May 1944–April 1945 year, for its work at the GOCO conventional explosives plants. This would represent a more than 30 percent reduction in the fees paid the previous year, when Du Pont earned $9.5 million. The Ordnance Department explained that the cuts were justified because of recent price reductions negotiated with Hercules Powder, another top plant operator, and because some members of Congress were complaining that Du Pont's profits were too high. In response, Du Pont executives protested that the fee cut was "entirely out of line" and that the company was effectively "being penalized for efficiency." But in the end, Du Pont agreed to reset its operating fee at $0.009 per pound for smokeless powder—about half the fee that it had received under the initial Indiana plant contract.[98]

Similar price-cutting efforts were made by the Navy Department. In 1942, the Navy established a special "Negotiation Section," which became housed in a new Office of Procurement and Material, based in Philadelphia. By March 1943, this office employed twenty-three full-time contract negotiators, many of whom were lawyers or experienced business executives.[99] According to their own estimates, the Navy negotiators typically reduced the prices offered by contractors by about 5 percent, thereby saving the government tens of millions of dollars a year.[100] One member of the Navy team was Morgan Adams, a Great War veteran who had become a successful banker in Los Angeles. During the first quarter of 1944 alone, Adams estimated, his tough negotiations had saved the Navy $31 million. One of the biggest of the contracts was an order for twenty-four LSTs, for which Bethlehem Steel wanted to charge $1,575,000 apiece. But Adams bargained Bethlehem down to $1,350,000 per unit, creating a nominal savings on this one deal of over $5 million.[101] One of Adams's colleagues was Mark E.

Andrews, a forty-year-old lawyer and businessman from Houston. In late 1944, Andrews worked on negotiations with the New York Shipbuilding Company for two new aircraft carriers. In the first meeting, the company came in asking $27.8 million for each carrier; Andrews and his Navy team offered $24.5 million. After two more meetings, the two sides agreed to a price of $26.5 million, along with a redetermination clause that allowed for price adjustments to be made later, once actual construction costs were better known.[102]

As the records of these negotiations suggest, the Navy and War Departments' top procurement officers assumed that they needed to question the prices quoted by their contractors. Typical was the experience of executives from the Yellow Truck Company (controlled by GM) who sat down with Ordnance Department officers in July 1942 to discuss a large order for Army trucks. Yellow Truck's president, I. B. Babcock, opened these negotiations by proposing prices that would allow for a pretax profit margin of 5.6 percent. After Ordnance Department officers replied that this was far too high, the two sides settled on a figure of 4 percent. High profit margins, even on smaller orders, were deemed unacceptable. In February 1943, the Narragansett Machine Company asked the Ordnance Department to provide it an allowance for profits, on a recently canceled contract, that appeared to amount to over 27 percent of its costs. This caused the chief of the Detroit Ordnance District, General Quinton, to speak up. "That's not the proper profit," Quinton insisted. "That's an unallowable profit," he said. "I think 6 percent is a big profit, myself."[103]

Starting in 1942, the military began to apply an additional layer of profit control to its suppliers: contract "renegotiation." Created by a new statute, renegotiation involved the lowering of already-negotiated contract prices, if it was determined that any profits earned under those agreements seemed "excessive." By war's end, the government's renegotiators forced contractors to return $10 billion worth of "excessive" gross earnings. After accounting for sums that would have been confiscated in any case by the EPT, this amounted to a net recovery of nearly $4 billion—about twice the cost of the atomic bomb program. In the eyes of many business leaders, renegotiation represented a form of profit control that seemed more intrusive and harsher than anything that had come before. Particularly for executives at smaller and midsize manufacturing firms, which were hard hit by profit controls, renegotiation seemed to go too far. So they launched a major campaign to have it revoked. Alienated by what they regarded as excessive profit control, many important contractors responded by openly resisting the authority of the wartime state.[104]

Statutory renegotiation was created in April 1942, amid widespread calls for strict limits on profiteering. In February, the Supreme Court had issued a decision in a long-litigated case involving allowable profits on some of the Great War contracts of Bethlehem Steel, one of the nation's leading munitions suppliers. Finding in favor of the company, the Supreme Court suggested that if the government wanted to regulate war profits more severely, Congress needed to pass appropriate legislation. Soon after, the House Naval Affairs Committee used a series of hearings to publicize its investigation of recent war profits. Some of these, committee chairman Carl Vinson (D-GA) argued, were far too high. Of all the companies investigated by the Vinson committee, the one that emerged as the most controversial was Jack & Heintz, Inc. of Cleveland, the recently founded, fast-growing producer of aircraft engine starters. In 1941, Jack & Heintz had paid its executives and employees nearly $1 million in bonuses. Especially shocking to the congressmen and members of the press was the revelation that the company president's secretary, Adeline R. Bowman, had received nearly $40,000 in compensation. These revelations, publicized in March 1942, fanned the flames of antiprofiteering activism in the press and in Congress, where legislators worked quickly to create new controls.[105]

The solution they chose—renegotiation—was, in effect, a compulsory version of something that was already being practiced voluntarily by a few companies. Nearly a year and a half earlier, in October 1940, Eastman Kodak had promised the War Department that it would voluntarily refund any profits that exceeded 10 percent of its costs.[106] During the early weeks of 1942, the declarations of voluntary refunds multiplied. At Douglas Aircraft, the board of directors resolved in February to return to the government any "unusual or excessive profits . . . as an evidence of its good faith with the Government, and in the establishment of good public relations with the Government." In late March, United Aircraft volunteered to adjust its contract prices to ensure that the company's after-tax profits in 1942 would be $15 million, the same as they had been the previous year. Other leading contractors that made similar promises included GM, Sperry, North American Aviation, and Continental Motors.[107]

Such voluntary price reductions were not enough for members of Congress, who created a new system of compulsory refunds: statutory renegotiation. Congress chose this approach as an alternative to flat percentage limits, such as the 10 percent cap on profit-cost ratios that had been applied to Navy contractors in the later 1930s, by the Vinson-Trammell Act, or the proposed 6 percent wartime cap on ratios of profits to invested capital, proposed by Treasury Secretary Morgenthau in autumn 1941. Those flat-percentage schemes had been opposed by business leaders, the War and Navy Departments, and the press, for being insufficiently sensitive to the vast differences among industries and firms.[108] A more flexible solution was offered by the renegotiation statute, which was part of legislation signed by President Roosevelt on 28 April 1942. It required the War and Navy Departments and the USMC to recover any "excessive profits" made by companies on future orders worth $100,000 or more, as well as on contracts that were not yet complete. Exactly what this would mean in practice was unclear because the law failed to define "excessive profits."

During the spring and summer of 1942, the War and Navy Departments each moved quickly to create a new national-level "price adjustment board," which would formulate policy. These central authorities would oversee the activities of dozens of local price adjustment boards, housed in district-level procurement offices like the Ordnance Department's regional districts and the regional offices of the AAF Materiel Command. By summer 1942, as the War and Navy Departments recruited hundreds of accountants, lawyers, and businesspeople to staff these new boards, some basic renegotiation policies were already emerging. Each company's case would be understood as unique; renegotiators would weigh several factors, including technical contributions to the war, levels of private and public plant investment, and sales volume. There were also some general rules of thumb. Early on, the price adjustment boards determined that no company should expect to retain dollar profits in 1942 higher than the ones earned in 1941, even though most would have a higher volume of sales. By February 1943, when renegotiation was well under way, the War and Navy Departments stated publicly that most companies should expect to make profit margins on sales only about half or a third of the ones that they had made in peacetime. The typical company could expect renegotiators to adjust its contract prices so that its pretax profit margin on sales would fall between 5 percent and 10 percent.[109] Assuming that the EPT pushed the company's effective tax rate up to 60 percent (a typical effective rate), this would mean that its after-renegotiation, after-tax margins (again on sales) would be between 2 percent and 4 percent.

Many business leaders disliked renegotiation, for a variety of reasons. One of these, naturally, was that it represented an additional limit on profits, which were already being controlled by original contract negotiations and the EPT. Renegotiation introduced new uncertainties for companies, which now had to await the end of their settlements before they had any clear idea of how much profit could be declared for 1942, or any future wartime year. Equally important, renegotiation imposed yet another paperwork burden—more red tape. As they prepared for renegotiation, many companies provided the military price adjustment boards with thick bound volumes describing their finances and contributions to the war effort.[110] Many business leaders claimed that in order to comply with the demands of renegotiation, they had to create new legal and accounting departments. This burden was especially irritating to executives at smaller companies, which started the war with limited clerical capacities and limited knowledge of how to deal with government agencies.[111]

Once business leaders realized the implications of the renegotiation activities being launched by the War and Navy Departments, many of them mobilized to demand that Congress modify or eliminate the statute. Among those calling for the repeal of renegotiation were the Chamber of Commerce and the NAM, the nation's two biggest business associations; and the *Wall Street Journal*. Repeal was favored openly by executives from some of the nation's leading military contractors, including Newport News Ship, GE, Westinghouse, and Bendix Aviation. At Du Pont, whose top executives avoided public comment on the matter, one vice president complained to his colleagues that the statute was "an absurdity and a monstrosity."[112]

The most outspoken critics of renegotiation were executives from independent midsize companies, rather than the nation's largest industrial corporations. These leaders were often less familiar with government agencies, and more fiercely independent, than their counterparts at the biggest corporations. They were disgusted with the settlements proposed by military renegotiators, who seemed to them to be more interested in confiscating dollars than in winning the war. The president of the Northern Pump Company, John B. Hawley, was the subject of one of the earliest major renegotiation actions. In 1941, when his fast-expanding, Army-Navy "E"-award-winning Minneapolis company became a major supplier of gun mounts for navy ships, Hawley received $448,000 in pretax compensation, which put him among the country's highest-paid executives. In June 1942, Hawley and his colleagues met with a team of sixteen Navy renegotiators,

who told Northern Pump officials that they must return $9 million of their
pretax profits for 1942. (This amounted to a net refund of $2.3 million,
beyond what would have been taken by taxes.) After the meeting, Hawley
flooded Congress with protests of the "dictatorship" represented by renegotiation and encouraged his fellow business leaders to do the same.

Over the months that followed, Hawley gained many allies. One was
Bill Jack, president of Jack & Heintz, the Cleveland-area company whose
big bonus payments in 1941 helped inspire Congress to pass renegotiation
in the first place. Another, also from Cleveland, was James F. Lincoln, head
of Lincoln Electric, the nation's leading independent manufacturer of welding equipment. After the Navy told Lincoln that his company must return
nearly $3.3 million of its $5.9 million in pretax profits on its 1942 military
sales, Lincoln publicly denounced renegotiation as "bureaucratic terror-
ism" and initiated a lawsuit that challenged its constitutionality. Lincoln
was joined by Willard F. Rockwell, chairman of Timken-Detroit Axle, who
had been outraged by the War Department's ruling that his company must
return $12.5 million of its $16.5 million in 1942 pretax profits. In December
1943, Rockwell, calling on members of Congress to repeal the statute, told
them that the War Department renegotiators dealing with his company had
been "arbitrary," "arrogant," "ignorant," "stubborn," and "stupid."[113]

Rockwell and his peers were ultimately outflanked by Pentagon officials,
led by undersecretaries Patterson and Forrestal, who succeeded in the winter of 1943–44 in persuading many influential newspaper columnists, along
with legislators, to oppose the immediate repeal of renegotiation. In February 1944, Congress made only minor changes to the statute. In this case,
there had been just enough support for regulation among pro-business
moderates, in the Pentagon and the private sector, to win the day. These
moderates claimed that even the appearance of profiteering might have
undesirable political effects, comparable with the more radical movements
that had followed the Great War. Such pragmatic calculations overlapped
with a more visceral discomfort with the stark inequalities that accompanied modern warfare. As Senator Harry Truman explained in January 1944,
as he defended renegotiation, "I don't think we should allow the creation
of mushroom war millionaires as happened in 1917 and 1918, while our
young men are being killed on the field of battle for fifty dollars a
month."[114]

Congress's decision to reauthorize renegotiation disappointed many
business leaders, especially the executives of midsize companies. One of

these was Edward G. Budd, president of Edward G. Budd Manufacturing of Philadelphia, a leading independent manufacturer of railcars and auto bodies that had become a major war contractor. Navy renegotiators had reduced the Budd Company's after-tax profits for 1943 to just $1.3 million, barely over 1 percent of its $115 million in sales. This paltry sum, Budd complained to Senator Truman, not only left the company unable to pay any dividends to stockholders but also had caused its managers "difficulty in meeting their expenses." Furthermore, Budd argued, the military price adjusters' boasts about the large refunds that they collected "produces a feeling of bitterness which has swept over this country among manufacturers especially among the smaller ones."[115]

The continuing "bitterness" of many business leaders over renegotiation was reflected in widespread refusals among contractors, during the latter part of the war, to compromise with military price adjusters. The most dramatic case involved Lord Manufacturing, a smaller enterprise that had grown in wartime thanks to military demand for its vibration-dampening mounts for delicate aircraft instruments. In October 1944, following a two-year struggle over prices and profits, the Navy seized the company's plants (and quickly brought in personnel from GE to operate them).[116] This was a unique case, but even when tensions over renegotiation remained below the boiling point, many contractors made their opposition clear. As late as February 1945, executives from the A. O. Smith Company, a top manufacturer of bombs, told Ordnance Department officers that they might not take on any new contracts because they were dissatisfied with renegotiation.[117] Their sentiments were shared by other business leaders, hundreds of whom simply refused to sign the refund agreements drawn up by price adjusters. In the end, Patterson, Forrestal, and USMC officials issued nearly 1,400 "unilateral determinations," which were used only as a last resort, after months of discussions between firms and the government. (If a company ignored a unilateral order, the government could simply seize the funds by deducting them from contract payments.)

Even as business leaders continued to resist renegotiation, they faced a redoubled effort by military procurement officers to bring down original contract prices. By the latter part of the war, procurement officers were building regular price adjustments into their orders from contractors. They also experimented with new forms of contracts, designed to create incentives to bring down costs. Immediately after Pearl Harbor, by some accounts, the military procurement bureaus had been "price takers," who were scrambling to place giant new orders without enough knowledge of costs to negotiate good contracts.[118] This characterization probably does not give them enough credit for their early achievements. But certainly by 1944, having accumulated a great deal of knowledge about the costs of munitions production, procurement officers were more confidently fine-tuning their price and profit control work.

Shipbuilders were among the contractors who experienced the most substantial shifts in procurement practices, as Navy Department and USMC officials worked during the latter part of the war to devise sharper contracting instruments. All the procurement agencies faced resistance from contractors when, in response to pressures from Congress, they sought to replace CPFF contracts with deals designed to create more incentives for cost-cutting.[119] In this enterprise, the War Department made relatively little headway; but the Navy carried out significant reforms. Out of $31.2 billion worth of contracts awarded by the Navy in 1940–44, CPFF orders accounted for nearly 42 percent of the total amount. But by the second half of 1944, the fraction of current orders using CPFF agreements had dropped to under 18 percent.[120]

In many cases, the Navy's preferred substitutes for the CPFF orders were not simple fixed-price agreements but sophisticated target-price, incentive contracts. In these deals, the Navy and the company began by estimating the likely final per-unit price, including a modest profit allowance. If the company managed to deliver the goods at lower prices, it would be rewarded with a higher profit margin.[121] The first major Navy order to use this sort of agreement seems to have been a contract for destroyers with Consolidated Steel, negotiated in June 1943.[122] By spring 1944, the Navy was starting to use these contracts more widely, including in its orders for fighter aircraft.[123]

Tinkering with the basic target-price method, Navy contract negotiator Morgan Adams created what he called a "fixed price limited incentive profit contract to be based on returned costs of contractor." Adams's version used a maximum price, at which the contractor would be allowed no profit, and above which he would take a loss. But the sliding scale also provided for profit margins as high as 14 percent, if contractors delivered at prices that the Navy estimated as the lowest that could possibly be reached.[124] Adams's scheme was soon used in real orders, including a May 1944 deal with the Dravo Corporation, which, until recently, had been resisting Navy efforts to convert its CPFF contracts. Now, in a new order for ninety more LSTs,

Dravo officials agreed to a contract with a maximum per-ship cost of $1.35 million. If the company could deliver the ships for $1.2 million a unit, which was the initial target price, it would receive a profit of 5.5 percent. As it turned out, Dravo delivered the LSTs for about $1.1 million apiece, which provided it a pretax profit of about 7 percent. Given that the company's pretax margins on sales had dropped from 12 percent in 1942 to just 6 percent in 1943, company officials probably regarded this as a reasonable outcome.[125]

Incentive contracts were also favored by the USMC, which handled the procurement of merchant ships. In its dealings with builders of the Liberty ships, the USMC contracts reimbursed all approved costs but reserved the most generous fees for contractors able to use the fewest man-hours and make the speediest deliveries. Depending on a contractor's performance in these areas, the preliminary "base fee" of $110,000 a ship (about 6 percent of average costs in 1941) could rise to as high as $140,000, or as low as $60,000. In practice, the fees awarded could vary widely, with Bethlehem-Fairfield and the Kaiser yards earning close to the maximum on some large orders, and Todd-Houston and others making close to the minimum. But the discrepancies were reduced by taxes and renegotiation, as well as by reforms to the contracts. Like the War and Navy Departments, the USMC cut fees significantly over the course of the war. In December 1942, they were halved, so that the standard fee declined to $55,000 a ship. In April 1943, the fees were cut again, by an additional 20 percent.[126]

Incentive contracts were not used as widely by the War Department. However, starting in 1943, War Department contracting officers began to exert even greater control over contractors' prices, by demanding that they be reset, in light of new information about actual costs, every three or six months. In 1944, the War Department procurement agencies began to use more "company pricing" arrangements, in which the repricing was done by reviewing all of a firm's contracts, instead of just one at a time. As they did this price control work, contracting officers sought what they called "fair and reasonable" prices, which included an allowance for profit. But any "excessive profits" needed to be eliminated by the regular repricing. So in effect, by 1944–45, renegotiation was being carried out by two bodies within any given regional military procurement agency: by contracting officers, as well as by the price adjustment teams. For some contractors, this price control on the front end could actually be preferable to renegotiation alone because it provided them with a more accurate day-to-day understanding of the profits that they would be allowed to retain, instead of the much higher uncertainties that came from waiting for the government's determination of a single annual refund.[127]

The Question of Net Results

At a conference in November 1943, Ordnance Department procurement officers reminded themselves of a maxim that they had been following for months: "the job is to introduce synthetically into war procurement, so far as we practically can, the peace-time force of competition."[128] Without the benefit of such competition, the wartime state tried to find ways to push down prices, as well as the fractions of prices that represented profits. As we have seen, the procurement agencies seem to have pursued this work with creativity and energy. From the point of view of most contractors, prices and profits seemed to be tightly regulated. They were controlled by a variety of mechanisms, including original contract negotiations, high taxes, statutory renegotiation, and contract reforms and adjustments that attempted to provide more incentives for contractors to lower their costs and prices. But how successful were these measures, in the end?

Certainly, the procurement agencies succeeded in their goal of achieving significant reductions in prices. As contractors' unit costs dropped—thanks to economies of scale, improving production techniques, or other factors—they were forced to offer lower prices to the government. As its orders multiplied after 1941, Boeing adopted what company president Philip Johnson called "mass production methods," which brought down unit costs on the B-17. By 1943–44, when output peaked at about sixteen planes a day, Boeing was selling a superior version of the B-17 for a third less than it had charged in 1941.[129] The AAF received similar reductions from North American Aviation, which, by summer 1944, was supplying its P-51 "Mustang" fighters—the speedy protectors of Allied bomber fleets in Europe—for $24,000 per unit, about 20 percent lower than the prices used the previous year.[130] Another top-notch fighter plane, Grumman's F6F "Hellcat," introduced in 1942, provided the U.S. Navy with air superiority in the Pacific. Initially, each Hellcat cost the Navy nearly $54,000. But most of the Hellcats were delivered in 1944, at a per-plane price of $39,100.[131]

The Navy and the USMC also received significant price reductions from the shipyards, where labor productivity improved dramatically over time.

By the end of 1943, the Liberty shipyards were taking only about one month to complete each of the merchant vessels, compared with an average of six months at the beginning of the war.[132] The most efficient Liberty yards, including North Carolina Ship and Oregon Ship, produced the basic vessels (not including government-furnished engines and other installed equipment) for under $800,000 apiece, less than half the price that the USMC had paid in early 1941.[133] On the Navy side, contractors also achieved large gains in labor productivity. But by the end of 1943, the Consolidated Steel yard in Texas had reduced the number of man-hours used on each DE to 560,000, down from a million. This allowed Consolidated to supply DEs for $1.8 million per vessel—about half of what the Navy was prepared to pay a year and a half earlier. Over the same period, at Bath Iron Works, a top builder of destroyers, man-hours per ship declined from about 1.7 million to 1.0 million. By December 1943, Bath was selling its destroyers for $5.9 million apiece, down from the $7.0 million contract price that it had received just six months earlier.[134]

Price reductions alone, of course, did not necessarily translate into tight profit control. If contractors' costs dropped faster than the prices that they renegotiated with the War and Navy Departments, they would see profits rise, not fall. Did this happen? According to many critics on the political left, including labor leaders and progressive journalists, business profits grew in wartime to unconscionable levels. One of the more restrained purveyors of this point of view was Hellen Fuller of the *New Republic*, who wrote in September 1943 that corporate "fat cats" were getting rich on war orders. Drawing on recent government reports, Fuller reported that corporations' gross income had grown from $19 billion in 1942 to $23 billion in 1943. After taxes, the profits were $8.5 billion and $7.5 billion, respectively. This was on par with the previous record year for American corporate profits, 1929, when after-tax earnings had been $8.1 billion.[135]

The allegations of excessive wartime profit-taking upset business leaders, who regarded profit controls as more than adequate. In October 1942, after OPA chief Leon Henderson made speeches suggesting that corporate profits had quadrupled since the start of the war, the NAM used pamphlets and press releases to try to set the record straight. While it was true that gross (pretax) profits in 1942 were double what they had been in 1939, the NAM explained, net profits had increased only 11 percent over that period, thanks to high taxes. And after-tax earnings for 1942 were actually lower than they had been in 1941, even though sales were considerably higher.[136]

These explanations continued throughout the war. After the left-leaning New York City newspaper *PM* reported in January 1943 that GM had made "huge profits" in 1942, the company responded by informing the press and government price adjusters that its profits were lower than they had been before the war.[137] In 1944, the NAM issued a new pamphlet that pointed out that business profit margins had dropped significantly since Pearl Harbor. "No 'war millionaires' are being made in anything like 1917 quantities," it assured its readers. Aggregate corporate profit margins during the Great War had been over 9 percent, the NAM noted; but during World War II, they were under 3 percent of gross revenues.[138] Such numbers, *Forbes* magazine claimed in early 1945, showed that the alleged "huge war profits" were simply "mythical."[139]

Most business executives believed sincerely that the American public, misled by the unions and a handful of leftist journalists, had little sense of how thoroughly their profits were being regulated. "[T]he profit margin of today is a matter of public policy," declared GM chairman Alfred P. Sloan, Jr., in 1942, "rather than a measure of competitive position and of other factors that normally determine the returns on the Corporation's operations."[140] GM executives, proud of their role as the nation's top producer of munitions, believed that they and their more than 400,000 employees were making huge contributions to the war effort, while keeping profits low. In 1942, the GM board, in recognition of the company's lower profits, had cut stock dividends nearly in half, from $3.75 to $2.00 a share.[141] It was not only executives from the largest corporations who shared this perspective. Ralph W. Carney was an executive with the Coleman Camp & Stove Company, based in Wichita. In 1944, in a speech to fellow businessmen, he claimed that his company had actually lost money the previous year on an ammunition contract. "You read of nothing but profits in the papers," Carney complained, when in truth, taxes were sky-high and margins low. "The businessman is just a middleman for money today," said Carney.[142]

As the divergent views of business leaders and progressive critics suggest, there will never be any fully satisfactory answer as to whether wartime profit controls were adequate because everything depended (and depends) on expectations and metrics. For those who believed that wartime profits should be zero, the actual earnings of American companies seemed far too high. For those who figured that businesses should be able to earn profits at rates comparable with the ones that they had enjoyed before the war, the earnings of most companies seemed modest. But we should not conclude that everything was in the eye of the beholder: we have evidence about aggregate and company-level profits in the World War II era, which allows us to make specific observations, even if they cannot settle debates about whether profits were too high.

For American business as a whole, the World War II years saw significant increases in sales volume and dollar profits, which tracked closely with the broader wartime growth of the national economy. From 1939 to 1944, the gross nominal sales of all U.S. corporations doubled, rising from $130 billion to $259 billion. Over the same period, net (after-tax) nominal profits also roughly doubled, from $6.0 billion to $11.7 billion.[143] Because of inflation, which reduced the value of a dollar by about 25 percent between 1939 and 1944, the nominal sales and profits in 1944 were really about 75 percent higher than those in 1939. And the ratio of corporate profits to GDP declined slightly over the same period, from about 6.5 percent to about 5.3 percent. (The most important reason for this was that wage increases outpaced the rise in profits.)[144] So any discussion of business profits during World War II needs to recognize that the early 1940s was a time of economic expansion, albeit an expansion that came largely from the increased output of weapons.[145]

Leading military contractors saw a greater rise in sales volume, as a whole, than did the average American company. The increases in sales were especially dramatic among companies in the aircraft industry, where many firms went from midsize to giant. However, during the all-out mobilization period of 1942–45, aggregate dollar profits of the top military contractors remained flat, in comparison with their prewar levels. This meant that during those years, the leading military contractors' profit margins (the ratio of net earnings to sales) dipped significantly. So in comparison with the "average" American company, which was less fully devoted to war production, the "average" top military contractor saw somewhat less wartime growth in nominal dollar earnings and significantly lower margins.[146] This is easy to see in the following graphs, which present financial data from twenty-seven leading prime contractors (see Figure 4 and Figure 5). Together, these companies experienced the 1942–45 period as one of very large sales, modest nominal dollar profits, and low margins. During the period of all-out mobilization, their aggregate nominal profits dropped well below what they had been during the defense period of 1940–41; their margins on sales dropped to about 3 percent, on average.

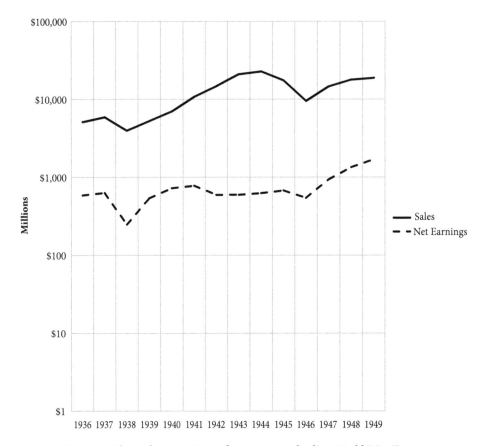

Figure 4. Sales and net earnings of twenty-seven leading World War II contractors, 1936–49 (log scale). *Moody's Manual of Investments, American and Foreign: Industrial Securities* (New York, 1939–50); corporate annual reports. The twenty-seven companies in the "top contractors" group used for Figures 4 and 5 were selected by combining two lists: the operators of the top thirty-five war plants by dollar value of prime contracts, and the operators of the top thirty-five war plants by dollar value of wartime investment in plant. This resulted in a group of thirty-two companies, five of which were omitted from the group because of a lack of good financial data. These five are Ford, Alcoa, Kaiser/Permanente Metals, Western Cartridge/Olin Industries, and Cities Service Corp. The twenty-seven companies included in the group, in order of 1944 sales volume, are General Motors, U.S. Steel, Bethlehem Steel, Curtiss-Wright, General Electric, Chrysler, Douglas, Consolidated-Vultee, Western Electric, United Aircraft, North American Aviation, Du Pont, Lockheed, Boeing, Martin, Republic Steel, Packard, Sperry, Studebaker, Anaconda Copper, Grumman, Eastman Kodak, New York Ship, Newport News Ship, Dow, Hercules Powder, and Atlas Powder.

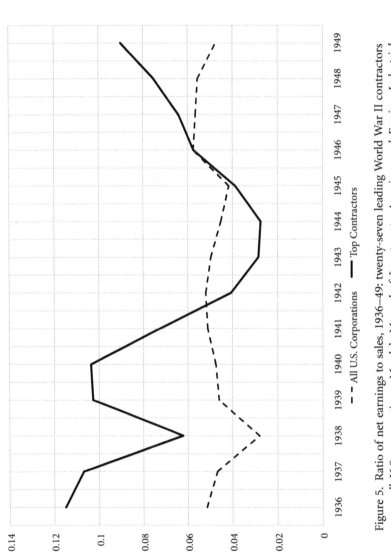

Figure 5. Ratio of net earnings to sales, 1936–49: twenty-seven leading World War II contractors versus all U.S. corporations. *Moody's Manual of Investments, American and Foreign: Industrial Securities* (New York, 1939–50); corporate annual reports; national aggregate data from *Historical Statistics of the United States, Colonial Times to 1957* (Washington, DC: U.S. Department of Commerce, 1960), 580. For methodology, please see the caption to Figure 4.

For the top prime contractors that had already been giant industrial corporations in the 1930s, the wartime experience was one of moderate increases in sales, relatively little change in dollar profits, and moderate drops in margins. Three of the nation's top prime contractors—Chrysler, GM, and Du Pont—actually recorded lower net earnings during the war years than they had enjoyed in the late 1930s. GE and Eastman Kodak saw no significant increase in net earnings, despite large increases in their sales. Several other top contractors, including the largest steel and mining companies, along with Hercules Powder and Atlas Powder, enjoyed only relatively small increases in after-tax earnings. So the leaders of these companies had little trouble convincing themselves that they had refrained from taking excessive war profits.

Even Du Pont, which enjoyed exceptionally high after-tax margins on sales in 1942–45 (thanks to tax and renegotiation policies that favored firms that had done well in the late 1930s), did not see any reason to apologize for its financial experience. Although Du Pont's after-tax profit margins on sales during the war years were about 12 percent—much higher than those of most contractors—they were far lower than before the war, when the margins were closer to 30 percent. Of course, much of this drop came from the near-doubling of the company's sales volume, thanks to its operation of several giant government-owned explosives plants. But even the company's return on its own private investment dropped during the war years, from about 9 percent to 6 percent.[147] Meanwhile, at other companies that had entered the war as highly profitable giants, such as GM, GE, and Westinghouse, after-tax margins on sales dropped to about 3 percent or 4 percent.[148] Thanks to higher sales, dollar earnings for this group remained relatively steady.

More specialized military contractors, which grew suddenly in wartime, had a different experience. Typically, these companies saw extraordinary increases in sales volume and a significant rise in dollar profits. But they, too, could plausibly claim not to be profiteers because their margins were so low. This distinction was evident even in the comparative experiences of the nation's two largest steel companies. The larger of these, U.S. Steel, participated in the modest wartime expansion of the steel industry; it saw its sales double, thanks to heavy demand from the construction industry, shipbuilders, and munitions makers. But at Bethlehem Steel, which served both as a big steelmaker and as a top builder of warships, the war years brought a much bigger spike in its sales volume, which came close to that of its rival. The differences between the two companies were appreciated by military renegotiators, as well as by the impersonal formulas of the EPT.[149] Bethlehem, a true military contractor, saw its margins on sales for 1942–45 kept at about 2 percent. U.S. Steel, whose wartime growth was more modest and which dealt less directly with the military, kept more than 3 percent. This meant that U.S. Steel, which was also allowed a slightly higher margin on invested capital, booked over $100 million more in wartime profits than did Bethlehem, despite their comparable sales volumes.

Bethlehem's financial experience was typical of the leading military contractors, whose expanding sales and dollar profits were accompanied by low margins. In the aircraft industry, companies that had only employed a few hundred people before the war suddenly became giant corporations, with tens of thousands of employees and hundreds of millions of dollars in sales. Most of these firms—including Lockheed, Boeing, Grumman, and Douglas—made far more in profits than they had ever seen before, but their after-tax margins on sales were kept well under 2 percent. The same was true of the second-tier auto companies that made aero engines, including Packard and Studebaker; it also applied to many smaller "war babies" in the aircraft industry. Among the shipbuilders, the margins were only slightly higher.[150] At Reynolds Metals, which had used government loans to become the nation's only producer of aluminum besides Alcoa, dollar profits in 1942–44 averaged less than $3 million a year, or about 2 percent of sales. From the point of view of Richard S. Reynolds, Sr., who struggled throughout the war to get the government to lower the interest rate on his loans from 4 percent to 3 percent, the profits did not seem excessive, nor were they sufficient to allow him to position his company to compete with Alcoa after the war.[151]

The contrasting experiences of the specialized military contractors, on the one hand, and the better-established industrial giants, on the other, are easy to see at a glance. Consider the experiences of four top munitions suppliers, each of which served as the top contractor in its field: Chrysler (tanks), Du Pont (explosives), Boeing (heavy bombers), and Newport News Ship (aircraft carriers). Two of these companies, Chrysler and Du Pont, were world-class industrial giants before 1939. In 1942–45, their dollar earnings were lower than they had been before the war, even though their sales had increased considerably. But they were still able to accumulate tens of millions of dollars in the early 1940s. This contrasted with the experience of Boeing and Newport News, whose sales jumped during the war; in

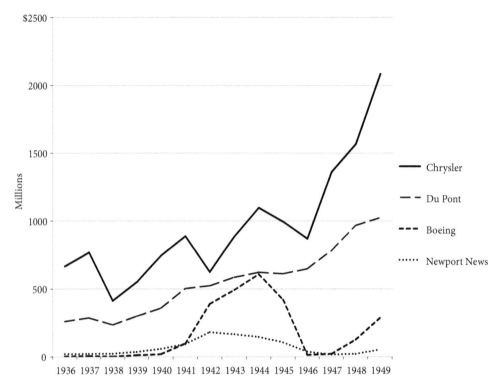

Figure 6. Representative top industrial corporations versus specialty military contractors: sales, 1936–49. *Moody's Manual of Investments, American and Foreign: Industrial Securities* (New York, 1939–50); corporate annual reports.

Boeing's case, the growth was so great that by 1944, sales volume was equal to that of Du Pont. However, neither Boeing nor Newport News ever came close to retaining the sort of profits that would impress the leaders of Du Pont, Chrysler, and other well-established corporations (see Figure 6 and Figure 7). Annual profits for the specialty military contractors—not just Boeing and Newport News but also Lockheed, Sperry, New York Ship, and many other top munitions makers—remained well below $10 million a year.

For the specialized military contractors, this was far more than they had seen over the previous two decades; it allowed most of them to come out of the war free of debt, along with money in the bank.[152] When the business

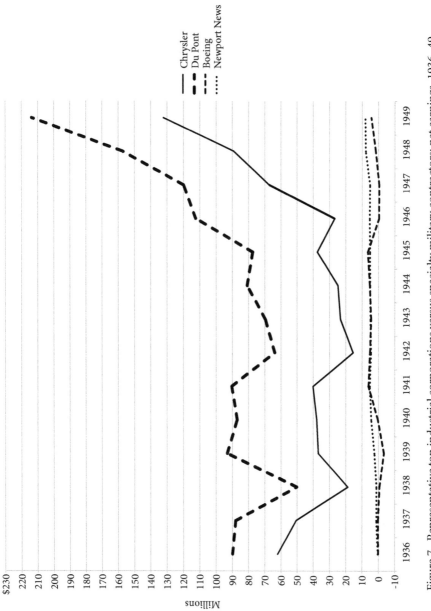

Figure 7. Representative top industrial corporations versus specialty military contractors: net earnings, 1936–49. *Moody's Manual of Investments, American and Foreign: Industrial Securities* (New York, 1939–50); corporate annual reports.

leaders' worst fears about a sharp postwar recession failed to materialize and when the government offered additional assistance in the form of tax refunds, that set-aside cash—much of which had been designated by corporate executives as reconversion "reserves"—began to be reclassified as profit. By war's end, the combined reserves of a dozen top companies in the aircraft industry reached over $100 million. By mid-1946, with the American economy doing much better than many people had expected, aircraft industry experts observed that "most companies will not find it necessary to use these rainy-day reserves during their reconversion period."[153] Nonetheless, the earnings of the specialized military contractors never seemed to their leaders to be terribly large, especially in comparison with the sums being retained by the big industrial corporations. Nor did the financial experience of the aircraft companies impress investors. Their stock prices failed to rise in wartime, even though their dollar profits climbed dramatically.[154]

*   *   *

In August 1947, when the Gallup polling organization asked Americans if companies had made too much profit during World War II, 73 percent said yes.[155] Given that the poll was conducted after a year of well-publicized congressional investigations into the profits of Liberty shipbuilders and Howard Hughes, the results may not be surprising. To the dismay of business leaders, the American public never did seem to appreciate how tightly their war profits had been regulated. Given that their companies retained millions of dollars in earnings, during an all-out war effort that pulled more than ten million citizens into the armed forces, this was perhaps unavoidable. But from the point of view of the executives, there was also plenty of evidence to support the notion that the controls had been sufficient. They believed that this was confirmed by the hard financial data and by the record of their personal experiences with government auditors, tax collectors, contracting officers, and price adjustment boards. Most business leaders saw the wartime state as a zealous regulator. Indeed, more than a few of them were exasperated by what they saw as excessive oversight. Their experiences, far from encouraging them to cozy up to the government in the hopes of earning easy profits, more often made business leaders more inclined to endorse a view of the war economy in which only the private sector seemed heroic.

Something similar occurred, as the following chapter will suggest, in another major field of wartime government-business interaction: labor-management relations. There, as in the case of profit control, the wartime state proved to be an intrusive regulator. The government, most business leaders believed, had been doing too much to support labor unions, since the early days of the New Deal. But the war years saw a dramatic new manifestation of government power in labor-management relations. This was the seizure—government takeover, most often by military authorities—of privately owned facilities. The record of these seizures, and of the broader wartime labor-relations story more generally, helps explain why many business leaders understood themselves not as privileged "fat cats" but as aggrieved victims of an overreaching, militarized national state.

Chapter 5

Of Strikes and Seizures

In mid-March 1945, President Roosevelt received a note from his wife, Eleanor. The First Lady was upset by reports of antiunion activity at Cocker Machine and Foundry, a textile machinery company in Gastonia, North Carolina. Her sources told her that the company was refusing to bargain with local unions affiliated with the American Federation of Labor (AFL), even after they had won a formal representation election certified by the federal government's National Labor Relations Board (NLRB). Cocker executives had reportedly pressured the local draft board to reclassify three machinists who had refused to cross picket lines during a recent strike by members of the molders' union. In other words, it appeared that company leaders were trying to get rid of pro-union employees by having them inducted into the armed forces. "This seems to me outrageous," Eleanor wrote to her husband. The First Lady suggested a response: "Why can't you take over the plant?"[1]

We might regard this suggestion—that the federal government should take over a privately owned factory because its managers were hostile to unions—as little more than the fantasy of a frustrated leftist. Sending in troops to take over a private company run by antiunion executives would surely have qualified as a truly radical act—especially in the South, where organized labor had never secured much of a foothold. So while the First Lady's ideas might have sent shivers up the spines of conservative business leaders, those executives could presumably take solace in the fact that her suggestion was too extreme even for most New Dealers, including her husband.

Or were they?

In fact, Eleanor Roosevelt's suggestion of a plant takeover in March 1945 was not so radical. Over the previous four years, the federal government had already carried out more than three dozen seizures of private enterprises. And during the year that followed FDR's death, the administration of President Harry Truman would conduct another two dozen takeovers. Nearly all these seizures were administered by the War and Navy Departments.

Although seizures were, in some sense, exceptional, they were neither rare nor peripheral. They touched many leading American companies and industries, along with several million workers. Among the prominent firms that experienced seizures in 1941–46 were a leading manufacturer of military aircraft (North American Aviation); a top warship producer (Federal Shipbuilding) that was itself a subsidiary of the world's largest steel company (U.S. Steel); a plant of the world's premier manufacturer of telecommunications equipment (Western Electric); one of the world's largest retailers (Montgomery Ward); and the refineries of two large oil companies (Humble Oil and Cities Service). In 1944, the U.S. Army took over the transit system of Philadelphia, one of America's largest cities. And between 1943 and 1946, the U.S. government seized and temporarily controlled the nation's coal mines (repeatedly); its railroads (twice); and much of the oil industry (see Figure 8).

In many of these seizures, government authorities understood themselves as intervening in response to bad behavior by workers who were engaging in unauthorized strikes that disrupted war production. In such cases, there was little or no intended censure of business leaders. However, in nearly half of the five dozen seizures undertaken in 1941–46, government officials blamed management. Occasionally, the military took over companies because their managers seemed incompetent—or corrupt. But more often, the seizures blamed on management were caused by business leaders' willingness to flout federal labor law.

In the eyes of many business leaders, the Roosevelt administration's labor policies ranked among its worst offenses. Thanks in part to the Wagner Act (1935), which set up the NLRB and provided government support for collective bargaining, union membership had more than doubled during the 1930s. By the end of the decade, there were more than eight million union members. This impressive growth continued during World War II: by 1945, more than fourteen million Americans (a third of all employees outside agriculture) belonged to unions. This would turn out to be a high-water mark for organized labor, even though union membership would not begin to recede significantly until the 1960s.

The growth of unions during World War II was not simply a natural continuation of patterns established in the 1930s. Organized labor had won

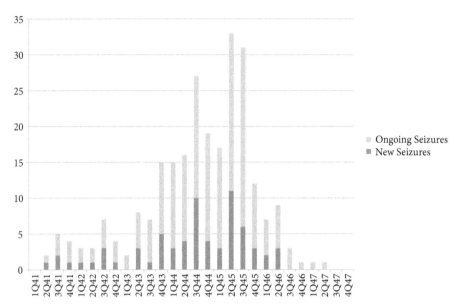

Figure 8. Seizures of war plants and other private business enterprises by the U.S. government, 1941–47. John L. Blackman, Jr., *Presidential Seizure in Labor Disputes* (Cambridge, MA: Harvard University Press, 1967), 257–78; John H. Ohly, *Industrialists in Olive Drab: The Emergency Operation of Private Industries during World War II* (Washington, DC: Center of Military History, 1999), 313–19.

dramatic victories in 1937, when the Supreme Court upheld the Wagner Act and new CIO-affiliated unions won recognition at General Motors and U.S. Steel, among other major companies. But then the movement stalled. After the impressive performance of conservatives in the 1938 congressional elections, union leaders and New Deal labor regulators found themselves on the defensive.[2] During World War II, however, government officials provided additional support for unions, just as they had during the Great War, in exchange for what they hoped would be stability and uninterrupted munitions production.[3] With good reason, then, many business leaders believed that without the war emergency—and without the wartime interventions of the federal government that pushed companies to accept "maintenance of membership" provisions and other measures favoring union growth—organized labor might have been far weaker.

In the eyes of many business leaders and conservative politicians, the government's wartime labor policies ranked as one of the most disturbing manifestations of the Roosevelt administration's abuse of executive power. That power was wielded most dramatically in the plant seizures, which became one battleground in a broader struggle over the legitimate boundaries of state authority. This struggle exposed and amplified the deep discontent in the American business community with the wartime state.

In that regard, the record of the World War II plant seizures is worth a close look because of what it suggests about politics on the home front. We already know that unions grew substantially in wartime and that the war years saw plenty of strikes, some of them ended by military takeovers. Occasionally, we even recall the government's brief spring 1944 seizure of Montgomery Ward, the giant retailing enterprise. That dramatic takeover was provoked by Ward chairman Sewell L. Avery, one of the most vocal critics of the Roosevelt administration and its labor policies.

But we need to understand that the well-publicized Ward episode was merely the tip of an iceberg of massive resistance, on the part of employers, to the wartime gains by unions. Amid an all-out war effort, more than a few business leaders decided that they would prefer to risk having the military take over their plants, rather than obey government policies that favored unionization. These hard-liners were in the minority. But they were applauded, in public and private, by large numbers of their peers. By the time Eleanor Roosevelt wrote her husband about the possibility of taking over the Cocker plant, in early 1945, employer resistance to federal labor law had become widespread, as had strikes and seizures.

This disorder was a telling indicator of the dynamics of government-business relations during World War II. Far from being content with the more militarized government that succeeded the New Deal, business leaders and their allies regarded the wartime state as especially dangerous. They resisted its unprecedented intrusions—including plant seizures—in a variety of ways, ranging from strong rhetoric to outright physical and legal defiance. In the sphere of industrial relations, as elsewhere, the effectiveness of this campaign would not be fully evident until after 1945. But it was a serious challenge, which again showed how war mobilization could amplify antistatist politics in the business community.

Defense-Sector Strikes and the Seizures of 1941

By mid-1940, when the U.S. industrial mobilization started, American business leaders were well aware of the possibility of government commandeering of private enterprise. Many were old enough to remember the seizures of Smith & Wesson and Western Union during World War I, as well as the massive government takeover of the railroads during that conflict.

During the interwar years, some business leaders had considered the prospect of future seizures. Executives at Sperry Gyroscope, one of the military's most important suppliers of aviation instruments and other high-tech military equipment, were disturbed in 1935 when one Navy officer "nonchalantly said that he felt that they would have to take over Sperry lock, stock and barrel" in the event of a new war because the company's entire production capacity would be so essential. Robert B. Lea, a Sperry vice president at the time, recalled that this remark led him and other company leaders to work with the War Department in 1938 to develop emergency expansion plans that would meet military needs but preserve private control. A year later, executives at Du Pont considered whether to formally segregate their military and civilian operations as a way of protecting themselves from unwanted government control in the event of war. In the end, the internal committee reporting on this issue downplayed the likelihood of a seizure. "The prospect of a Major General on the 9th floor of the Du Pont building," it concluded, "is, we believe, so extremely remote as to be entirely negligible."[4] Despite this conclusion, the fact that this conversation was taking place in the boardroom of one of the nation's leading industrial corporations, one week before Germany's invasion of Poland, suggests that business leaders remembered the Great War takeovers.

The seizure issue was openly discussed in Washington in the late summer of 1940, as Congress prepared to establish the first peacetime draft in the nation's history. Wendell Willkie, the Republican candidate for president, condemned an amendment that added seizure powers to the bill. According to Willkie, the measure would represent an important step in the direction of the "socialization or Sovietization" of American business. Willkie's fears were shared by Reuben H. Fleet, president of Consolidated Aircraft, one of the nation's top airframe manufacturers. Fleet announced that because of the bill's plant commandeering provisions, which might lead to the sort of nationalization of the aircraft industry that had occurred in France, his company would hold off on its planned plant expansion.[5]

In mid-September 1940, after lively debate over the seizure issue, the Democrat-controlled Congress passed the Selective Training and Service Act by comfortable majorities. According to the statute's Section 9, in the event that a company resisted filling military contracts, the government was allowed to issue a compulsory order. If a company failed to fill this order, the government could seize and run its plants; company executives were subject to criminal penalties. Congress was warning companies that they could not reject war orders, by brandishing a weighty stick. This complemented the carrot of special tax breaks for investment in war plant, provided three weeks later in the Second Revenue Act. But would the stick actually be used? Just after the draft bill was passed, Undersecretary of War Robert Patterson reassured business leaders that he did not expect to have to issue compulsory orders, because industry was already cooperating so nicely.[6]

But business leaders continued to worry about the government's seizure power and its potential threat to their autonomy. The National Association of Manufacturers (NAM) devoted one of its bulletins for company labor-relations specialists to the subject of the Great War seizures. The problem was also discussed within individual firms. In January 1941, Sun Oil president J. Howard Pew asked the advice of his lawyer, George Wharton Pepper, as he considered whether the company's Sun Shipbuilding subsidiary should sign a contract to build vessels for the Navy. Pepper advised Pew that he could ill afford to reject a Navy order. "If the contract is not accepted," wrote Pepper, "an attempt to commandeer the plant is a very real and practical possibility with some doubt on our part as to whether it could be successfully resisted." Pepper predicted that the courts would almost certainly uphold such wartime "industrial compulsion," just as they would the conscription of soldiers.[7]

By the beginning of 1941, then, business leaders anticipated that defiance of the wartime state might well result in seizure. Over the months that followed, events showed that this was indeed the case. Before the Pearl Harbor attacks in December, there were three major plant takeovers. But even before the first of those, there were several near-seizures. The context was a major wave of labor-management disputes, which made 1941 one of the most strike-ridden years of the century.

This trouble had several causes. As the economy heated up, some union leaders gambled that companies—especially those under pressure to complete military contracts—would prefer concessions to strikes. Others, anticipating that wages might be frozen if the United States entered the war, hoped to win raises beforehand. And until late June 1941, when Germany invaded the Soviet Union, at least a few radical labor leaders regarded defense-industry strikes as non-problematic, if not desirable. (After the Soviets joined the Allies, by contrast, labor leaders with communist sympathies often led the effort to prevent strikes.) Meanwhile, most American business leaders, as they continued to call for revision of the Wagner Act, worked hard to prevent further unionization of their plants.[8]

All these factors contributed to the rise in labor disputes in 1940–41 in the growing defense sector. In 1940–41, there were serious strikes at the facilities of Boeing, Alcoa, International Harvester, Remington-Rand, Bethlehem Steel, American Car & Foundry, and Mack Truck. In the defense plants alone, 1941 saw five million person-days lost because of labor disputes.[9]

The longest of the defense-industry strikes in 1940–41 was the seventy-six-day work stoppage at the main plant of Allis-Chalmers, which employed nearly ten thousand workers in Milwaukee. A major producer of electric motors and ship turbines for the Navy, Allis-Chalmers had rocky relations with United Autoworkers (UAW) Local 248, the CIO-affiliated union that had represented workers at its largest plant since 1937. The local called on the company to make the plant a union shop, in which every employee would have to be a dues-paying member of the UAW. On 21 January 1941, after Allis-Chalmers president Max Babb insisted that the company was committed to an open shop (in which workers could refuse to join the union), the workers struck.[10]

As the Allis-Chalmers strike stretched into March, it attracted a great deal of attention from industrial mobilization officials, Congress, and the press. Business leaders and their allies in Washington had the upper hand. Because Local 248 leader Harold Christoffel was known to have connections to the Communist Party, pro-business commentators could easily characterize the strike as part of a radical campaign to sabotage the defense effort. Some critics, including Senator Styles Bridges (R-NH), warned of a dangerous "Fifth Column" in the United States. Edward R. Stettinius, Jr., the U.S. Steel executive who had become a top official at the Office of Production Management (OPM), actually believed that company leaders deserved much of the blame. But when he communicated with members of Congress about the strike in late March, Stettinius warned them that "labor is out of control and the radical element is out of control and will be until you do something on the Hill." Here he was parroting Benjamin F. Fairless, president of U.S. Steel, who had used exactly the same phrases in a phone conversation with Stettinius only hours earlier.[11]

Meanwhile, executive branch officials and members of Congress began to encourage Roosevelt to seize the Allis-Chalmers plant. At the Navy Department, where officials were concerned that the strike was slowing the completion of destroyers, formal seizure plans were already being drawn up.[12] On 27 March, Navy Secretary Frank Knox, joined by OPM's William Knudsen, telegraphed Allis-Chalmers managers and union leaders to demand that the plant reopen. Although this order implied that seizure might soon follow, the company and the union ignored it; the following days saw growing crowds and violence along the picket lines in Milwaukee. The FBI reported to Roosevelt that the area around the plant was "virtually insurrection." After cabling the White House to report unruly mobs, Wisconsin's governor called out the National Guard to restore peace. Secretary of War Stimson now advised Roosevelt to seize the plant; several congressmen did the same, and prepared bills that would give the president even more extensive seizure powers than he had had under the 1940 draft law.[13] On 11 April, Roosevelt and his cabinet agreed that the government should seize the plant if the strike was not settled within seventy-two hours.[14]

Meanwhile, conditions were also deteriorating at an even larger enterprise, the Ford Motor Company. At the beginning of April, a major strike involving tens of thousands of workers started at Ford's immense River Rouge plant. In contrast with GM and Chrysler, which had recognized the UAW back in 1937, Ford had fought to remain union-free. Since summer 1940, officials in Washington had been struggling to determine how the company's flagrant defiance of the Wagner Act should affect its ability to take military contracts. In September, Interior Secretary Harold Ickes, perhaps only half in jest, had suggested to Roosevelt that he would be happy to lead a seizure of the Ford plants. By February 1941, after at least one military contract was withheld from the company because of the labor-relations issue, the prospect of a seizure at Ford was being was discussed seriously in the business press.[15]

Despite the growing pressures on him to seize the Allis-Chalmers plant and intervene at Ford, the president worked to find another solution. On 15 March, Roosevelt used a fireside chat to criticize "war profiteering," as well as "unnecessary strikes"; he called on business and labor leaders alike "to make common sacrifice for the great cause."[16] Four days later, he created a new national labor-relations authority, the National Defense

Mediation Board (NDMB). Composed of labor, industry, and "public" representatives, the NDMB quickly took up some of the nation's most pressing labor disputes. In April, the NDMB helped settle the Allis-Chalmers and Ford strikes. In a major about-face, Ford agreed to recognize the UAW. Henry Ford's reluctant capitulation was encouraged by one of his top lieutenants, Charles E. Sorensen, who suggested to his boss that the government might seize the company's plants in the name of national defense.[17]

Although the settlements at Ford and Allis-Chalmers had prevented seizures, the possibility of takeovers remained. On 27 May 1941, President Roosevelt took a step toward war, by declaring an "unlimited national emergency." In a fireside chat announcing this action, the president warned labor and business leaders that they were both expected to choose patriotism over self-interest. Immediately after this radio address, a news service for business leaders published a story entitled "Your Business Now Belongs to Uncle Sam." Businessmen should now expect "rigid control in the realm of your business activity," it explained. "Above all, the President has the power to commandeer any industry."[18]

Americans did not have to wait long for the first seizure. In early June, the War Department took over a large plant of North American Aviation (NAA), in Inglewood, California, near Los Angeles. At the time, the NAA facility, which was partly owned by the government, accounted for nearly a fifth of the nation's total output of military aircraft. In the preceding months, it had been the site of a bitter struggle between the CIO-affiliated UAW and the AFL-affiliated International Association of Machinists (IAM), which were competing across the country to represent aircraft workers.[19] When six thousand NAA workers voted in a NLRB-certified representation election in early 1941, the UAW prevailed by just seventy votes. After winning the election, the UAW local demanded wage increases. On June 4, NAA president J. H. "Dutch" Kindelberger once again refused to raise the starting minimum wage. The next day, the UAW local set up picket lines and shut down the plant.[20]

Once the NAA strike started, most officials in Washington agreed that unless the workers went back to work immediately, the plant should be seized. UAW and CIO leaders at the national level had refused to sanction the actions of the local. Indeed, the national UAW moved quickly to dismiss the local's leaders. Confident that he would do little to offend labor, Roosevelt ordered seizure. However, he told his cabinet and the War Department that they should regard this as a temporary action, aimed at getting the union and management to resume production, as well as mediated contract negotiations.[21]

Although Roosevelt wanted the NAA seizure to be a temporary measure, it was achieved with a dramatic show of military force. On the morning of June 9, local police tried, with little success, to use tear gas to disperse a growing crowd of hundreds of picketers. But the U.S. Army, operating under the authority of the president's seizure order, had little trouble taking the plant. Commanding a force of 2,500 men marching with fixed bayonets, Lieutenant Colonel Charles E. Branshaw (a top Air Corps procurement officer) entered the facility and drove away the picketers. A day later, more than seven thousand employees returned to work.[22]

Under the watch of three Army battalions, NAA workers and managers resumed production. But with the contract dispute still unsettled, War Department officials scrambled to figure out what the seizure might actually involve. Some of them began to prepare fallback plans for turning the NAA plant into a fully government-owned and operated (GOGO) facility. Alternatively, the War Department might create some kind of semi-nationalized operation, in which military money and managers would be used to run the plant as long as necessary. However, many War Department officials were eager to avoid the financial and legal complexities of such action; they knew, as Colonel Branshaw put it, that staying in the plant for very long would mean "capitalists on your neck," complaining of interference in private enterprise.[23]

To the relief of Branshaw and officials in Washington, the NDMB, working with national UAW leaders, succeeded in negotiating a contract agreement before the end of June. NAA officials agreed to a $0.60 minimum hourly wage that would rise within three months to $0.75, along with an across-the-board ten-cent raise. Beyond this, the NDMB awarded the UAW local a novel benefit, which would become known as "maintenance of membership." Under this clause, any employee who had belonged to the union at the beginning of May would have to remain a member of the union—and pay monthly dues—for the duration of the new contract.[24]

Although the NAA seizure evidently encouraged the company to make contract concessions, its political implications were not necessarily damaging to business. Because the seizure had been imposed to break a strike, it was unionists, more than businessmen, who complained loudest about the government's use of the sword. Some union leaders believed that the event had weakened their hand. Business leaders and conservative politicians were cheered by public opinion polls, which indicated that the well-publicized Allis-Chalmers and NAA strikes had turned public opinion against organized labor in general.[25]

But for some business conservatives, the NAA seizure represented an unwelcome step in government-business relations. Reacting to news of the takeover, Senator Arthur H. Vandenberg (R-MI) suggested that the move had been instigated by "those who want to precipitate nationalization of industry." Editors at the *New York Times*, noting that some congressmen were already preparing bills extending the president's seizure powers, warned their readers against seeing the NAA seizure as a model for future policy. In fact, the newspaper argued, "it would be difficult to imagine any step more dangerous to democratic traditions and our system of free enterprise than wholesale plant seizures."[26]

Such concerns were intensified by the next seizure, undertaken in August 1941 at one of the nation's largest naval shipyards. The Federal Shipbuilding and Dry Dock Company was the nation's top producer of destroyers. It was also a subsidiary of U.S. Steel, one of the largest business enterprises in the world. By summer 1941, when Federal Ship had nearly $500 million in Navy contracts, its yards at Kearny, New Jersey (adjacent to Newark), already employed sixteen thousand workers. They were at work on two $14 million cruisers, as well as six destroyers.[27]

The takeover of Federal Ship, like the NAA seizure, followed a dispute between the company and a CIO-affiliated union. Since 1937, workers at Federal Ship had been represented by Local 16 of the Industrial Union of Marine and Shipbuilding Workers of America (IUMSWA). In 1941, the IUMSWA was still struggling to organize several of the biggest private warship yards on the East Coast, including the facilities of Electric Boat, Bath Iron Works, and Bethlehem–Fore River. At Federal Ship, Local 16 already enjoyed status as the official bargaining agent for shipyard workers. But it had never succeeded in getting company president Lynn H. Korndorff to agree to a union shop. After Federal workers struck briefly in June 1940, Korndorff agreed to a pay raise but not the union shop. In 1940–41, as Federal's workforce grew, Local 16 appeared to enjoy wide support among the workers but was having trouble collecting dues from more than a minority.[28]

The dispute at Federal Ship was taken up by the NDMB, which in July 1941 offered the compromise solution of maintenance of membership. This would mean that workers could avoid joining the union but only if they took the deliberate step of opting out, immediately after their hire. Beyond that point, they would need to remain dues-paying members of the union for the duration of the contract. The NDMB order upset Korndorff, who did not believe that the company should be forced to help the union by firing workers who didn't pay their dues. Maintenance of membership, Korndorff complained, impinged on "the freedom of the American worker to choose."[29] The NDMB order also failed to satisfy the leaders of Local 16, who wanted a true union shop, without any opt-out mechanism. Fed up with Korndorff and federal labor officials, the workers struck on August 6.

Inconveniently, President Roosevelt spent the next several days on a ship off the Canadian coast, in meetings with British prime minister Winston Churchill that would produce the Atlantic Charter (in which the Allies promised a postwar global order of free trade and peace). As they waited for Roosevelt to return, officials at the Navy Department and the OPM urged Korndorff to obey the NDMB. They also started to draft plans for a seizure, which had been invited by the union. Then, on 11 August, U.S. Steel—perhaps eager to keep labor developments at this one company from strengthening unions across all its national operations—suddenly offered to sell Federal Ship to the government. As Korndorff met with Navy Secretary Knox to discuss this possibility, Adlai E. Stevenson, a lawyer who had just started work as an aide to Knox, helped draft a seizure order. This document in hand, Stevenson flew to Maine in search of the president. Bursting in upon Roosevelt at dinner, Stevenson told the president that he needed to sign the paper immediately. Bemused by the younger man's agitation, Roosevelt pocketed the order and said that they could wait to discuss it until he was back at the White House. On 19 August, Roosevelt told Korndorff and IUMSWA leader John Green to go back to the bargaining table. But they failed to agree on the union security issue. So on 23 August, Roosevelt ordered the Navy to seize the yard.[30]

As the Navy officers moved in, they were cheered by workers. Contrary to Korndorff's prediction that it would be difficult for the Navy to get the shipyard running again, employees came back to work immediately and production resumed. On 6 September, the yard launched the *Atlanta*, a light cruiser.

Even more than in the case of NAA, the takeover of Federal Ship was surrounded with uncertainties about the extent and duration of government control. Because the Navy had long run its own network of shipyards, it was more than capable of nationalizing Federal Ship. As Stevenson put it, a full-blown Navy takeover of the facility would present only "minor technical obstacles." Admiral Harold G. Bowen, who led the takeover, was a smart, proud officer who had managed several Navy yards, besides serving as chief of the Navy's Bureau of Engineering. Since 1939, Bowen had been director of the Naval Research Laboratory, which, among other things, was helping develop the new technology of radar.[31]

However, the Navy's GOGO shipyards, like other government agencies, did not engage in formal collective bargaining with unions. This meant that an all-out nationalization would have the effect of punishing the union local. With this complication in mind, Stevenson and his Navy Department colleagues considered the possibility of creating a new semiprivate corporate entity that might be able to contract with the union.[32] But Navy officials, uncertain about the best course of action, failed to settle on any clear policy. On 17 September, almost a month into the seizure, Secretary Knox admitted that the Navy still hadn't decided much about the ownership status of the plant. For the moment, he claimed, Navy control remained temporary; it would support the NDMB policy of maintenance of membership. But in November, when the union demanded the firing of eighteen workers who were not paying dues, it turned out that the Navy would not enforce maintenance of membership, after all. After the NDMB told the Navy to uphold the union's request, Bowen and Knox chose to ignore the order.[33]

As the Federal Ship seizure demonstrated, Bowen and most of his fellow Navy officers were not committed to providing additional protections to unions. But neither did they always sympathize with business leaders. In October, Bowen told a group of Cleveland businessmen that the U.S. economy needed to be "quite completely regimented," no less so than the war economies of "the totalitarians." Bowen and his peers believed that when it came to production management, they were capable of outdoing executives in the private sector. Even at Federal Ship, which was already a leading warship maker in 1941, Bowen saw room for improvement (see Figure 9). Under his watch, he claimed, productivity rose by 20 percent, and profits increased, as the Navy hired four thousand new workers. This record disturbed the business community, Bowen recalled later, because it allowed the "left-wing" press to tout the achievements of public enterprise, while contradicting business leaders' claims that seizures would always be clumsy and damaging to the private plant.[34]

Figure 9. Christening of the USS *Aaron Ward* (DD-483), November 1941. In this photo, Hilda Ward christens a new destroyer named for her late father, who had retired as a rear admiral in 1913. (The ship was sunk in action in April 1943.) This event occurred on 22 November 1941, at the Federal Shipbuilding and Dry Dock Company shipyard in Kearny, New Jersey, which at the time was being run by the U.S. Navy. This was the second of what would end up being several dozen U.S. government seizures of private enterprises during World War II. Standing at far left is Rear Admiral Harold G. Bowen, who emerged as the Navy's leading administrator of seizures. Courtesy Naval History & Heritage Command, image NH 57706.

Business leaders were indeed disturbed by the Federal Ship seizure, in which the national government seemed to be violating the sanctity of private property, while punishing corporate executives for standing up to unions. In early September 1941, NAM president Walter D. Fuller used his Labor Day letter to business leaders to comment on the Federal Ship case.

This seizure, Fuller said, threatened "the immediate future of the American system of free enterprise and the American system of representative democracy." More specifically, the Federal Ship case seemed, as the *Wall Street Journal* suggested, "a test of whether or not the defense emergency is going to be used by organized labor as a vehicle to enforce some form of the closed shop as a price of its cooperation." If the union won security at Federal Ship, labor leaders might provoke more seizures across the country, in an effort to extend these results.[35]

Before Pearl Harbor, as the Navy continued to run Federal Ship, there was one more seizure. On October 30, Roosevelt ordered the War Department to take over the Bendix, New Jersey, plant of Air Associates Inc., a midsize manufacturer of landing gear cylinders and other aircraft parts. Here again, as in the case of Federal Ship, company managers were ousted by military officers who interceded on the side of a CIO union.

Labor-management relations at the Bendix plant had been miserable since July 1941, when the UAW's Local 969 narrowly won a representation election, 206 votes to 188. F. Leroy Hill, president of Air Associates, clashed with union leaders. Hill dismissed several union members, claiming that temporary layoffs were necessary because of shortages of materials. On 12 July, workers at the Bendix plant started a strike; the NLRB charged the company with multiple violations of the Wagner Act. On 20 July, the UAW asked Roosevelt to seize the plant. But when the dispute was referred to the NDMB for settlement, the employees returned to work.[36]

Over the following weeks, the situation at Air Associates deteriorated. Even after the War Department threatened to cancel the company's $1.4 million in prime contracts and suggested that it might force a change in management, Hill refused to budge. The union then called another strike. On 9 October, the NDMB ordered that the union stop the strike but also demanded that Hill rehire all the fired workers immediately. When Hill replied that he would need another thirty days to reinstate the workers, the UAW restarted its plans for a strike. Hill responded by encouraging non-UAW members to continue working and by recruiting replacements. The result was chaos. At least two people were injured when cars full of strikebreakers sped through picket lines. On 23 October, the local sheriff decided to close all roads to the plant, so that strikers and their opponents wouldn't engage in pitched battles at its gates. But twenty or thirty cars full of strikebreakers reached the plant via a back road before the sheriff managed to close it. On the morning of 24 October, an agitated William L. Nunn, chairman of New Jersey's state labor mediation board, telephoned the War Department to report that in Bendix, there was something "pretty close to being open warfare." Even after the governor and several New Jersey businessmen asked Hill to obey the NDMB order, he refused. Although public opinion seemed to be running against the company, the workers remained bitterly divided. Dozens of pro-Hill employees appeared at the governor's home to voice their discontent with the UAW.[37]

As the situation worsened in Bendix, Air Associates executives met with top officials from the OPM and the War Department in Washington. The company promised that it would reinstate the UAW members as quickly as possible. But because this would require dismissing many of the recently hired replacement workers, more troubles loomed. When Colonel Roy M. Jones of the AAF arrived on 30 October to oversee the process, he found UAW and non-UAW employees brawling with stones, clubs, and iron bars. Buildings were burning. Local police, along with growing numbers of workers and picketers, were brandishing firearms. As night fell, Jones feared a massacre. Working fast, War Department Undersecretary Patterson asked Roosevelt to sign a seizure order, which he did at 10:15 PM. At 2:00 AM, Colonel Jones seized the plant. By dawn on 31 October, 2,100 troops had moved in.[38]

Upon seizing the plant, Colonel Jones started rehiring from the UAW picket lines and worked to restore production in Bendix. After some hesitation, the War Department decided to seize Air Associates' seven small branch offices across the country. War Department lawyers drafted plans to set up a special government corporation to run the business. But before this step was taken, the War Department persuaded the Air Associates board to dismiss Hill. In late November, Frederic G. Coburn, a retired Navy officer and aircraft industry executive, was named the company's new president. Meanwhile, the War Department reached a deal with the company that would allow the Army to operate the plant using regular company funds, without any elaborate legal transfer of ownership.[39]

After he was forced out, an undaunted Hill criticized the government. He managed to get more than five hundred workers to call for his return by having them sign a petition that was sent to members of Congress. Hill protested the seizure in a letter to Patterson. "I have no apologies to make," Hill said. Days later, the War Department issued its own press release, which explained that the seizure was necessary because "rioting was in progress" in Bendix, where valuable war production had been disrupted.

Within the War Department, members of a growing industrial-relations department had few reservations about the seizure. They had discovered "sweatshop conditions" in the plant, with nearly all employees working for under $0.45 an hour. More generally, as Captain John H. Ohly put it, "the entire history of the company is one of outrageous labor violations."[40]

Although Hill evidently had little public support, the Bendix takeover still caused consternation in the business community. According to the *Wall Street Journal*, the Air Associates seizure showed that the Roosevelt administration was considering only a false "choice between government operation, likely to result in government ownership, and capitulation to aggressive unionism." After Hill was forced out, the *Journal* questioned whether the government had abandoned the rule of law. The Air Associates case was also watched closely by the NAM, where staffers prepared a draft resolution to be considered at the organization's annual meeting in December, protesting "Government-Dictated Ouster of Private Plant Managers." According to the resolution, "If the action taken in this case represents settled government policy, we have already passed the line between liberty and dictatorship."[41]

At the NAM's large "Congress of American Industry" conference, in New York in December 1941, several business leaders used their speeches to demand that the war not be used as an opportunity to encroach further upon private enterprise. If the United States were to abandon its tradition of competitive capitalism "and supinely rely on government control and operation," declared J. Howard Pew of Sun Oil, "then Hitlerism wins even though Hitler himself be defeated." Fuller, the outgoing NAM president, suggested that using seizures as a technique for achieving stability in industrial relations was akin to Hitler shooting hostages in France. Such concerns resonated with conservatives in Congress, including Senator Robert A. Taft (R-OH), who at the same moment was decrying "the complete lack of interest of the present administration in preserving private industry." With the Federal Ship and Air Associates cases in mind, Taft wondered: "Will those plants ever be surrendered?"[42]

Just hours after the NAM conference ended, Americans heard the news from Pearl Harbor. After a year and a half of industrial mobilization, the country was now truly at war. This turn of events appeared to transform the political climate surrounding labor relations. Before the end of December, a large labor-management conference promised Roosevelt that strikes and lockouts would be abandoned for the duration of the conflict. In early

January, the president created a new National War Labor Board (NWLB), which was supposed to settle any labor disputes. It represented a more powerful version of the NDMB, which had fallen apart just before Pearl Harbor.

With patriotic goodwill running high, the Navy and War Departments restored the seized facilities to private control. Air Associates was reprivatized on 29 December. A new contract between the UAW and the company provided a ten-cent hourly wage increase for all eight hundred employees, minimum starting wages of $0.60 and $0.75 for women and men, respectively, and a union security clause. The new regime helped improve output at Air Associates, which, by mid-1942, was judged by War Department officials to be adequate.[43]

At Federal Ship, which was returned to private control at the beginning of January, company officials still resisted the idea of providing the union local with maintenance of membership. But in April 1942, the public and labor members of the NWLB issued a sharp pro-labor order in the case. Praising the "patriotic zeal" of Federal Ship workers, the NWLB accused management of "a lack of acceptance of the democratic process." The board would not "allow the most powerful corporation in the world to take advantage of the no-strike pledge," it declared. Confronted with this forceful NWLB position, the company reluctantly accepted the union security measure that had been at issue over the last year. Although Federal Ship workers would continue to struggle to get the company to implement NWLB orders, this represented a major victory for the union.[44]

Even though the three 1941 seizures represented a small fraction of all the takeovers that would occur during World War II, they were especially important. As the United States entered fully into the war, business and labor leaders alike were already familiar with the possibility of defense plant seizures. At the War and Navy Departments, top officials, lawyers, and procurement and engineering officers had become experienced with the mechanics of takeovers and the operation of seized properties. And among American conservatives, the use of seizure was already understood as one significant part of the broader threat to private enterprise that was posed by the mobilization for war.

The 1941 seizures were also important because of their connections to government mediators' growing reliance on maintenance of membership. By spring 1942, when the NWLB finally succeeded in imposing maintenance of membership at Federal Ship, the board was starting to use the measure widely. In its standard version, the measure contained a fifteen-day "escape clause."[45] This meant that if a worker did not opt out of the union within two weeks of being hired, he or she was obliged to remain in it (and keep paying dues) for the life of the union's contract with the company. Union leaders commonly referred to this as a "weak" form of security because it allowed, in theory, for large numbers of nonunion workers at a given plant. Nevertheless, it provided locals with relatively stable membership rosters, and therefore more leverage and a steady income stream.[46]

Given the intensity of the AFL-CIO rivalry and the challenges posed by company-sponsored unions at many plants, the benefits provided by maintenance of membership were substantial. In practice, very few workers used the fifteen-day escape clause. Even in plants where unions encountered the most resistance from rank-and-file workers, fewer than 10 percent of employees typically chose to use the clause. According to NWLB chairman William H. Davis, a champion of maintenance of membership, by mid-1944 it was still the case that "you can put in a thimble" all the workers who had chosen to use escape clauses. In the eyes of many business leaders, this record showed that they had been right all along to say, as the Chamber of Commerce and the NAM did in early 1942, that maintenance of membership was nothing more than a "variant of the closed shop" and a violation of the "freedom to work."[47]

The 1941 seizures were also remarkable, at least as it turned out, for their unusual legal status. A decade later, in its important *Youngstown* decision of 1952, the Supreme Court would imply that they may not have been legal at all. The 1941 seizures were not challenged in the courts at the time, despite the business community's serious concerns about them. A couple of years later, there would be legal challenges. However, by that time, the nation was technically at war; also, starting in mid-1943, there was a new labor law in play, following an upsurge in strikes.

From the No-Strike Pledge to the Smith-Connally Act

In the months that followed the shock of Pearl Harbor, when the no-strike, no-lockout pledge was still fresh, serious labor disturbances and seizures were rare. In 1942, which saw far fewer strikes than the previous year, there were only five seizures. During the first half of 1943, which saw a major increase in strikes, the government resorted to takeovers on only three

occasions. Given that the number of American plants engaged in war production had grown significantly, this meant that the seizure rate for this
period was far below what it had been in 1941.[48]

Among the relatively small number of seizures during the first two years
after Pearl Harbor, moreover, several did not involve labor disputes. On six
occasions between April 1942 and January 1944, the Navy Department
seized plants because of what it regarded as management failures to achieve
adequate production.

The seizures in response to production problems were really a subset
of a larger group of cases, in which authorities in Washington pressured
underperforming contractors to change management. One of these
occurred at Consolidated Aircraft, a top producer of bomber aircraft. During 1941, War and Navy Department officials became dissatisfied with the
leadership of Reuben Fleet, the company's founder and president. Fleet's
persistent conflicts with unionists did not help matters, but officials in
Washington also believed that the company's plants in San Diego and Fort
Worth were failing to respond quickly enough to growing military demand.
So in November 1941, they pushed Fleet into retirement, by arranging to
have his company purchased by the smaller Vultee Aircraft. Brought in to
head the new enterprise was Tom M. Girdler, president of Republic Steel.
This move was hardly applauded by labor leaders, who knew Girdler as a
fervent opponent of unions. But the reorganized company, which would
eventually change its name to Consolidated-Vultee, succeeded in mass-
producing its B-24 bombers.[49]

Government officials forced changes in management in a variety of
other companies, including ten suppliers of merchant ships. One of these
was Savannah Shipyards, an upstart enterprise led by Frank Cohen.
Although he had little knowledge of the shipbuilding business, Cohen had
managed in October 1941 to get a Maritime Commission (USMC) contract
for twelve Liberty ships. Using several million dollars in government funds,
Cohen set up his own construction company to build the yard, in Savannah, Georgia. But when there was little evidence of progress by the time of
Pearl Harbor, the USMC canceled Cohen's contract and brought in new
management. The yard was completed and run by a new entity, the South-
eastern Shipbuilding Corporation. There were comparable developments at
an even larger yard in South Portland, Maine, where Liberty ship production was delayed by poor management, as well as labor troubles. In January
1943, after months of subpar output, congressional investigations, and

strikes, the USMC ousted the old management team, which had been headed by Pete Newell of Bath Iron Works. The USMC installed a new group of managers from the Seattle-Tacoma Shipbuilding Company, part of the Todd Shipbuilding Corporation.[50]

Although most of the forced changes in management were achieved without resorting to outright commandeering, the government also achieved the reforms via seizure. The first of the Navy takeovers in 1942 was imposed on Brewster Aeronautical, a small aircraft company based on Long Island, New York. In 1938, Brewster managed to get a prime contract from the Navy for fifty-four of its own F2 "Buffalo" fighters; it also took on large foreign orders. In 1940, as industrial mobilization heated up, the Navy ordered three hundred more F2s, along with 1,115 units of the SB2A, an entirely new model that Brewster had started to design only a few months earlier. In 1941, Brewster fell far behind on its scheduled deliveries. Meanwhile, the Brewster workforce jumped from a few hundred to nearly ten thousand employees. The company was still relying heavily on an expanded version of its old Long Island plant, where workers had to move pieces of aircraft vertically among six floors. The longtime company president, a former Navy officer named James Work, was often absent because of illness.[51]

Well aware of Brewster's production problems in 1941, the Navy continued to work with the struggling company because its needs for aircraft were so great. At one time, Navy officials considered asking Grumman, its best producer of carrier-based fighters, to take over Brewster. But this idea was scrapped because the Navy thought it might detract from Grumman's performance. Finally, on 20 April 1942, with production delays mounting at Brewster, the Navy seized the company. The takeover team was led by Captain George C. "Scrappy" Westervelt, a graduate of the Naval Academy and MIT who had directed the Navy's own aircraft plant for most of the 1920s. Westervelt was instructed by Navy Department undersecretary James Forrestal, who felt that the Navy was busy enough with other jobs, "to restore the operation to private management, at the earliest moment" possible.[52] The Navy did keep the seizure brief. After operating Brewster for just a month, it installed a new president and returned the company to private control. (Because the company continued to suffer from production and labor problems, the Navy ended up exerting considerable indirect control over Brewster for the remainder of the war.)[53]

Six months after the Brewster seizure, in October 1942, the Navy again took over a poorly run company and installed new executives. This takeover, which involved one of the war's seamiest cases of white-collar crime, occurred at the Triumph Explosives, based in Elkton, Maryland. At the beginning of World War II, Triumph, a small fireworks manufacturer, won large contracts for 40mm antiaircraft shells; it expanded its facilities using $6.5 million of Navy money. By the mid-1942, there were 9,200 employees at the Elkton plant, which formerly had only four hundred workers. Triumph's sales and profits were high. But in October, the company's leaders, Gustave Kann and Joseph Decker, were arrested by the FBI. Convicted of bribing inspectors, overcharging the government on contracts, and illegally diverting profits via a shell corporation, they were sentenced to three years in jail. (Decker would kill himself in April 1944, a few days after the Supreme Court denied his appeal.) Following the arrests, the Navy took over the company. A team led by Commander A. B. McCrary ran it for three months, before the Navy installed a new private management team.[54]

In 1943–44, management failures caused four more Navy seizures. In three of these, the leading player was Admiral Harold Bowen, the same top engineering officer who had headed the Federal Ship seizure in 1941. As his memoirs show, Bowen was critical of the management of the several underperforming plants that he seized. In June 1943, Bowen oversaw the Navy's takeover of the Howarth Pivoted Bearings Company near Philadelphia, one of two suppliers of the thrust bearings required in hundreds of naval vessels and merchant ships. At the Howarth plant, which was running six months behind schedule, Bowen criticized the company's use of outdated machine tools and manufacturing practices, excessive production errors, and poor accounting methods. Five months later, Bowen led a surprise seizure of a struggling new GOCO bombsight manufacturing plant, operated by Remington Rand, in Elmira, New York. There, Bowen found serious problems in the flow of parts and materials among various parts of the plant, which left too many workers idle.[55] Just after he arrived in Elmira, Bowen was ordered west, to the facilities of the Los Angeles Shipbuilding and Drydock Corporation. After Bowen seized the yards, on 8 December, he concluded that the company had "no vestige" of a modern cost accounting system; among workers, there was a "scandalous" level of "loafing."[56]

Disgusted as they were with the record of managers at these underperforming plants, Bowen and his fellow Navy officials did not scorn private enterprise in general. In fact, as the takeovers became more numerous, they outsourced the management of seized properties to more competent companies. The Navy turned the operation of the Howarth plant over to Westinghouse, the prominent electrical equipment firm that had long served as a major Navy supplier of turbines for warships. In Los Angeles, Bowen handed over the seized facility to Todd Shipyards, one of the country's leading makers of merchant vessels.[57]

Although the Navy seizures undertaken in response to allegedly subpar production could be disturbing to individual companies, they caused little public outcry. For example, there was little media coverage of the Navy's takeover of the plants of York Safe & Lock, a major ordnance manufacturer in Pennsylvania, at the beginning of 1944. In what turned out to be the war's last seizure for reasons of alleged managerial incompetence, the Navy sacked eleven top York Safe & Lock executives, who were replaced by a seven-man military team led by Captain R. N. Ducey. These events were covered only briefly by daily newspapers, far away from the front pages.[58] They inspired little protest from the business community, which preferred not to draw attention to the seizures that called into question the production capabilities of private management.

The business community was more concerned with takeovers caused by labor disputes, such as the three that occurred in 1941. In the very first seizure after Pearl Harbor, undertaken in mid-March 1942, the Roosevelt administration faced an employer who openly challenged the authority of the new NWLB. This was George P. McNear, Jr., an owner of the Toledo, Peoria, and Western Railroad Company, a small midwestern line. When the NWLB instructed the workers and the company to settle an ongoing strike through arbitration, McNear refused. His company was then seized by the Office of Defense Transportation, which ended up controlling the railroad for more than three years, through the end of the war.[59] (After the road was returned to McNear, in late 1945, a bitter labor dispute followed. In March 1947, someone murdered McNear with a shotgun blast.)[60]

Overt company resistance to the NWLB also caused the seizure of S. A. Woods Machine, a Boston-area manufacturer of woodworking machinery that was making artillery shells. Longtime company president H. C. Dodge was upset by an August 1942 ruling by the NWLB that granted maintenance of membership to the CIO-affiliated United Electrical Workers. The NWLB told Dodge that if he resisted this ruling, "you must be considered as engaging in an employer strike against the government in time of war." Dodge was unmoved. On 19 August, the Army seized the plant. Over the next few weeks, the War Department canceled S. A. Woods's contracts, settling with the company for $1.75 million. The Army maintained formal control over the company through the end of the war but outsourced its management to the Murray Company, a Dallas-based maker of cotton-ginning machinery. Disgusted, Dodge spent the second half of the war distributing thousands of copies of a pamphlet describing his company's ordeal, titled "The Fifth Freedom—Freedom to Work."[61]

It was another, shorter seizure in 1942 that inspired more public protest from business leaders. In Bayonne, New Jersey, at a plant owned by General Cable, a thousand workers staged a wildcat strike to protest an NWLB order denying their request for a raise. Admiral Bowen of the Navy seized the facility on 13 August. Bowen left just a week later, when the AFL electrical workers' union representing the Bayonne workers promised that there would be no strikes.[62] This episode disturbed NAM president William P. Witherow, who, in an open letter to the NWLB, argued that it had created "a dangerous and un-American precedent." Instead of taking over the plant, he argued, the government should have punished the striking workers, by helping the company install replacements for them. The General Cable seizure was also criticized by editors at the *Wall Street Journal*, who suggested that national labor policy might need a complete overhaul.[63]

By the late spring of 1943, two years after the NAA seizure, there had still been only a handful of takeovers. But by seizing just a few companies, the government signaled to the business community that violators of its labor policies risked losing control of their enterprises. By the end of the war, the NWLB would settle some twenty thousand labor-management disputes; of these, only a few dozen cases ended in seizures or other naked acts of coercion. According to George W. Taylor, a chairman of the NWLB, such figures showed that the vast majority of workers and managers were willing to set aside their differences while they focused on getting the production job done. There was some truth to this interpretation. But on this subject, more revealing was the assessment of Taylor's colleague Lloyd K. Garrison, a public member of the NWLB who served as its last chair. Although seizure powers were rarely used, Garrison observed, "the possibility of their use was always in the background and undoubtedly gave an added measure of force to the Board's decisions."[64]

This deterrent effect was difficult to measure but was no doubt important, as business leaders and union officers struggled to decide how far to push each other during the wartime emergency. Military officials and federal labor mediators seem to have wielded the seizure threat often. A more direct approach was used in early 1942 by Navy Undersecretary Forrestal, who told Allis-Chalmers officials that "the Government is loath to take possession of and operate" its plant but would do so if output did not improve. Often, the threat to employers was more tacit. This was suggested by remarks made at the end of 1943 by William E. Umstattd, president of Timken Roller Bearing. When the NWLB ordered his company in January 1943 to provide maintenance of membership, Umstattd told a congressional committee that "there was no direct threat" of seizure of Timken's plants. However, Umstattd recalled, the board's authority to use seizure to force compliance was mentioned in discussions with company officials, who agreed to go along with the union security rules only reluctantly, under a sort of half-voiced protest.[65]

Such compromises remained far more common than outright defiance, throughout the war. But by mid-1943, growing labor-management conflict was causing government officials to prepare for more seizures. The most important factor in this transition was a strike by coal miners, led by the hard-nosed United Mineworkers (UMW) union president, John L. Lewis.

Serious labor-management problems in the coal industry were nothing new. When miners struck in April and November 1941, the Roosevelt administration had come close to seizing the mines. But Lewis and the miners managed to extend a string of successful bids for higher wages and union security, without a takeover. As the nation's all-out war effort started in early 1942, Lewis presided over a big, strong union, with half a million members and $6 million in the bank.[66]

Unlike most union leaders, Lewis never embraced the no-strike pledge. Nor did he accept the strict wage controls that were central to the Roosevelt administration's wartime domestic economic policy. In July 1942, the NWLB used a decision in the cases of several midsize steel companies to outline a general policy on wage controls. Its "Little Steel formula" used the figure of 15 percent as the standard measure of how much the cost of living had increased since January 1941. The NWLB would generally allow wage adjustments to match that figure but not exceed it, except in cases of unusual inequities. Using the Little Steel formula and other wage and price controls, the government pursued an aggressive wartime anti-inflation policy that made it hard for unions to win wage increases before 1945.[67]

By spring 1943, as the coal miners' two-year contract expired, Lewis had expressed his disdain for the NWLB and its wage policy. Since the miners had already gained the union shop in most mines across the country, they could not be influenced with the carrot of union security. They wanted a pay raise of $2 a day, which would violate the Little Steel cap. In late April, aware that the NWLB would refuse to grant this raise, Lewis led the miners out on strike, in what would be the first in a series of stoppages. Well-publicized in the national media, these coal strikes were among the most hotly debated domestic events of 1943. They became the most widely discussed of a growing number of serious labor-management disputes, which included a machinists' strike in San Francisco shipyards; a strike by rubber workers in Akron; and a major stoppage at Chrysler. These events suggested workers' growing discontent with the NWLB, which approved few pay raises and took months to resolve most disputes.[68]

Faced with strikes that posed a serious threat to the war economy, the Roosevelt administration started to rely more heavily on takeovers. The first of the new seizures started on 1 May 1943, when the president ordered Interior Secretary Harold Ickes to take over the coal mines. In terms of actual operations, this was mostly a token gesture: Ickes raised American flags over about 3,300 mines, but the coal companies continued to run their own facilities, for all practical purposes. In early June, after President Roosevelt insisted that Ickes and Lewis reach a settlement that could satisfy the NWLB, Lewis responded by encouraging the miners to strike again. Meanwhile, owners of the mines, along with many members of Congress, became agitated. "The operators have been getting more and more nervous," Ickes noted in his diary. "They are not in control of their own properties and some are beginning to worry that they might never get their mines back, or at least for the duration of the war."[69]

Ickes reassured the operators that he was not interested in any permanent nationalization of the coal mines. But the government would continue to rely on seizure as a basic regulatory device in the coal industry for the next three years. In late June 1943, Lewis agreed to send the miners back to work through October but only if the government continued its takeover. Mine operators learned to live with the seizure, which provided most of them with relatively stable labor relations, production, and profits. But by mid-October, as Lewis's deadline approached, Ickes had returned the mines to private control. When the miners started another giant strike at the beginning of November, Roosevelt had Ickes re-seize the mines. This time, Ickes and Lewis were allowed to bypass the NWLB. They ended up with a deal that provided the miners with a raise of $1.875 a day but a shorter lunch break—the "dyspepsia formula." By the end of June 1944, Ickes had returned nearly all the mines to their private owners.[70]

Although Lewis eventually succeeded in negotiating a better contract for the miners, his actions altered labor's broader political fortunes, as well as federal labor law. In 1941–42, when the editorial content of most newspapers and radio stations was critical of unions, public opinion polls indicated widespread support for a total ban on strikes in wartime. Such a ban was favored by many congressional conservatives, led by Representative Howard W. Smith (D-VA). Thanks to the lull in labor-management conflict that followed Pearl Harbor, President Roosevelt had been able to hold off Smith and his allies. But during the coal strikes of April–June 1943, the calls for more antiunion legislation mounted.[71]

In June 1943, during the coal strike, congressional conservatives succeeded in passing the first significant revision to the 1935 Wagner Act. Enacted over Roosevelt's veto, this was the War Labor Disputes Act, also known as the Smith-Connally Act. The new law imposed a thirty-day "cooling off" period on would-be strikers, who were now required to register their intentions with the government, wait a month, and then conduct a federally supervised election in which each worker was asked whether he or she was willing to have war production interrupted by a strike. The new law also banned direct union contributions to political candidates and provided criminal penalties for those who struck seized plants.

One reason that the Smith-Connally Act appealed to many congressmen and their constituents was because it seemed to discourage strikes. However, it did so in a way that promised to make seizure more central to wartime labor policy.[72] Section 3 of the statute extended the commandeering provisions of the 1940 Selective Service and Training Act by empowering the president, in the case of a strike or other labor disturbance, to seize and run "any plant, mine, or facility equipped for the manufacture, production or mining" of anything useful to the war effort. The law required that seized facilities be returned to their private owners within sixty days of the restoration of efficient production—a measure that reassured some business leaders who had been asking for more formal legal limits on the takeovers.[73] But because judgments about efficiency were left to the discretion of the public authorities, the law would not prevent seizures from lasting far longer than two months.

Thanks in part to the ways in which it expanded executive power, the Smith-Connally Act was criticized by some conservatives, as well as union leaders and other progressives. As Roosevelt observed when he vetoed the bill, one of the most obvious flaws of Smith-Connally was that it undermined the no-strike pledge, by suggesting that if workers followed the rules and waited thirty days, a strike became perfectly legal. This apparent legitimation of strikes also worried some business leaders and their allies, as did the law's apparently broad grant of seizure powers. As the *New York Times* complained, the law seemed to promise that more employers would be punished by the loss of control of their companies, as well as the stigma of seizure, when workers misbehaved.[74]

The Smith-Connally Act pointed the way to a wartime labor-relations policy that would be more forceful, if not more effective. In a 16 August 1943 executive order, Roosevelt announced that violators of NWLB orders should henceforth expect a variety of penalties, including contract cancellations, denials of raw materials, and the removal of draft exemptions, as well as plant takeovers. Roosevelt promised that any seizures should be conducted with "the least possible interference with existing management."[75] But it was clear that by the second half of 1943, the Roosevelt administration, encouraged by Congress, had adopted a more hard-line approach to violators of its labor policies, whether unions or employers. Would this more confrontational posture succeed in limiting disobedience? Developments over the next few months suggested that it did not.

In the months following the passage of Smith-Connally, from October 1943 to April 1944, there were nine new seizures. Several of these were imposed to end strikes that caused minor disruptions in war production, such as those that occurred at several small leather tanneries and textile mills in Massachusetts. The Massachusetts strikes were caused by jurisdictional disputes among competing unions—a common problem during an era of struggles among the AFL, CIO, and independent organizations.[76] Different problems sparked the War Department's six-month takeover, starting in November 1943, of a large Western Electric radio and radar equipment plant at Point Breeze, Maryland. There, a majority of the members of an independent employees' association started a strike to protest the racial integration of work crews and to demand more segregated toilet facilities.[77] This was one of two military takeovers (the other being the Army's seizure of Philadelphia's transit system in August 1944) in response to strikes staged by white supremacist, segregationist workers.[78]

More national attention was given the Army's brief, token seizure of the nation's railroads, which ran from late December 1943 into early January

1944. The Roosevelt administration used this nominal takeover to stave off a threatened strike and buy more time for negotiations of a wage increase. The brief episode evidently did little to disturb railroad executives, who continued to run their roads as usual.[79] But to many conservative critics, the railroad takeover was, as the *Wall Street Journal* put it, nothing less than a "deplorable" act, in which the Smith-Connally Act was used, perversely, to punish innocent companies.[80] In Congress, the railroad seizure was denounced by Harold Knutson (R-MN), who remarked that the whole affair made him wish that he could somehow magically replace Roosevelt with Calvin Coolidge. Another prominent Republican critic was Wendell Willkie, who had called attention to the dangers of seizure during the 1940 presidential campaign. Now, more than three years later, Willkie referenced Roosevelt's recent admission that the exigencies of the military crisis had transformed him from "Dr. New Deal" into "Dr. Win the War." The physician-president, Willkie complained, was still administering unneeded "drugs" to the American people. Among these narcotics were the recent seizures, which, for Willkie and many business leaders, demonstrated the administration's incompetence and its excessive use of executive power.[81]

The Montgomery Ward Case and the Spread of Seizures

Several seizures of late 1943 and early 1944, which were directed at disciplining unruly workers, lacked the sort of bitter government-business conflict that had occurred in a handful of earlier takeovers, such as the Federal Ship seizure of 1941. But a few seizures during the months after the passage of Smith-Connally did involve employer defiance of federal labor authorities. These cases were the most important antecedents of the well-publicized April 1944 takeover at the Chicago headquarters of Montgomery Ward, the giant retailer.

Employer resistance caused the very first of the seizures after Smith-Connally, which took place in September 1943, at the Atlantic Basin Iron Works, in Brooklyn. This midsize shipyard, which specialized in repair work, had seen its workforce grow during the war to nearly four thousand employees. Company officials, led by president Bernard A. Moran, had been struggling for several years with an IUMSWA (CIO) local. The seizure came after Moran refused to provide the local with maintenance of membership, which had recently been ordered by the NWLB. Like many business leaders, Moran disparaged this measure as nothing less than the union shop. But he and his lawyers introduced a new challenge by claiming that, in the wake of the Smith-Connally Act, the NWLB was no longer allowed to impose maintenance of membership. This was not the view of the Roosevelt administration, which appointed Admiral Emory S. Land, in his capacity as war shipping administrator, to oversee a seizure of the Atlantic Basin shipyard. After being occupied for two weeks, the company agreed to implement maintenance of membership, but only under formal protest.[82]

Employer defiance of the NWLB also caused the two plant seizures that began in April 1944, just before the Montgomery Ward incident. One of these, handled by the Navy Department, involved Jenkins Brothers, a midsize manufacturer of valves, based in Bridgeport, Connecticut. The other seized company was Ken-Rad Tube and Lamp, whose main plant was in Owensboro, Kentucky. A midsize manufacturer of radio sets and tubes, Ken-Rad had become an important supplier to the Army's Signal Corps. Ken-Rad executives had refused to bargain seriously with the AFL-affiliated autoworkers local, even after it won an NLRB-supervised representation election. At both Ken-Rad and Jenkins Brothers, company executives refused to obey NWLB orders to provide their employees with pay raises that were supposed to be retroactive to the autumn of 1942.[83] These disputes were watched closely by the War Department, by officers such as Lieutenant Colonel Paul M. Hebert, longtime dean of the law school at Louisiana State University, who served during the war as a top Pentagon labor lawyer. "We think," Hebert noted, "that this case far transcends the importance of Ken-Rad." Hebert and his colleagues reasoned that if these two companies were allowed to disregard the NWLB orders, many others might do the same. "The prestige and fairness of the Army in its relations with labor and management as groups," Hebert observed, "may well be at stake."[84]

The Ken-Rad case became even more significant because of how the company, led by president Roy Burlew, reacted to the seizure. On 14 April 1944, a day after President Roosevelt signed an executive order authorizing the takeover, Colonel Carroll Badeau of the Signal Corps took possession of the Owensboro plant. At first, it seemed that Burlew and his fellow executives might cooperate. But then they abandoned their plant and challenged the seizure with a lawsuit. This meant that Colonel Badeau and his team became the genuine managers of the company. They proceeded to seize its four smaller feeder plants, in Kentucky and Indiana, so that they could continue production. For the next six weeks, Badeau's team managed all five plants, which together employed more than three thousand people, most of them women. So the Ken-Rad takeover became one of a handful of cases in which the military's managerial role was real, rather than merely formal. The case was also special because of the company's legal challenge, which claimed that the seizure violated the Constitution, as well as the Smith-Connally Act's requirement that the NWLB provide "fair and equitable" settlements.[85]

The Ken-Rad case resulted in decisive legal victories for the government and the union. On 9 May 1944, a federal district court judge, Mac Swinford, rejected the company's request for an injunction. By suggesting that the president had constitutional powers to seize wartime plants without specific statutory authorization, Swinford made what would turn out to be the most sweeping court endorsement of presidential seizure power.[86] Faced with this legal defeat, Ken-Rad executives gave in. The UAW-AFL would now represent Ken-Rad workers at the smaller feeder plants, as well as the main facility; the union also won a retroactive pay raise, maintenance of membership, and a checkoff provision that required the company to collect dues for the union.[87] Here was a case in which the government succeeded in using seizure to impose its labor policies on a defiant employer. This might have attracted more attention from the business community, had it not been overshadowed by a far more celebrated seizure, which started before the Ken-Rad struggle was resolved.

Montgomery Ward, with some 78,000 employees and six hundred retail stores across the United States, ranked as one of the largest business enterprises in the world.[88] Millions of Americans, including rural residents who continued to use the company's famous mail-order catalogs, were Ward customers. Any serious conflict between this enterprise and the U.S. government, let alone an outright seizure of its properties, was bound to attract a great deal of attention. The April 1944 takeover certainly did so. It generated a heated public-relations contest in which many business leaders, journalists, and politicians joined forces to challenge the legitimacy of seizures and, more broadly, the wartime state's labor policies.

The April 1944 seizure of Montgomery Ward was the culmination of years of conflict between the Roosevelt administration and the company's seventy-year-old president, Sewell L. Avery. The latter was a politically active, conservative Republican, who had been a founding member of the Liberty League back in the 1930s.[89]

The seizure originated with a standoff between Avery and the NWLB. Beginning in 1940, most workers at the company's large mail-order house, central warehouse, and retail store in Chicago were represented by the United Retail, Wholesale, and Department Store Employees of America (URWDSE), a CIO-affiliated union. Like many of his fellow business leaders, Avery had refused union demands for a closed shop. On 5 November 1942 (just two days after the big Republican gains in the midterm elections), the NWLB ordered the company to provide maintenance of membership. A week later, Avery said that he would refuse this command because maintenance was merely "the starting phase which leads inevitably to the closed shop." Avery said that he would carry out the order only if the president demanded it directly. Meanwhile, Ward started to spend large sums on a public-relations effort that included reproductions of Avery's protest letters to the NWLB, in full-page ads in newspapers around the nation. After President Roosevelt told him—twice—that he must obey the board, Avery finally signed a contract, in which the company noted that it had agreed only "after protest."[90]

This 1942 faceoff received considerable public reaction, which confirmed Avery's belief that he was doing right. His mailbags were full of gushing tributes from leaders of small and large businesses alike. The editor of *Nation's Business*, the U.S. Chamber of Commerce's magazine, assured Avery that he enjoyed widespread support, even if not all business leaders were so brave. "You fought the good fight," explained Merle Thorpe, "and heartened a great many other employers who certainly were with you in spirit." Loretta Moushey, assistant director of the department of industrial relations at Monsanto Chemical in St. Louis, wrote: "I sincerely hope that industry will follow your lead in publicly opposing the closed shop." Among smaller businessmen, Avery's fans included David Swift, secretary of the Los Angeles Society of Magicians; and Edward N. Kett, owner of Ace Laundry in Peoria, Illinois. "Many small concerns such as ours experience the same problems," explained the owner of the Seattle-based Northwest Bolt & Nut, "but unfortunately we are not financially able to withstand long strikes or to publicize the unfair treatment at the hands of certain labor unions and governmental bureaus as you have done."[91]

To Avery, this reaction suggested that he should have done even more to resist unionization. Of the three thousand letters that Avery had received by January 1943, his staff calculated, 93 percent were "vigorously favorable." The remainder, Avery believed, was "made up from a small list of

New Dealers, easily identified, non-argumentative letters from wives of union members who gently threaten not to buy until we stop, etc., and the rest are radicals." The national press coverage, from Avery's point of view, was also overwhelmingly favorable. Of 453 newspaper editorials published on the Avery-NWLB conflict, 85 percent were favorable to Ward.[92]

Avery also received plenty of support in Congress, where Republicans and conservative Democrats applauded him. "Every day it becomes clearer that the New Deal administration is a labor government," declared Congressman Knutson, the Minnesota Republican, "and that the President is prepared to trample over Constitutional rights in order to meet the wishes of labor leaders." Another U.S. House member, Dan R. McGehee (D-MS) wrote Avery directly to offer praise. "If the labor policy of this Administration continues," McGehee asserted, "it will be only a short time until it will control all industries and the business of this country."[93]

Reassured by this support in the winter of 1942–43, Avery was ready, when the contract with the Chicago union expired a year later, to press even harder. Despite the contract, Ward had never done much to enforce maintenance of membership. The company argued that, given the high turnover among its workforce, there was considerable doubt about whether most Chicago workers still favored the URWDSE. Union leaders, for their part, detested the Ward chief, whom they enjoyed calling "S. L. Avery." With no new agreement in sight, the contract expired in December 1943. In early 1944, the NWLB ruled that the old contract must be extended, up until the time of a new federally supervised election. When Avery rejected this compromise, the NWLB asked Fred M. Vinson, director of the Office of Economic Stabilization, to recommend that President Roosevelt draw up an order allowing the seizure of Ward properties. Vinson agreed, telling Roosevelt that the Ward case involved "the defiant conduct of a contumacious employer."[94] Taking Vinson's advice, Roosevelt signed a seizure order. Because Ward was a retailer, not obviously linked to the war effort, the president ordered that the operation be handled not by the military but by the Department of Commerce.

This seizure did not go well. On 26 April 1944, a small team of second-tier officials, led by Undersecretary of Commerce Wayne G. Taylor, arrived at the Ward national headquarters in Chicago to announce the takeover. To their surprise, Avery refused to accept their authority. After Taylor and his team returned with a U.S. marshal and eight of his deputies, Avery said that he would not leave unless the U.S. Army moved in. (The government's hand was probably weakened by the conspicuous absence of Commerce Secretary Jesse Jones, who, after the war, would recall the Ward seizure as "[a]bout the most awkward thing the White House asked me to do." Jones dealt with this awkwardness by staying away from Chicago.) Faced with Avery's resistance, the White House called for help from the War Department. Just after 6 PM, a detachment of forty soldiers entered the Ward offices to serve notice of the seizure. After talking briefly with his lawyer, Avery declared that it was time for him to go home for dinner.[95]

Avery managed to return to his office the next morning, on 27 April. He spoke there with Attorney General Francis Biddle, who had rushed to Chicago on an overnight flight. Biddle would recall later that Avery had "deeply shocked" him, by saying "to hell with the government." After Avery refused to leave, Biddle ordered the soldiers on the scene to "throw him out." This was acceptable to Avery, who knew that by then, a large crowd of reporters and photographers was outside. Carried out of the building in his chair by two military policemen, Avery enjoyed a remarkable media moment (see Figure 10).[96]

The photograph of Avery's ejection became a national sensation. Over the next few days, as one small-town editor observed, "practically every daily newspaper in the nation" ran some version of the Avery photo on its front page. For many conservatives, the image perfectly illustrated the excesses of the New Deal and the wartime state. This single photograph, Avery's friend and fellow Chicago business leader Sterling Morton noted, "will, I think, become one of the nightmares of the New Deal." Editors at *Life*, the popular weekly magazine, agreed that the photo—which they reproduced on a full page—was remarkable. "In this picture," *Life* explained, "half the great social and political issues of America's last ten years lie riven and exposed, their ends twitching."[97]

By aggravating so many raw nerves, the Ward seizure of April 1944 generated a sort of impromptu referendum on the wartime state's domestic policies. In the short run, the Roosevelt administration did poorly. Many journalists observed that no issue since Roosevelt's disastrous court-packing initiative of 1937 had generated so much criticism of the administration.[98] At Ward, Avery's assistants calculated that of the 1,657 letters and telegrams that it received in the first three days after the seizure, nearly two-thirds were strongly pro-Avery. Among the members of Indiana's congressional delegation, each of whom had received more than two hundred letters on the subject by early May, the mail reportedly ran 5–1 in favor of Avery. At

Figure 10. Sewell L. Avery being carried out of his Montgomery Ward Company office, Chicago, April 1944. Of all the seizures that occurred on the home front, the Ward takeover was the one that received the most public attention. A second, larger, U.S. Army–run seizure of Montgomery Ward started in December 1944 and ran through the end of the war. Courtesy of Chicago History Museum, ICHi-74221; photographer unknown.

the White House, an analysis of one batch of correspondence found that although pro-Roosevelt telegrams outnumbered pro-Avery telegrams by 183 to 75, there were 278 regular letters that sided with Avery, against 191 letters favoring the government. A month after the takeover, the Gallup polling organization reported the results of its survey of three thousand Americans that had been conducted on 9 May, the day that the seizure ended. Observing that the Ward case had "attracted more public attention than almost any other domestic event of recent months," Gallup found that 60 percent of those surveyed sided with Avery.[99]

Although American public opinion as a whole might have been only marginally tilted against the Ward seizure, the episode energized conservatives. In the business community, there was a fresh wave of attacks on the Roosevelt administration, especially from the grass roots. Local chambers of commerce, from Wyoming to New Jersey, mobilized immediately to protest the Ward takeover. The American Association of Small Business passed a formal resolution stating that "the seizure of Montgomery Ward is a form of regimentation and contrary to our American way of life and freedom of enterprise." As in 1942, much of Avery's strongest support seemed to come from leaders of smaller enterprises. "Thousands of small business firms," the president of the Williams Radiator Company in Los Angeles told Avery, "are indebted to you for challenging and bringing to public attention bureaucratic rulings which smaller firms must accept in silence, regardless of how wrong they are." One letter that Avery received from the owner of a New York floor-coverings company was telling: "As one of the many small business men wondering where we are headed in these unbelievable times," Arthur C. Watson wrote, "I want to express my admiration for your courage in sticking to what you believe is right, regardless of threats from our self appointed Gestapo." But Watson predicted that the seizure would probably turn out to have good results: "It would appear you may have started something that will put these Bureaucrats back in their boxes."[100]

As the language of these letters suggests, the April 1944 Ward seizure fit almost perfectly into the framing narrative that the American business community had been propagating since before Pearl Harbor. The Ward seizure, represented so dramatically in the photographs of Avery being carried out of his office, seemed to show how management—the only true hero on the home front—was distracted and abused by a bureaucratic, semi-totalitarian government. For those sympathetic to business, it was easy to read the event as evidence of the excesses of a government that wrongly indulged organized labor, even at the cost of stopping war production, and that was happy to use the iron fist of militarized plant seizures to punish management, even when labor was to blame.

Besides energizing business leaders, the April 1944 Ward seizure also fueled antiadministration attacks by members of Congress and the press. To be sure, a handful of editors, including those at the pro-labor Chicago *Sun*, ran stories attacking Avery; others published columns that provided at least mild defense of Roosevelt's actions.[101] But for hundreds of conservative newspaper editors across the country, the episode offered a chance to ramp up antistatist rhetoric. The *Los Angeles Times* saw in the Ward episode "an extraordinarily resemblance to the Hitlerism we are fighting a war supposedly to destroy." Several newspapers, along with Representative Charles S. Dewey (R-IL), denounced the administration's "Gestapo methods." Many critics, including the syndicated columnist Westbrook Pegler, argued that the Ward case demonstrated that the wartime state seemed to observe no constitutional limits to its power. As Senator James Eastland (D-MS) put it, the episode suggested that Roosevelt might next "take over a grocery store or butcher shop in any hamlet in the U.S." Senator Kenneth S. Wherry (R-NE) was more blunt. "This is dictatorship," Wherry announced, "and the end of private enterprise."[102]

Even allies of the president had their doubts. Several members of Roosevelt's cabinet second-guessed the action. Interior Secretary Ickes observed that Attorney General Biddle, with whom he lunched on May 15, seemed to be rather "downhearted" about the whole affair. Ickes kindly reassured Biddle that the episode would be quickly forgotten. However, Ickes actually believed that the Ward seizure might well hurt the Democrats in the November elections. "As a matter of fact," he confided to his diary, "I think that this has done a good deal of harm." Certainly the situation did not seem favorable to the administration in early May 1944, when, after the CIO-affiliated union won another NLRB-sponsored election, the Commerce Department ended its seizure. Washington-based journalist Alan Drury observed in his own diary that "the Republicans have been handed another good issue on a silver platter."[103]

Over the longer run, conservatives found it hard to leverage the Ward seizure controversy into broader political gains. In September 1944, when a special House committee issued its report on the takeover, it divided strictly on party lines. Whereas the three Republicans on the committee concluded that the Ward seizure had been completely illegal, its four Democratic members called it a justifiable response to an impending strike that might have spread across the home front. The Roosevelt administration was also helped by news of the progress of Allied forces in Europe. By the time that Avery testified in Congress that he had endured seizure as a way of protesting "the march of dictatorship in this Nation," the public was more interested in reports of the recent D-Day landings. To the extent that Americans did continue to pay attention to Avery, according to *Time* magazine, many were becoming disenchanted with his unending abrasiveness and self-promotion.[104] Certainly, the Ward seizure does not seem to have provided much help to conservatives in the elections of November 1944, when Roosevelt won a fourth term and Democrats took back some seats in Congress.

The shifting political winds help explain why Roosevelt was willing, in December 1944, to order a second Ward seizure. This takeover, which would last through the end of the war, caused less public controversy but involved a far more substantial challenge to private control.

After the May 1944 election that recertified the CIO-affiliated union as the bargaining agent of many Ward workers in Chicago, Avery had continued to defy labor leaders and the NWLB. The conflict came to a head in mid-December 1944, when Ward employees in Detroit started a major strike. This was the last straw for President Roosevelt and home-front mobilization czar James F. Byrnes, who agreed that there must be another seizure. This time, the seizing agency would be the War Department.[105] On 28 December, the Army began a new takeover of Ward. This time, the government seized retail stores and mail-order houses in six cities across the country, as well as most of the company's main facilities in Chicago. Avery, predictably, refused to cooperate with this second takeover. So, too, did more than a dozen of the company's branch managers, who were immediately fired by the Army.[106] As 1945 opened, the War Department was faced with managing a significant part of one of the world's largest business enterprises.

For the War Department, the new Ward takeover presented two serious problems. One problem was legal: it was not clear whether the seizure would be allowed by the courts. The other problem had to do with business administration. The War Department had taken over several important pieces of Ward, but most of the company's national operations remained under the control of Avery and his lieutenants. This semi-seizure would have been very difficult to administer under any circumstances, but the company's lack of interest in cooperating with the War Department made it even more unwieldy.

The second Ward seizure was vulnerable to a serious legal challenge. As a retailer serving civilian customers, Montgomery Ward was not obviously covered by the seizure provisions laid out in the Smith-Connally Act, which referred to plants engaged in the "production" of war goods. Well aware of this issue, Avery and his lawyers challenged the second seizure. The case was heard by a federal district court in Chicago, which, on 27 January 1945, declared the seizure illegal. Drawing on the minority report of the Republican members of the congressional committee that had investigated the first Ward takeover, Judge Philip L. Sullivan used dictionary entries to distinguish between "production" and "distribution." Because Ward was engaged in the latter but not the former, Sullivan found, the seizure was not authorized by Smith-Connally. Nor could this takeover be justified by the president's inherent constitutional powers, Sullivan wrote, because those could be used for seizures only in cases of "immediate" or "extreme" danger, "when the emergency is so great that the national safety would be imperiled before Congress could act." Able to find no legal justification for the seizure, Sullivan nonetheless allowed it to continue, until an appeals court had time to rule on the case.[107]

Needless to say, Sullivan's ruling complicated the second Ward seizure. As it awaited the ruling of a higher court, the War Department was reluctant to make any changes in the management of the properties that it held, or to provide the union with any of the privileges awarded it by the NWLB. This delay alienated workers, who came to believe that the seizure gained them little.[108] By the time President Roosevelt died, in April 1945, the situation was still in limbo. In a cabinet meeting on 18 May, Attorney General Biddle told President Truman that the government expected to lose in the appeals court; at that point, Biddle suggested, any effort to press the case further might damage the president's authority. However, Truman and his friend Fred Vinson, director of the Office of Economic Stabilization, agreed that, if necessary, they would appeal the case to the Supreme Court. In early June, the administration received some good news, in the form of a 2–1 decision by the Seventh Circuit Court of Appeals, in favor of the government. Defining war "production" very broadly, the majority concluded that the seizure of Ward was covered by the Smith-Connally Act, after all.[109]

For the War Department, the appeals court decision was welcome; but it did not end the messy management difficulties at Ward. At the heart of the problem was the incompleteness of the seizure, which covered only the company's main Chicago facilities and a handful of other properties across the country. Hundreds of other stores and warehouses remained under the control of Avery and his colleagues, who were far from cooperative. From the beginning, Army officers realized that they were paralyzed by the incompleteness of the takeover, which prevented them from controlling the revenues that they would need to provide workers with the retroactive wage increases ordered by the NWLB. Equally bad, the War Department's control of the main Ward warehouses in Chicago left it in the position of filling the orders of the still privately held stores, using public funds. Because Avery and his lieutenants were refusing to pay the War Department–controlled warehouses for the goods that they shipped out to local stores, the government was already losing as much as $1 million a week on its own account. So as it awaited the appeals court ruling, the War Department decided to return the big Chicago warehouses to the company, while cutting its own seizure staff from more than three hundred down to about 170 people.[110]

After the favorable appeals court ruling in June, the War Department considered whether to institute a more substantial seizure. By summer 1945, many junior officers in charge of legal and labor issues in the Ward case were concerned about the damage that it was doing to the reputation of the War Department. The seizure had failed to do much for the union, which, they believed, had suffered unfairly from Avery's intransigence. Meanwhile, the end of the war in Europe reduced public sympathy for takeovers. Under these circumstances, these officers believed, there were only two good options. One would be for the War Department to get out of the business of seizure entirely, so that a civilian agency could handle the difficult job of enforcing government labor policy. Barring this, as Captain John Chapman put it, "the time has come to adopt a tougher policy and a more hard-boiled technique." Here was the second option: in the Ward case and others, Chapman argued, the Army should stop using token or partial seizures; instead, it would be better off handling "all aspects of management control."[111]

These ideas were taken seriously at the Pentagon, which, by early August 1945, was making serious preparations to take over Montgomery Ward's entire national operation. On 19 July and 1 August 1945, as it searched for a way to do more to implement NWLB policies, the War Department re-seized the company's two main shipping warehouses in Chicago. After the second of these actions, Avery—backing away from an earlier promise—announced that he would continue to refuse to pay for goods shipped by the Army. This time, the War Department responded by stopping ship-ments to the privately controlled stores. On 4 August, Robert A. Lovett, the acting secretary of war, demanded that Avery begin to work with the government, "in accordance with your duty as an American citizen." Two days later, when Avery still had not complied, the War Department was preparing for an all-out seizure that would have involved thousands of soldiers moving into hundreds of Ward stores across the nation. This was an extraordinary crisis in American government-business relations. How-ever, it was defused, thanks to even more extraordinary developments, in the Pacific theater. On 7 August, President Truman announced that the United States had dropped an atomic weapon on Hiroshima. By 9 August, as Americans received news of the second bombing at Nagasaki, Avery and his colleagues told the War Department that they would start to pay for the shipments from Chicago.[112]

The end of the Pacific War prevented any expansion of the War Depart-ment seizure of Ward, which ended on 18 October. Reviewing the history of the War Department's operation, which lasted nearly ten months, *Time* mag-azine dismissed it as "a fumbling, inept experiment."[113] This assessment cor-rectly pointed to the many problems with the operation, which had proved unsatisfactory to all sides—the workers, the Army, and the company. How-ever, it favored the story told by Avery, who claimed that the Army's in-competent management was harming the enterprise. In fact, the Army's operational problems came mostly from the halfway nature of the seizure. Even under these difficult circumstances, the Army managed to run its own concerns at a profit; despite the long semi-seizure, the whole company's earn-ings for 1945 were higher than they had been the previous year.[114]

Once he was back in full control of the company, Avery ended mainte-nance of membership and the dues checkoff at facilities that had been recently controlled by the Army. He resumed his conflict with the union, which responded with more strikes and boycotts. This was one of the costs of Avery's uncompromising leadership style, which also made it very diffi-cult for him to hold on to managers. By the early 1950s, Montgomery Ward had fallen further behind Sears, whose leaders were somewhat less prickly, if no more enamored of CIO unions and government regulators.[115]

Although Sewell Avery ranked as the most famous provocateur of seizure, he was hardly a lone wolf. Indeed, his actions seem to have encouraged other business leaders to pursue a similar strategy of stiff resistance to government labor policy. By the time of the second Ward seizure, the nation had already begun to see a sharp rise in the number of government takeovers of war plants. One reason for this was the sharp rise in wildcat strikes, which signaled the disintegration of the post–Pearl Harbor "no-strike pledge"[116] But the growing number of seizures in 1944–45 was also caused by the willingness of larger numbers of business owners to openly defy the government. By war's end, this attitude was particularly noticeable in the South, which had previously been untouched by seizures. All in all, the uptick in government takeovers in 1944–45 suggested an alarming unraveling of industrial relations at the national level.

As Americans anticipated news of victory in Europe, there were growing numbers of seizures intended to control unruly workers. In late August 1944, just after its dramatic seizure of the Philadelphia transit system, the War Department took over a large nickel mine in West Virginia, where members of the steelworkers' local had violated an NWLB order not to strike. A few days later, at the beginning of September, Interior Secretary Ickes seized ten coal mines in Pennsylvania because of wildcats. Later that month, the Navy started a yearlong seizure of machine shops in the San Francisco Bay Area, after machinists there refused to work more than eight hours a day until they received a raise.[117] The military also intervened briefly in Cleveland and Toledo in several complicated disputes involving workers belonging to an independent union called the Mechanics Educational Society of America (MESA).[118]

But the final months of the war also saw several new seizures of companies whose executives, following the lead of Avery at Montgomery Ward, were refusing to implement NWLB orders. It was no accident that several of these occurred in Texas and elsewhere in the South, where employers tended to be especially hostile to unions and to government regulation.[119]

The first of the late-war seizures in the South occurred at Hughes Tool, the leading manufacturer of oil drilling equipment, based in Houston. In October 1940, the NLRB banned the company-sponsored organizations that had represented Hughes Tool workers for most of the 1930s. In 1941, the Independent Metal Workers (IMW), led by former members of the company union, defeated the USW-CIO in a representation election. But the CIO continued its efforts at Hughes Tool, which, after Pearl Harbor, became a major manufacturer of ordnance, as the operator of $38 million worth of new government-owned plant in Houston. In a new representation election, held in December 1942, the USW-CIO managed to prevail, by the close margin of 1,680 votes to 1,538. (Both local unions were segregated by race.) In April 1943, the company signed a one-year contract with the USW-CIO. But it did not include maintenance of membership, which union leaders continued to demand. After a few months, the NWLB ordered Hughes Tool to provide it. In late June 1944, the USW-CIO local held a one-week strike. As Hughes Tool executives continued to defy their rulings, officials at the NWLB asked the White House to prepare a seizure order.[120]

In September 1944, the War Department took over Hughes Tool plants, using a staff of thirty-nine people, led by Colonel Frank Cawthon. This was the start of a seizure that would last a whole year, through the end of the war. Soon after the takeover, IMW president R. H. Epperson warned the Pentagon that the Army had better not push maintenance of membership "down the throats of Hughes Tool Co. employees." To the dismay of CIO leaders, War Department authorities heeded Epperson's warning. Worried about the chaos that might ensue if it fired several hundred workers no longer in good standing with the USW local, the Army opted to oversee an uneasy status quo.[121]

Meanwhile, a similar labor dispute pushed another major Texas company toward a government takeover. Humble Oil, controlled by Standard Oil of New Jersey, qualified on its own as a large enterprise. It was a leading supplier of aviation gasoline, which it made in two giant plants—one privately financed, the other government-owned—in Baytown, Texas, just outside Houston. During the war, Humble, like its peers in the oil industry, was the target of organization drives by the CIO-affiliated Oil Workers International Union (OWIU). In Baytown, Humble employees were represented by a company-friendly independent union. However, the OWIU won a representation election in 1942 at Humble's refinery in Ingleside, Texas, which made butadiene for the synthetic rubber program. Although the Ingleside plant had only about five hundred unionized workers, Humble managers were dismayed by what was the CIO's first victory in any of their plants. In May 1943, the company and the union signed a contract that settled some wage disputes but not the question of union security. After the NWLB's regional board in Dallas sided with the company, the union appealed to the national board in Washington. In April 1944, the national authority, in a split decision accompanied by energetic dissents from industry members, ordered Humble to provide maintenance of membership.[122]

Instead of capitulating, Humble executives fought the government in court. In September 1944, the company succeeded in getting a U.S. district court judge to enjoin any contemplated seizure.[123] In December, after workers voted to strike, a circuit court ended the injunction, leaving the government free to enforce the NWLB order.[124] Over the weeks that followed, Humble executives continued to defy the government. Finally, on 5 June 1945, after Humble workers voted again to strike, President Truman ordered Harold Ickes, in his capacity as petroleum administrator for war, to seize the Ingleside plant. Again, the company challenged the seizure in court; on 20 June 1945, a federal judge rejected Humble's arguments. On 22 June, the PAW began a mostly token seizure that left the company's managers in charge of day-to-day operations.

The PAW seizure of the Humble refinery, in and of itself, qualified as a remarkable event. Here again—as in the Montgomery Ward case—one of the nation's largest companies, having repeatedly defied government orders in favor of a union, was taken over. Yet the Humble case received relatively little notice at the time. One reason for this was that the June 1945 takeover occurred soon after V-E Day, when Americans were occupied with other matters. But another reason the Humble seizure did not stand out was that it coincided with a broader, national crisis in management-labor relations.

One sector of the economy that saw a jump in strikes was the oil industry, which suddenly became the target of a rash of government seizures. These began in April 1945, when the PAW, backed by a deployment of Army troops, seized the giant GOCO aviation gasoline plant in Lake Charles, Louisiana, run by the Cities Service Company. In this case, relations between the company and the AFL-affiliated local union were stable, but some plant employees set up roadblocks and picket lines to protest an increase in the rents that they were charged for their housing. The picketing ended soon after the troops arrived, but tensions evidently remained high, because the seizure lasted through the end of the war.[125] By then, the PAW was the nominal operator of five facilities. In early June, it seized the Pure Oil Company's "Cabin Creek" fields at Dawes, West Virginia, where workers had been striking for three weeks over maintenance of membership. The PAW seizures continued into July, when Ickes took over two large war plants in Texas. One of these was the Texas Company's refinery in Port Arthur, Texas, a major aviation gasoline plant that was partly owned by the government. The other was a $30 million GOCO butadiene plant in Houston, operated by a subsidiary of Sinclair Oil. In both cases, longtime disputes between the oil companies and OWIU locals had turned into threatened strikes.[126]

Labor-management conflict in the South drove another cluster of seizures in May 1945, which involved three smallish textile companies in the Piedmont. The first of the three involved Cocker Machine and Foundry, a textile machinery company in Gastonia, North Carolina. This was the same firm that Eleanor Roosevelt suggested that the president seize, in her note of March 1945, after she learned of apparently illegal antiunion activities on the part of Cocker executives. Franklin Roosevelt never seized Cocker, but his successor did. After Harry Truman signed an executive order on 19 May 1945, the Army's Quartermaster Corps took over the company. Although this seizure lasted through the end of the war, the Army left most day-to-day operations in the hands of Cocker managers, who began to comply with federal orders.[127]

The other two seizures in the Piedmont had larger implications for labor's fortunes in the South, because they involved locals of the CIO-affiliated Textile Workers of America (TWUA). For most of the twentieth century, the TWUA fought an uphill battle against the Southern textile mills, most of which avoided unionization. However, with the help of the Wagner Act, the TWUA succeeded in organizing a few mills. One of these was Gaffney Manufacturing, in Gaffney, South Carolina, a midsize mill that employed about seven hundred people. The Gaffney facility was controlled by Deering-Milliken, based in New York, which owned textile mills across the South. Company executives wanted to avoid recognizing the TWUA, even if it won representation elections. So, rather than obey federal orders, they chose to endure an all-out seizure. In May 1945, before the War Department arrived, company managers fled the plant. For the next three months, the mill was run by Army officers, who managed to bring production back close to its wartime peak.[128]

Meanwhile, the Army conducted a less elaborate takeover of the Mary-Leila Cotton Mills, in Greensboro, Georgia, a manufacturer of cotton sheeting that was used in incendiary bombs being dropped on Japan. At Mary-Leila, the TWUA local had begun a strike back in early April, after the company refused to obey NWLB orders to provide maintenance of membership. Once the Army moved in, the strike ended, and company executives made a temporary, uneasy truce with the union.[129]

As the takeovers in the South suggest, President Truman proved to be even more willing than his predecessor to use his power to take over private enterprises. During Truman's first weeks as president, he focused on the Potsdam conference, the atomic bomb, and other aspects of foreign policy. But the summer of 1945 also saw Truman struggle with a major crisis in industrial relations on the home front, which would continue into the "reconversion" year of 1946. Both before and after V-J Day, Truman made free use of the seizure authority provided him under the Smith-Connally Act, which did not expire until mid-1947.[130]

In 1945, strikes and seizures became far more frequent. Besides the takeovers in the South, there were plenty of other seizures and near-seizures in other regions. One of the most serious of the near-seizures involved the giant Chrysler-Dodge truck plant in Detroit, where about fifteen thousand workers struck in February 1945, to protest the firing of seven workers who refused to file new reports on the pace of production. In this case, leaders of the UAW local, defying the union's national leaders, briefly tried to force an Army seizure. Before the strike ended, the War Department prepared seriously for such a takeover, which would have been one of the largest of the war.[131] So, too, would have been a seizure of Higgins Industries, the landing craft producer in New Orleans where about five thousand workers briefly struck in June 1945 to protest the company's plans to modify its contracts with AFL-affiliated locals. Here again, there was serious talk of a government takeover, without one ever taking place.[132]

Elsewhere, unresolved disputes resulted in real seizures. In May 1945, Interior Secretary Ickes again took over several coal mines, after more strikes.[133] Meanwhile, the Office of Defense Transportation, with the help of twelve thousand troops, responded to a strike of Chicago truckers by taking over the trucking companies.[134] In mid-June, the War Department started a monthlong seizure of the Diamond Alkali plant in Painesville, Ohio, which made magnesium chloride used in incendiary bombs.[135] In early July, the Navy Department seized Goodyear's main tire plant in Akron, where nearly twenty thousand workers went out on strike. Later that month, another of the big four tire companies, U.S. Rubber, saw one of its large Detroit facilities seized by the War Department, again in response to a strike.[136]

At the end of the war, when President Truman issued an executive order directing government agencies to return seized properties "as soon as practicable," the United States was acting as legal manager of more than twenty seized industrial facilities. These included more than a dozen manufacturing plants, the Montgomery Ward warehouses and stores, several refineries, and six coal mines. Beyond this, the government controlled several railroads in the Midwest and about a hundred small machine shops around San Francisco.[137]

In autumn 1945, as the seized facilities were returned to their owners, it appeared that the companies that had defied government labor boards had made a winning bet. In nearly every seizure case involving companies that refused to provide union security, the unions failed, during the reconversion months of 1945–46, to win maintenance of membership or any comparable protection.[138] This was especially true in the South. At Humble Oil, executives found a simple way to rid themselves of the OWIU local at the Ingleside, Texas, plant that had been seized in 1945: they simply closed that facility. Meanwhile, executives at Gaffney Manufacturing, once the company regained control over its seized textile mill, dug in for a fight. The TWUA local in Gaffney began a long strike that ended in 1947 with the company having broken the union. This was a major defeat for the CIO in the South, where organized labor would continue to struggle to find a foothold for years to come.[139]

During the reconversion months of late 1945 and early 1946, there was a wave of massive but mostly peaceful strikes. Some of the nation's largest companies, including General Motors, U.S. Steel, and General Electric, experienced lengthy stoppages. Many strikes ended with compromise agreements that provided workers with hourly pay raises of 10 percent to 20 percent.[140] On the face of it, this seemed to be a generous increase. However, because less overtime work was required after war's end and because price controls were lifted in 1946, the nominal raise failed to provide some workers with any meaningful increase in take-home pay.

During the reconversion period, the Truman administration continued to use seizures. From August 1945 to June 1946, President Truman ordered at least eight new takeovers. In one of the first, in early October 1945, he directed the Navy Department to begin a nominal takeover of much of the nation's oil industry. This seizure ended in the spring, after most companies and unions compromised on a wage increase of about 18 percent. In late January 1946, in the midst of a strike by meatpacking workers, the secretary of agriculture formally took charge of much of that industry. This takeover, which affected 255 packing plants, stockyards, and other facilities, lasted three months. It ended after the parties reached an agreement that allowed the companies to raise prices slightly, in order to go along with a raise of sixteen cents an hour for the workers.[141] This episode was an important (if poorly remembered) chapter in a longer-running dispute between the meat companies and the OPA, which became even more intense as the 1946 elections approached.[142]

Of all the seizures of the reconversion period, the two that received the most attention were the brief takeovers, in May 1946, of the railroads and the coal mines. The 21 May seizure of the coal mines, where strikes were already under way, was not especially surprising. The Interior Department had seized the mines repeatedly during the war years; President Truman had long despised John L. Lewis, the leader of the miners' union. In contrast, Truman had friendlier relations with the railroad union chiefs. They were present at the White House on 17 May, when the president announced that he would seize the railroads to prevent a strike that could cripple the national transportation network. When the railroad workers struck anyway, on 23 May, Truman, as Interior Secretary Ickes put it, "went haywire."[143]

In a cabinet meeting the next day, Truman startled his aides by saying that he would ask Congress for the power to induct the strikers into the armed forces. Truman also drafted a speech including language suggesting that it might be necessary to "hang a few traitors." (Truman's aides persuaded him to tone down his rhetoric.) As the president addressed Congress on 25 May, he received a note informing him that the railroad strike had been settled. The coal strike was settled three days later; but in November, yet another walkout by coal miners was met with yet another seizure. In early 1947, that takeover, the last of the World War II years, came to an end, as the mines were returned to private operators.[144] The Smith-Connally Act, which had ostensibly authorized the several dozen seizures that had occurred over the last four years, expired in June 1947.[145]

* * *

Thanks to the Republican victory in the 1946 midterm elections, which gave the GOP control of Congress for the first time in a decade and a half, conservatives were able to make substantial revisions to the Wagner Act. They did so with the Taft-Hartley Act of 1947, which passed over Truman's veto. This statute did not, in the short run, devastate existing unions, many of which managed to flourish for another generation, despite tougher hurdles set up by the new law. After the act was passed, some companies fought unions tooth and nail; others, including GM and Ford, settled into an entente with them. Still, Taft-Hartley undermined the labor movement over the longer run, by allowing individual states to pass "right-to-work" (open shop) laws. Over time, unions based in the North shrank, as companies moved more jobs to right-to-work locales, which included most of the states in the South.[146]

Among the many features of the Taft-Hartley Act were new procedures for dealing with strikes. Significantly, the Taft-Hartley Act—whose cosponsor, Senator Robert Taft, had long questioned the necessity of seizures—did not authorize government takeovers of private enterprises. Instead, it said that in the event that a looming strike appeared to threaten a national emergency, the president could appoint a special board of inquiry. After this board reported, the attorney general could ask a federal judge to issue an injunction that would impose an eighty-day cooling-off period.[147] These provisions were comparable with those that had been provided in 1943; but Taft-Hartley, unlike Smith-Connally, said nothing about the president's powers to seize private enterprises.

Controversy over seizure reemerged during the Korean War. In August 1950, the Department of Defense began a token seizure of the nation's railroads to prevent a strike over a wage dispute. President Truman was able to claim legal authority for this action from the 1916 statute that allowed the government to operate railroads "in time of war." (Although Congress never actually declared war during the Korean conflict, the United States would remain technically at war—with Japan—until spring 1952, when the Senate ratified a World War II peace treaty.) During the railroad seizure, which lasted until May 1952, nine company executives were commissioned as Army officers; private companies continued to manage day-to-day operations of the rails. The takeover soon alienated workers because until they settled their differences with the companies, they were forced to work without a contract and without the legal right to strike.[148] But the revival of seizures also bothered business leaders. In early 1951, the National Association of Manufacturers approved a new policy statement on takeovers, stating that if they were to take place at all, they must be accompanied by mechanisms for review by the courts and must not be used to alter the status quo of wages, hours, or working conditions.[149]

When the NAM was devising its policy statement on seizures in 1951, few Americans imagined that a year later, a new government takeover would lead to a serious constitutional crisis. But one did occur, starting in early April 1952, when Truman ordered the Commerce Department to seize the American steel industry, which was in the midst of dispute with unions and the government about wages and prices.[150] This takeover was met with fierce resistance from steel company executives and their fellow business leaders, who used the occasion to mount a major public-relations campaign.[151] Like the first Montgomery Ward seizure, eight years previously, this takeover became a sensational political event, in which the White House found itself on the defensive. In early June 1952, eight weeks after the seizure started, the U.S. Supreme Court delivered its opinion in the case of *Youngstown Sheet & Tube v. Sawyer*. In a 6–3 decision, the high court ruled that the steel seizure was illegal. This case still stands as a landmark ruling on the subject of the limits of executive power.[152] More narrowly, but significantly, it marked the end of an era of frequent government seizures of private enterprises.

Truman's defeat in the 1952 steel-seizure dispute was part of a broader repudiation of the intense regulation and state coercion that had been so central during the American industrial mobilization for World War II. Between 1941 and 1946, Presidents Roosevelt and Truman signed off on dozens of seizures, nearly all of which were managed by the military. Although many of those takeovers came in response to illegal strikes, the seizures should not be understood simply as a militarized form of discipline over labor. In fact, as the 1952 dispute showed again, the seizures often pitted government against business. The World War II takeovers were among the most spectacular results of a much broader struggle over the national state's labor policies. From the point of view of most business leaders, those policies—including the widespread use of maintenance of membership—were biased in favor of unions. Only a few executives pressed their objections so far that their enterprises ended up being seized. But as the contents of Sewell Avery's mailbags suggest, the business community's dissatisfaction with wartime labor policy was strong. So were its objections to the seizures, which seemed to confirm pro-business conservatives' long-running warnings against the rise of a New Deal dictatorship.

There were many reasons for the Truman administration's defeat in the steel-seizure case of 1952. These included its ineffective legal arguments, as

well as the Korean War's status as something less than the all-out emergency that had existed in World War II. But the 1952 result should also be
attributed to two broader forces, which were interconnected. One, about
which Truman himself complained,[153] was the political savvy and energy of
the business community, which came out of World War II well prepared
to challenge any new threats to the autonomy of private enterprise. This
continuing political mobilization contributed to the second factor: a
broader trend in the American political economy, which had changed significantly since 1945. By the 1950s, the nation had already started down the
path of deregulation. Among the most important pieces of this process were
developments in the biggest single arena of government-business interaction: the military economy. Starting with the reconversion efforts of 1945–
46—and continuing through the 1950s, 1960s, and beyond—the military-
industrial sphere was transformed by a new wave of privatization.

Chapter 6

Reconversions

On the evening of 10 December 1943, GM chairman Alfred P. Sloan, Jr. stood before hundreds of his fellow business executives to deliver a speech called "The Challenge." The occasion was the annual meeting of the National Association of Manufacturers (NAM), the group that had already done so much to spread pro-business messages about the war economy. Now, as Allied forces advanced in Italy, Sloan asked his audience to consider the problem of postwar reconversion. "Is it not as essential to win the peace, in an economic sense," he asked, "as it is to win the war, in a military sense?" For Sloan, winning the peace meant securing a postwar political-economic order in which private enterprise could again reign supreme. To achieve this, business leaders would need to meet the challenge of creating jobs for veterans. If they failed, Sloan predicted, the government would likely set up enterprises of its own, just as it had during the Depression. This, Sloan warned, would be "the beginning of the socialization of enterprise."[1]

By late 1943, Sloan and his fellow business leaders were optimistic about the prospects for a good demobilization and reconversion. With munitions production at full tilt and a more conservative Congress seated in Washington, the business community's political position was stronger than it had been for over a decade. Even so, many questions about reconversion remained unsettled. Manufacturers, still busy filling war orders, would have to find a way to settle their contracts and transition from military to civilian production. Even more worrisome, the government still owned about $15 billion worth of manufacturing plant, which represented roughly a fifth of the nation's industrial capacity. So there seemed to be plenty of potential for a postwar recession and for the sort of "socialization" of industry that Sloan and his colleagues feared.

As it turned out, reconversion proceeded in a way that mostly satisfied Sloan and his peers. Business-friendly contract termination and tax policies contributed to an economic transition that was remarkably smooth. To the surprise of many economists—and more than a few business leaders—the nation was able to avoid a postwar slump.[2] This eased the anxieties of Sloan and his fellow executives, who did not have to defend themselves against charges that free markets were again failing to provide jobs.

When it came to the disposal of government-owned war plant, there was more contention. This was understandable, given that plant disposal represented the largest privatization of public property in American history since the land sales of the nineteenth century. The property in question represented the largest set of state-owned assets outside the Soviet Union.[3] Business leaders favored a rapid sell-off of these assets, which they regarded as a potential threat to private enterprise. They were pleased in 1944, when Congress passed a plant-disposal law that explicitly favored privatization. But the process of plant disposal remained controversial. The privatization of the government's aluminum and steel plants, which was mostly done during 1946, inspired new debates about how to deal with the problem of monopoly. The disposal of government-owned capacity in basic industry was not finished until 1955, when the government sold off the last of its synthetic rubber plants. By then, Congress had already killed off the Reconstruction Finance Corporation (RFC), the public infrastructure bank that had paid for much of the American arsenal in World War II.

The problem of plant disposal was connected to another important part of the reconversion story: the privatization of the defense sector. The American military had always relied on private contractors, especially in wartime. But after World War II, this reliance grew, until it reached levels previously unknown in U.S. history. Because this privatization was a slow process, and one that developed during a period of unprecedented levels of military mobilization in peacetime, it was easy to overlook. But it was well under way by 1961, when President Eisenhower, in his farewell address, warned Americans about a "military-industrial complex." By the end of the 1960s, as some of the more astute critics of the Vietnam War–era defense sector pointed out, the American military economy was far more privatized than the one that fought World War II.

This privatization of the military-industrial complex was influenced by technological changes and, perhaps, by sober assessments of the cost savings promised by outsourcing. But it was also driven by an ongoing, highly ideological campaign to minimize public enterprise throughout the American economy, including the defense sector. This campaign was rooted in developments before and during World War II. In the late 1940s and early 1950s, it was continued by conservative business leaders and their allies, including Herbert Hoover. Hoover and his colleagues did not find it easy to reform the Cold War military establishment, a sprawling, secretive apparatus that included many departments with decades-long traditions of public enterprise. However, by the time Hoover and Alfred Sloan died—in the mid-1960s—the military was shedding most of its in-house industrial capacities. During World War II, when business conservatives boasted of an American war economy created by the genius of private enterprise, there was plenty of distortion and fantasy involved. Over the decades that followed, the dream of a fully privatized defense sector moved much closer to reality.

Soft Landings

In 1943–44, as business leaders and legislators turned their attention to reconversion, one of their main concerns was the cancellation and settlement of military contracts. In this area, policymakers were influenced by memories of the Great War. At the time of the armistice in November 1918, the United States military and its suppliers were transacting business under 24,000 contracts, worth about $7.5 billion. In World War II, the contract volume was about ten times larger. This was troubling, given that the smaller Great War termination job had been so difficult. By late 1919, about a third of contracts remained unsettled; over 10 percent remained unsettled in 1921. About three thousand World War I contracting disputes ended up in the U.S. Court of Claims, where they took an average of over three years to settle.[4]

"If war contracts are terminated in the ruthless manner of World War I," Eugene E. Wilson of United Aircraft declared in early 1944, "the [aircraft] industry can hardly survive." This was extreme rhetoric; but even outside business circles, most key players agreed that contract cancellations needed to be better handled than they had been in 1918–19. As one Ordnance Department officer put it in 1943: "The War Department is determined to profit from the costly lessons to be learned from World War I terminations." So, too, were most members of Congress, along with Roosevelt's cabinet and other civilian officials in Washington. Some believed that poor reconversion policies after the Great War had contributed to the sharp recession of 1920–21, an event that World War II mobilization czar James Byrnes remembered as "one of the sharpest economic collapses in history."[5] This time around, civilian and military leaders were determined to provide faster settlements, which would improve business confidence and speed reconversion.[6]

In comparison with their predecessors, reconversion policymakers in World War II expected to have the advantage of a less abrupt shift to peacetime. The sudden end to the Great War in November 1918 had come as a surprise, at a time when war production was still rising. Deliveries of merchant ships did not peak until May 1919, when the government was still spending large sums on munitions.[7] During World War II, by contrast, U.S. munitions output peaked in the winter of 1943–44, long before the end of combat operations. In autumn 1944, American policymakers hoped to enjoy a gentle, two-phase reconversion. Because the Pacific War was expected to continue for many months after V-E Day, it seemed likely that many military contractors would be able to transition gradually to civilian production.[8]

By 1943, the War and Navy Departments had already gained considerable experience with contract cutbacks and cancellations. This forced the military to begin to craft contract termination policies, well before Congress passed controlling legislation. Indeed, the Contract Settlement Act, which became law in July 1944, was largely an affirmation of policies that the War and Navy Departments had already put into practice. Two early cancellations in the tank program, involving Guiberson Diesel Engine and International Harvester (see Chapter 4), had convinced the War Department of the necessity of negotiated lump-sum settlements. Under these agreements, which became the rule, the government would reimburse the contractor for completed goods and the cost of incomplete units, along with a small allowance for profit. No full audit was used, unless there was evidence of fraud.[9]

Working ahead of civilian policymakers, military officers created a set of termination practices that emphasized speed and goodwill. As one senior civilian employee of the Chicago Ordnance District explained to an Army contracting officer in 1943, "we believe the prompt payment of termination charges in an amount that is _fair_ and that is _liberal_ instead of restrictive is truly important." If the military failed to issue fast termination payments, he noted, "national bankruptcy" after the war might result. This approach was established well before November 1943, when the War and Navy

Departments set up a Joint Contract Termination Board to help standardize policy.[10]

The military's quick-settlement approach was endorsed by civilian policymakers—most notably, in the "Baruch-Hancock Report" of January 1944. The authors of this influential reconversion blueprint were Bernard Baruch and John Hancock, who had been top industrial mobilizers during the Great War. In November 1943, James Byrnes, chief of the Office of War Mobilization (OWM), asked them to begin a study of the major issues surrounding reconversion. In their report, Baruch and Hancock called for quick termination settlements, handled by the same procurement agencies that were already overseeing contracts. Certainly, there should be no comprehensive audits by the comptroller general, which would be slow and impractical and might "quibble the Nation into a panic." Even if the government and a contractor could not immediately agree on a full settlement, Baruch and Hancock recommended, at least 90 percent of the claim should be paid immediately as an advance.[11]

This policy was endorsed by Byrnes, who used his clout as OWM director to institute it. Even before the Baruch-Hancock report was released, Byrnes ordered all procurement agencies to insert a "Uniform Termination Article" in all their contracts. This clause, which formalized existing War Department practices, called for termination settlements within sixty days. After the Baruch-Hancock report appeared, Byrnes encouraged Congress to adopt legislation that would provide for fast, easy settlements. "When you provide for contract terminations," Byrnes advised Congress in June 1944, "you are not giving contractors something, you are simply providing for the government to promptly pay what it owes. That's being honest."[12]

Congress needed little convincing. The idea of fast settlements appealed not only to the friends of larger corporations but to progressive champions of small business, such as Senator James E. Murray (D-MT), who worried that long audits might devastate subcontractors. Few congressmen sympathized with Comptroller General Lindsay C. Warren, who suggested that the General Accounting Office, rather than the military, should handle terminations.[13]

In the Contract Settlement Act, passed on 1 July 1944, Congress demanded that procurement agencies use quick settlements with their contractors. Except in cases of suspected fraud, there would be no detailed, time-consuming audits by the comptroller general. The law established a new civilian office to oversee termination, led by a director of contract settlement. In September 1944, the director proclaimed that in all cases, contractors should receive immediate partial payments of 75 percent to 90 percent of the estimated cost of any undelivered articles, materials, and parts. So as the nation moved closer to the end of the war, there was a clear termination policy, validating existing military practices, which promised to prevent significant delays in the payment of termination claims. According to one top Navy contract administrator, "the specter of ruinous inventory losses, which hung over war contractors until the passage of the Contract Settlement Act of 1944, has now vanished."[14]

These policies pleased the business community. Since 1943, the NAM, along with professional accountants, had been calling for negotiated settlements and fast payments. At the Automotive Council for War Production, in Detroit, George Romney and his staff, in consultation with Chrysler executives, had made lobbying on termination policy a high priority. The auto industry's best friends in Congress, including Senator Arthur H. Vandenberg (R-MI), were happy to endorse the Baruch-Hancock blueprint, which they regarded as the best policy for minimizing postwar unemployment, besides being good for business.[15]

By the time the Contract Settlement Act passed, in July 1944, Allied forces were already moving across northern France. On the home front, the military prepared for a wave of contract cutbacks and cancellations. By September, the War Department employed more than 6,500 people on contract terminations. The Army Air Forces created a new Readjustment Division, which provided training to more than two thousand military personnel. It also conducted meetings for contractors and subcontractors across the nation, which were attended by at least 27,000 people.[16]

Starting in summer 1944, military bureaus and contractors faced a sharp uptick in cutbacks and terminations. These amounted to $3.6 billion in the third quarter of 1944 alone. After reports of shortages and setbacks for Allied forces, they actually dropped in late 1944 and early 1945, to an average of about $2.1 billion per quarter. After V-E Day, there were huge cutbacks, especially for items such as tanks and artillery. In April–June 1945, the procurement bureaus reduced their orders by more than $14 billion; munitions schedules were cut by a third.[17]

The cutbacks of late 1944 and early 1945, like earlier ones, were applied unevenly across the war economy. Some of them, such as the Navy's May 1944 cancellation of its remaining orders with the troubled Brewster Aeronautical Corporation, were protested by workers and local officials. After

the Brewster episode, Byrnes demanded that all major cutbacks and terminations be cleared by the War Production Board, which would attempt to
dull the pain.[18] The military, together with the WPB, attempted to apply
cutbacks in a way that minimized disruption. However, in many cases,
mass layoffs were impossible to avoid. As the AAF reduced its schedules by
thousands of planes, its top contractors, including North American Aviation and Consolidated-Vultee, dismissed thousands of workers.[19]

The partial demobilization of 1944–45 involved complex political and
economic struggles. In June 1944, WPB chief Donald Nelson approved a
"spot authorization" plan that would allow some contractors to transition
early to civilian production. But the Pentagon resisted. The controversy
over Nelson's plan highlighted an emerging struggle among private companies. Some complained that the Pentagon's attitude favored big business
because it prevented smaller firms from getting a head start in the race for
postwar civilian markets.[20] This problem was real but was easily overstated.
The Pentagon was already making all sorts of major cutbacks that affected
hundreds of smaller subcontractors, as well as larger prime contractors.
Even when military officials appeared to act in ways that favored big business's postwar position, the realities could be more complicated. This was
the case when the Ordnance Department decided after V-E Day to terminate its orders of .50-caliber machine guns from GM's Frigidaire Division,
the low-cost producer. This certainly helped Frigidaire, which could return
more quickly to making consumer appliances. But the military also
intended to help Colt and Savage, the smaller specialty arms manufacturers,
which were much less eager to absorb drastic cuts in war orders.[21]

Debate over the early-reconversion issue ended abruptly because of the
shocking events of August 1945. World War II was over several months
earlier than expected. This meant that V-J Day caused a sudden demobilization, which was not so different from that of November 1918, after all. The
military immediately issued contract terminations amounting to $24 bil-
lion, half of the remaining war economy.[22]

For some companies, this change was not much more severe than the
one that they had experienced a few months earlier, after V-E Day. However, for those contractors who had been major Pacific War suppliers,
reconversion came very fast indeed. At the beginning of August 1945, Boeing's plants in the Seattle area were turning out 160 B-29s a month; the
plant that it operated in Wichita had a monthly output of an additional
hundred. Immediately after V-J Day, the AAF canceled orders for more

than two thousand B-29s, which had been intended for use in what would have been an enormously destructive, nonnuclear endgame to the Pacific War. On 14 August, the AAF ordered Boeing, along with its other contractors: "Immediately stop all work, terminate all subcontracts and place no further orders except as to additional work or material required to complete any unterminated portion of your contract." By October, Boeing had ceased B-29 production in Wichita; its output in Seattle had been cut by over 80 percent, to just twenty units a month. Boeing had no choice but to dismiss thousands of workers, as did many of its peers. At North American Aviation, for example, nearly twenty thousand workers were let go during the week following V-J Day.[23]

Although the cutbacks in the late summer of 1945 were severe, the generous termination policies devised in 1944 allowed most contractors to avoid financial ruin. By all accounts, the terminations went smoothly. About half of the claims were settled before the end of 1945; by mid-1946, the War Department had reached final settlements on over 80 percent of the dollar value of its canceled contracts.[24]

Contractors facing the stresses of reconversion benefited from generous tax laws. In the Revenue Act of 1942, Congress created two tax policies that would help businesses enjoy more working capital during reconversion. First, it required the Treasury to set aside 10 percent of all excess profits tax (EPT) payments, which would be returned to companies at war's end as an automatic refund. For the many contractors who paid millions of dollars in EPT payments, this amounted to a substantial, government-mandated reserve fund. The second provision allowed companies to "carry back" postwar losses—or even subpar profits—to one or more profitable wartime years. This would allow many companies to retroactively reduce their wartime tax bills, generating cash refunds.[25]

Even after Congress passed these provisions, many business leaders and accountants continued to lobby for new rules that would allow companies to avoid paying taxes on profits set aside in special reconversion reserve funds, so that they could better prepare for the stresses of the postwar months.[26] They never received this gift, but Congress did approve the calls by many business groups, including the NAM and the Chamber of Commerce, for a significant postwar tax cut. The Tax Adjustment Act, passed in the summer of 1945, ordered the Treasury to issue refunds more quickly. And a new Revenue Act, passed at the end of the year, canceled the EPT, thereby dropping the highest marginal rate faced by corporations, from 95 percent down to 38 percent. Ending the EPT provided the single biggest piece of the $5.7 billion tax cut provided by the Revenue Act. Here was a government stimulus that almost every business leader could appreciate.[27]

The business-friendly contract termination and tax policies contributed to the postwar boom, which saw unemployment levels stay well under 5 percent, far below the level that had been predicted by many government officials and economists. The aggregate profits of U.S. corporations in 1946–48, which averaged nearly $20 billion a year, were nearly twice as high as they had been during the war years.[28] Traditionally, the postwar expansion has been explained as a product of pent-up consumer demand. More recently, economists have emphasized the importance of exports.[29] But many business leaders, including the executives of leading military contractors, could also credit their soft landing to termination and tax rules. Many companies were helped by tax refunds, which in 1946 alone amounted to $1.1 billion. In the circles of leading military contractors, the refunds were especially important. Twelve top aircraft industry companies lost $150 million before taxes in 1946 and 1947 combined, but tax credits trimmed their net losses to $53 million. The Treasury also sent multimillion-dollar refunds in 1946 to important war contractors from the auto and electrical equipment industries, including GM, Packard, Westinghouse, and GE.[30] For these companies, and for the American business community as a whole, the reconversion era turned out to be less painful than expected.

Postwar Plant Sales

Although the contract termination and reconversion tax policies attracted some critical scrutiny, there was more controversy over a different aspect of the industrial mobilization: the disposal of government-owned war plant. A large part of the American "arsenal of democracy" consisted of government-owned industrial plant (buildings and machinery), much of which was built in 1940–43. Even without counting the more than $1 billion in off-the-books facilities created for the secret atomic weapons program, there was about $15 billion worth of government-owned plant. This represented about 20 percent of the nation's manufacturing capacity. It worried the champions of free enterprise, including many business leaders.

To be sure, there were reasons to question whether the government-owned plant amounted to much of a threat. The agencies that owned the most plant, including the War and Navy Departments, the Maritime Commission, and the Defense Plant Corporation (DPC), were not exactly bastions of socialism. The DPC owed its origins to left-leaning New Deal lawyers but was overseen by Jesse Jones, the most conservative member of Roosevelt's cabinet. Many DPC leases provided the operating companies with options to buy the plant at war's end. Moreover, there was good reason to believe that government-owned assets were less valuable than they seemed. This was pointed out in early 1944 by Louis Kahn, a practicing architect, who would soon emerge as one of the leaders of his profession. Many of them had been done on the cheap, Kahn reassured business leaders, and were meant to last only about five years. Many executives agreed. A majority of them, *Fortune* magazine reported, believed that fewer than half of the government-owned plants would be usable for civilian production.[31]

Despite signs that the disposal of government-owned war plant would not threaten capitalism, many Americans regarded it as a serious issue. On the left, it was assumed that war-plant disposal would be rigged to favor the big industrial corporations. This was the view of Interior Secretary Harold Ickes, as least in 1941–42, when he worried that the Alcoa leases of GOCO aluminum plants were too generous and that plant disposal would aid monopoly. Even less politically progressive officials, such as Ferdinand Eberstadt and James Forrestal, were sensitive to the problem. In January 1941, Eberstadt told Forrestal that he was worried that some manufacturers were already looking ahead "to the time when they will purchase these plants for a song." Certainly, Eberstadt predicted, plant disposal "will be an economic problem of first importance."[32]

For many business leaders, the real problem presented by the huge stock of government-owned plant was the encouragement that it might provide to New Deal–style schemes of state enterprise. Many of the most politically active business leaders, including Walter D. Fuller, head of Curtis Publishing, and Frederick C. Crawford, president of Thompson Products, warned that the GOCO plants must never be allowed to be operated by the government after the war, as "yardsticks" or otherwise. By late summer 1941, according to the official magazine of the Chamber of Commerce, the government plant problem had already become the "ghost that stalks at every business conference, the object of fear and misgiving, the destroyer of national unity."[33]

After Pearl Harbor, as dozens of new government-owned plants were authorized, business leaders and their allies became even more wary.

"Many of the new industrial plants," explained Senator Robert A. Taft (R-OH), "will be owned by the government. Whether they will ever be returned to private industry, any more than Muscle Shoals [the basis for the TVA] was returned to private industry, may well be doubted, unless Congress is constantly on guard, and determined to restore a system of privately owned and operated enterprise." Throughout the war, members of leading business associations, including the NAM and the Chamber, issued warnings about the problem; at their annual meetings, they passed resolutions calling for a ban on any government competition with private industry.[34]

For conservatives worried about war-plant disposal, one bête noire was the National Resources Planning Board (NRPB). This small agency, staffed by New Deal economists such as Eveline M. Burns and Alvin H. Hansen, was working on plans for a "full employment" postwar economy. As part of their plans for using public works to boost employment, NRPB economists suggested that some government-owned war facilities, such as the aluminum and rubber plants, might be used as the basis for new public-private partnerships in manufacturing, or for TVA-style public corporations.[35]

The NRPB proposals were denounced by most business associations. They also found little support in Congress, which moved swiftly in early 1943 to kill the agency. President Roosevelt, whose pollsters advised him that there was not much public support for a big new welfare state, let it die.[36]

Although the downfall of the NRPB pleased conservatives, their struggle to contain the threat posed by government-owned plant was far from over. According to public opinion polls, a large segment of the American public was open to many of the NRPB's proposals, including the idea of creating more public enterprises and public-private partnerships in industry.[37] Clifford J. Durr, the New Deal lawyer who helped create the DPC, continued to believe that some public facilities should be retained by the government, perhaps as TVA-style public enterprises or "yardsticks." This idea appealed to left-wing economists, such as Colston E. Warne and Maynard C. Krueger, along with James G. Patton, leader of the National Farmers' Union.[38] A more novel scheme was floated briefly by Interior Secretary Ickes, who suggested in an April 1944 speech that the public plant could be operated after the war by new public corporations, whose shares would be issued to veterans. But he never pursued this idea.[39] A few weeks later, Congress passed the GI Bill, which provided veterans with a variety of substantial benefits but no stake in the government plants.

Creative postwar uses of the public-owned facilities were also proposed by union leaders. "This wealth of factories and goods belongs to the American people," one CIO-issued comic book explained in 1944, "and must be used for their welfare."[40] CIO leaders, including UAW officials Walter Reuther and Donald Montgomery, usually stopped short of calling for the government to run the plant. Instead, they suggested, the government might use strict leases or purchase agreements, which would require private operators of the plant to keep them running full blast, with large (and presumably unionized) workforces. As the war came to a close, Reuther proposed that Willow Run and other large plants might be converted to the production of useful civilian goods, such as prefabricated housing and rail equipment.[41]

The CIO proposals came in the context of a larger public discussion of how to create a postwar economy that would provide "full employment." The more progressive proposals, which echoed some of the suggestions of the NRPB, envisioned a powerful new federal "Work Administrator," which could use public works projects to ensure jobs for all. In 1945–46, energetic lobbying by the Chamber, the NAM, and other business associations helped persuade Congress to create a less invasive law. The Employment Act of 1946 created a new Council of Economic Advisors, charged with helping the White House minimize unemployment. But it provided no big new public works agency; instead, it demanded that government employment policies must "foster and promote free private enterprise."[42]

The business community enjoyed similar success with surplus property disposal policy, which began to take shape in 1944. However, this victory was preceded by plenty of anxiety, which continued long after Congress rebuffed the NRPB. In fact, American business leaders did not resemble the oblivious creatures envisioned by *Business Week* magazine, which claimed in June 1943 that "almost without anyone's noticing it, large sectors of American industry have been socialized. . . . The old bugaboo of government ownership of industry has become an accomplished fact" during the war emergency, without any outcry: "no one has cared much."[43] This was a provocative claim; however, it was wrong.

Many conservative business leaders saw the public-owned plant as a serious threat. According to NAM president Frederick Crawford, James F. Lincoln, *Forbes* magazine, and others, government-owned plant might easily be used by New Dealers to compete unfairly with private enterprise. If this were allowed to happen, they warned, it would cause "the socialization of all industry" and the end of American freedom. When Crawford shared these thoughts with Alfred Sloan in 1943, the GM chairman agreed. In fact, Sloan claimed, the prospect of direct government competition was the problem that worried him most—more, even, than taxes, or labor relations. "If government once moves toward private industry," Sloan predicted, "private industry is finished."[44]

The problem of government plant was of special concern to executives in the aircraft industry, in which well over three-quarters of production capacity was now publicly owned. Throughout the war, aircraft industry executives and their allies urged their friends in Washington to stay alert, in order to resist the inevitable schemes for nationalization. They often called attention to the French case, where a (partial) nationalization in the 1930s had been followed by military failures in 1940. According to aircraft industry executives, the "miracle" of America's wartime production was a testament to the superiority of private enterprise, so any suggestion of government-operated plants after the war should be out of the question.[45] As a study by Harvard Business School, commissioned by the aircraft industry, warned in early 1945, "the possibility of government operation is still real. Final determination of policy on this issue of government versus private operation is of far-reaching importance."[46]

Although these concerns endured through the war's end, business leaders were pleased by policy developments in 1944. The influential Baruch-Hancock report, released in January of that year, recommended that Congress should insist on having "[n]o Government operation of surplus war plants in competition with private industry." Indeed, the report issued a large-font "Warning" against this outcome; on its very first page, it announced that one of the top priorities for reconversion should be "taking the government out of business."[47]

The business community received more good news in February 1944, when, in response to the Baruch-Hancock report, President Roosevelt used an executive order to create a new Surplus War Property Administration. Progressives hoped that this agency would be headed by David Lilienthal, head of the TVA, or another of their friends. When Roosevelt named Will L. Clayton, a top RFC administrator, they were stunned. Clayton, a wealthy cotton broker from Houston, was a friend of Jesse Jones; like Jones, he ranked as one of the most business-friendly high officials in the executive branch. When the Clayton-led agency began its operations in spring 1944, its members used the Baruch-Hancock report as a starting point. They also knew, and noted in their early meetings, that Congress seemed strongly opposed to any postwar government operation of the GOCO plant.[48]

In the end, Congress created a law that favored quick privatization but not economic concentration. According to the Surplus Property Act, which became law in October 1944, the government's disposal practices must "give maximum aid in the reestablishment of a peacetime economy of free independent private enterprise." It would have to "discourage monopolistic practices," by giving preference to smaller firms, as well as veterans.[49]

During the ten months between the passage of the Surplus Property Act and V-J Day, there was little disposal. It did seem clear, given the policies that took shape in 1944, that there would be some kind of massive sell-off of state-owned property. This did not prevent some business leaders from fearing the worst. As the July 1945 electoral victories of the Labour Party in Britain demonstrated, conservatives needed to remain vigilant.[50] A month later, the war was over; the problem of surplus property disposal became urgent.

By late 1944, Americans were already looking ahead to what promised to be an astonishing amount of war surplus. This would include not only government-owned plant, which had cost more than $15 billion, but also mountains of weapons and equipment. Much of this enormous stockpile would be sold off. According to *Fortune* magazine, this would certainly require "the greatest merchandising job in all history."[51] Some observers, including Interior Secretary Ickes, compared the coming sell-off to the government's post–Louisiana Purchase land sales of the nineteenth century, in which millions of acres of national territory were transformed into private property.[52]

This time around, what were the chances that the mass disposal of property would offer anything to average Americans? Some progressive critics of the war economy, who assumed that big business had taken over in Washington, were pessimistic. But at least a few voices were more hopeful. According to the editors of *Life* magazine, who addressed a readership of several million, there was still a chance to organize the disposal so that it would favor "veterans, small farmers and small business men." If this could be done, it might allow for "a rebirth of economic freedom in America." One way or another, *Life* announced, the disposal of the war surplus would "have a vast effect on the character of our postwar economy."[53]

In the end, the disposal of the public-owned war surplus did not help a new wave of small proprietors displace the large industrial corporations.

Indeed, much of the surplus property was acquired by "big business," including many of the larger war contractors. Did this amount to a giant government handout to monopoly capital? Did plant disposal boost economic concentration in America? Many critics have answered these questions in the affirmative. According to the journalist Robert Allen, writing in early 1947, the government's sell-off of its war plants to big corporations qualified as "the greatest scandal arising out of the war." The disposal program provided a big windfall for the nation's biggest war contractors, some historians have concluded.[54]

These claims are misleading. They exaggerate the extent to which surplus property disposal offered easy gains to America's largest companies. The disposal program did little to affect economic concentration at the national level; in a few cases, it clearly worked against monopoly. Much of the property was sold in competitive auctions, which allowed the government to recover something close to the real value of its holdings. So on the whole, we should not understand the process of World War II surplus property disposal as one in which big business triumphed by getting the people's assets for a steal.

However, we do need to understand this process as a giant privatization of public property. By 1955, the government's holdings of industrial plant—which, a decade earlier, had included steel mills, aluminum plants, the entire synthetic rubber industry, and a variety of other facilities—had been mostly liquidated. Certainly, some of this sell-off gave away too much to individual purchasers, at least in retrospect. But to focus on the dollar gains (or losses) associated with specific deals is to miss much of the larger significance of what was happening. From the point of view of the American business community, the outcome of the surplus property disposal process was really more of a political victory than an economic one. It eliminated much of the threat of a new wave of "government competition," revived by the World War II mobilization. And it reinforced and valorized the business community's strident political claims about the superiority of private enterprise.

Much of the political struggle over disposal focused on the plants. However, the volume of surplus movable property was also immense; its disposal qualified as a huge project in its own right. After V-J Day, the government found itself with tens of thousands of airplanes and trucks that it no longer wanted, along with hundreds of ships. It would also try to unload $2 billion worth of food, along with an endless number of

Figure 11. Surplus Curtiss P-40 "Warhawk" fighters, stacked at the Army Air Forces scrapyard, Walnut Ridge, Arkansas, ca. 1946. The scrapping of obsolete weapons was one important part of the job of surplus disposal after 1945. More politically controversial was the disposal of still-viable, costly industrial facilities, such as aluminum and synthetic rubber plants. National Archives photo, courtesy of Nick Veronico.

miscellaneous items, which included seven million tubes of toothpaste and seventeen thousand homing pigeons.[55]

To see the incredible waste and financial loss associated with their war effort, Americans needed look no further than the "boneyards," where thousands of airplanes sat in 1945–46, parked, awaiting their fate (see Figure 11). These were familiar not only to AAF veterans but to millions of moviegoers, who saw dramatic images of the boneyards in newsreels and in the powerful Hollywood reconversion film, *The Best Years of Our Lives* (1946). The parked aircraft, once so precious, were now unwanted. As the Surplus Property Administration (SPA) put it, they were "white elephants with wings." Many were damaged; most were already obsolete. Not everything would be scrapped immediately. About 1,500 of the still-world-class B-29 bombers were stored in military reserve. As many as 2,000 planes were "cocooned" in a spray-on plastic to prevent them from deteriorating. But these were the exceptions. By June 1946, the government had already declared 68,000 planes, including 21,000 bombers and 10,000 fighters, to be surplus.[56] How, exactly, was the government supposed to dispose of the aircraft that had been designed as fearsome weapons of war?

The answer came later in 1946, when the War Assets Administration (WAA; successor to the SPA) started to liquidate the boneyards. Most of the planes, once the pride of the AAF, would be sold for scrap. The numbers were not pretty. In September 1946, in one of the largest disposal transactions, the government sold 21,000 planes that had been sitting in boneyards in Arkansas, Oklahoma, Arizona, and California. This giant sale, which involved aircraft that had cost the government $3.9 billion, brought only $6.6 million—well under 1 percent of the original cost. Most of the planes were bought by just five companies, which became part of a single entity, called the Aircraft Conversion Company. Among the leaders of this enterprise were George and Herman Brown, of Brown & Root, the Texas-based construction company that served during World War II as an important builder of ships, as well as military bases. The Browns and their associates tore the planes apart, so that their components could be separated and melted down. They ended up with 200 million pounds of aluminum, along with smaller amounts of silver, platinum, and some usable fuel. The Browns and their associates turned a profit on the deal—and probably a bigger one than they had any right to expect, given that postwar aluminum prices ended up being higher than anticipated.[57]

Like obsolete planes, aging warships had limited value. Most would end up being scrapped. A few, however, experienced a demise that was far more spectacular. In 1946, the Navy gathered a small fleet of surplus ships at Bikini Atoll, in the middle of the Pacific Ocean. The vessels assembled at Bikini included four old battleships, two carriers, two cruisers, thirteen destroyers, eight submarines, and six LSTs, along with several dozen smaller craft. According to the Pentagon, the ships had originally cost nearly half a billion dollars but were now worth only about $3.7 million, if sold as scrap. Instead of being auctioned off, they served as targets of the first atomic explosions since Nagasaki. In July 1946, the U.S. military dropped two bombs at Bikini: one that exploded in the air; and another—far more impressive to observers—that detonated underwater. Several of the surplus warships sunk on site; most of the rest, badly contaminated, were scuttled before the end of 1948.[58]

In comparison with old warships and military aircraft, merchant ships held more of their original value. But even here, government sales agencies knew that the task would not be easy. After the Great War, the government had sold off 220 merchant ships for $41 million, only about 8 percent of their original cost. Now, in 1945, the United States faced the aftermath of a much bigger merchant shipbuilding effort, which had produced 5,300 ships. This amounted to about 55 million deadweight tons of shipping, five times what the United States had held before the war and more than the global market could absorb. Only the best, fastest American-made ships, which included more than six hundred C-types, five hundred Victory ships, and six hundred high-speed oil tankers, would be in high demand. There would be fewer customers for the far more numerous Liberty ships, the so-called Ugly Ducklings.[59]

The disposal of these vessels was governed by the Merchant Ship Sales Act, passed by Congress in March 1946. Of the nearly 1,400 merchant ships sold off by mid-1947, more than two-thirds were purchased by foreign parties. American firms, which were given preference, snapped up most of the C-ships. Europeans proved to be especially interested in the T2 tankers, which they used to alleviate serious postwar fuel shortages. Most of the more than two thousand surplus Liberty ships were never used again.[60]

Although the sale of surplus aircraft, ships, and other equipment was a big job, it never caused the same sort of struggles that accompanied the disposal of industrial plant. This problem also existed in 1918, when the government held plant that had originally cost about half a billion dollars. After 1918, the government sold most of it, for only about 5 percent of what it had originally cost. But in 1945, the stakes were far higher. The government now held thousands, not hundreds, of facilities, including over ten thousand acres worth of factory floor space. These plants, which represented 15 percent to 25 percent of the nation's industrial capacity in 1945, were worth not millions of dollars but billions.[61]

"Plant disposal is perhaps the most complex of all surplus problems," reported the Office of War Mobilization and Reconversion in July 1945. The complexity came in part from the mismatch between the nature of the property and the hopes for its use. In Washington and across the country, there was a popular consensus that the surplus plant should be used to favor smaller, innovative enterprises. But many of the facilities, built for high-volume war production, were immense. And nearly a quarter of the government-owned plant, worth about $4 billion, consisted of so-called scrambled facilities, in which the public assets were distributed amid private plant, on the same sites. Many of these, which would be very difficult to sell to anyone but their operators, were run by large corporations.[62]

Despite these obstacles, most government officials were committed to keeping plant disposal from adding to economic concentration. Such was the view of one of the most influential congressmen working on disposal policy, Senator Joseph C. O'Mahoney (D-WY). The former chair of TNEC, the body that had conducted a massive investigation of economic concentration in America in 1938–41, O'Mahoney wanted to avoid socialism, on the one hand, and monopoly, on the other. "[B]oth the economic and the political future of this country," O'Mahoney said in autumn 1945, "will be deeply affected by what is done with these Government-owned facilities."[63]

What was done, for the most part, was that the plants were sold off for the highest prices that the government could obtain. Following their congressional mandate, surplus disposal agencies favored quick privatization. "Disposal to private interests," the SPA explained in one of its publications, "will be given preference over any form of Government financing, ownership, or control."[64] Disposal was a big enterprise. The lead selling agency at the outset was the SPA; it was succeeded in early 1946 by the WAA. The WAA's operations peaked in early 1947, when it had 57,000 employees. By 1949, when it was absorbed by the new General Services Administration, the WAA and its predecessors had acquired real property (mostly war plant) with an original cost of about $7.8 billion. By mid-1949, 82 percent of this real property had been sold, for an average of 36 percent of the cost of the government's original investment.[65]

This aggregate performance seems respectable, especially if measured against the post–Great War sales. By 1946–48, when most of the disposal took place, few plants were worth as much as the government had paid for them five years earlier, before they had been used hard for war production. Many plants were simply too big to be used efficiently, at least by the vast majority of American firms.[66] This was evident in the mixed performance of those companies that did buy or lease giant war plants. For smaller, independent companies, these acquisitions rarely worked out. Playboy Motors failed in its attempt to make money-producing convertible cars at the big facility in Tonawanda, New York, where GM had recently been making aero engines. The Kaiser-Frazer Corporation, cofounded by Henry Kaiser, the famous Liberty shipbuilder, spent about $1 million a year in the late 1940s and early 1950s to lease Willow Run, where Ford had recently been mass-producing B-24 bombers. This enterprise was a bust: in five years, Kaiser-Frazer lost over $100 million. In late 1953, the government sold Willow Run to GM, for $26 million. This transfer was telling: in general, it was only the largest corporations, such as GM and International Harvester, that had much success using the big GOCO war plants.[67]

As SPA and WAA officials went about the business of selling, they learned that there could be huge disparities between the original cost of a plant and its postwar market value. Behind the aggregate, average sale-cost ratio of 36 percent, there were enormous variations. In some cases, the government recovered nearly 100 percent of what it had originally paid. This was true in the case of one of the largest of the early plant sales, in 1945, when Bethlehem Steel agreed to pay $22 million—full cost—for the government-owned part of a scrambled facility in Pennsylvania.[68]

The government's single biggest success, in terms of cost recovery, came in 1947, with the sale of its "Big Inch" and "Little Inch" pipelines. Built with RFC funds in 1942–44, the pipelines—each of which ran over 1,300 miles, from the Gulf Coast to the Northeast—had helped keep oil and gasoline flowing to the nation's biggest population centers during the war. Together, the two pipelines had cost the government $140 million. In late 1946, the WAA tried to auction them off, but the highest bid (for both pipelines together) came in at just $66 million. Instead of letting them go for this price, WAA director Robert M. Littlejohn, a retired major general from the Army's Quartermaster Corps, decided to reject all bids. Littlejohn then got permission from Congress to allow the pipelines to be used for natural gas transmission, not just for liquid fuels. In a second auction, held in 1947, the winning bidder, the Texas Eastern Transmission Corporation, agreed to pay $143 million—the full wartime cost.[69]

Usually, the government recovered far less. Most of the government-owned aviation gasoline plant, nearly all of which was in scrambled facilities run by the leading oil companies, was sold to the operators for well under the wartime costs.[70] A few big plants sold for less than 10 percent of the initial costs. One of them was the giant magnesium facility in Velasco, Texas, purchased for $5 million by Dow Chemical, the wartime operator. The government found few parties willing to pay high prices for the big GOCO ordnance plants. This appeared to work to the benefit of state universities, several of which—including Texas A&M and Iowa State—acquired large facilities for next to nothing.[71] However, in many cases, these ordnance plants were at least partially reappropriated by the military, for Cold War production.[72]

At the national level, plant disposal turned out to do little to affect aggregate levels of industrial concentration. Progressive critics, including the Smaller War Plants Corporation, whose oft-cited report on the subject was issued by Congress in 1946, claimed that the sell-off of the public plant, along with wartime contracting, had boosted concentration. But this was not true, as several careful studies have shown. If anything, there seems to have been a very small decrease in concentration—including in inter-regional terms, thanks to the surfeit of new war plant that went up in Texas and California. But even this industrialization of the Sunbelt appears to have done less than might be expected to change prewar trends of U.S. regional economic development.[73] More akin to a lumbering battleship than a sleek destroyer, the national economy proved harder to reform—in any direction—than many observers had anticipated.

Such was the situation at the macro level. But the record of plant disposal is only comprehensible if we also consider developments in specific sectors, such as aluminum and synthetic rubber, in which the GOCO plant was especially important. Together, these industry-level developments suggest that the antimonopoly orientation of American public policy helped prevent any outrageous giveaways to the nation's biggest corporations, even if it did not prevent some companies from profiting from plants formerly held by the public.

In the case of aluminum, the disposal of GOCO plant wrought a significant change in industrial organization. Before World War II, there had been only one domestic producer of aluminum metal: Alcoa. During the war, Alcoa operated under the shadow of an ongoing antitrust prosecution by the Justice Department. Meanwhile, RFC loans had allowed a second company, Reynolds Metals, to get started in the business. But Reynolds's capacity remained small (at about 7 percent of domestic ingot production). Nearly all the GOCO plant, which represented over half of all production capacity, was run by Alcoa. On V-J Day, the fate of the industry remained uncertain and highly dependent upon the disposal of the GOCO plant.[74]

In summer 1945, Alcoa was still hoping to acquire at least some of the most desirable of the GOCO aluminum plants, including facilities in Arkansas, Oregon, and Washington.[75] But Alcoa's offers were rejected by W. Stuart Symington, Jr., the new Surplus Property Administrator. (Symington, who led Emerson Electric during the war, would later become the first

secretary of the Air Force, and then a U.S. senator.) Symington, well aware
of the attitude of Congress, the courts, and the Justice Department, knew
that he could not dispose of the plants in a way that perpetuated Alcoa's
monopoly. But it would not be easy to offer them to others because the
leases under which Alcoa had been operating the DPC-owned plant were
not set to expire until 1948. On 27 August 1945, Symington met with
Arthur V. Davis, Alcoa's eighty-year-old chairman, to ask him to end the
leases voluntarily. Davis refused. Symington responded by unilaterally can-
celing the leases, under the legal cover of a clause that allowed the government to do so if the plants had been operating below 40 percent of capacity
for at least six months.[76]

Symington then turned to Reynolds Metals, which ended up leasing or
purchasing nine GOCO plants, which had originally cost the government
nearly $200 million.[77] Reynolds was soon joined by the ubiquitous Henry
Kaiser, who arranged a $16 million line of credit from Bank of America, in
San Francisco, to help him enter the aluminum industry. Starting in 1946,
Kaiser negotiated with the government to lease several major GOCO aluminum facilities.[78] These maneuvers, approved by Symington and his colleagues, ended the Alcoa monopoly. "Never before," *Fortune* magazine
claimed in 1946, "has a one-company industry been cracked open so fast,
so wide, and so handsome for competition."[79] By the mid-1950s, Kaiser
and Reynolds each had about a quarter of U.S. aluminum production
capacity; the remainder rested with Alcoa, still the industry leader.[80] By
then, when American aluminum production was 800 percent higher than
it had been in 1940, it was clear that the postwar leases negotiated by Reynolds and Kaiser were good deals for the companies. Back in 1945–46, when
postwar demand for aluminum remained uncertain, it had not been quite
so obvious.[81]

Soon after the first Reynolds and Kaiser deals were announced, Americans
interested in the politics of plant disposal turned their attention to the steel
industry. Although the postwar months saw the sell-off of several large
GOCO steel plants, public attention was directed at the largest of them: the
giant integrated steelworks in Geneva, Utah. Outside the atomic bomb program, this $200 million facility, located near Salt Lake City, was the most
expensive of all the plants financed by the United States during World War
II. During the war, it had been built and operated by U.S. Steel, for no fee.
The fate of this behemoth was of great interest to Westerners, who imagined
that it might be a key to their region's postwar economic development.

Would U.S. Steel, the biggest company in the industry, be allowed to acquire it? Many observers doubted it. In early 1945, Attorney General Francis Biddle suggested that it should not be allowed to do so.[82]

But U.S. Steel did acquire the giant Geneva steelworks. In May 1946, it agreed to take ownership by paying the government $47 million—under a quarter of the plant's original cost. Not surprisingly, this deal was subjected to widespread criticism, especially from champions of small business and antimonopoly progressives.[83] Was this an outrageous giveaway to monopoly capital, as they maintained? Neither the details of the Geneva sale nor the plant's postwar fate suggests that it was quite so bad.

Like so many other GOCO plants, the big Geneva steelworks were disposed of by the WAA, via competitive auction. Clearly, competition for the property was limited by the sheer size of the facility. In the end, the WAA received just six bids. The only all-cash bid came from U.S. Steel, which offered to pay $40 million for the plant itself, plus $7.5 million for the inventory on site. The other bidders, who offered only to lease the plant, all asked for substantial government loans. One of them, Pacific-American Steel & Iron, based in Seattle, offered to co-manage the plant with the government, in the sort of public-private partnership that had been envisioned a few years earlier by the NRPB. Many observers expected a bid from Henry Kaiser, who had publicly expressed interest in leasing the Geneva works. In September 1945, Kaiser suggested privately to Symington that he might even use the plant as the core of "a giant ordnance center" in Utah. But Kaiser, who was still paying off the government loans that had financed his own large steelworks in Fontana, California, never submitted a formal bid. From the point of view of the WAA, the offer from U.S. Steel was clearly superior. As soon as Attorney General Tom C. Clark approved the deal, it went forward.[84]

Although U.S. Steel's acquisition of the Geneva works made it more of a player in the postwar West, the company never became the sort of bullying regional monopoly that many had feared. The Geneva plant may not have been a white elephant, but neither was it a steal. Because of its location, it was always struggling with the high cost of transporting metal to the West Coast. This helps explain why Kaiser's Fontana complex, which had only half of Geneva's capacity in 1946, grew faster than its Utah competitor over the next two decades. By the 1960s, the Geneva facility, like other American steel plants, was already having trouble competing with Japanese imports.[85]

Most of the major GOCO plant leases and sales, including those in the aluminum and steel industries, were completed by mid-1947. But one group of plants remained under government ownership much longer: the synthetic rubber industry. One reason for the delayed sales in this sector was concerns about national security. Everyone remembered the rubber crisis after Pearl Harbor. In 1946, Congress and military policymakers agreed that the government should retain synthetic rubber plant with a combined capacity of about 600,000 long tons a year—about two-thirds of peak wartime output—in case the nation again faced an unwelcome interruption of imports of natural rubber. This reserve policy allowed for some sales. Between October 1946 and December 1948, the government auctioned off eighteen of its fifty-one plants, which had originally cost $270 million, for $74 million. Five plants were mothballed (to be revived only in case of war); another five were scrapped.[86]

Even after these early disposals, the government still owned a substantial GOCO synthetic rubber industry. Its twenty-three active facilities included several large butadiene plants (which originally cost between $10 million and $60 million each), most of them operated by large chemical and oil companies. The butadiene was combined with other chemicals in copolymerization plants, which produced GR-S rubber. Most of these were run by tire companies, just as they had been during the war. For the tire companies, along with other buyers of rubber, the synthetic rubber plants were a valuable source of supply.[87]

Such was the situation in early 1948, when Congress passed new legislation that provided a path to privatization. In the 1948 Rubber Act, Congress demanded that the nation establish a "free, competitive synthetic rubber industry" that would require the end of government ownership. However, it allowed over a year for the RFC and the White House to come up with a privatization plan. In January 1950, the Truman administration, emphasizing the dangers of the Cold War, asked Congress to extend the Rubber Act for a full decade. This did not fly. It was only because of the Korean War emergency that Congress agreed to delay action, until 1954.[88]

As the Korean War ended, government and industry moved toward a final privatization of the synthetic rubber plants. The plants had proved valuable during the Korean War, when natural rubber prices had spiked. Furthermore, recent technological innovations, including "cold rubber" and "oil extended" methods of manufacture, had made synthetic rubber even more competitive. So by 1953, when Congress passed the Rubber

Producing Facilities Disposal Act, there were high hopes for a good return on the government's investment. In 1954–55, the government sold twenty-six plants, for a total of about $275 million. This transaction provided the United States with a net profit of roughly $10 million, over and above its initial investment, and a decade's worth of net operating costs. Nearly all the plants were sold to the same set of big oil, chemical, and tire companies that had been operating them since the war.[89]

Thanks to continuing demand for synthetic rubber, the privatized GOCO plants were well used by their buyers. However, they do not seem to have provided extraordinarily high profits. Analysis of the first few years of private control suggested that even with a healthy market for synthetic rubber, the companies' rates of return on their net investment in the GOCO plant hovered between 6 percent and 9 percent.[90]

Although the privatization of the synthetic rubber industry may not have qualified as a windfall for business in purely economic terms, it represented a clear victory for business leaders and their allies in their long-running fight against "government competition" with private industry. This was the certainly the view of William O'Neal, president of General Tire & Rubber, who said in March 1954 that he and his fellow executives were united in their effort to "wrest their industry from the clutches of government control." Their goal, O'Neal explained, was "to get the government out of private industry and keep it out." This dimension of the sale of the rubber plants was also understood by the news media, which correctly characterized the transactions as part of a broader exercise by the Eisenhower administration in "avoiding government competition with taxpaying private enterprise." According to much of the national press coverage, the sale of the rubber plants in 1954–55 was the furthest thing from a boon to monopoly capital. Rather, it was the "end of a monopoly"—a monopoly that had been held for over a decade by the federal government.[91]

Privatizing the Military-Industrial Complex

Although the sale of the synthetic rubber plants in 1955 involved the last big group of publicly held, DPC-financed GOCO war plants in basic industry, there remained a large set of government-owned manufacturing facilities. These included dozens of aircraft and ordnance plants, as well as naval shipyards, which the military retained long after 1945. But in the 1950s and 1960s, even these facilities were being let go, as part of an ongoing privatization of the defense sector. By the time of President Eisenhower's famous warning about the rise of the military-industrial complex (MIC), which he delivered in his farewell address in 1961, the privatization of the American military economy was well under way. It was driven not merely by technical calculations but also by the partisan, pro-business public-relations campaign, which had been pursued energetically since the New Deal, including throughout World War II. After 1945, this campaign continued to influence the structure of the defense industry.[92]

As World War II ended, many Americans expected that there would be a true demobilization, ushering in an era of low defense spending. At the same time, the emergence of new technologies—including rockets and the atomic bomb—suggested that the United States would never again be able to carry out a two- or three-year industrial mobilization. As Senator Harley M. Kilgore (D-WV) put it, in August 1945: "The next war will be lost in 8 to 10 weeks—or won." This was also the view of many top military officers, whose requests for bigger budgets were informed not just by self-interested jockeying for more resources but also by genuine concerns about how they could provide adequate defense.[93]

In Washington, the Truman and Eisenhower administrations found themselves doing battle against a large group of proponents of higher defense outlays, including many Pentagon officials and members of Congress, as well as contractors. President Truman approved much higher military outlays only after the start of the Korean War, in the summer of 1950. By 1951, after the alarming intervention of Chinese forces, Truman was endorsing a large military-industrial "mobilization base," capable of making 50,000 planes and 35,000 tanks a year. This was not just a temporary wartime expedient but a more long-term realization of the goals suggested in NSC-68, the influential national security blueprint that was drafted after the first Soviet atomic bomb test, in 1949.[94]

The budget struggles were resumed by President Eisenhower, who came into office in 1953 determined to scale back defense outlays. Hawks were dissatisfied with Eisenhower's "New Look" policy, which sought to save money by relying heavily on nuclear weapons, instead of large conventional forces. Eisenhower prevented huge increases in military spending but failed to shrink it: by the time he left office in 1961, it had stabilized at about 9 percent of GDP. This was well under the military's share of economic output in the Soviet Union. But it was still more than enough to sustain a large military establishment, which accumulated the means of destroying much of humankind.[95]

In these struggles over military budgets in the late 1940s and throughout the 1950s, some business firms had more than a casual interest. But the ranks of companies that pressed for more spending were rather small. The most active of them were the manufacturers of airplanes and their components, the members of what would soon be known as the "aerospace industry."

Immediately after V-J Day, most companies in the aircraft industry expected to have to reorient their enterprises dramatically. Thanks to their enormous sales volume during the war years, most companies had a cushion of several millions of dollars in cash and government securities. However, most of them lost money in 1946 and 1947. Future demand—for civilian and military products alike—remained uncertain. In Seattle, directors of Boeing were concerned about finances in late 1946, even though they were sitting on $45 million in cash and Treasury notes. To remain competitive in the emerging markets for commercial and military jets, they believed, they would have to quickly borrow an additional $15 million from private banks. Elsewhere, aircraft company executives attempted to blunt the shock of demobilization by diversifying. Several top war contractors, including Consolidated-Vultee (Convair) and Grumman, began to produce civilian goods such as appliances, buses, and boats.[96]

Given the uncertain conditions in 1946–47, few aircraft companies were interested in trying to lease or buy many of the large GOCO facilities that they had operated in wartime.[97] There were some exceptions. Douglas Aircraft, which came out of the war with a net worth of about $60 million, decided to buy part of the government-owned plant in Long Beach for about $3.7 million.[98] But for the most part, the GOCO airframe plant was unwanted. This was true even of the brand-new facility in Renton, Washington, where Boeing had been making B-29 bombers. "[W]e don't want to retain the Renton plant," Boeing president William Allen told the AAF in mid-1946. "As rapidly as we can get rid of it, we want to." So the military kept the plant as a storage facility.[99]

Even as aircraft companies were struggling to survive without huge war contracts, they were lobbying in Washington to keep military demand from falling too far. They drafted a former top AAF procurement chief, General Oliver P. Echols, to head the Aircraft Industries Association, which functioned as the industry's main lobbying organization. In 1946, it hired Hill &

Knowlton, a top public-relations firm, to create the "Air Power Is Peace Power" campaign, which educated Congress and the public about the need for a strong air defense. This campaign influenced the presidentially appointed Air Policy Commission, which recommended that the newly independent Air Force (USAF) be allowed to maintain seventy groups, which meant about 12,400 state-of-the-art planes. In the wake of the Air Policy Commission report and the communist takeover in Czechoslovakia (also in early 1948), Congress provided nearly $1 billion more for aircraft than Truman requested.[100]

The aerospace industry's lobbying successes of the late 1940s suggested that the United States was already seeing the rise of a MIC, in which anxieties about national security were being harnessed to promote private economic interests. But at this point, a large fraction of the nation's defense plant was still owned by the government. During the industrial demobilization of 1945–47, while most of the DPC-owned plant was auctioned off by the WAA, the Navy and War Departments joined the sell-off, after designating several billion dollars' worth of their own goods and plant as salable surplus. However, the military departments held back about $2 billion worth of their own GOCO plant (including tens of thousands of machine tools), for use in a future emergency. The Navy, which took delivery of twelve large aircraft carriers and 129 other new warships during the year and a half after V-J Day, also created a "reserve fleet" of more than two thousand vessels.[101]

As the Cold War deepened, this emergency industrial reserve grew. In early 1948, President Truman temporarily froze all surplus plant sales and leases. Later that year, Congress passed the National Industrial Reserve Act, which authorized a "Departmental Industrial Reserve," consisting of government-owned facilities controlled by the military services. It also established a "National Industrial Reserve," composed of plants that were sold to private firms but with contract clauses that would force their buyers to return them to war production in case of emergency. By the time of the Korean War, about two hundred plants were in each of these two reserves.[102]

At the local level, some politicians and business leaders regarded military reserve facilities as far from ideal because they could tie up large properties without adding many jobs or generating tax revenue. Such was the case in Groton, Connecticut, where the Navy was interested, in 1946, in mothballing its "Victory Yard," where the Electric Boat Company made submarines during the war. Thanks to pressure from local interests, the property was instead sold, for just 8 percent of its original cost, to Charles Pfizer & Company, the pharmaceutical company. This transaction was a great deal for Groton, which gained a high-tech research facility that would boost the local economy for decades to come.[103]

As the Cold War intensified, more of the military's reserve facilities were actually used, so the political calculus changed. Increasingly, government-owned plants became valued by localities, sometimes more so than by the companies operating them. Such was the case in Wichita, site of a large government-owned airframe plant where Boeing made B-29s during the war. In 1948, against the wishes of Boeing, the USAF decided to give a large order for B-47 bombers to the Wichita plant, instead of to Boeing's privately owned facilities in Seattle. Ostensibly, this was part of a new (and ultimately halfhearted) "industrial dispersion" initiative, designed to limit the Soviets' ability to knock out American war production with a small number of atomic weapons. It was also entangled with domestic political struggles over the location and control of defense production. Because the military still owned so much plant, it could choose to have most of its manufacturing done in its own GOCO and GOGO facilities, where it had even greater control than it did over the private plants of its contractors.[104]

During the Korean War, this public-private balance in the defense sector began to shift. This was not because of any immediate reduction in the stock of government-owned reserve plant, much of which—including the big USAF airframe plants in Marietta, Georgia, and Tulsa, Oklahoma—was now reactivated.[105] However, when it came to the construction of new defense plant, there was now a striking departure from World War II practices. This time around, American companies made fuller use of the accelerated amortization provisions allowing fast (five-year) depreciation of defense plant. These tax benefits, available from 1950 to 1956, were similar to those that Congress created back in 1940. But during the Korean War, about 90 percent of the new war plant was financed privately, across the economy, compared with just 40 percent in World War II. By 1956, American companies had built $22 billion worth of new defense-related plant and research facilities, for which the amortization law provided a tax break of about $5 billion.[106]

Thanks to the new crop of privately financed defense plant during the Korean War era, the American military economy became less dominated by publicly owned facilities. Even then, the military retained a great deal of plant. In mid-1954, 249 plants remained in the Departmental Industrial Reserve (owned by the military), worth nearly $9 billion. As late as 1961, when President Eisenhower delivered his warning about the MIC, the military still owned half the manufacturing capacity in the aircraft industry.[107] Two decades after they had become the basis for Roosevelt's "arsenal of democracy," GOCO and GOGO plants were still important. But they were in decline, thanks in part to the growing political strength of the champions of free enterprise.

After V-J Day, pro-business conservatives enjoyed new success in the arena of domestic politics. In the first national elections held after war's end, in November 1946, Republicans, running against government regulation, took back control of Congress, where they had been in the minority for a decade and a half.[108] Even before this major electoral defeat, American progressives recognized that they had lost ground. As Senator Claude Pepper (D-FL) explained to a California audience in September 1946, the recent public-relations efforts of business conservatives had won the day. "We have almost enshrined the words 'free enterprise'—propagated by the National Association of Manufacturers and the organs of monopoly—into a national taboo beyond the reach of inquiring minds," Pepper said. "We are swept into the current of those who thrust at government bureaucracy and we privately rail at government controls." Thanks to the "selling job" done in recent months by war contractors and other members of the business community, Pepper claimed, Americans had turned against the New Deal state.[109] This analysis was supported by the results of a Gallup poll of early 1948, which found that when Americans were asked to choose between freedom and economic security, 83 percent preferred the former.[110]

The appearance of a rightward drift in domestic politics was encouraging to pro-business conservatives but was not enough of a triumph to allow them to rest. During the late 1940s, they continued to raise millions of dollars for public-relations campaigns, which touted the superiority of free enterprise and traditional American political liberties. After the election of 1948, in which Truman won a surprise victory, disappointed conservatives redoubled their efforts.[111] In many fields, they prevailed. Truman's "Fair Deal," which included proposals for national health care, more public housing, and more TVA-style public enterprises, was blocked in Congress.[112]

As Truman turned into a lame duck, the ongoing Cold War seemed to help push the nation's political center of gravity further to the right. Thanks to the Soviet atomic bomb test and the "loss" of China in 1949, anticommunism was becoming even more powerful. This trend was evident not only in the growing influence of conservatives like Joseph McCarthy and Richard Nixon but in the orientation of ostensibly liberal Democrats. In the 1940s and early 1950s, the rhetoric of left-leaning Democrats such as John F. Kennedy, Paul Douglas, and Adlai E. Stevenson contained more criticisms of economic regulation (in health care, among other fields) and more emphasis on liberty. In 1952, Stevenson, the Democratic Party's candidate for the presidency, went so far as to tell *Newsweek* magazine, "I don't like subsidies, doles, or interference with free markets, free men, and free enterprise."[113]

One of the more remarkable manifestations of this postwar conservatism was the reemergence of Herbert Hoover, who left the White House back in 1933. Since then, Hoover had worked mostly behind the scenes in Republican Party politics. But after the elections of 1946, in which Republicans retook Congress, Hoover assumed a more public role. In 1947, at the age of seventy-three, he was named chairman of the new Commission on Organization of the Executive Branch of the Government.[114] This body, widely known as the "Hoover Commission," was ostensibly a bipartisan operation charged with making government more efficient. But it—along with a second Hoover-led commission, which operated in the early 1950s— was also an important player in the postwar drive for privatization.

The first Hoover Commission, which operated in 1947–49, had only limited influence, thanks in part to Truman's unexpected reelection. The recommendations that had the most influence, such as those that informed the National Security Act of 1949 (reorganizing the Defense Department), were the least partisan ones.[115] But the first Hoover Commission called openly for more privatization. Several of the "task forces" established by Hoover, as well as the management consultants they hired to assist them, were focused on the problem of "federal business enterprises" competing unfairly with private business. When it came to the controversial question of the TVA and other public utilities, the commissioners were too divided to agree on a recommendation. But they did criticize the government-run postal system, along with federal agencies that offered loans to farmers. They also called for the liquidation of the RFC, the great financier of World War II plant.[116]

Even before the Hoover Commission attacked it, the RFC was in a weak position. Restricted by Congress to making only those loans that private capital would not make, the RFC had few legitimate customers in the booming postwar economy. In 1948, the Republican-majority Congress started to plan for its dismantling. The RFC's opponents were energized in 1950–51, when the press reported that some RFC staffers had done paid work for companies, after helping them get loans. Although the scandals turned out to be less serious than the initial reports suggested, they hurt the Truman administration, as well as the RFC. In 1953, Congress put the RFC out of business.[117]

That the RFC would die off during the Korean War was remarkable, given that it had been so central to the nation's war mobilization just a decade earlier. But this was just one example of the very large differences between the two war efforts. On the surface, there were many parallels: many of the mobilization agencies that cropped up in 1950–51, including the Office of Defense Mobilization, looked similar to those that had appeared in World War II. Again, there were some strict price and wage controls. President Truman, like his predecessor, called for an "equality of sacrifice," among consumers, business, and labor.[118]

However, the industrial mobilization for the conflict in Korea, which remained a "limited war," did not involve the kind of sustained, powerfully regulated, all-out effort that had occurred in the early 1940s. This was evident in the operations of companies such as Chrysler, which, during World War II, sent its entire output to the military. During the Korean War, Chrysler was as an important producer of tanks and other weapons. But even at their peak, in 1952–53, military sales amounted to only 20 percent of Chrysler's total revenues. Meanwhile, across the whole economy, defense spending in 1952–53 absorbed about 14 percent of national output, compared with over 40 percent in 1943–44. In this semi-mobilized economy, there seemed to be even more resentment of government controls among business leaders and consumers than there had been during World War II. In 1951, Congress lifted many of those controls, which had been operating for only a few months. Even taxes, which remained relatively high in the late 1940s and were hiked to pay for the Korean War, did not bite business as hard. There was a new excess profits tax, but it took only about 30 percent of earnings above those during the designated prewar base period, instead of the 90 percent nominal rate that had prevailed for much of World War II.[119]

As they completed a war mobilization that involved a comparably small role for government regulation and public enterprise, American business leaders became further heartened by the election of President Eisenhower. Even for politicians and business executives who stood to Eisenhower's right, there was no question that he qualified as an improvement over his predecessors. Certainly, this was the case when it came to industrial policy. During the 1952 campaign, and early in his presidency, Eisenhower made it clear that he would battle any form of "creeping socialism," such as new TVA-style government enterprises or national health insurance. He went beyond this, by promising to do more to take the government out of business, along the lines recommended by the Hoover Commission of 1947–49.[120]

Eisenhower was joined in Washington by Hoover, now seventy-eight, who again headed up a commission on the organization of the executive branch. This new Hoover Commission ("Hoover II"), like the first, used task forces to examine the ways in which executive agencies could become more efficient. Some accounts of Hoover II's work, observing that Eisenhower and the press regarded Hoover and his task forces as too ideologically extreme, have suggested that the second commission, like the first, was never too influential.[121] Certainly, Hoover and his team never dismantled the whole New Deal state, a task that became especially difficult after the 1954 elections, when Democrats regained control of Congress. But Hoover II's influence should not be so easily dismissed. Especially over the longer run, much of its vision of reform was realized.

Even more than its predecessor, Hoover II was focused on the problem of government competition with private business enterprise. This made sense, given that Congress, in the same statute that created Hoover II, had stated explicitly that such government competition should cease, whenever possible.[122] Hoover and his team members agreed. According to the authorized summary of Hoover II findings, written by two of the commission's staffers, the average American citizen was a foe of "Big Government" who shared the perspective of the average business leader. This was someone who "dread[ed] bureaucrats," opposed "regimentation," and was sick and tired of having to fill out government forms and "obey scores of petty regulations." Business leaders were especially dismayed, according to the Hoover II summary, that they "must face the unfair competition of Government-financed and tax-free business." Working from this basic assumption, members of Hoover II condemned the network of government enterprises left over from the New Deal and World War II, which "threaten[ed] the efficient operation, if not the very foundation, of the free enterprise system."[123]

Hoover II took a special interest in the government enterprises on the military side of the national state, which, at the time, was far larger than its civilian side. Hoover's task forces found at least 2,500 separate government-run enterprises under the auspices of the Department of Defense (DoD). At least a thousand of these, Hoover II concluded, were ripe for immediate elimination. Some of these operations, including military-run laundries, bakeries, and butcher shops, were small. But Hoover II also called for the privatization of some of the military's largest industrial holdings, including the more than two hundred government-owned plants then in the Departmental Industrial Reserve. Hoover II urged Congress and the White House to "return these facilities," which were valued at nearly $9 billion, "to private industry." Given that nearly all the plants had always been government-owned, the use of the word "return" was misleading. But members of Hoover II were intent on correcting what they regarded as the military's misguided "desire for self-sufficiency" in weapons production.[124]

This critique extended into warship construction, in which the Navy—which owned and operated its own shipyards on both coasts—had long held substantial in-house production capacity. In 1954, Hoover II commissioners noted with dismay, the Navy's own yards employed 105,900 people, about half of all American shipyard workers. Over the last five years, these GOGO facilities had built a third of the Navy's new warships. Hoover II attacked this state of affairs, which it called "an alarming intrusion into the private shipbuilding industry of this country." More generally, members of Hoover II declared, the DoD needed to practice "procurement from private industry whenever possible." This would allow the DoD to benefit from "the genius of the private enterprise system," which, unlike public enterprise, offered superior "initiative, ingenuity, inventiveness and unparalleled productivity."[125]

Behind Hoover II's calls for reform in the nation's military economy, it promoted a selective memory of what happened during the nation's biggest war effort, a decade earlier. "Private enterprise has proved its ability to produce for the national defense in preparing this country to meet the needs of war," members of Hoover II declared. "It manifested an inventiveness and productivity which second only to the valor of our troops, made possible victory in both World War I and World War II."[126] This was the message that had been broadcast strongly during World War II by business leaders and trade associations. It contained much truth but also much distortion. Now, this vision of the American political economy—in which the government figured only as an incompetent bureaucratic menace—was being used to generate the findings of a major, congressionally sponsored commission on political and economic reform.

Ironically, the realization of many of Hoover II's recommendations would not come until the 1960s, when Democrats controlled the White House and Congress. Nevertheless, Hoover and his colleagues could point to good results in the shorter term, during the Eisenhower years. By the time Hoover II wrapped up its work, in 1955, the RFC and the synthetic rubber industry had been privatized. So, too, had a variety of other public enterprises, including the Inland Waterways Corporation and an assortment of small-scale, in-house Navy and Army operations. The USAF, which previously used in-house facilities to maintain most of its planes, declared that at least half that maintenance and repair work would be given to private firms.[127] The Eisenhower administration worked to ensure that there would be no expansion of public enterprise in electric power generation and transmission.[128] And with the Atomic Energy Act of 1954, Congress ended the public monopoly over atomic power by encouraging private utilities to plan their own nuclear plants. (In the 1960s, they would build them.)[129]

Hoover's vision of a more privatized political economy was also realized in the defense sector, but not all at once. Certainly, it was pushed during the Eisenhower years, by Congress, the White House, and the Pentagon. In early 1953, the Joint Committee on Defense Production, a congressional body, declared: "It is national policy to hold Government lending and Government ownership of defense facilities to a minimum." Eisenhower's secretary of defense, Charles E. Wilson (former GM president) agreed. In 1955, Wilson announced that the Pentagon "supports the basic principle that free competitive enterprise should be fostered by government."[130] The changing policy environment was noted by leaders of Boeing, the top military contractor, in their 1958 annual report to stockholders. "In recent years," they explained, "the Department of Defense has requested or directed the airframe industry to make maximum use of private funds in acquiring necessary new facilities and in supporting an expanded independent research program."[131]

This trend was welcome to many business leaders who had long championed more privatization. As World War II ended, members of the for-profit business community maneuvered to prevent the military from expanding its in-house capacities. Testifying before Congress a few days after V-J Day, Harry Woodhead, president of Consolidated-Vultee Aircraft, said: "We strongly recommend that the Army and Navy should not undertake to design, to develop, or to manufacture aircraft." This was little more than a request for the continuation of wartime practices. But Woodhead and his peers wanted to be sure that the Navy would not revive the in-house aircraft plant that it had used in the 1920s and that the AAF's big facility at Wright Field, which included engineering divisions and testing facilities, would not try to expand into new enterprises.[132] Elsewhere, representatives of private industry asked more directly for the downsizing of military-run facilities. In 1947–48, for instance, the director of AT&T's Bell Laboratories, Oliver Buckley, led a group of industry officials in calling for major cutbacks in the Naval Research Laboratory, which then employed about three thousand people. Its work, Buckley and his peers argued, could be done better by the private sector.[133]

The early Cold War push for a heavier reliance on contractors also came from actors within the military establishment. One important move came in 1950, when the Navy awarded its first contracts for nuclear-powered submarines. During the interwar years and World War II, there had been two premier submarine producers: one public (Portsmouth Navy Yard), and one private (Electric Boat). In the months after World War II, the Navy continued to order conventional submarines from both these yards. In winter 1949–50, Admiral Hyman G. Rickover, chief of the Navy's nuclear power program, was working with GE and Westinghouse, the Navy's long-time suppliers of ship turbines, on different atomic power plants for use in submarines. Rickover arranged to have GE partner with Electric Boat, which would build the first nuclear sub. But Rickover also met with the top officers at Portsmouth to ask whether they would be willing to work with Westinghouse on a different nuclear sub. When the officers at Portsmouth hesitated, Rickover immediately telephoned Electric Boat to offer it the entire program.[134]

This 1950 episode makes for a good story about the shortsightedness of Navy bureaucrats. But as some of Rickover's biographers have pointed out, his rush to make Electric Boat a sole source indicated that he may have desired that outcome all along. A talented, ambitious officer who wanted tight control over the programs that he administered, Rickover knew that he might enjoy more influence as the Navy boss of the Electric Boat project than he would if part of the job were handled by his peers at Portsmouth. In the end, Portsmouth did build nuclear submarines—ten of them, in all.

But its position had shifted, from coequal rival of Electric Boat to secondary supplier. And it would soon be replaced by Newport News Ship, the Navy's premier supplier of aircraft carriers, which entered the field of submarine construction in the 1950s. More and more, the Navy sent the bulk of its orders to private shipyards, which started to take the lead in designing the vessels that they built.[135]

Even within the USAF, which had always relied on private contractors more heavily than had the Navy, the public-private equation changed. During and immediately after World War II, the AAF's large facility at Wright Field, Ohio, made important contributions to the design of engines and planes. The AAF's in-house departments were also master managers of weapons acquisition projects. During World War II, the engines, avionics instruments, and many other key parts of the AAF's finished fighters and bombers were purchased directly by Wright Field, which supplied this mass of "government-furnished equipment" (GFE) to the airframe contractors. Immediately after the war, there were signs of a growing reliance on private expertise—such as that contained in the new RAND Corporation, whose employment by the USAF was regarded by some Wright Field officers as "a slap in the face." Still, in the late 1940s, the AAF held a great deal of in-house expertise in the engineering and the acquisition of weapons.[136]

In the early 1950s, the USAF shed some of this in-house capacity. One reason for this was its adoption of the "weapon system" approach to procurement. Under this method, the military provided less GFE; lead prime contractors became responsible for ordering more of the important pieces of a finished weapon. This was done only in a very limited way during World War II, in aspects of the B-29 project. It was first employed more fully in 1949, when two lead contractors—Convair and Hughes Aircraft— were allowed to manage the procurement of most elements of the F-102 fighter. In 1953, Convair (which became part of General Dynamics in 1954) was allowed to manage almost all the acquisition work associated with the B-58 bomber. These aircraft projects, which allowed the USAF to do less acquisition work internally, did not prove especially successful. But they were early examples of a change that was gaining momentum.[137]

The most important new developments in defense acquisition in the 1950s came in the production of weapons that were not used during World War II: ballistic missiles. By 1960, missiles, guided by sophisticated electronics, had become the most expensive class of weapons in the American arsenal. This was one reason that the USAF—which oversaw more missile procurement than did the Navy and Army—accounted for about half the overall military budget.[138]

The dynamics of government-business relations in first-generation American missile programs were complicated, but by the time of Eisenhower's MIC address in 1961, it was evident that the Pentagon favored pushing management and production capacity toward the private sector. This represented a rejection of the Army's approach to the Jupiter missile program, which built on the War Department's long tradition of carrying out substantial peacetime research and small-scale production in its own arsenals. In late 1956, Secretary of Defense Wilson effectively closed the door on the Army's missile-building operations, by handing the entire land-based, long-run missile program to the USAF.[139] The USAF's program, which produced the Atlas, the first intercontinental ballistic missile, was led by Major General Bernard A. Schriever. He had a substantial office of his own but also relied heavily on a contractor, Ramo-Wooldridge, which served as a "systems integrator" or "systems engineer."[140] Whereas the production of the actual finished missile was led by Convair, the prime contractor for the weapon, the USAF used Ramo-Wooldridge to handle much of the work of organizing the many elements of the whole project.[141]

It may be possible to characterize the shifts in American weapons procurement practices in the 1950s as nothing more than a rational move, under the pressure of the existential threat of the Cold War, toward more optimal arrangements. But it seems clear that within the military establishment, there was a constant, ideologically driven pressure, from Congress and civilian authorities at the Pentagon, to do more contracting out. This pressure was applied even in the face of evidence that some in-house capacity was desirable. For instance, in the late 1950s, the Navy's Bureau of Aeronautics used a fairly traditional, World War II–style arrangement to procure the new F-4 Phantom fighter, built by McDonnell. While the design and manufacture of the airframe was handled by McDonnell, the Navy had served as overall project manager and had supplied a good deal of GFE. The F-4, which was tested in 1958 and entered service in 1960, turned out to be one of the most successful aircraft in history. Nevertheless, the Navy's Bureau of Aeronautics was immediately pushed by the DoD and Congress to do more contracting out. Army and Navy officers complained of similar pressures.[142]

The push to do more contracting out also affected the new space program, overseen by NASA. In 1960, as NASA was setting up shop, its procurement practices were influenced by a report from McKinsey &

Company, the management consultant firm. According to McKinsey, NASA needed to rely heavily on the advantages of "free enterprise"; its in-house capacities, the consultants insisted, should be kept to a "bare minimum." This became the approach favored by NASA chief James E. Webb, who oversaw a decentralized acquisition system that relied mainly on private contractors. By 1964, as the Apollo program ramped up, NASA itself had about 32,000 in-house employees, but its contractors employed more than ten times as many people. After Apollo, NASA's in-house capacities would become considerably smaller. By the 1980s, it was even contracting out the job of preparing the space shuttle for launch to Lockheed.[143]

Although the Eisenhower administration presided over important shifts in the direction of the privatization of the defense sector, the most dramatic steps in that direction did not come until the 1960s. They were overseen by a new secretary of defense, Robert S. McNamara, who came to the Kennedy administration from the Ford Motor Company. (A former Harvard Business School professor, McNamara had served during World War II as an analyst in the AAF.) Thanks in part to Kennedy's emphasis on "flexible response," which called for more conventional forces, McNamara oversaw defense budgets that were actually growing.[144] But he was still determined to make major reforms.

McNamara brought to the Pentagon a new emphasis on formal, quantified cost-benefit analysis, which he expected to be able to use to make major improvements in military acquisition practices. He increased civilian control, decreased cost-plus contracting, and introduced "total package procurement" (which created more winner-take-all competitions).[145] The complexities of these reforms should not allow us to overlook McNamara's important role in extending the privatization of the defense sector. When Assistant Secretary of Defense Thomas D. Morris announced in 1963 that the DoD was "dedicated to the preservation and strengthening of a free enterprise economy," this was nothing new.[146] But under McNamara, the Pentagon's actions did even more to live up to the language.

Immediately after he took office, McNamara started to liquidate the military's large holdings of industrial plant, which dated from World War II. Soon after he set up office in the Pentagon, McNamara ordered the military to give up a quarter of the two hundred government-owned plants remaining in its "industrial reserve." He also managed to close bases and other military installations, despite protests of localities and their representatives in Congress. In his first three years as defense secretary, McNamara closed more than five hundred military installations; the Pentagon shed about 81,600 employees. But the biggest news came in November 1964, when McNamara said that he would be closing or consolidating another ninety-five facilities, which would mean another 63,000 job cuts. Among the operations slated to be shut down were several of the military's most prominent in-house production facilities. One of these was the Brooklyn Navy Yard, a longtime producer (and refitter) of big warships, which still had 11,000 employees. Another was the Navy's main submarine yard at Portsmouth, which had 7,000 workers. Also on the block was the Springfield Armory, the Army's arsenal in Massachusetts, which had been one of the world's most important designers and producers of small arms for more than a century.[147]

McNamara's decision to close major GOGO weapons production facilities represented a sharp break with tradition, as well as an important new step in the privatization of the American political economy. Some of McNamara's reforms at the Pentagon hurt individual contractors in the private sector; but at the macro level, they were creating a new kind of defense sector, in which the military would no longer have in-house production capacities. Private contractors discovered that it was now possible to eliminate competition from the government side that had existed for many decades.

When McNamara took office in 1961, the Springfield Armory was struggling with production of the M14 rifle. The M14, which made only modest improvements to the Springfield-designed M1 that had performed so well in World War II, was being manufactured by two private contractors—Winchester and Harrington-Richardson—as well as by the Springfield Armory itself. When McNamara arrived at the Pentagon, all three M14 producers were experiencing problems and delays. After he was briefed on the status of the rifle program, McNamara called it "a disgrace." He was happy to learn of a privately developed alternative, the AR-15, which had recently been acquired by Colt, an experienced small arms manufacturer. More innovative than the Army's M14, the AR-15 (which would become the M16) was a lightweight, fully automatic assault rifle. It was favored by the USAF and by the DoD's Advanced Research Projects Agency (DARPA). In 1963, McNamara ordered the Army to adopt the M16 instead of the M14. Colt received large orders for the M16, which became the military's new standard.

Although it is easy to read the M14 and M16 rifles as a case of a stodgy military bureaucracy being outperformed by an agile private sector, it also needs to be understood as part of the broader story of an ideologically driven defense-sector privatization. Colt and its allies (including DARPA) exaggerated the effectiveness of the M16, just as they exaggerated the deficiencies of the M14 and the problems with its production. Careful tests of the two weapons in 1962–63 showed that while the M16 had the advantage of being lighter and was effective at closer ranges, the M14 (as designed) was better for longer-range shooting. To some extent, the Springfield Armory was being penalized for developing a weapon that was better suited for a future conflict in Europe than it was for fighting in Southeast Asia. The penalty, imposed by McNamara, was death. When the Springfield Armory closed for good in 1968, some of its functions were transferred to the Rock Island Arsenal, in Illinois. But much of the Army's in-house capacity for small arms production was lost for good.[148]

McNamara followed the same path in naval shipbuilding. In 1945, the Navy's in-house production capacities, which included ten of its own shipyards, were very strong. Certainly, the Navy could have continued to make at least half its ships in its own yards, as it had done during the interwar years. This capability bothered private shipbuilders and their allies, who worked to keep the Navy from ordering new vessels from its own yards. Part of this effort required a creative manipulation of common knowledge about the U.S. Navy yards and their recent history. In one influential report on postwar shipbuilding policy, issued in 1945, a team from Harvard Business School argued that the wartime record of contractors had been so impressive that they deserved to be first in line for any new orders in peacetime. According to the Harvard team, which provided no evidence to support its claims, "the private yards have shown that they are the best place to preserve the know-how" of warship construction.[149] In another dimension of this effort, the Harvard team and other contractor-friendly experts explained matter-of-factly that the construction of new warships was only an emergency, secondary function of the Navy's yards, which had always been focused on refitting and repair.[150] This amounted to a very misleading rewriting of history, especially the record of the Navy yards since the Great War.

Although contractors and their allies succeeded in having most orders for new warships go to the private sector during the early Cold War, they were not satisfied with a partial victory. The second Hoover Commission was dismayed to find that about a third of the orders in the late 1940s and 1950s had gone to the Navy's own yards. During the Eisenhower years, the contractors did a bit better: in 1955–61, eighty-three of the 107 new ships purchased by the Navy (78 percent) were built in private shipyards. However, the Navy yards were still doing about 80 percent of the repair and refitting work. This bothered the private shipbuilders, whose trade associations, including the Atlantic & Gulf Coast Dry Dock Association and the Shipbuilders' Council of America, pressed Congress and the Pentagon for change.[151]

In 1962, Congress responded by passing a new law that required at least 35 percent of the repair work to go to private yards. Meanwhile, the private shipbuilders, the Navy, and Congress debated the evidence on the comparative costs of the public and private yards. These were analyzed in studies prepared by management consultants, including Ernst & Ernst and Arthur Andersen & Company, which concluded that the most efficient private yards were at least 10 percent cheaper, at least in new construction. According to the Navy's own analysis of the consultants' reports, the lower costs for new construction came almost entirely from the more generous fringe benefits received by the Navy's own employees; in the field of repair, the Navy believed, there was no evidence of a difference in costs.[152] But private shipbuilders continued to argue for their superior efficiency; they accused the Navy of hiding the truth.[153]

Although private shipbuilders were obviously on the offensive, it still seemed unlikely, during the first months of McNamara's tenure at the DoD, that the Navy's long-established shipyards would cease to be major players in the big business of refitting warships. As *Fortune* magazine reported in 1962, "the situation is likely to remain pretty much as it is."[154] But this was wrong. In the new round of base closings announced by McNamara in November 1964, the Brooklyn and Portsmouth yards both appeared on the list. Although the closing of Portsmouth took many years, it launched its last new submarine in 1967. By that time, all the Navy's new construction, along with nearly half its repair work, was done in private yards. The privatization trend would continue in the last decades of the twentieth century, which saw the Navy shut down most of the rest of its in-house production facilities.[155]

McNamara's decisions to minimize the military's in-house production capacities, which came just as President Johnson was ramping up the American war effort in Vietnam, were part of a broader cost-cutting effort that was generally applauded. "These cutbacks," *Life* magazine declared right after the 1964 announcement that included the news about the Springfield

Armory and the Brooklyn and Portsmouth shipyards, "are about as free of political or regional favoritism as they can be."[156] At this moment, much of the press was impressed with McNamara, whose willingness to offend Congress and the military bureaucracy seemed salutary and bold. But the media's coverage of the reforms failed to note their significance for the business community's broader, long-run political struggle against public enterprise. For the business executives who had worked hard to frame the story of the World War II industrial mobilization, as well as for their postwar allies, including congressional conservatives and members of the Hoover Commission, the net effect of McNamara's actions was almost unbelievably favorable. As the United States began a major new war effort, the defense sector was finally on a clearer path to privatization.[157]

The new order was obvious during the Vietnam War, which was sustained with a set of military-industrial arrangements that were a far cry from those that existed during World War II. In a reversal of the situation that existed in the 1940s and 1950s, most of the aircraft for Vietnam were made in privately owned plants, instead of publicly owned ones. Leading military contractors for the Vietnam War, unlike their predecessors, faced very few direct economic controls. They also avoided the hyper-regulation of war profits. Indeed, even though the war was preceded by a major tax cut, the Johnson and Nixon administrations avoided calling for much economic sacrifice, other than a special 10 percent war tax "surcharge," which lasted only eighteen months. Profits of military contractors were still subject to statutory renegotiation, as they had been during World War II and the Korean War. But during the Vietnam era, the sums demanded by the Renegotiation Board dropped dramatically, to about a fifth of what they had been in the 1950s. This was a new kind of American war economy, in which regulation—along with the military's in-house production and management capacities—was vastly reduced. And there were related changes under way in the theater of war abroad, where many American troops found themselves supplied by contractors (as well as some surviving military enterprises) with a growing abundance of consumer goods and services.[158]

*   *   *

In 1946, Harold Ickes, President Roosevelt's longtime secretary of the interior, reflected on the political and economic lessons of the recent war mobilization. "The bomb that imposed the hush of death upon Hiroshima,"

Ickes wrote, "shattered with equal force and effectiveness the wails of a few little men that the Government should not engage in business but should rely upon private enterprise and individual initiative to invent and to develop."[159] For this observation to have come from Ickes, who had overseen many of the New Deal's large government-financed construction projects during the 1930s, was no great surprise. What is striking is how little traction his perspective had during the reconversion period and the longer Cold War era that followed. In those years, many of the most powerful American policymakers acted as if the lessons of World War II were essentially the opposite of the ones that Ickes was suggesting. Instead of looking for areas in which government action and investment might advance the public good, they favored privatization.

The reconversions of the American economy after World War II helped launch a much longer-run transformation. Seen in isolation, the sell-off of government-owned industrial plant in 1946–55, which had been expected by many Americans, was far from revolutionary. But that effort was connected, economically and politically, to a longer-run development that saw a broader privatization of the American political economy. At the heart of this process, and a leading force in it, was the transformation of the defense sector. Recent changes in the structure of the MIC, including the rise of the USAF and the military's abandonment of its in-house capacities, contributed to the rise of a new "contract state." Thanks to choices of McNamara and other policymakers, as the economist Walter Adams observed, "the government is forced to buy what it no longer can make."[160] Robust public capacities had been replaced with dependency and deference.

Did this matter? Certainly, it is possible to exaggerate the drawbacks of the new, more privatized MIC, and its friendliness to firms in the private sector. There were still pressures on contractors from their competitors and from military contracting authorities, who could be exacting.[161] During the Cold War and after, some American military contractors failed entirely; many others were compelled to merge.[162] Perhaps the shift toward more contracting out helped the United States to win the Cold War faster, and at a lower cost, than it might otherwise have done.[163]

This book cannot adequately evaluate the various claims about the drawbacks and advantages of the sort of defense sector favored by Hoover, McNamara, and their allies. However, it does suggest how different that model was from the American military-industrial machine during World War II. Obviously, the American war effort of the early 1940s, like those before and after it, relied heavily on private contractors. But in World War II, as contractors knew only too well, the defense sector was subject to a dense web of robust regulation. Some of this was provided by high taxes and price and profit controls; some came from the military's large in-house capacities, for project oversight and for weapons production. By the time of the Vietnam War—and certainly since then—the defense sector had become less regulated. No doubt, contractors still had many legitimate complaints about red tape, change orders, and other drawbacks of doing business with the Pentagon. But in comparison with their predecessors, they were freer from special regulation and freer to act more like ordinary firms. This may help explain why the larger American business community, which had long associated war with undesirable taxes and regulations, seems to have grown more comfortable, by the late 1950s and early 1960s, with large defense budgets.[164] Business leaders had not overhauled their political views. Instead, the defense sector was changing, in ways that made war-fighting more compatible with capitalism.

Conclusion

The scale and complexity of the American industrial mobilization for World War II, a campaign that enlisted thousands of organizations and millions of people, have made it vulnerable to misinterpretation. Some authors have portrayed the nation's war production as a vindication of free-market capitalism; others have described it as forging a sinister military-corporate alliance. This book rejects both views, by showing the ways in which business and government were reluctant, contentious, and even bitter partners. Business leaders were disturbed, and sometimes enraged, by the government's active role in manufacturing matériel, buying industrial plant, and regulating prices and profits. Already opposed to the New Deal, business leaders worked hard during the war to denigrate government action, while touting their own contributions to the war effort. This campaign was a success, especially during the postwar reconversion period and over the longer run, as the U.S. defense sector became increasingly privatized. Over the last half-century, as politicians deregulated the broader economy, American war-fighting has become only more reliant on market mechanisms and for-profit companies.[1]

Although this book focuses on military-industrial relations, it also speaks to the broader history of struggles between progressives (the left-liberals who tended to support the New Deal) and conservatives.[2] Over the course of the twentieth century, the business community sought continuously to contain state enterprise and regulation. The battles of the 1940s shaped modern American conservatism. Although I should not dismiss the contributions of ordinary citizens and traditional intellectuals (including economists, journalists and editors, religious leaders, and novelists),[3] it was the business community's organic intellectuals—executives and their hired hands—who developed much of the conservative message.[4]

The history of the World War II mobilization offers sobering lessons about the power of economic elites to shape American politics. During the early 1940s, business leaders downplayed the role of the public sector while hyping the contributions of private enterprise. Although they faced formidable rivals—the Roosevelt administration and organized labor, among others—conservative business leaders bested their opponents by spending more money on public relations and refining a more coherent, forceful message. Had the labor movement been less divided and had the Roosevelt administration been more unified and disciplined when it came to public relations, more Americans might have heard messages that touted the crucial contributions of public institutions—military as well as civilian—to the nation's victory in the war of production. But during World War II, the business community was more unified and energetic than its ostensible rivals. Although this unity and energy have waxed and waned over the years since 1945,[5] American business leaders and their allies have mostly continued to prevail over trade unionists and left-leaning policymakers in struggles over ideas, language, and power. Decades of mainstream political discourse denigrating government, along with widespread reticence about the contributions of military and civilian governmental authorities, have almost certainly damaged public welfare and the ability of Americans to engage in constructive citizenship.[6]

Does the record of the industrial mobilization of World War II offer any significant lessons for policymakers in the twenty-first century? Some have suggested that absent the crisis of an all-out global war, the public will never endorse the sort of dramatic government interventions that occurred in the 1940s.[7] This sort of caution fails to recognize the extent to which the American approach to all-out war mobilization created a balanced, flexible style of government-business interaction, which might well be as effective as the more privatized version that ascended after 1945.

Decades of energetic lobbying have fueled an overreliance on contracting out. Policymakers interested in improving national and global security will likely need to do more to scale back privatization in certain areas. The lesson of World War II is that difficult challenges can be managed successfully with creative approaches, combining contracting with robust regulation and targeted public enterprise and investment.[8] Perhaps the rise of China as a military and economic power will force American policymakers to ponder this issue.

If American policymakers had applied the lessons of World War II mobilization to the toughest challenges of the later twentieth century, people around the world would be better off today. As the leading historian of the Defense Plant Corporation once observed, there might be valuable payoffs to more direct, World War II–style public investments and enter-prises in energy policy.[9] But for decades, the celebration of private enter-prise led American policymakers to reject such ideas. This rejection of targeted governmental action has delayed, if not prevented entirely, an ade-quate response to a major global environmental crisis. Similarly, ideology limits the American public health system in its ability to respond to pan-demics and other major challenges.[10]

Such is the political-economic environment of our day. More than we have imagined, that environment was shaped by American business leaders of the World War II era. In the early 1940s, as they churned out the muni-tions that allowed the Allies to win the titanic struggle against fascism, they also found time to fight for a future in which they would be less constrained by public authority. In the long run, victory in that war was theirs.

Abbreviations

ACWP Records	Records of the Automotive Council for War Production, Detroit Public Library, Detroit
AFHRA	U.S. Air Force Historical Research Agency, Maxwell Air Force Base, AL
BHA	Boeing Historical Archives, Bellevue, WA
Byrnes Papers	Papers of James F. Byrnes, Special Collections Library, Clemson University, Clemson, SC
Chamber Records	Records of the United States Chamber of Commerce, Hagley
CPA	Civilian Production Administration
CPA-*Contracts*	CPA, *Alphabetic Listing of Major War Supply Contracts, Cumulative, June 1940 Through September 1945*, 4 vols. (Washington, DC: CPA, 1946)
CPA-*Facilities*	CPA, *War Industrial Facilities Authorized, July 1940–August 1945: Listed Alphabetically by Company and Plant Location* (Washington, DC: CPA, 1946)
CPA-*History*	CPA, *Industrial Mobilization for War: History of the War Production Board and Predecessor Agencies, 1940–1945* (Washington, DC: GPO, 1947)
DPED	Records of the Explosives Department, E. I. Du Pont de Nemours & Co., accession 2144, Hagley
Ford Records	Ford Motor Co. Records, Benson Ford Research Center, Dearborn, MI
Forrestal Papers	Papers of James V. Forrestal, Seeley G. Mudd Manuscript Library, Princeton University, Princeton, NJ
Hagley	Hagley Museum & Library, Wilmington, DE
Ickes Diaries	Unpublished diaries, papers of Harold LeClair Ickes, LOC

Johnson Papers	Papers of Louis A. Johnson, Albert and Shirley Small Special Collections Library, University of Virginia, Charlottesville
Kaiser Papers	Papers of Henry J. Kaiser, Bancroft Library, University of California, Berkeley
Knudsen Papers	Papers of William S. Knudsen, Detroit Public Library, Detroit
LOC	Library of Congress, Manuscript Division, Washington, DC
MWCR	Montgomery Ward Company Records, American Heritage Center, Laramie, WY
NAM Records	Records of the National Association of Manufacturers, Hagley
NARA	National Archives and Records Administration, College Park, MD
NARA-GL	National Archives and Records Administration, Great Lakes Regional Depository, Chicago
NDAC Minutes	CPA, *Minutes of the Advisory Commission to the Council of National Defense* (Washington, DC: GPO, 1946)
NDU	National Defense University Library, Fort McNair, Washington, DC
NYT	*New York Times*
Patterson Papers	Papers of Robert P. Patterson, LOC
Pew Personal Papers	Personal papers of J. Howard Pew, Hagley
PSF-FDR	President's Secretary's File, Franklin D. Roosevelt Presidential Library and Museum, Hyde Park, NY
RG 21	Record Group 21: Records of District Courts of the United States, NARA-GL
RG 80	Record Group 80: General Records of the Department of the Navy, NARA
RG 107	Record Group 107: Records of the Office of the Secretary of War, NARA
RG 156	Record Group 156: Records of the Office of the Chief of Ordnance, NARA and NARA-GL
RG 160	Record Group 160: Records of Headquarters, Army Service Forces, NARA
RG 200	Record Group 200: Gift Collection Records, NARA

RG 253	Record Group 253: Records of the Petroleum Administration for War, NARA
RG 270	Record Group 270: Records of the War Assets Administration, NARA
RG 334	Record Group 334: Records of Interservice Agencies, NARA
Reynolds Papers	Papers of R. S. Reynolds, Sr., Virginia Historical Society, Richmond
SPA	Surplus Property Administration
Sperry Records	Sperry Gyroscope Company Division Records, accession 1915, Hagley
Stettinius Papers	Papers of Edward R. Stettinius, Jr., Albert and Shirley Small Special Collections Library, University of Virginia, Charlottesville
TPL	Harry S. Truman Presidential Library and Museum, Independence, MO
VSD	*Vital Speeches of the Day*
WAA	War Assets Administration
WPB	War Production Board
WPB *Minutes*	CPA, *Minutes of the War Production Board, January 20, 1942 to October 9, 1945* (Washington, DC: GPO, 1946)
WSJ	*Wall Street Journal*

Notes

Introduction

1. For details about the military hardware used and unloaded at Normandy, see Dwight D. Eisenhower, *Crusade in Europe* (Garden City, NJ: Doubleday, 1948), 53; Gordon A. Harrison, *Cross-Channel Attack* (Washington, DC: Office of the Chief of Military History, 1951), 301–35, 447; Max Hastings, *Overlord: D-Day and the Battle for Normandy* (New York: Simon & Schuster, 1984), 80–86, 191; Stephen E. Ambrose, *D-Day: The Climactic Battle of World War II* (New York: Simon & Schuster, 1994), 239–58; Richard Overy, *Why the Allies Won* (New York: W. W. Norton, 1995), 156–71; Williamson Murray and Allan R. Millett, *A War to Be Won: Fighting the Second World War* (Cambridge, MA: Harvard University Press, 2000), 411–45; Olivier Wieviorka, *Normandy: The Landings to the Liberation of Paris*, trans. M. B. DeBevoise (Cambridge, MA: Harvard University Press, 2008), 103; Paul Kennedy, *Engineers of Victory: The Problem Solvers Who Turned the Tide in the Second World War* (New York: Random House, 2013), 250–82; Rick Atkinson, *The Guns at Last Light: The War in Western Europe, 1944–1945* (New York: Henry Holt, 2013), 23–24; Craig L. Symonds, *Neptune: The Allied Invasion of Europe and the D-Day Landings* (New York: Oxford University Press, 2014), 150–61, 225–327.

2. To be sure, the Soviet and British home fronts were also critical to Allied success. For overviews and comparisons, see Mark Harrison, ed., *The Economics of World War II: Six Great Powers in International Comparison* (New York: Cambridge University Press, 1998); Overy, *Why the Allies Won*; Phillips Payson O'Brien, *How the War Was Won: Air-Sea Power and Allied Victory in World War II* (New York: Cambridge University Press, 2015); Jeffrey Fear, "War of the Factories," in *The Cambridge History of the Second World War*, vol. 3: *Total War Economy, Society, and Culture*, ed. Michael Geyer and Adam Tooze (New York: Cambridge University Press, 2015), 94–121. For outstanding English-language accounts of other national war economies, see Mark Harrison, *Soviet Planning in Peace and War, 1938–1945* (New York: Cambridge University Press, 1985); Adam Tooze, *The Wages of Destruction: The Making and Breaking of the Nazi Economy* (New York: Viking, 2006); David Edgerton, *Britain's War Machine: Weapons, Resources, and Experts in the Second World War* (New York: Oxford University Press, 2011); Yoshiro Miwa, *Japan's Economic Planning and Mobilization in Wartime, 1930s–1940s: The Competence of the State* (New York: Cambridge University Press, 2015). On the Allied commanders' reliance on their abundance of munitions, see John Ellis, *Brute Force: Allied Strategy and Tactics in the Second World War* (New York: Viking, 1990).

3. Another important interpretive strain stresses the contributions of male and female war workers, or "soldiers of production," on the home front. See, e.g., Maureen Honey, *Creating Rosie the Riveter: Class, Gender and Propaganda During World War II* (Amherst: University of Massachusetts Press, 1984); James T. Sparrow, *Warfare State: World War II Americans and the Age of Big Government* (New York: Oxford University Press, 2012). I address this subject in Chapter 3.

4. Among the most celebratory of these are Francis Walton, *Miracle of World War II: How American Industry Made Victory Possible* (New York: Macmillan, 1956); Arthur Herman, *Freedom's Forge: How American Business Produced Victory in World War II* (New York: Random House, 2012). Less boosterish, but nevertheless part of this school, are Overy, *Why the Allies Won*; Richard E. Holl, *From the Boardroom to the War Room: America's Corporate Liberals and FDR's Preparedness Program* (Rochester, NY: University of Rochester Press, 2005); Maury Klein, *A Call to Arms: Mobilizing America for World War II* (New York: Bloomsbury, 2013); Charles K. Hyde, *Arsenal of Democracy: The American Automobile Industry in World War II* (Detroit: Wayne State University Press, 2013).

5. One of the early architects of this view was the progressive journalist I. F. Stone. For a sampling of his wartime publications, see I. F. Stone, *A Nonconformist History of Our Times: The War Years, 1939–1945* (Boston: Little, Brown, 1988). For the foundational, New Left histories, see Barton J. Bernstein, "The Removal of War Production Board Controls on Business, 1944–1946," *Business History Review* 39 (summer 1965): 243–60; Bernstein, "The Automobile Industry and the Coming of the Second World War," *Southwestern Social Science Quarterly* 47 (June 1966): 22–33; Bernstein, "The Debate on Industrial Reconversion: The Protection of Oligopoly and Military Control of the Economy," *American Journal of Economics and Sociology* 26, no. 2 (Apr. 1967): 159–72; Paul A. C. Koistinen, "The Hammer and the Sword: Labor, the Military, and Industrial Mobilization, 1920–1945" (Ph.D. diss., University of California, Berkeley, 1965), published later as *The Hammer and the Sword: Labor, the Military, and Industrial Mobilization, 1920–1945* (New York: Arno, 1979). This early work served as the foundation of Koistinen's more recent treatment of the subject, part of a multivolume survey of the history of American military-industrial relations: *Arsenal of World War II: The Political Economy of American Warfare, 1940–1945* (Lawrence: University Press of Kansas, 2004). Elements of the Bernstein-Koistinen account have been reproduced, in various forms, in many of the most influential works of the last half-century. See, e.g., Richard Polenberg, *War and Society: The United States, 1941–1945* (Philadelphia: J. B. Lippincott, 1972), 12–13; David Brody, "The New Deal and World War II," in *The New Deal: The National Level*, ed. John Braeman, Robert H. Bremner, and David Brody (Columbus: Ohio State University Press, 1975), 287–97; John Morton Blum, *V Was for Victory: Politics and American Culture During World War II* (New York: Harcourt Brace, 1976), 110–46; Gregory Hooks, *Forging the Military-Industrial Complex: World War II's Battle of the Potomac* (Urbana: University of Illinois Press, 1991); Alan Brinkley, *The End of Reform: New Deal Liberalism in Recession and War* (New York: Alfred A. Knopf, 1995), 175–200; David M. Kennedy, *Freedom from Fear: The American People in Depression and War, 1929–1945* (New York: Oxford University Press, 1999), 619–23; Brian Waddell, *The War Against the New Deal: World War II and American Democracy* (DeKalb: Northern Illinois Press, 2001); Robert Higgs, *Depression, War, and Cold War: Studies in Political Economy* (New York: Oxford University Press, 2006), 30–60. Leading labor historians generated a compatible story, by emphasizing the role of governmental and union bureaucracies in dulling radicalism. See Nelson Lichtenstein, *Labor's War at*

Home: The CIO in World War II (New York: Cambridge University Press, 1982); Christopher L. Tomlins, *The State and the Unions: Labor Relations, Law, and the Organized Labor Movement in America, 1880–1960* (New York: Cambridge University Press, 1985). Similar themes are sounded in parts of the best-selling, ironically titled, neo-populist oral history of the broader war experience: Studs Terkel, *"The Good War": An Oral History of World War II* (New York: Ballantine, 1985).

6. On framing and social and political contestation, see David A. Snow and Robert D. Benford, "Master Frames and Cycles of Protest," in *Frontiers in Social Movement Theory*, ed. Aldon D. Morris and Carol McClurg Mueller (New Haven, CT: Yale University Press, 1992), 133–55; Marc W. Steinberg, "Tilting the Frame: Considerations on Collective Action Framing from a Discursive Turn," *Theory and Society* 27 (Dec. 1998): 845–72; Neil Fligstein and Doug McAdam, *A Theory of Fields* (New York: Oxford University Press, 2012).

7. Robert H. Connery, *The Navy and Industrial Mobilization in World War II* (Princeton, NJ: Princeton University Press, 1951); R. Elberton Smith, *The Army and Economic Mobilization* (Washington, DC: Office of the Chief of Military History, 1959); Irving Brinton Holley, Jr., *Buying Aircraft: Matériel Procurement for the Army Air Forces* (Washington, DC: Office of the Chief of Military History, 1964); Gary E. Weir, *Forged in War: The Naval-Industrial Complex and American Submarine Construction, 1940–1961* (Washington, DC: Naval Historical Center, 1993); Bartholomew H. Sparrow, *From the Outside In: World War II and the American State* (Princeton, NJ: Princeton University Press, 1996), 161–257; Rodney K. Watterson, *32 in '44: Building the Portsmouth Submarine Fleet in World War II* (Annapolis, MD: Naval Institute Press, 2011); Thomas Heinrich, "'We Can Build Anything at Navy Yards': Warship Construction in Government Yards and the Political Economy of American Naval Shipbuilding, 1928–1945," *International Journal of Maritime History* 24 (Dec. 2012): 155–80; Gerald T. White, "Financing Industrial Expansion for War: The Origin of the Defense Plant Corporation Leases," *Journal of Economic History* 9, no. 2 (Nov. 1949): 156–83; Gerald T. White, *Billions for Defense: Government Financing by the Defense Plant Corporation During World War II* (University: University of Alabama Press, 1980); Hooks, *Forging the Military-Industrial Complex*; George Vincent Sweeting, "Building the Arsenal of Democracy: The Government's Role in the Expansion of Industrial Capacity, 1940 to 1945" (Ph.D. diss., Columbia University, 1994); John H. Ohly, *Industrialists in Olive Drab: The Emergency Operation of Private Industries During World War II*, ed. Clayton D. Laurie (Washington, DC: Center of Military History, 1999); Robert P. Patterson, *Arming the Nation for War: Mobilization, Supply, and the American War Effort in World War II*, ed. Brian Waddell (Knoxville: University of Tennessee Press, 2014). On price control on the civilian side of the World War II economy, see, esp., Meg Jacobs, *Pocketbook Politics: Economic Citizenship in Twentieth-Century America* (Princeton, NJ: Princeton University Press, 2005); Lizabeth Cohen, *A Consumer's Republic: The Politics of Mass Consumption in Postwar America* (New York: Alfred A. Knopf, 2003); Joanna L. Grisinger, *The Unwieldy American State: Administrative Politics Since the New Deal* (New York: Cambridge University Press, 2012). On the wartime state's impressive fiscal achievements, see Sparrow, *Warfare State*.

8. The struggle at the WPB is at the center of most of the best-known early postwar accounts, including Donald M. Nelson, *Arsenal of Democracy: The Story of American War Production* (New York: Harcourt Brace, 1946); Bruce Catton, *The War Lords of Washington* (New York: Harcourt Brace, 1948); Eliot Janeway, *The Struggle for Survival: A Chronicle of*

Economic Mobilization in World War II (New Haven, CT: Yale University Press, 1951). The WPB and its antecedents are also the focus of two major government-issued histories: U.S. Bureau of the Budget, *The United States at War: Development and Administration of the War Program by the Federal Government* (Washington, DC: Bureau of the Budget, 1946); CPA, *Industrial Mobilization for War: History of the War Production Board and Predecessor Agencies, 1940–1945* (Washington, DC: CPA, 1947).

9. Joseph Schumpeter, *Capitalism, Socialism, and Democracy* (New York: Harper & Row, 1942); Thomas K. McCraw, *Prophet of Innovation: Joseph Schumpeter and Creative Destruction* (Cambridge, MA: Harvard University Press, 2007), 303–425.

10. We already know a good deal about the mid-twentieth-century public-relations efforts of business leaders, companies, and business associations, thanks to a fast-growing literature: Howell John Harris, *The Right to Manage: Industrial Relations Policies of American Business in the 1940s* (Madison: University of Wisconsin Press, 1982); Elizabeth A. Fones-Wolf, *Selling Free Enterprise: The Business Assault on Labor and Liberalism, 1945–60* (Urbana: University of Illinois Press, 1995); Sanford M. Jacoby, *Modern Manors: Welfare Capitalism Since the New Deal* (Princeton, NJ: Princeton University Press, 1997); Roland Marchand, *Creating the Corporate Soul: The Rise of Public Relations and Corporate Imagery in American Big Business* (Berkeley: University of California Press, 1998); Andrew A. Workman, "Manufacturing Power: The Organizational Revival of the National Association of Manufacturers, 1941–1945," *Business History Review* 72, no. 2 (summer 1998): 279–317; Jennifer Klein, *For All These Rights: Business, Labor, and the Shaping of America's Public-Private Welfare State* (Princeton, NJ: Princeton University Press, 2003); Gregory Teddy Eow, "Fighting a New Deal: Intellectual Origins of the Reagan Revolution, 1932–1952" (Ph.D. diss., Rice University, 2007); Allan J. Lichtman, *White Protestant Nation: The Rise of the American Conservative Movement* (New York: Atlantic Monthly Press, 2008); Wendy L. Wall, *Inventing the "American Way": The Politics of Consensus from the New Deal to the Civil Rights Movement* (New York: Oxford University Press, 2008); Kim Phillips-Fein, *Invisible Hands: The Making of the Conservative Movement from the New Deal to Reagan* (New York: W. W. Norton, 2009); Darren Dochuk, *From Bible Belt to Sunbelt: Plain Folk Religion, Grassroots Politics, and the Rise of Evangelical Conservatism* (New York: W. W. Norton, 2011); Elizabeth Tandy Shermer, *Sunbelt Capitalism: Phoenix and the Transformation of American Politics* (Philadelphia: University of Pennsylvania Press, 2013); Kevin M. Kruse, *One Nation Under God: How Corporate America Invented Christian America* (New York: Basic Books, 2015). For rich historiographical essays, see Julian E. Zelizer, "Rethinking the History of American Conservatism," *Reviews in American History* 38, no 2 (June 2010): 367–92; Kim Phillips-Fein, "Conservatism: A State of the Field," *Journal of American History* 98, no. 3 (Dec. 2011): 723–43.

11. See Herman E. Krooss, *Executive Opinion: What Business Leaders Said and Thought on Economic Issues, 1920s–1960s* (Garden City, NY: Doubleday, 1970), 210; Richard S. Tedlow, *Keeping the Corporate Image: Public Relations and Business, 1900–1950* (Greenwich, CT: JAI, 1979), 140; David L. Stebenne, "Thomas J. Watson and the Business-Government Relationship, 1933–1956," *Enterprise & Society* (2005): 61. Other studies imply that the rivalry heated up again late in the war, as reconversion loomed: Harris, *Right to Manage*; Fones-Wolf, *Selling Free Enterprise*. Recent studies that describe longer-run continuities include Eow, "Fighting a New Deal"; Wall, *Inventing the "American Way"*; Phillips-Fein, *Invisible Hands*. For discussions of how geopolitical developments in the World War II era caused many New Deal

liberals to reassess their view of the proper roles of the national state, see David Ciepley, *Liberalism in the Shadow of Totalitarianism* (Cambridge, MA: Harvard University Press, 2006); Anne M. Kornhauser, *Debating the American State: Liberal Anxieties and the New Leviathan, 1930–1970* (Philadelphia: University of Pennsylvania Press, 2015).

12. Some readers may find such statements about the American "business community" implausible because they seem to collapse what must have been enormous disparities in the political and economic interests—and experiences—of different industries, firms, and business leaders. Certainly, those disparities did exist; parts of this book, including its discussions of corporate taxes and profit-control policies, point to their importance. But it also contends that some generalizing is justified. For studies that point to heterogeneity in the mid-twentieth-century business community, see Robert M. Collins, *The Business Response to Keynes, 1929–1964* (New York: Columbia University Press, 1981); Thomas Ferguson, "From Normalcy to New Deal: Industrial Structure, Party Competition, and American Public Policy in the Great Depression," *International Organization* 38 (1984): 41–94; Kim McQuaid, *A Response to Industrialism: Liberal Businessmen and the Evolving Spectrum of Capitalist Reform, 1886–1960* (New York: Garland, 1986); Colin Gordon, *New Deals: Business, Labor, and Politics in America, 1930–1935* (New York: Cambridge University Press, 1994); Stebenne, "Thomas J. Watson and the Business-Government Relationship." For a sophisticated analysis that points out differences among firms and executives without exaggerating them, see Harris, *Right to Manage.* There is a large literature on business and political mobilization in the later twentieth century, which explores ideology, shifting coalitions, and collective action problems. See, e.g., David J. Vogel, *Fluctuating Fortunes: The Political Power of Business in America* (New York: Basic Books, 1989); Benjamin C. Waterhouse, *Lobbying America: The Politics of Business from Nixon to NAFTA* (Princeton, NJ: Princeton University Press, 2013).

13. On the wartime fate of the New Deal and its endurance after 1945, see Brody, "New Deal and World War II"; Steve Fraser and Gary Gerstle, eds., *The Rise and Fall of the New Deal Order, 1930–1980* (Princeton, NJ: Princeton University Press, 1989); John W. Jeffries, "The 'New' New Deal: FDR and American Liberalism, 1937–1945," *Political Science Quarterly* 105, no. 3 (autumn 1990): 397–418; Brinkley, *End of Reform*; Karen Orren and Stephen Skowronek, "Regimes and Regime Building in American Government: A Review of the Literature on the 1940s," *Political Science Quarterly* 114, no. 4 (winter 1998–99): 689–702; Nelson Lichtenstein, "Class Politics and the State During World War II," *International Labor and Working Class History* 58 (fall 2000): 261–74; Jefferson Cowie and Nick Salvatore, "The Long Exception: Rethinking the Place of the New Deal in American History," *International Labor and Working-Class History* 74, no. 1 (fall 2008): 3–32; Sparrow, *Warfare State.* On deregulation, see Shane Hamilton, *Trucking Country: The Road to America's Wal-Mart Economy* (Princeton, NJ: Princeton University Press, 2008); Marc Allen Eisner, "Markets in the Shadow of the State: An Appraisal of Deregulation and Implications for Future Research," in *Government and Markets: Toward a New Theory of Regulation*, ed. Edward J. Balleisen and David A. Moss (New York: Cambridge University Press, 2010), 512–37; Eduardo Federico Canedo, "The Rise of the Deregulation Movement in Modern America, 1957–1980" (Ph.D. diss., Columbia University, 2008).

14. On the whole, historians and social scientists remain blind to the military side of the American state and political economy, despite its obvious importance and despite some admirable calls to pay it more attention. In recent years, a few scholars have called for more

attention to the American state's military side: Hooks, *Building the Military-Industrial Complex*; Ira Katznelson, "Flexible Capacity: The Military and Early American Statebuilding," in *Shaped by War and Trade: International Influences on American Political Development*, ed. Katznelson and Martin Shefter (Princeton, NJ: Princeton University Press, 2002), 82–110; Jenifer Van Vleck, *Empire of the Air: Aviation and the American Ascendancy* (Cambridge, MA: Harvard University Press, 2013). For a recent discussion that points to the importance of the military side of the American state but also suggests the thinness of the historical literature about it, see William J. Novak, "The Myth of the 'Weak' American State," *American Historical Review* 113, no. 3 (June 2008): 752–72; Novak et al., "AHR Exchange: On the 'Myth' of the 'Weak' American State," *American Historical Review* 115, no. 3 (June 2010): 766–800.

15. The shift to an "all-volunteer" army and the privatization of military manpower, which should also be considered an important part of the broader changes in U.S. political economy, coincided more directly with other moves in the direction of deregulation and privatization. See P. W. Singer, *Corporate Warriors: The Rise of the Privatized Military Industry* (Ithaca, NY: Cornell University Press, 2003); Deborah D. Avant, *The Market for Force: The Consequences of Privatizing Security* (New York: Cambridge University Press, 2005); Beth Bailey, *America's Army: Making the All-Volunteer Force* (Cambridge, MA: Harvard University Press, 2009); Jennifer Mittelstadt, *The Rise of the Military Welfare State* (Cambridge, MA: Harvard University Press, 2015).

Chapter 1

1. Samuel Crowther to Irving S. Olds, 22 Oct. 1940, and Crowther to Edward R. Stettinius, Jr., 22 Oct. 1940, folder Crowther (1), box 119, Stettinius Papers.

2. William E. Leuchtenburg, "The New Deal and the Analogue of War," in *Change and Continuity in Twentieth-Century America*, ed. John Braeman, Robert H. Bremner, and Everett Waters (Columbus: Ohio State University Press, 1964), 81–143; Robert H. Wiebe, *The Search for Order, 1877–1920* (New York: Hill & Wang, 1967), 293–99; Ellis W. Hawley, *The Great War and the Search for a Modern Order: A History of the American People and Their Institutions, 1917–1933* (New York: St. Martin's, 1979); Alan Brinkley, *Liberalism and Its Discontents* (Cambridge, MA: Harvard University Press, 1998), 79–93; Marc Allen Eisner, *From Warfare State to Welfare State: World War I, Compensatory State Building, and the Limits of the Modern Order* (University Park: Pennsylvania State University Press, 2000). On military-industrial relations specifically, see Paul A. C. Koistinen, "The 'Industrial-Military Complex' in Historical Perspective: World War I," *Business History Review* 41 (winter 1967): 378–403; Paul A. C. Koistinen, "The Industrial-Military Complex' in Historical Perspective: The Interwar Years," *Journal of American History* 56, no. 4 (Mar. 1970): 819–39; Paul A. C. Koistinen, *Mobilizing for Modern War: The Political Economy of American Warfare, 1865–1919* (Lawrence: University Press of Kansas, 1997).

3. For a detailed contemporary listing, see Richard J. Beamish and Francis A. March, *America's Part in the World War* (Philadelphia: John C. Winston, 1919), 300–381.

4. David M. Kennedy, *Over Here: The First World War and American Society* (New York: Oxford University Press, 1980), 93–143; Ronald Schaffer, *America in the Great War: The Rise of the War Welfare State* (New York: Oxford University Press, 1991). For an extended discussion of the historiography, see Mark R. Wilson, "Economic Mobilization," in *A Companion to Woodrow Wilson*, ed. Ross A. Kennedy (New York: Wiley-Blackwell, 2013), 289–307.

5. Charles Hirschfeld, "Nationalism Progressivism and World War I," *Mid-America* 45, no. 3 (July 1963): 139–56; Christopher N. May, *In the Name of War: Judicial Review and the War Powers Since 1918* (Cambridge, MA: Harvard University Press, 1989), 26–59; Gail Radford, *The Rise of Public Authority: Statebuilding and Economic Development in Twentieth-Century America* (Chicago: University of Chicago Press, 2013).

6. David E. Lilienthal and Robert H. Marquis, "The Conduct of Business Enterprises by the Federal Government," *Harvard Law Review* 54, no. 4 (Feb. 1941): 547.

7. Historians have failed to do enough point this out, in part because they have not paid enough attention to what Robert Cuff, the greatest historian of the American mobilization for the Great War, called "the gap between the rhetoric and reality of the WIB experiment." Robert D. Cuff, *The War Industries Board: Business-Government Relations During World War I* (Baltimore: Johns Hopkins University Press, 1973), 265.

8. Bernard M. Baruch, *American Industry in the War* (New York: Prentice Hall, 1941), 77, 389; Melvin I. Urofsky, *Big Steel and the Wilson Administration: A Study in Business-Government Relations* (Columbus: Ohio State University Press, 1969), 213–16; Robert D. Cuff and Melvin I. Urofsky, "The Steel Industry and Price Fixing During World War I," *Business History Review* 44, no. 3 (autumn 1970): 291–306; Jordan A. Schwarz, *The Speculator: Bernard M. Baruch in Washington, 1917–1965* (Chapel Hill: University of North Carolina Press, 1981), 71–82. Wilson reportedly considered the prospect of seizing the mills as early as July 1917. See Cuff, *War Industries Board*, 58–59, 125–28. On Brookings, see Stuart D. Brandes, *Warhogs: A History of War Profits in America* (Lexington: University Press of Kentucky, 1997), 171–72. On Baruch's clashes with lumbermen, see James E. Fickle, "Defense Mobilization in the Southern Pine Industry," *Journal of Forest History* 22, no. 4 (Oct. 1978): 206–23.

9. Robert D. Cuff, "The Dilemmas of Voluntarism: Hoover and the Pork-Packing Agreement of 1917–1919," *Agricultural History* 53 (1979): 727–47.

10. Frank Freidel, *Franklin D. Roosevelt: The Apprenticeship* (Boston: Little, Brown, 1952), 326; Geoffrey C. Ward, *A First-Class Temperament: The Emergence of Franklin Roosevelt* (New York: Harper & Row, 1989), 227–28; Brandes, *Warhogs*, 171.

11. Melvyn Dubofsky, *The State and Labor in Modern America* (Chapel Hill: University of North Carolina Press, 1994), 58–75; Joseph A. McCartin, *Labor's Great War: The Struggle for Industrial Democracy and the Origins of Modern American Labor Relations, 1912–1921* (Chapel Hill: University of North Carolina Press, 1997).

12. Valerie Jean Conner, *The National War Labor Board: Stability, Social Justice, and the Voluntary State in World War I* (Chapel Hill: University of North Carolina Press, 1983), 124–37.

13. "Plan Strike at War Plant," *NYT*, 12 July 1918; "Strike at Pistol Plant," *NYT*, 13 July 1918; "Rejects Decision of War Labor Board," *NYT*, 31 Aug. 1918; "Smith & Wesson Labor Concessions," *NYT*, 6 Sept. 1918; McCartin, *Labor's Great War*, 139, 163, 178.

14. "President to Put Strikers in Army," *NYT*, 14 Sept. 1916.

15. Michael Kazin, *A Godly Hero: The Life of William Jennings Bryan* (New York: Random House, 2006).

16. Conner, *National War Labor Board*, 35–48, 161–70; H. M. Gitelman, "Being of Two Minds: American Employers Confront the Labor Problem, 1915–1919," *Labor History* 25, no. 2 (spring 1984): 209–10; May, *In the Name of War*, 28–54; McCartin, *Labor's Great War*, 92; Richard R. John, *Network Nation: Inventing American Telecommunications* (Cambridge, MA:

Harvard University Press, 2010), 365–406. On the relationships among wartime mobilization, government-business relations in the telephone industry, and corporate political and public relations activity, see also Roland Marchand, *Creating the Corporate Soul: The Rise of Public Relations and Corporate Imagery in American Big Business* (Berkeley: University of California Press, 1998).

17. William G. McAdoo, *Crowded Years: The Reminiscences of William G. McAdoo* (Boston: Houghton Mifflin, 1931), 295–316; Richard Sicotte, "Economic Crisis and Political Response: The Political Economy of the Shipping Act of 1916," *Journal of Economic History* 59, no. 4 (Dec. 1999): 861–84; Gail Radford, "William Gibbs McAdoo, the Emergency Fleet Corporation, and the Origins of the Public-Authority Model of Governmental Action," *Journal of Policy History* 11 (1999): 59–88. On McAdoo as a practitioner of "state capitalism"—a term used by the New Dealers in the 1930s, as well as historians—see Jordan A. Schwarz, *The New Dealers: Power Politics in the Age of Roosevelt* (New York: Knopf, 1993), 13–21.

18. Bernard Mergen, "The Government as Manager: Emergency Fleet Shipbuilding, 1917–1919," in *Business and Its Environment: Essays for Thomas C. Cochran*, ed. Harold Issadore Sharlin (Westport, CT: Greenwood, 1983), 50–74; Robert H. Ferrell, *Woodrow Wilson and World War I* (New York: Harper & Row, 1985), 99–101; Deborah Hirschfield, "From Hog Islanders to Liberty Ships: The American Government and Merchant Ship Construction in Two World Wars," *American Neptune* 54 (1994): 86–87.

19. David Sarasohn, *The Party of Reform: Democrats in the Progressive Era* (Jackson: University Press of Mississippi, 1989), 204–18; Jon R. Huibregtse, *American Railroad Labor and the Genesis of the New Deal, 1919–1935* (Gainesville: University Press of Florida, 2010), 22–23.

20. Charles Whiting Baker, *Government Control and Operation of Industry in Great Britain and the United States During the World War* (New York: Oxford University Press, 1921), 58; McAdoo, *Crowded Years*, 448–61; K. Austin Kerr, "Decision for Federal Control: Wilson, McAdoo, and the Railroads, 1917," *Journal of American History* 54, no. 3 (Dec. 1967): 550–60; Douglas B. Craig, *Progressives at War: William G. McAdoo and Newton D. Baker, 1863–1941* (Baltimore: Johns Hopkins University Press, 2013), 198–204.

21. Lee A. Craig, *Josephus Daniels: His Life & Times* (Chapel Hill: University of North Carolina Press, 2013).

22. Benjamin Franklin Cooling, *Gray Steel and Blue Water Navy: The Formative Years of America's Military-Industrial Complex* (Hamden, CT: Archon, 1979), 85–160; Earl A. Molander, "The Emergence of Military-Industrial Criticism, 1895–1915," in *The Military-Industrial Complex: Eisenhower's Warning Three Decades Later*, ed. Gregg B. Walker, David A. Bella, and Steven J. Sprecher (New York: Peter Lang, 1992), 237–67; Brandes, *Warhogs*, 111–14.

23. Josephus Daniels, *The Wilson Era: Years of Peace, 1910–1917* (Chapel Hill: University of North Carolina Press, 1946), 358–61.

24. Urofsky, *Big Steel*, 122–48; Cooling, *Gray Steel and Blue Water Navy*, 161–212; Joe H. Camp, Jr., "Birch Rod to Arsenal: A Study of the Naval Ordnance Plant at South Charleston, West Virginia, and the Search for a Government Industrial Policy" (Ph.D. diss., University of West Virginia, 2002), 10–37.

25. John W. Adams, "The Influences Affecting Naval Shipbuilding Legislation, 1910–1916," *Naval War College Review* 22, no. 4 (1969): 55; Freidel, *Franklin D. Roosevelt: The Apprenticeship*, 217–19.

26. *Annual Report of the Secretary of the Navy for the Fiscal Year, Including Operations and Recommendations to December 1, 1918* (Washington, DC: GPO, 1918), 43.

27. Daniel Thomas Campbell, "New York Shipbuilding Company: The First Two Decades" (Ph.D. diss., Temple University, 2001), 171–82.

28. Daniels, *Wilson Era: Years of Peace*, 299–345.

29. *Activities of the Bureau of Yards and Docks, Navy Department: World War, 1917–1918* (Washington, DC: GPO, 1921), 19, 216; Josephus Daniels, *Our Navy at War* (Washington, DC: Pictorial Bureau, 1922), 300–303; Albion, "Brief History of Civilian Personnel in the U.S. Navy Department," 13; Paul H. Silverstone, *U.S. Warships of World War I* (Garden City, NY: Doubleday, 1970), 30–55, 116–50; William J. Williams, "Josephus Daniels and the U.S. Navy's Shipbuilding Program During World War I," *Journal of Military History* 60, no. 1 (Jan. 1996): 7–38; Thomas R. Heinrich, *Ships for the Seven Seas: Philadelphia Shipbuilding in the Age of Industrial Capitalism* (Baltimore: Johns Hopkins University Press, 1997), 179.

30. Hugh G. J. Aitken, *The Continuous Wave: Technology and American Radio, 1900–1932* (Princeton, NJ: Princeton University Press, 1985), 254–94.

31. Daniels, *Our Navy at War*, 252; idem, *Wilson Era: Years of Peace*, 344–68, 496; William F. Trimble, "The Naval Aircraft Factory, the American Aviation Industry, and Government Competition, 1919–1928," *Business History Review* 60 (summer 1986): 175–98; Thomas Wildenberg and Norman Polmar, *Ship Killer: A History of the American Torpedo* (Annapolis, MD: Naval Institute Press, 2010), 33–55; David K. Van Keuren, "Science, Progressivism, and Military Preparedness: The Case of the Naval Research Laboratory, 1915–1923," *Technology and Culture* 33 (1992): 710–36; Larry G. Gerber, *The Limits of Liberalism: Josephus Daniels, Henry Stimson, Bernard Baruch, Donald Richberg, Felix Frankfurter and the Development of the Modern American Political Economy* (New York: New York University Press, 1983), 173, 235–36.

32. Daniel R. Beaver, *Newton D. Baker and the American War Effort, 1917–1919* (Lincoln: University of Nebraska Press, 1966); Craig, *Progressives at War*, 46–151.

33. "Government Manufacture of Arms, Munitions, and Equipment," Senate Doc. 664, 64th Cong., 2nd Sess. (1917).

34. Daniel R. Beaver, *Modernizing the American War Department: Change and Continuity in a Turbulent Era, 1885–1920* (Kent, OH: Kent State University Press, 2006), 161.

35. Julie Z. Strickland, "War Making and State Building: The Dynamics of American Industrial Development, 1917–1935" (Ph.D. diss., Stanford University, 1988); Terrence James Gough, "The Battle of Washington: Soldiers and Businessmen in World War I" (Ph.D. diss., University of Virginia, 1997).

36. William B. Williams, *History of the Manufacture of Explosives for the World War* (n.p., 1920), 8; Baruch, *American Industry in the War*, 188; Beaver, *Modernizing the American War Department*, 47.

37. Grosvenor B. Clarkson, *Industrial America in the World War: The Strategy Behind the Line, 1917–1918* (Boston: Houghton Mifflin, 1923), 390–410.

38. R. Eugene Harper, "Wilson Progressives vs. Du Pont: Controversy in Building the Nitro Plant," *West Virginia History* 48 (Mar. 1989): 93–107.

39. Clarkson, *Industrial America in the World War*, 390–410; Williams, *History of the Manufacture of Explosives*, 13–16; Alfred D. Chandler, Jr. and Stephen Salisbury, *Pierre S. Du Pont and the Making of the Modern Corporation* (New York: Harper & Row, 1971), 402–55;

Robert Cuff, "Private Success, Public Problems: The Du Pont Corporation and World War I," *Canadian Review of American Studies* 20 (fall 1989): 175–82.

40. John Milton Cooper, Jr., *Woodrow Wilson: A Biography* (New York: Alfred A. Knopf, 2009), 392–93.

41. Chandler and Salisbury, *Pierre S. Du Pont*, 359–71; Cuff, "Private Success, Public Problems," 173–74.

42. Brandes, *Warhogs*, 136–40.

43. Urofsky, *Big Steel and the Wilson Administration*, 91–106, 228–23; Matthew Ware Coulter, *The Senate Munitions Inquiry of the 1930s: Beyond the Merchants of Death* (Westport, CT: Greenwood, 1997), 42–43, 69; Brandes, *Warhogs*, 134–37, 165–69; Ajay K. Mehrotra, "Lawyers, Guns, and Public Moneys: The U.S. Treasury, World War I, and the Administration of the Modern Fiscal State," *Law and History Review* 28, no. 1 (Feb. 2010): 212.

44. Hugh Rockoff, "Until It's Over, Over There: The U.S. Economy in World War I," in *The Economics of World War I*, ed. Stephen Broadberry and Mark Harrison (New York: Cambridge University Press, 2005), 316; Julia C. Ott, *When Wall Street Met Main Street: The Quest for an Investor's Democracy* (Cambridge, MA: Harvard University Press, 2011), 2–99.

45. Seward W. Livermore, *Politics Is Adjourned: Woodrow Wilson and the War Congress* (Middletown, CT: Wesleyan University Press, 1966), 58–61; Kennedy, *Over Here*, 106–13; Brandes, *Warhogs*, 134–35; W. Elliott Brownlee, *Federal Taxation in America: A Short History*, 2nd ed. (New York: Cambridge University Press, 2004), 60–73; Rockoff, "Until It's Over, Over There," 321; Steven A. Bank, Kirk J. Stark, and Joseph J. Thorndike, *War and Taxes* (Washington, DC: Urban Institute Press, 2008), 49–78; Mehrotra, "Lawyers, Guns, and Public Moneys," 211–20.

46. Urofsky, *Big Steel*, 122–48; Kenneth S. Davis, *FDR: The Beckoning of Destiny, 1882–1928* (New York: G. P. Putnam's Sons, 1972), 573–74; Gerber, *Limits of Liberalism*, 333.

47. K. Austin Kerr, *American Railroad Politics, 1914–1920: Rates, Wages, and Efficiency* (Pittsburgh: University of Pittsburgh Press, 1968); Robert Hessen, "Charles Schwab and the Shipbuilding Crisis of 1918," *Pennsylvania History* 38 (Oct. 1971): 389–99.

48. May, *In the Name of War*, 44; Schwarz, *Speculator*, 82.

49. Burl Noggle, *Into the Twenties: The United States from Armistice to Normalcy* (Urbana: University of Illinois Press, 1974), 47–51; Schwarz, *Speculator*, 102–4.

50. Baker, *Government Control and Operation of Industry*, 121; McAdoo, *Crowded Years*, 507–9; Kerr, *American Railroad Politics*, 135–42, 16–71; Ari Hoogenboom and Olive Hoogenboom, *A History of the ICC: From Panacea to Palliative* (New York: W. W. Norton, 1976), 95–105; Susan H. Armitage, *The Politics of Decontrol of Industry: Britain and the United States* (London: Weidenfeld and Nicolson, 1969), 93–95; May, *In the Name of War*, 50–54; Huibregtse, *American Railroad Labor*, 31–32; Craig, *Progressives at War*, 205–6.

51. Aitken, *Continuous Wave*; Jonathan Reed Winkler, *Nexus: Strategic Communications and American Security in World War I* (Cambridge, MA: Harvard University Press, 2008), 256–59.

52. Daniels, *Wilson Era: Years of Peace*, 363.

53. Morton Keller, *In Defense of Yesterday: James M. Beck and the Politics of Conservatism, 1861–1936* (New York: Coward-McCann, 1958), 170.

54. Dubofsky, *State and Labor in Modern America*, 76–96; Joseph Slater, "Public Works: Labor and the Boston Police Strike of 1919," *Labor History* 38, no. 1 (winter 1996–97): 7–27;

Donna T. Haverty-Stacke, "Creative Opposition to Radical America: 1920s' Anti-May Day Demonstrations," *Labor: Studies in Working-Class History of the Americas* 4, no. 3 (fall 2007): 59–80; Beverly Gage, *The Day Wall Street Exploded: A Story of America in Its First Age of Terror* (New York: Oxford University Press, 2009).

55. Livermore, *Politics Is Adjourned*, 67–102.

56. "Resolutions Adopted at Sixth Annual Meeting" and "Declarations Adopted at the War Emergency and Reconstruction Conference," 1918, in folder Board Resolutions, 1917–1918, and miscellaneous Board Resolutions folders, 1919–1941, box 1, Chamber Records; James Warren Prothro, *The Dollar Decade: Business Ideas in the 1920s* (Baton Rouge: Louisiana State University, 1954), 27, 143, 160; Kerr, *American Railroad Politics*, 195; Lynn Dumenil, "'The Insatiable Maw of Bureaucracy': Antistatism and Education Reform in the 1920s," *Journal of American History* 77, no. 2 (Sept. 1990): 499–524; Douglas B. Craig, *After Wilson: The Struggle for the Democratic Party, 1920–1934* (Chapel Hill: University of North Carolina Press, 1992), 138.

57. H. Larry Ingle, "The Dangers of Reaction: Repeal of the Revenue Act of 1918," *North Carolina Historical Review* 44, no. 1 (winter 1967): 72–88; Ajay K. Mehrotra, *Making the Modern American Fiscal State: Law, Politics, and the Rise of Progressive Taxation, 1877–1929* (New York: Cambridge University Press, 2013), 349–408.

58. U.S. House of Representatives, *Inquiry into Operations, Policies, and Affairs of United States Shipping Board and Emergency Fleet Corporation*, House Report 2, 69th Cong., 1st Sess. (Washington, DC: GPO, 1925), 10–11, 18, 26–27, 52; Noggle, *Into the Twenties*, 59; Armitage, *Politics of Decontrol of Industry*, 39–42; Ferrell, *Woodrow Wilson and World War I*, 102.

59. Prothro, *Dollar Decade*, 224; Otis L. Graham, Jr., *An Encore for Reform: The Old Progressives and the New Deal* (New York: Oxford University Press, 1967); Robert Mason, *The Republican Party and American Politics from Hoover to Reagan* (New York: Cambridge University Press, 2012), 16–25.

60. Arthur S. Link, "What Happened to the Progressive Movement in the 1920s?," *American Historical Review* 64, no. 4 (July 1959): 833–51; Stanley Shapiro, "The Twilight of Reform: Advanced Progressives After the Armistice," *Historian* 33, no. 3 (May 1971): 349–61; Jackson K. Putnam, "The Persistence of Progressivism in the 1920s: The Case of California," *Pacific Historical Review* 35, no. 4 (Nov. 1966): 395–411; Ronald L. Feinman, *Twilight of Progressivism: The Western Republican Senators and the New Deal* (Baltimore: Johns Hopkins University Press, 1981); Daniel Amsterdam, "The Roaring Metropolis: Business, Civic Welfare, and State Expansion in 1920s America" (Ph.D. diss., University of Pennsylvania, 2009).

61. J. Leonard Bates, "Josephus Daniels and the Naval Oil Reserves," *United States Naval Institute Proceedings* 79 (Feb. 1953): 170–79; Burl Noggle, *Teapot Dome: Oil and Politics in the 1920s* (New York: W. W. Norton, 1962); 100–101; Craig, *After Wilson*, 94–119.

62. The standard history of Muscle Shoals is Preston J. Hubbard, *Origins of the TVA: The Muscle Shoals Controversy, 1920–1932* (Nashville, TN: Vanderbilt University Press, 1961). See also Daniel Schaffer, "War Mobilization in Muscle Shoals, Alabama, 1917–1918," *Alabama Review* 39 (1986): 110–46; Pisani, *Water and American Government*, 220–27.

63. Hubbard, *Origins of the TVA*, 71.

64. John D. Hicks, *Republican Ascendancy, 1921–1933* (New York: Harper & Bros., 1960), 64; Hubbard, *Origins of the TVA*, 118.

65. Hubbard, *Origins of the TVA*, 233, 254–55, 266; Thomas K. McCraw, *TVA and the Power Fight, 1933–1939* (Philadelphia: J. B. Lippincott, 1971), 5; Philip J. Funigiello, *Toward*

a National Power Policy: The New Deal and the Electric Utility Industry, 1933–1941 (Pittsburgh: University of Pittsburgh Press, 1973), 10–19.

66. Ellis W. Hawley, "Herbert Hoover, the Commerce Secretariat, and the Vision of an 'Associative State,' 1921–1928," *Journal of American History* 61, no. 1 (1974): 116–40.

67. Glen Jeansonne, *The Life of Herbert Hoover: Fighting Quaker, 1928–1933* (New York: Palgrave Macmillan, 2012).

68. Hubbard, *Origins of the TVA*, 293; McCraw, *TVA and the Power Fight*, 24; Craig, *After Wilson*, 164; Eisner, *From Warfare State to Welfare State*, 297.

69. McCraw, *TVA and the Power Fight*, 30–31; James David Bennett II, "Struggle for Power: The Relationship Between the Tennessee Valley Authority and the Private Power Industry, 1933–1939" (Ph.D. diss., Vanderbilt University, 1969), 78–79, 123–24; Camp, "Birch Rod to Arsenal," 120–22.

70. Hubbard, *Origins of the TVA*, 256, 312–14.

71. McCraw, *TVA and the Power Fight*, 161.

72. Thomas K. McCraw, *Morgan vs. Lilienthal: The Feud Within the TVA* (Chicago: Loyola University Press, 1970), 27, 76; McCraw, *TVA and the Power Fight*, 48–51, 83; Bennett, "Struggle for Power," 135–66, 179–295; Schwarz, *New Dealers*, 219–34.

73. Schwarz, *New Dealers*, 317; Sarah T. Phillips, *This Land, This Nation: Conservation, Rural America, and the New Deal* (New York: Cambridge University Press, 2007), 230.

74. Patterson, *Congressional Conservatism*, 38–58.

75. "Fight This Destructive Wheeler-Rayburn Bill," *New Orleans Times-Picayune*, 7 May 1935; Funigiello, *Toward a National Power Policy*, 102.

76. George Wolfskill, *The Revolt of the Conservatives: A History of the American Liberty League, 1934–1940* (Boston: Houghton Mifflin, 1962), 225–37; Michael Stephen Czaplicki, "The Corruption of Hope: Political Scandal, Congressional Investigations, and New Deal Moral Authority, 1932–1952" (Ph.D. diss., University of Chicago, 2010), 52–65.

77. Funigiello, *Toward a National Power Policy*, 174–205; Adams, *Mr. Kaiser Goes to Washington*; Christopher James Tassava, "Multiples of Six: The Six Companies and West Coast Industrialization, 1930–1945," *Enterprise & Society* 4, no. 1 (Mar. 2003): 1–27; David P. Billington and Donald C. Jackson, *Big Dams of the New Deal Era: A Confluence of Engineering and Politics* (Norman: University of Oklahoma Press, 2006), 189–92.

78. Bonnie Fox Schwartz, *The Civil Works Administration, 1933–1934: The Business of Emergency Employment in the New Deal* (Princeton, NJ: Princeton University Press, 1984), 45, 215; Jason Scott Smith, *Building New Deal Liberalism: The Political Economy of Public Works* (New York: Cambridge University Press, 2006), 108–11.

79. Louis Galambos and Joseph Pratt, *The Rise of the Corporate Commonwealth: U.S. Business and Public Policy in the Twentieth Century* (New York: Basic Books, 1988), 124.

80. Keller, *In Defense of Yesterday*, 245.

81. Herbert Hoover, *The Challenge to Liberty* (New York: Charles Scribner's Sons, 1934), 76–103, quotation at 90.

82. Mason, *Republican Party*, 45; Clyde P. Weed, *The Nemesis of Reform: The Republican Party During the New Deal* (New York: Columbia University Press, 1994), 101.

83. Craig, *After Wilson*, 278. See also James T. Patterson, *Congressional Conservatism and the New Deal: The Growth of the Conservative Coalition in Congress, 1933–1939* (Lexington: University of Kentucky Press, 1967), 13–31, 179–82.

84. Kim McQuaid, *A Response to Industrialism: Liberal Businessmen and the Evolving Spectrum of Capitalist Reform, 1886–1960* (New York: Garland, 1986).

85. Robert F. Burk, *The Corporate State and the Broker State: The Du Ponts and American National Politics, 1925–1940* (Cambridge, MA: Harvard University Press, 1990).

86. Burk, *Corporate State and Broker State*, 112–32.

87. Wolfskill, *Revolt of the Conservatives*; Burk, *Corporate State and Broker State*, 206; Craig, *After Wilson*, 292; David Farber, *Everybody Ought to Be Rich: The Life and Times of John J. Raskob, Capitalist* (New York: Oxford University Press, 2013), 289–309.

88. Weed, *Nemesis of Reform*, 62–76; Dubofsky, *State and Labor in Modern America*, 129–60; Burk, *Corporate State and Broker State*, 181–93; Sarah R. Hammond, "'God Is My Partner': An Evangelical Business Man Confronts Depression and War," *Church History* 80, no. 3 (Sept. 2011): 498–519; Peter van Horn to Marvin H. McIntyre, 12 May 1936, folder Politics 1933–43, box 156, PSF-FDR.

89. Ira Katznelson, *Fear Itself: The New Deal and the Origins of Our Time* (New York: Liveright, 2013), 249.

90. William E. Leuchtenburg, *Franklin D. Roosevelt and the New Deal, 1932–1940* (New York: Harper & Row, 1963), 190; Wolfskill, *Revolt of the Conservatives*, 187, 219; James Holt, "The New Deal and the American Anti-Statist Tradition," in *The New Deal: The National Level*, ed. John Braeman, Robert H. Bremner, and David Brody (Columbus: Ohio State University Press, 1975), 39–40; Burk, *Corporate State and Broker State*, 211; David M. Kennedy, *Freedom from Fear: The American People in Depression and War* (New York: Oxford University Press, 1999), 279–82.

91. "Poll Vote Heavy Against Private Munitions Making," *Dallas Morning News*, 8 Mar. 1936.

92. John E. Wiltz, *In Search of Peace: The Senate Munitions Inquiry, 1934–1936* (Baton Rouge: Louisiana State University Press, 1963); Coulter, *Senate Munitions Inquiry*.

93. For a general discussion of the many problems with the "isolationist" label as applied to the interwar United States, see Brooke L. Blower, "From Isolationism to Neutrality: A New Framework for Understanding American Political Culture, 1919–1941," *Diplomatic History* 38, no. 2 (Apr. 2014): 345–76.

94. "Private Enterprise and Public War," *New Republic* (16 Nov. 1921): 26–30; Jari Eloranta and Mark Wilson, "Thwarting the 'Merchants of Death' Accusation: The Political Economy of Military Procurement in Industrial Democracies During the Interwar Period," *Essays in Economic and Business History* 28 (2010): 91–106.

95. Wiltz, *In Search of Peace*, 14–15; Brandes, *Warhogs*, 173, 186–94; Paul A. C. Koistinen, *Planning War, Pursuing Peace: The Political Economy of American Warfare, 1920–1939* (Lawrence: University Press of Kansas, 1998), 212–19; Stephen R. Ortiz, *Beyond the Bonus March and GI Bill: How Veteran Politics Shaped the New Deal Era* (New York: New York University Press, 2010), 89–90, 116–17.

96. *War Policies Commission: Message from the President of the United States Transmitting Report of the War Policies Commission Created by Public Resolution No. 98* (Washington, DC: GPO, 1931), 22, 494, 669–71; Wiltz, *In Search of Peace*, 1–15; Coulter, *Senate Munitions Inquiry*, 54, 79; Brandes, *Warhogs*, 205–6; Koistinen, *Planning War, Pursuing Peace*, 220–52.

97. "Arms and the Men," *Fortune* (Mar. 1934): 52–57, 113–26; Coulter, *Senate Munitions Inquiry*, 22.

98. David G. Anderson, "British Rearmament and the 'Merchants of Death': The 1935–36 Royal Commission on the Manufacture of and Trade in Armaments," *Journal of Contemporary History* 29, no. 1 (Jan. 1994): 5–37; David Edgerton, "Public Ownership and the British Arms Industry, 1920–1950," in *The Political Economy of Nationalisation in Britain, 1920–1950*, ed. Robert Millward and John Singleton (Cambridge: Cambridge University Press, 1995), 171–78; Jeffrey J. Clarke, "The Nationalization of War Industries in France, 1936–1937: A Case Study," *Journal of Modern History* 49, no. 3 (Sept. 1977): 411–30; John F. Godfrey, *Capitalism at War: Industrial Policy and Bureaucracy in France, 1914–1918* (New York: Berg, 1987), 219–20; Martin S. Alexander, *The Republic in Danger: General Maurice Gamelin and the Politics of French Defence, 1933–1940* (Cambridge: Cambridge University Press, 1992), 112–17.

99. Coulter, *Senate Munitions Inquiry*; Brandes, *Warhogs*, 207–25. Not all women's associations supported Detzer's initiative. See Christine K. Erickson, " 'So Much for Men': Conservative Women and National Defense in the 1920s and 1930s," *American Studies* 45, no. 1 (spring 2004): 85–102.

100. Coulter, *Senate Munitions Inquiry*, 36, 48.

101. "Legion Outlines Program to Take Profit from War," *Dallas Morning News*, 25 Sept. 1934.

102. Wiltz, *In Search of Peace*, 74–85; Coulter, *Senate Munitions Inquiry*, 36; Burk, *Corporate State and Broker State*, 152–66; Craig, *After Wilson*, 249–51.

103. Wiltz, *In Search of Peace*, 72.

104. Barton to Carpenter, 15 Aug. 1934, folder C-55, box 824, Papers of Walter S. Carpenter, Jr., in Records of E. I. Du Pont de Nemours & Co., Ser. II, Part 2, Hagley.

105. "Remington Arms Co." reminiscences, 17 Feb. 1972 [*sic*], folder Remington Arms Co., box 2, Donald F. Carpenter Papers, Hagley; "Stockholders' Bulletin: The Du Pont Company as a Munitions Manufacturer," 10 Aug. 1934, and Walter Carpenter memo on Nye Committee hearings, 19 Sept. 1934, both in folder C-55, box 824, Walter Carpenter Papers, Hagley; Cuff, "Private Success, Public Problems," 183–86.

106. "Curbing the Profiteer," *Cleveland Plain Dealer*, 25 May 1935; Coulter, *Senate Munitions Inquiry*, 81–85; Schwarz, *Speculator*, 339–40; Koistinen, *Planning War, Pursuing Peace*, 272–73.

107. *Munitions Industry: Report on Government Manufacture of Munitions*, 74th Cong., 2nd Sess., Senate Report 944, Part 7 (Washington, DC: GPO, 1936), 133.

108. Wiltz, *In Search of Peace*, 92, 96.

109. Ibid., 95–96; Charles F. Elliott, " 'The Genesis of the Modern U.S. Navy,' " *United States Naval Institute Proceedings* 92 (Mar. 1966): 64–65; Coulter, *Senate Munitions Inquiry*, 58, 122.

110. Wiltz, *In Search of Peace*, 95–98; Coulter, *Senate Munitions Inquiry*, 132.

111. "Nye Urges Drastic Tax to Take Profit from War in Address to Veterans," *New Orleans Times-Picayune*, 17 Sept. 1935; "To Prevent Profiteering in Time of War," House Report 808, 75th Cong., 1st Sess. (1937), copy in folder War Dept. 1937, box 81, PSF-FDR; "Promises to Aid V.F.W. in Getting Service Officer," *New Orleans Times-Picayune*, 3 July 1937.

112. *Taking the Profits Out of War: Hearings Before the Committee on Military Affairs* (Washington, DC: GPO, 1935), 116–18.

113. Ernest Angell, "Shall We Nationalize Munitions?," *Harper's Magazine* 170 (Mar. 1935): 407–17.

114. *Munitions Industry: Report on Government Manufacture of Munitions*, 86, 122.

115. *Commercial Shipyards and the Navy* (New York: National Council of American Shipbuilders, 1937), 11, 87–88; Elliott, "Genesis of the Modern U.S. Navy," 64; Robert H. Levine, *The Politics of American Naval Rearmament, 1930–1938* (New York: Garland, 1988), 30–31, 375–76; Thomas Heinrich, "'We Can Build Anything at Navy Yards': Warship Construction in Government Yards and the Political Economy of American Naval Shipbuilding, 1928–1945," *International Journal of Maritime History* 24 (Dec. 2012): 155–80. On political efforts to preserve U.S. Navy yards, see Adams, "Influences Affecting Naval Shipbuilding Legislation," 59; Fritz Peter Hamer, "A Southern City Enters the Twentieth Century: Charleston, Its Navy Yard, and World War II, 1940–1948" (Ph.D. diss., University of South Carolina, 1998), 14–20.

116. Elliott, "Genesis of the Modern U.S. Navy," 62–69; Robert Gordon Kaufman, *Arms Control During the Pre-Nuclear Era: The United States and Naval Limitation Between the Two World Wars* (New York: Columbia University Press, 1990), 204; William M. McBride, "The Unstable Dynamics of a Strategic Technology: Disarmament, Unemployment, and the Interwar Battleship," *Technology and Culture* 38 (Apr. 1997): 410; John S. Olszowka, "From Shop Floor to Fight: Work and Labor in the Aircraft Industry, 1908–1945" (Ph.D. diss., State University of New York, Binghamton, 2000), 39; James F. Cook, *Carl Vinson: Patriarch of the Armed Forces* (Macon, GA: Mercer University Press, 2004), 89–102.

117. McBride, "Unstable Dynamics," 390–91, 406–9.

118. Levine, *Politics of American Naval Rearmament*, 54–58; Coulter, *Senate Munitions Inquiry*, 128.

119. *Commercial Shipyards and the Navy*, 19, 36, 72, 79–80.

120. Levine, *Politics of American Naval Rearmament*, 448–66; Camp, "Birch Rod to Arsenal," 132–33; McBride, "Unstable Dynamics," 417–20.

121. Lt. Col. G. M. Barnes, "Procurement Planning: The Basis of the New American System of National Defense," *Army Ordnance* 18 (July–Aug. 1937): 22–23; Col. Harry B. Jordan, "A School of Supply Strategy: The Aims and Methods of the Army Industrial College," *Army Ordnance* 19 (Sept.–Oct. 1938): 77–78; Michael Geyer, "Professionals and Junkers: German Rearmament and Politics in the Weimar Republic," in *Social Change and Political Development in Weimar Germany*, ed. Richard Bessel and E. J. Feuchtwanger (London: Croom Helm, 1981), 85–86; Peter Mansfield Abramo, "The Military and Economic Potential of the United States: Industrial Mobilization Planning, 1919–1945" (Ph.D. diss., Temple University, 1995).

122. Dwight F. Davis, "Industrial Mobilization as Insurance Against War," 18 Feb. 1924, folder Major Addresses by Others, box 6, Frank A. Scott Papers, Seeley G. Mudd Manuscript Library, Princeton University; "Chicago Ordnance District, Unit War Plans, January 1, 1925," and "1928 Mobilization Plan," box 24, RG 156, NARA-GL; Hanford MacNider, "The War Department Business Council," *Army Ordnance* 6 (May–June 1926): 417; Albert A. Blum, "Birth and Death of the M-Day Plan," in *American Civil-Military Decisions: A Book of Case Studies*, ed. Harold Stein (Birmingham: University of Alabama Press, 1963), 63–64; Abramo, "Military and Economic Potential," 38–53; Koistinen, *Planning War, Pursuing Peace*, 26–29, 83–112.

123. U.S. War Policies Commission, *Report* (Washington, DC: GPO, 1931), 34–38, 50, 368–73; Maj. Dwight D. Eisenhower, "Brief History of Planning for Procurement and Industrial Mobilization Since the World War," 2 Oct. 1931, Army Industrial College (AIC) Lectures Collection, NDU; *Industrial Mobilization Plan*, rev. 1933 (Washington, DC: GPO, 1933), 1–10; *Industrial Mobilization Plan*, rev. 1936 (Washington, DC: GPO, 1936), 1–10; Kerry E. Irish, "Apt Pupil: Dwight Eisenhower and the 1930 Industrial Mobilization Plan," *Journal of Military History* 70, no. 1 (Jan. 2006): 31–61.

124. *Taking the Profits Out of War*, 39–56; Col. C. T. Harris, "The Planning Branch and Its Problems," 6 Dec. 1935, AIC lectures, NDU; "Conclusions and Recommendations" on Problem #27: "Nationalization of the Munitions Industry," AIC, 5 Apr. 1937, box 2, entry 45, RG 334, NARA; Johnson, "Procurement Plans in Theory and Practice," 11 Oct. 1939, folder Speeches, box 80, Johnson Papers; Camp, "Birch Rod to Arsenal," 108; Spurlock, "Bell Telephone Laboratories and the Military-Industrial Complex," 185.

125. Johnson, "The Business of National Defense," 5 Apr. 1939, and "The Railroads and National Defense," 26 Apr. 1940, both in folder Speeches, box 80, Johnson Papers.

126. Maj. Frank W. Gano, *A Study of Priorities* (Washington, DC: Army Industrial College, 1938), 169; Col. F. H. Miles, Jr., "Industrial Preparedness," 20 May 1940, in vol. "Staff II," box 19, entry 43, RG 334.

127. Terrence J. Gough, "Origins of the Army Industrial College: Military-Business Tensions After World War I," *Armed Forces & Society* 17, no. 2 (winter 1991): 259–75; Terrence J. Gough, "Soldiers, Businessmen and US Industrial Mobilization Planning Between the World Wars," *War & Society* 9, no. 1 (May 1991): 63–98.

128. Harris, "Planning Branch and Its Problems"; Dwight F. Davis address to AIC, 21 Feb. 1924; Lt. Col. A. B. Quinton, Jr., "Duties of a District Procurement Planning Officer," 27 Feb. 1937, both in AIC lectures, NDU.

129. "Conclusions and Recommendations" on Problem #27: "Nationalization of the Munitions Industry," AIC, 5 Apr. 1937, box 2, entry 45, RG 334; Harris testimony, 12 Mar. 1937, in *To Prevent Profiteering in Time of War: Hearings Before the Committee on Military Affairs, United States Senate*, 75th Cong., 1st Sess., Part 2 (Washington, DC: GPO, 1937), 142; Col. James H. Burns, "What the Individual Manufacturer Would Be Called Upon to Do in Time of War," in *Industry's Preparation for National Defense* (Washington, DC: Chamber of Commerce of the United States, 1939), 6, 12.

130. Cuff, *War Industries Board*, 191.

131. Baruch to Frank Scott, 29 May 1924, folder Baruch, box 3, Scott Papers.

132. Lt. Col. C. B. Ross, "Priorities for the Nation in Arms: Munitions Production with the Iron Hand in the Velvet Glove," *Army Ordnance* 13 (Nov.–Dec. 1932): 161–62; Harris statement in discussion following Capt. Charles E. Cheever, "Emergency Legislation—War-Time Contracts," 11 Jan. 1936, AIC Lectures, NDU Library; Col. H. K. Rutherford, "Mobilizing Industry for War," *Harvard Business Review* 18, no. 1 (autumn 1939): 9.

133. Ickes quoted in Blum, "Birth and Death of the M-Day Plan," 77; Frank B. Blumenfield, *A Blueprint for Fascism: What the Industrial Mobilization Plan Holds for America* (New York: American League Against War and Fascism, 1937).

134. On the demise of such plans in 1937–38, see William E. Leuchtenburg, "Roosevelt, Norris, and the 'Seven Little TVAs,'" *Journal of Politics* 14, no. 3 (Aug. 1952): 418–41.

135. "American Institute of Public Opinion—Surveys, 1938–1939," *Public Opinion Quarterly* 3, no. 4 (Oct. 1939): 586–87; George H. Gallup, *The Gallup Poll: Public Opinion,*

1935–1971 (New York: Random House, 1972), 1:145, 1:234, 1:251; Richard Polenberg, "The National Committee to Uphold Constitutional Government, 1937–1941," *Journal of American History* 52, no. 3 (1965): 582–98; Richard Polenberg, *Reorganizing Roosevelt's Government: The Controversy over Executive Reorganization, 1936–1939* (Cambridge, MA: Harvard University Press, 1966), 55–57; Patterson, *Congressional Conservatism*, 77–127, 289–90, 328; Richard Polenberg, "The Decline of the New Deal, 1937–1940," in *New Deal: The National Level*, 246–66; Wendy L. Wall, *Inventing the "American Way": The Politics of Consensus from the New Deal to the Civil Rights Movement* (New York: Oxford University Press, 2008), 48–62.

136. Walter S. Carpenter, Jr., "Comments for the Board of Directors Meeting," 10 Sept. 1937, folder 4, box 817, Walter Carpenter Papers, Hagley.

137. Charles R. Hook, "Industry Does Not Want War," *Forbes* 44 (1 July 1939): 15–17.

Chapter 2

1. Alan Clive, *State of War: Michigan in World War II* (Ann Arbor: University of Michigan Press, 1979), 25; Richard Overy, *Why the Allies Won* (New York: W. W. Norton, 1995), 190–98; David M. Kennedy, *Freedom from Fear: The American People in Depression and War, 1939–1945* (New York: Oxford University Press, 1999), 619–22, 650–55. Contemporary press coverage of the Knudsen meeting was less admiring: "OPM Flops Again," *Time* (19 Jan. 1942): 12–13.

2. Richard Polenberg, *War and Society: The United States, 1941–1945* (Philadelphia: J. B. Lippincott, 1972), 219; Paul A. C. Koistinen, "Mobilizing the World War II Economy: Labor and the Industrial-Military Alliance," *Pacific Historical Review* 42, no. 4 (Nov. 1973): 446.

3. Because the American military-industrial mobilization involved dozens of government agencies and tens of thousands of business firms and products, we cannot hope for any truly comprehensive account of how it worked. Nevertheless, we can capture much of the story by concentrating on a handful of the largest wartime industries. From July 1940 through August 1945, the United States spent a little over $300 billion on the war. About $100 billion went to pay, train, and transport soldiers and sailors, leaving about $200 billion spent on war plant (buildings and machinery) and munitions (defined broadly as all the finished goods supplied to the armed forces). Nearly half this spending on plant and munitions was devoted to just two industrial sectors: those that made aircraft and ships. More than another quarter of the total spending went to just two other categories of goods: ordnance (guns, ammunition, and explosives) and Army vehicles (tanks and trucks). Most of the vehicles, guns, and ammunition were procured by the U.S. Army's Ordnance Department, which spent $33 billion during the war. Another $33 billion was spent by the Army Air Forces (AAF), which before 1941 had been called the Air Corps. For ships, the United States spent about $31 billion: about $18 billion for warships and landing craft, procured by the Navy, and $13 billion for cargo ships and tankers, procured by the U.S. Maritime Commission (USMC). The Navy also bought several billion dollars' worth of aircraft and ordnance, via its technical bureaus dedicated to handling those items. So well over half the dollar value of all munitions was procured by four main actors: the Navy, the USMC, the U.S. Army's Ordnance Department, and the AAF. Certainly, many other goods—including food, clothing, and communications equipment— were important to American soldiers and sailors. But focusing on ships, aircraft, ordnance, and tanks and trucks, goes a long way toward describing the heart of the American military-industrial effort. R. Elberton Smith, *The Army and Economic Mobilization* (Washington, DC:

GPO, 1959), 4–7; CPA-*History*, 962; Frederic C. Lane, *Ships for Victory: A History of Shipbuilding Under the U.S. Maritime Commission in World War II* (Baltimore: Johns Hopkins University Press, 1951), 3–10; Paul A. C. Koistinen, *Arsenal of World War II: The Political Economy of American Warfare, 1940–1945* (Lawrence: University Press of Kansas, 2004), 227. All dollar figures are in the dollars of the time (early 1940s). Readers who want to convert these amounts into rough early twenty-first-century equivalents may multiply by ten. For a careful accounting that puts the direct cost of World War II at $3.3 trillion in 2008 dollars, see Hugh Rockoff, *America's Economic Way of War: War and the US Economy from the Spanish-American War to the Persian Gulf War* (New York: Cambridge University Press, 2012), 217.

4. Peter C. Smith, *Dive Bomber! An Illustrated History* (Annapolis, MD: Naval Institute Press, 1982), 41–45, 106–7.

5. Rockoff, *America's Economic Way of War*, 162–63.

6. Robert Charles Ehrhart, "The Politics of Military Rearmament, 1935–1940: The President, the Congress, and the United States Army" (Ph.D. diss., University of Texas at Austin, 1975), 148–87.

7. Rodney K. Watterson, *32 in '44: Building the Portsmouth Submarine Fleet in World War II* (Annapolis, MD: Naval Institute Press, 2011), 5.

8. Stephen Roskill, *Naval Policy Between the Wars*, vol. 1: *The Period of Anglo-American Antagonism* (London: Collins, 1968), 575–88.

9. Rear Admiral W. R. Furlong, "Naval Ordnance: Procurement from Government and Private Sources," *Army Ordnance* 20 (Jan.–Feb. 1940): 220–24; Joel R. Davidson, *The Unsinkable Fleet: The Politics of U.S. Navy Expansion in World War II* (Annapolis, MD: Naval Institute Press, 1996), 57; Jeffery M. Dorwart with Jean K. Wolf, *The Philadelphia Navy Yard: From the Birth of the U.S. Navy to the Nuclear Age* (Philadelphia: University of Pennsylvania Press, 2000), 166; Thomas B. Heinrich, " 'We Can Build Anything at Navy Yards': Warship Construction in Government Yards and the Political Economy of American Naval Shipbuilding, 1928–1945," *International Journal of Maritime History* 24 (Dec. 2012): 155–80.

10. Horace N. Gilbert, "The Expansion of Shipbuilding," *Harvard Business Review* 20, no. 2 (winter 1942): 157–58; Paul H. Silverstone, *U.S. Warships of World War II* (New York: Doubleday, 1970), 13; Watterson, *32 in '44*, 13; Ralph L. Snow, *Bath Iron Works: The First Hundred Years* (Bath: Maine Maritime Museum, 1987), 271–311; Frederick R. Black, *Charlestown Navy Yard, 1890–1973* (Boston: National Park Service, 1988), 2:596–97.

11. George W. Mowry, *The Naval and Maritime Shipbuilding Programs* (Washington, DC: WPB, 1944), 1; Davidson, *Unsinkable Fleet*, 10–11.

12. Stephen S. Roberts, "U.S. Navy Building Programs During World War II," *Warship International* 18, no. 3 (1981): 220; Bath Iron Works Corp., *Annual Reports*, 1936–39 (Bath, ME, 1937–40); Electric Boat Co., *Annual Reports*, 1935–39.

13. Snow, *Bath Iron Works*, 271–311; David Palmer, "Organizing the Shipyards: Unionization at New York Ship, Federal Ship, and Fore River, 1898–1945" (Ph.D. diss., Brandeis University, 1990), 855–59; Kenneth Warren, *Bethlehem Steel: Builder and Arsenal of America* (Pittsburgh: University of Pittsburgh Press, 2008), 144; G. B. Arthur, "A Ship Has to Be Right," *Nation's Business* 34 (Apr. 1946): 74.

14. Snow, *Bath Iron Works*, 267–69; Thomas B. Heinrich, "Industry and Sea Power: U.S. Naval Shipbuilding in Comparative Perspective," unpublished paper in author's possession.

15. Tom Lilley et al., *Problems of Accelerating Aircraft Production During World War II* (Boston: Harvard Graduate School of Business Administration, 1946), 16–17.

16. "Aircraft Manufacturing" fact sheet, *Aviation* 37 (Oct. 1938): 35; Lilley, *Problems of Accelerating Aircraft Production*, 5; Irving Brinton Holley, Jr., *Buying Aircraft: Matériel Procurement for the Army Air Forces* (Washington, DC: Office of the Chief of Military History, 1964), 17–22; Jacob A. Vander Meulen, *The Politics of Aircraft: Building an American Military Industry* (Lawrence: University Press of Kansas, 1991), 186–98; Donald M. Pattillo, *Pushing the Envelope: The American Aircraft Industry* (Ann Arbor: University of Michigan Press, 1998), 91–93.

17. Vander Meulen, *Politics of Aircraft*, 186.

18. Morgenthau to FDR, 8 May 1940, folder Morgenthau May–June 1940, box 79, PSF-FDR; Lilley, *Problems of Accelerating Aircraft Production*, 15; Holley, *Buying Aircraft*, 202; John McVikar Haight, Jr., *American Aid to France, 1938–1940* (New York: Atheneum, 1970), 101; Louis R. Eltscher and Edward M. Young, *Curtiss-Wright: Greatness and Decline* (New York: Twayne, 1998), 84; Gavin J. Bailey, *The Arsenal of Democracy: Aircraft Supply and the Anglo-American Alliance, 1938–1942* (Edinburgh: Edinburgh University Press, 2013).

19. Robert E. Gross to E. O. McDonnell, 11 May 1938, and Gross to Lawrence C. Ames, 2 Sept. 1938, both in box 6, Gross Papers, LOC; T. C. Sullivan, "Lockheed's Current Production Program Most Ambitious in History of Industry," *WSJ*, 4 Apr. 1939; "How Many Planes When?," *Fortune* 22 (Aug. 1940): 49–53, 89–90; Pattillo, *Pushing the Envelope*, 108; Maury Klein, *A Call to Arms: Mobilizing America for World War II* (New York: Bloomsbury, 2013), 69–70.

20. "New French and British Orders Help Establish Record Backlog," and "Steady Growth Revealed by Employment Figures," both in *North American Skyline* 1 (Jan. 1940): 2, 14; Board of Directors minutes, 6 Mar. 1939 and 21 Feb. 1940, unboxed folders Douglas Board Minutes 1932–39 and 1940–45, BHA; John R. Breihan, "Between Munich and Pearl Harbor: The Glenn L. Martin Aircraft Company Gears Up for War, 1938–1941," *Maryland Historical Magazine* 88, no. 4 (winter 1993): 392–98.

21. Gross to Lawrence C. Ames, 2 Sept. 1938, box 6, Gross Papers, LOC; T. C. Sullivan, "Lockheed's Current Production Program Most Ambitious in History of Industry," *WSJ*, 4 Apr. 1939; "How Many Planes When?," *Fortune* 23 (Mar. 1941): 82, 184; "United Aircraft," *Fortune* 23 (Mar. 1941): 168–69; Edward R. Stettinius, Jr., *Lend-Lease: Weapon for Victory* (New York: Macmillan, 1944), 13–31; Holley, *Buying Aircraft*, 201; Haight, *American Aid to France*, 140; Eltscher and Young, *Curtiss-Wright*, 90; Koistinen, *Arsenal of World War II*, 59.

22. "Annual Report Shows 1939 Loss," *Boeing News* (Apr. 1940): 3; Lilley, *Problems of Accelerating Aircraft Production*, 14; Holley, *Buying Aircraft*, 61–71; Jeffery S. Underwood, *The Wings of Democracy: The Influence of Air Power on the Roosevelt Administration, 1933–1941* (College Station: Texas A&M University Press, 1991), 84; Rondall Ravon Rice, *The Politics of Air Power: From Confrontation to Cooperation in Army Aviation Civil Military Relations* (Lincoln: University of Nebraska Press, 2004), 142–49.

23. Johnson, "Preliminary Report on Expansion of Aircraft Production," 28 Oct. 1938, folder Aircraft Expansion, box 34, Johnson Papers; Johnson to FDR, 2 Nov. 1938, folder War Dept. 1933–41, box 10, PSF-FDR; Keith D. McFarland and David L. Roll, *Louis Johnson and the Arming of America: The Roosevelt and Truman Years* (Bloomington: Indiana University Press, 2005), 58–66.

24. Holley, *Buying Aircraft*, 169–75; Underwood, *Wings of Democracy*, 130–37.

25. Maj. Alfred J. Lyon to Harry L. Hopkins, 3 Nov. 1938, folder Aircraft Expansion, box 34, Johnson Papers.

26. "Meeting with Aircraft Industry and Minutes of Meeting," 21 Nov. 1938, folder Aircraft Expansion Conference, box 34, Johnson Papers; "To the President of the United States," *Aviation* 37 (Dec. 1938): 19; Proceedings of Aircraft Procurement Conference Held at Washington, DC, July 10, 1939, copy in box 418, BHA; Gen. B. K. Yount to Johnson, 26 July 1939, folder Aircraft Expansion Conference, box 34, Johnson Papers; Robert R. Russel, "The Expansion of Industrial Facilities Under Army Air Forces Auspices, 1940–1945," reel A2040, AFHRA; George Vincent Sweeting, "Building the Arsenal of Democracy: The Government's Role in the Expansion of Industrial Capacity, 1940 to 1945" (Ph.D. diss., Columbia University, 1994), 67–69; Holley, *Buying Aircraft*, 182–85.

27. Eltscher and Young, *Curtiss-Wright*, 84–85; James F. Nagle, *A History of Government Contracting*, 2nd ed. (Washington, DC: George Washington University, 1999), 385–87.

28. "Air Corps in Biggest Spending Splurge," *Aviation* 38 (Sept. 1939): 52; Holley, *Buying Aircraft*, 179–80; Breihan, "Between Munich and Pearl Harbor," 395.

29. CPA-*History*, 14; Lilley, *Problems of Accelerating Aircraft Production*, 12–17.

30. Unboxed folder "NAA History 1928–1945," BHA; Lockheed Aircraft Corp., *Annual Report*, 1940 (Burbank, CA, 1941).

31. Sweeting, "Building the Arsenal," 79.

32. Davidson, *Unsinkable Fleet*, 19.

33. CPA-*History*, 41–47; Holley, *Buying Aircraft*, 228.

34. Robert P. Patterson, *Arming the Nation for War: Mobilization, Supply, and the American War Effort in World War II*, ed. Brian Waddell (Knoxville: University of Tennessee Press, 2014), 87; U.S. Bureau of the Budget, *The United States at War: Development and Administration of the War Program by the Federal Government* (Washington, DC: GPO, 1946), 21; CPA-*History*, 15, 42–43; Ehrhart, "Politics of Military Rearmament," 394.

35. Rockoff, *America's Economic Way of War*, 162–63.

36. NDAC *Minutes*, 74; CPA-*History*, 19–20; Koistinen, *Arsenal of World War II*, 13–190.

37. CPA-*History*, 140; J. Carlyle Sitterson, *Aircraft Production Policies Under the National Defense Advisory Commission and the Office of Production Management, May 1940 to December 1941* (Washington, DC: CPA, 1946), 159; Lenore Fine and Jesse A. Remington, *Corps of Engineers: Construction in the United States* (Washington, DC: Office of the Chief of Military History, 1972), 408; Warren F. Kimball, *The Most Unsordid Act: Lend-Lease, 1939–1941* (Baltimore: Johns Hopkins University Press, 1969), 228.

38. "Camps for 1,418,000," *Fortune* 23 (May 1941): 57–63, 162; Sweeting, "Building the Arsenal," 205.

39. Gerald T. White, *Billions for Defense: Government Financing by the Defense Plant Corporation During World War II* (University: University of Alabama Press, 1980), 2; Sweeting, "Building the Arsenal," 1–2.

40. Those four industries accounted for three-quarters of all the wartime capital investments that used the tax breaks. Calculated from micro-level data in CPA-*Facilities*. Standard Oil of New Jersey used the amortization provisions for $104 million worth of new plant. Charles Sterling Popple, *Standard Oil Company (New Jersey) in World War II* (New York: Standard Oil, 1952), 240.

41. White, *Billions for Defense*, 6; Sweeting, "Building the Arsenal," 260–71.

42. James S. Olson, *Saving Capitalism: The Reconstruction Finance Corporation and the New Deal, 1933–1940* (Princeton, NJ: Princeton University Press, 1988).

43. Robert H. Connery, *The Navy and Industrial Mobilization in World War II* (Princeton, NJ: Princeton University Press, 1951), 119.

44. Roberts, "U.S. Navy Building Programs," 223; Mowry, *Naval and Maritime Shipbuilding Programs*, 1–2; Charles H. Coleman, *Shipbuilding Activities of the National Defense Advisory Commission and Office of Production Management* (Washington, DC: CPA, 1946), 14; CPA-*History*, 45; Bartholomew H. Sparrow, *From the Outside In: World War II and the American State* (Princeton, NJ: Princeton University Press, 1996), 167–68; Davidson, *Unsinkable Fleet*, 16–21, 61; Dorwart, *Philadelphia Navy Yard*, 166–80; Klein, *A Call to Arms*, 325–28; Heinrich, "'We Can Build Anything at Navy Yards.'" On Electric Boat, see Gary E. Weir, *Forged in War: The Naval-Industrial Complex and American Submarine Construction, 1940–1961* (Washington, DC: Naval Historical Center, 1993), 21–23; Weir, "Coming Up to Speed in American Submarine Construction, 1938–1943," *War & Society* 11, no. 2 (Oct. 1993): 87. Data on public and private investment in every substantial new war plant may be found in CPA-*Facilities*. Estimates of the Navy's spending on its own yards range from $590 million to $1 billion; estimates of investment in plant run by contractors range from under $300 million to $681 million. See *Shipyards and Facilities: Report of the Surplus Property Administration to the Congress, January 31, 1946*, copy in folder Committees and Committee Work: Surplus Property 1946, box 153, Joseph C. O'Mahoney Papers, American Heritage Center, Laramie, WY; *Administrative History of the Bureau of Ships*, 2:186.

45. Coleman, *Shipbuilding Activities*, 22–32, 116; Lane, *Ships for Victory*, 3–10, 35–36; Christopher James Tassava, "Launching a Thousand Ships: Entrepreneurs, War Workers, and the State in American Shipbuilding, 1940–1945" (Ph.D. diss., Northwestern University, 2003), 53–59, 107; Timothy Lang Francis, "Poseidon's Tribute: Maritime Vulnerability, Industrial Mobilization and the Allied Defeat of the U-Boats, 1939–1945" (Ph.D. diss., University of Maryland, 2001), 87–90.

46. Coleman, *Shipbuilding Activities*, 22–32, 116; Lane, *Ships for Victory*, 93–95; Klein, *A Call to Arms*, 176–88.

47. Mark S. Foster, *Henry J. Kaiser: Builder in the Modern American West* (Austin: University of Texas Press, 1989), 69–71; Tassava, "Launching a Thousand Ships," 111–14.

48. "Report of Operations, Quarterly Period Ended December 31, 1941, Morrison-Knudsen Co. Inc.," folder Morrison-Knudsen, carton 9, Kaiser Papers; Foster, *Henry J. Kaiser*, 70–71; Snow, *Bath Iron Works*, 367–83; Stephen B. Adams, *Mr. Kaiser Goes to Washington: The Rise of a Government Entrepreneur* (Chapel Hill: University of North Carolina Press, 1997), 95; Tassava, "Launching a Thousand Ships," 90.

49. Lane, *Ships for Victory*, 73–100.

50. Ibid., 50–53, 472.

51. Gilbert, "Expansion of Shipbuilding," 162; Coleman, *Shipbuilding Activities*, 36–41; Lane, *Ships for Victory*, 56–59; Snow, *Bath Iron Works*, 367–83; Mark Reutter, *Sparrows Point: Making Steel—the Rise and Ruin of American Industrial Might* (New York: Summit, 1988), 305; Albert P. Heiner, *Henry J. Kaiser, American Empire Builder: An Insider's View* (New York: Peter Lang, 1989), 135, 152–53; Ralph Scott, *The Wilmington Shipyard: Welding a Fleet for Victory in World War II* (Charleston, SC: History Press, 2007).

52. Lane, *Ships for Victory*; Klein, *A Call to Arms*, 315–22.

53. WPB *Minutes*, 14, 16–17; Coleman, *Shipbuilding Activities*, 43; Tassava, "Launching a Thousand Ships," 136–47.

54. Levin H. Campbell, Jr., *The Industry-Ordnance Team* (New York: Whittlesey House, 1946), 253–55.

55. F. W. Bradway memo, 9 Sept. 1939, and Executive Committee memo, 13 Sept. 1939, both in folder Smokeless Powder—General Correspondence (1 of 2), box 5, DPED; Gen. C. M. Wesson to Johnson, 2 Dec. 1939, folder Smokeless Powder, box 79; Brig. Gen. Earl McFarland to Louis Johnson, 10 Feb. 1940, folder Baruch, box 2, both in Johnson Papers.

56. "Indiana Ordnance Works," folder History File, box 2, DPED; Col. Charles Hines memo, 19 Feb. 1940, folder War Reports: Foreign Inquiries for Production of Munitions, Dec. 1939–Apr. 1940, box 85; Col. J. H. Burns to Brig. Gen. Edwin M. Watson, 16 Mar. 1940, folder War Dept. 1940, box 81, both in PSF-FDR; Joe Harden Camp, "Birch Rod to Arsenal: A Study of the Naval Ordnance Plant at South Charleston, West Virginia, and the Search for a Government Industrial Policy" (Ph.D. diss., West Virginia University, 2002), 142.

57. "Indiana Ordnance Works," folder History File, box 2, DPED.

58. E. B. Yancey to Gen. C. T. Harris, Jr., 2 July 1940, folder 48, box 839, Walter Carpenter Papers; "Alabama Ordnance Works" typescript history, folder History File, box 2; undated table on employment, folder Misc. Reports (1 of 4), box 1, both in DPED.

59. Campbell, *Industry-Ordnance Team*, 102–10, 217; Thompson and Mayo, *Ordnance Department*, 43. The lead contractor in the small arms ammunition program was Remington, a subsidiary of Du Pont. Thompson and Mayo, *Ordnance Department*, 189, 204–12; Thomas G. Alexander and Leonard J. Arrington, "Utah's Small Arms Ammunition Plant During World War II," *Pacific Historical Review* 34, no. 2 (May 1965): 185–96.

60. John K. Christmas, "Development of the Medium Tank," folder Minutes of Meetings, box L72, entry 930, RG 156, NARA; Nagle, *History of Government Contracting*, 397; Kevin Thornton and Dale Prentiss, *Tanks and Industry: The Detroit Tank Arsenal, 1940–1954* (Warren, MI: U.S. Army Tank-Automotive and Armaments Command, 1995), 3, 20–32; Klein, *A Call to Arms*, 252–55; Hyde, *Arsenal of Democracy*, 121–27.

61. "Full Tracked Vehicle Facility Production Summary, 1 Jan. 1940 to 1 July 1945," box 21, entry 3430, RG 200; "American Locomotive," *Fortune* 25 (Feb. 1942): 78–83, 112–22; R. P. Hunnicutt, *Sherman: A History of the American Medium Tank* (Belmont, CA: Taurus Enterprises, 1978).

62. Leslie E. Neville, "What Next in Aircraft Expansion?," *Aviation* (June 1941): 172; Sitterson, *Aircraft Production Policies*, 86–93; Holley, *Buying Aircraft*, 305–10; Sweeting, "Building the Arsenal," 215–19; Richard Macias, "'We All Had a Cause': Kansas City's Bomber Plant, 1941–1945," *Kansas History* 28 (winter 2005–6): 247; Hyde, *Arsenal of Democracy*, 75–80.

63. NDAC *Minutes*, 29; Leslie E. Neville, "What Next in Aircraft Expansion?," *Aviation* (June 1941): 42–43, 172–74; Col. J. G. Vincent, "Engines for Mustangs," *North American Skyline* 5 (Sept.–Oct. 1944): 14; Gerald T. White, "Financing Industrial Expansion for War: The Origin of the Defense Plant Corporation Leases," *Journal of Economic History* 9, no. 2 (Nov. 1949): 156–83; White, *Billions for Defense*, 30, 63–65; Sweeting, "Building the Arsenal," 136–51.

64. Roy A. Foulke, "Financial Management Problems in a War Economy," *Dun's Review* (Jan. 1942): 10–22, 44–50; Holley, *Buying Aircraft*, 298–99; Breihan, "Between Munich and Pearl Harbor," 400; White, "Financing Industrial Expansion for War," 171–74; Sweeting, "Building the Arsenal," 178–82.

65. John P. Gaty to Truman, 17 Oct. 1941, folder National Defense Aircraft Production, box 113, Truman Senatorial Papers, TPL.

66. White, who worked in the 1940s as an RFC historian and interviewed many of the major players, told this story in an article published in 1949: "Financing Industrial Expansion for War." White's book-length account, *Billions for Defense*, was published three decades later. See also John A. Salmond, *The Conscience of a Lawyer: Clifford J. Durr and American Civil Liberties, 1899–1975* (University: University of Alabama Press, 1990); Steven Fenberg, *Unprecedented Power: Jesse Jones, Capitalism, and the Common Good* (College Station: Texas A&M University Press, 2011).

67. "North American Dedicates Dallas Plant," *Aviation* (May 1941): 36; bound report, "North American Aviation Inc. Analysis of Performance, 1944 Fiscal Year, Prepared for War Contracts Price Adjustment Board," folder NR1371–07–02, BHA; Lilley, *Problems of Accelerating Aircraft Production*, 72; Holley, *Buying Aircraft*, 302; Pattillo, *Pushing the Envelope*, 137; Jacob Vander Meulen, *Building the B-29* (Washington, DC: Smithsonian Institution Press, 1995), 38.

68. FDR to Stimson, 4 May 1941, folder War Dept., Jan.–Aug. 1941, box 82, PSF-FDR; W. C. Folley memo on B-24 contract negotiations, 27 Nov. 1943, in folder Papers Drawn for Renegotiation Purposes, box 106, Accession 38, Ford Records. For a detailed summary of Willow Run's history, see Hyde, *Arsenal of Democracy*, 87–105.

69. Sorensen Diary Notes, 1940–44, drafts, 736–46, folder 1, in box 69, Accession 65, and "Aircraft Engine Manufacture," vol. 1, box 3, Accession 435, both in Ford Records; Allan Nevins and Frank Ernest Hill, *Ford: Decline and Rebirth, 1933–1962* (New York: Charles Scribner's Sons, 1963), 177–79; Timothy O'Callaghan, *Ford in the Service of America: Mass Production for the Military During the World Wars* (Jefferson, NC: McFarland, 2009), 90.

70. Leslie E. Neville, "What Next in Aircraft Expansion?," *Aviation* (June 1941): 174; Charles M. Wiltse, *Aircraft Production Under the War Production Board and Predecessor Agencies* (Washington, DC: WPB, 1944), 10; Russel, "Expansion of Industrial Facilities"; Sitterson, *Aircraft Production Policies*, 65–66, 95–98; Lilley, *Problems of Accelerating Aircraft Production*, 33–34; J. Carlyle Sitterson, *The Automotive Industry in War Production, May 1940 to December 1943* (Washington, DC: WPB, 1944), 27; Hyde, *Arsenal of Democracy*, 44–65.

71. Gen. H. H. Arnold to G-4, 28 May 1941, folder Aluminum Co., box 856, entry 154, RG 107, NARA; Daryl F. White, "Multinational Patriots: Business-Government Relations in the Canadian Aluminum and Nickel Industries, 1914–1945" (Ph.D. diss., University of Western Ontario, 2006), 225, 273.

72. R. S. Reynolds, Sr. to Assistant Secretary of War, 21 May 1940, folder Defense Commission, box 17, Reynolds Papers; "Exhibits on Aluminum," 1940–41, box 76, and Stettinius notes on 7 Jan. 1941, in Record Notes, 31 Aug. 1940–8 Jan. 1941, box 102, all in Stettinius Papers; "Aluminum: Competitors for Alcoa," *Time* (12 Aug. 1940): 56–57.

73. Normally, the depreciation of buildings was spread over twenty years and the depreciation of industrial equipment—such as machine tools—over ten years. Under the new amortization rule, companies could write off the cost of all new war plant, for tax purposes, in just five years—or, if the war ended earlier, even faster. *Excess Profits Taxation, 1940: Joint Hearings Before the Committee on Ways and Means, House of Representatives, and the Committee on Finance, United States Senate* (Washington, DC: GPO, 1940), 21–47; White, *Billions for Defense*, 7–9; Sweeting, "Building the Arsenal," 99–119.

74. "Aluminum and the Emergency," *Fortune* 23 (May 1941): 145; Raymond Headley, "Aluminum and Magnesium: How Much Will We Need in the Next 12 Months?," *Aviation* (June 1941): 70; Charles M. Wiltse, *Aluminum Policies of the War Production Board and Predecessor Agencies, May 1940 to November 1945* (Washington, DC: CPA, 1946); Margaret B. W. Graham and Bettye H. Pruitt, *R&D For Industry: A Century of Technical Innovation at Alcoa* (New York: Cambridge University Press, 1990), 228; Koistinen, *Arsenal of World War II*, 137.

75. "Aluminum Co. to Build, Operate 3 New Plants Under RFC Agreement," *WSJ*, 21 Aug. 1941; Jones to Truman, 24 Mar. 1943, folder Commerce–Jesse Jones, box 54, PSF-FDR; Wiltse, *Aluminum Policies*, 69–70; George David Smith, *From Monopoly to Competition: The Transformations of Alcoa* (New York: Cambridge University Press, 1988), 218; Keith E. Eiler, *Mobilizing America: Robert P. Patterson and the War Effort, 1940–1945* (Ithaca, NY: Cornell University Press, 1997), 176–79; Koistinen, *Arsenal of World War II*, 138.

76. R. S. Reynolds, Sr. to Sen. Lister Hill, 28 Apr. 1941, folder Senator Lister Hill, box 29; Walter L. Rice memo to R. S. Reynolds, Jr., "Conference with W. L. Batt and J. A. Krug," 6 Sept. 1941, folder OPM, box 47, both in Reynolds Papers.

77. Mark R. Wilson, "Making 'Goop' Out of Lemons: The Permanente Metals Corporation, Magnesium Incendiary Bombs, and the Struggle for Profits During World War II," *Enterprise & Society* 12 (Mar. 2011): 10–45.

78. Minutes of Ordnance Dept. meetings, 10 Mar.–16 Apr. 1941, box A131, entry 638, RG 156, NARA; CPA-*History*, 169–70.

79. Eiler, *Mobilizing America*, 230–31.

80. F. B. Vose to R. B. Lea, 2 Jan. 1942, folder 7, box 53, Sperry Records; Russel, "Expansion of Industrial Facilities"; CPA-*History*, 201–2, 279; Lilley, *Problems of Accelerating Aircraft Production*, 29–30; Connery, *Navy and Industrial Mobilization*, 139; Klein, *A Call to Arms*, 292–94.

81. CPA, *Industrial Mobilization for War*, 385; Koistinen, *Arsenal of World War II*, 289.

82. WPB *Minutes*, 1; Nevins and Hill, *Ford: Decline and Rebirth*, 129; Koistinen, *Arsenal of World War II*, 288.

83. Virginia Turrell, *Rubber Policies of the War Production Board and Predecessor Agencies* (Washington, DC: WPB, 1944), 1, 16; Vernon Herbert and Attilio Bisio, *Synthetic Rubber: A Project That Had to Succeed* (Westport, CT: Greenwood, 1985), 6–9.

84. Stettinius to Roosevelt, 12 Sept. 1940, folder Synthetic Rubber, box 86; "Rubber-Summary of Negotiations," bound vol. Special Summaries on Industrial Materials, June 1940–Mar. 1941, box 79, both in Stettinius Papers; George W. Auxier, *Rubber Policies of the National Defense Advisory Commission and the Office of Production Management, May 1940 to December 1941* (Washington, DC: CPA, 1947), 31–43; White, *Billions for Defense*, 40; Herbert and Bisio, *Synthetic Rubber*, 41–59; Koistinen, *Arsenal of World War II*, 150–52; Klein, *A Call to Arms*, 233–38.

85. Herbert and Bisio, *Synthetic Rubber*, 64–132. Standard Oil–NJ's subsidiaries did spend nearly $20 million of their own money on feeder plants. Henrietta M. Larson and Kenneth Wiggins Porter, *History of Humble Oil & Refining Company* (1959; New York: Arno, 1976), 597–98.

86. Harold M. Fleming, "Good News on Synthetic Rubber," *Harper's Magazine* (Dec. 1942): 66–75; "New Crisis in Rubber," *United States News* (6 Apr. 1945): 21; Popple, *Standard Oil Company (New Jersey) in World War II*, 75; William M. Tuttle, Jr., "The Birth of an

Industry: The Synthetic Rubber 'Mess' in World War II," *Technology and Culture* 22, no. 1 (Jan. 1981): 35–67; Herbert and Bisio, *Synthetic Rubber*, 69–71; Peter Neushul, "Science, Technology, and the Arsenal of Democracy: Production Research and Development During World War II" (Ph.D. diss., University of California, Santa Barbara, 1993), 67–72, 104–5; Klein, *A Call to Arms*, 406–11, 505–10.

87. WPB *Minutes*, 14–17, 258; Coleman, *Shipbuilding Activities*, 33; William Chaikin and Charles H. Coleman, *Shipbuilding Policies of the War Production Board, January 1942– November 1945* (Washington, DC: CPA, 1947), 6; Lane, *Ships for Victory*, 64, 138–49, 202–7, 250; Tassava, "Launching a Thousand Ships," 136–47, 361–69.

88. "Alabama Ordnance Works" typescript history, folder History File, box 2; "Statement on TNT and Smokeless," 12 Aug. 1942, folder Smokeless Powder—General Correspondence (2 of 2), box 5, both in DPED; E. B. Yancey, "Status of Military Plants and Contracts," 11 Aug. 1942, folder 5.0, box 830, Walter Carpenter Papers, Hagley.

89. Printed letter to Du Pont employees, 24 Aug. 1945, folder 5.1, box 830, Walter Carpenter Papers; Harry Thayer, *Management of the Hanford Engineer Works in World War II: How the Corps, Du Pont and the Metallurgical Laboratory Fast Tracked the Original Plutonium Works* (New York: American Society of Engineers, 1996), 17; Marcia L. Rorke, "The Manhattan Project, the Du Pont Company, and the Management of New Product Development" (Ph.D. diss., George Washington University, 2004), 180.

90. *Forty-Third Annual Report of the Eastman Kodak Company, for the Year Ended December 29, 1945* (Rochester, NY: Eastman Kodak, 1946), 24–29; Thompson and Mayo, *Ordnance Department*, 136; Vincent C. Jones, *Manhattan: The Army and the Atomic Bomb* (Washington, DC: Center of Military History, 1985); Klein, *A Call to Arms*, 731–33.

91. Albert Bradley to Carpenter, 23 May 1942, folder 33b, box 837, Walter Carpenter Papers, Hagley; Eltscher and Young, *Curtiss-Wright*, 93, 105; Vander Meulen, *Building the B-29*; Pattillo, *Pushing the Envelope*, 139; Richard S. Combes, "Aircraft Manufacturing in Georgia: A Case Study of Federal Industrial Investment," in *The Second Wave: Southern Industrialization from the 1940s to the 1970s*, ed. Philip Scranton (Athens: University of Georgia Press, 2001), 24–42; Jeffrey L. Holland, *Under One Roof: The Story of Air Force Plant 6* (Wright-Patterson Air Force Base, 2006), 3–25; Klein, *A Call to Arms*, 656–61; Hyde, *Arsenal of Democracy*, 84–86.

92. Vander Meulen, *Building the B-29*, 88–89; Hyde, *Riding the Roller Coaster*, 140–44.

93. Patterson, *Arming the Nation for War*, 173; Larson and Porter, *History of Humble* Oil, 566; Kevin Neptune, "Heart of the Matter: The Phillips Petroleum Company During World War II" (M.S. thesis, Texas A&M University–Commerce, 2003), 29.

94. "Construction Progress, Major 100-Octane Plants" [tables], 10 Jan. 1944, folder 2, box 13, Ser. IV, Byrnes Papers; plant-level data in CPA-*Facilities*; Porter and Larson, *History of Humble Oil*, 589–96; Beaton, *Enterprise in Oil*, 575–76; Popple, *Standard Oil Company (New Jersey) in World War II*, 247; Harold F. Williamson et al., *The American Petroleum Industry: The Age of Energy, 1899–1959* (Evanston, IL: Northwestern University Press, 1963), 772. The government paid another $150 million to build two giant pipelines, running from Texas to New Jersey, nicknamed "Big Inch" (twenty-four inches in diameter) and "Little Inch" (twenty inches). Beaton, *Enterprise in Oil,* 604; Klein, *A Call to Arms*, 227–28, 498–500. But most of the oil transported in these pipelines, built in 1942–44, was destined for civilian use. The postwar sale of the pipelines is discussed in Chapter 6.

95. Nagle, *History of Government Contracting*, 427.

96. Jim F. Heath, "American War Mobilization and the Use of Small Manufacturers, 1939–1943," *Business History Review* 46 (autumn 1972): 295–319.

97. Careful quantitative studies have found that conventional political variables do little to explain the pattern of wartime plant building. They also suggest that the mobilization did surprisingly little to alter the prewar balance of industrialization from state to state. See Sweeting, "Building the Arsenal," 260; Fred Bateman and Jason E. Taylor, "Was 'V' for Victory or Votes? A Public Choice Analysis of World War II Federal Spending," *Public Choice* 114, nos. 1–2 (Jan. 2003): 161–74.

98. H. J. Miller, "Report on State Efforts to Secure Defense Business for Minnesota Industries," ca. April 1941, copy in folder Industrial Resources and Production, box 5, RG 25, Nebraska State Historical Library, Lincoln, NE; NDAC *Minutes*, 56; Reginald Charles McGrane, *The Facilities and Construction Program of the War Production Board and Predecessor Agencies, May 1940 to May 1945* (Washington, DC: CPA, 1946), 57–62. On efforts by Connecticut and New York, see Jennifer M. Jensen and Jenna Kelkres Emery, "The First State Lobbyists: State Offices in Washington During World War II," *Journal of Policy History* 23, no. 2 (2011): 117–49.

99. Karl Stefan to Andrew Soulek, 4 Nov. 1941, folder 115, box 13, Karl Stefan Papers, Nebraska State Historical Library; Lockheed et al., 21 Jan. 1942, folder National Defense Aircraft Production, box 113, Truman Senatorial File, TPL; Donald J. Mrozek, "Organizing Small Business During World War II: The Experience of the Kansas City Region," *Missouri Historical Review* 71 (1977): 174–92.

100. NDAC *Minutes*, 147–48; Minutes of Conference of Committee on Production of the Council of State Governments with Officials of the Office of Production Management, Washington, DC, 30 July 1941, folder 329, box 11, RG 25, Nebraska State Historical Library; Minutes of Ordnance Dept. meeting of 9 Aug. 1941, box A131, entry 638, RG 156, NARA; Paul A. C. Koistinen, "The Hammer and the Sword: Labor, the Military, and Industrial Mobilization, 1920–1945" (Ph.D. diss., University of California at Berkeley, 1964), 129; Koistinen, *Arsenal of World War II*, 52, 167–68; Holley, *Buying Aircraft*, 308; Sweeting, "Building the Arsenal," 193–94. It was true that lobbying by politicians and local chambers of commerce might sometimes help determine why a plant was located in one city in a given region, rather than another. See, e.g., Thomas A. Scott, "Winning World War II in an Atlanta Suburb: Local Boosters and the Recruitment of Bell Bomber," in *The Second Wave*, ed. Scranton, 1–23; Kathryn Currie Pinkney, "From Stockyards to Defense Plants, the Transformation of a City: Fort Worth, Texas, and World War II" (Ph.D. diss., University of North Texas, 2003), 81–91; Elizabeth Tandy Shermer, *Sunbelt Capitalism: Phoenix and the Transformation of American Politics* (Philadelphia: University of Pennsylvania Press, 2013), 73–83.

101. William W. Dulles to Forrestal, 15 Mar. 1941, box 162, entry 114, RG 80; Minutes for Ordnance Department meeting of 19 Nov. 1940, box A131, entry 638, RG 156, NARA.

102. L. L. Bollinger, "Is Subcontracting the Answer?," *Harvard Business Review* 20, no. 2 (winter 1942): 171–83, quotation at 179; Lilley, *Problems of Accelerating Aircraft Production*, 37–38.

103. Patterson to chiefs of supply arms & services, 20 May 1941, folder Investigations, box 137, Patterson Papers, LOC; Robert Wood Johnson, *"But, General Johnson—": Episodes in a War Effort* (Princeton, NJ: Princeton University Press, 1944), 17; Holley, *Buying Aircraft*,

496–99; Jonathan J. Bean, *Beyond the Broker State: Federal Policies Toward Small Business, 1936–1961* (Chapel Hill: University of North Carolina Press, 1996), 99–126; Eiler, *Mobilizing America*, 193–95; Klein, *A Call to Arms*, 257–58.

104. Campbell notes, 6 Aug. 1941, box 13H2, entry 636, RG 156, NARA; Sparrow, *From the Outside In*, 200.

105. Sitterson, *Automotive Industry*, 20; Campbell, *Industry-Ordnance Team*, 92; Sparrow, *From the Outside In*, 199; Richard K. Fleischmann and R. Penny Marquette, "The Impact of World War II on Cost Accounting at the Sperry Corporation," *Accounting Historians Journal* 30, no. 2 (Dec. 2003): 88–89; Klein, *A Call to Arms*, 388–91; Allen Kaufman, "In the Procurement Officer We Trust: Constitutional Norms, Air Force Procurement and Industrial Organization, 1938–1948" (unpublished paper, 1996), 38, copy in folder 1997, box 1000, Procurement 1986–2000, Record Series VIII (Installations and Logistics), Historical Office, Office of the Secretary of Defense, Rosslyn, VA. I thank Elliott Converse for providing me with a copy of this paper. On Chrysler as especially reliant on subcontracting in the interwar period, see Michael Schwartz, "Markets, Networks, and the Rise of Chrysler in Old Detroit," *Enterprise & Society* 1, no. 1 (Mar. 2000): 63–99.

106. "A. O. Smith at War," *Fortune* 24 (Oct. 1941): 87–89, 134–40.

107. "The Conversion of Forry Laucks," *Fortune* 25 (Apr. 1942): 88–90, 153–58; Samuel E. Dyke, "War Production at Armstrong Cork Company, 1940–1945," *Journal of the Lancaster County Historical Society* 100, no. 4 (1998): 453–62; Klein, *A Call to Arms*, 258–62.

108. Philip Samporano, Jr., "The Times of Their Lives: Women, Men, and the Clock and Watch Industry in Bristol, Connecticut, 1900–1970" (Ph.D. diss., University of Connecticut, 2003), 248–61.

109. "Case History of Emerson Electric Manufacturing Company," reel 2078, AFHRA; Russel, "Expansion of Industrial Facilities"; Emerson Electric Manufacturing Co., *53rd Annual Report* (St. Louis, 1943); James C. Olson, *Stuart Symington: A Life* (Columbia: University of Missouri Press, 2003), 29–49.

110. Fleischmann and Marquette, "Impact of World War II on Cost Accounting at the Sperry Corporation," 89; Hyde, *Arsenal of Democracy*, 170.

111. Nevins and Hill, *Ford: Decline and Rebirth*, 195–203; McFarland, *America's Pursuit of Precision Bombing*, 138–44.

112. "Case History of the Elastic Stop Nut Corporation of America," reel A2075, AFHRA.

113. Solar Aircraft Co. annual reports, in folder Committees 1942–43, box 153, O'Mahoney Papers.

114. Jack & Heintz, Inc. company timeline, folder 276, box 15, IAM district #54 Papers, Western Reserve Historical Society, Cleveland; "History" section, SEC Form S-1, 22 July 1946, in binder J&H Precision Industries, Inc.: Organization and Financing 1946, box 3, new accession, Records of Jack & Heinz, Inc., Bedford Historical Society, Bedford, OH.

115. Calculated from CPA-*Contracts* and CPA-*Facilities*.

116. Cost breakdowns in Marcelle Size Knaack, *Encyclopedia of U.S. Air Force Aircraft and Missile Systems*, vol. 2: *Post–World War II Bombers, 1945–1973* (Washington, DC: Office of Air Force History, 1988), 482. See also Vander Meulen, *Building the B-29*, 21, 28.

117. "History: Ordnance Department Industry Integration Committee for Light Tanks from 10 September 1942 to 30 September 1943," box L42A, entry 926A, RG 156, NARA.

118. Col. J. H. Burns to Johnson, 16 Dec. 1938, folder Aircraft Expansion—Memoranda to Johnson, box 34, Johnson Papers; Leonard H. Engel, "Behind Scenes as America Tests New Winged Might," *New Orleans Times-Picayune*, 28 May 1939.

119. Ray M. Klein, "Marvels Abound at Wright Field," *Cleveland Plain Dealer*, 17 Dec. 1944; Holley, *Buying Aircraft*, 469.

120. Boeing, the designer of the B-17, would receive licensing fees of 1.2 percent from Douglas and Vega. See Board of Directors Meeting Minutes, 22 Oct. 1941, box 3584, BHA; Holley, *Buying Aircraft*, 540–544; Kaufman, "In the Procurement Officer We Trust," 39–43.

Chapter 3

1. Pew remarks in *Vigilance Today for a Free Enterprise Tomorrow* (New York: NAM, 1941), folder Promotional Material for 1941, box 846, Ser. III, NAM Records.

2. Undated flyer, "Free Enterprise and the Automotive Industry," folder Public Relations Committee: Free Enterprise, unboxed material in drawer 1, cabinet 6, ACWP Records.

3. Merle Thorpe, "Defenders Without Benefit of Drums," *Nation's Business* 29 (May 1941): 13; Richard S. Tedlow, *Keeping the Corporate Image: Public Relations and Business, 1900–1950* (Greenwich, CT: JAI, 1979); Robert M. Collins, *The Business Response to Keynes, 1929–1964* (New York: Columbia University Press, 1981), 42; Colleen Ann Moore, "The National Association of Manufacturers: The Voice of Industry and the Free Enterprise Campaign in the Schools, 1929–1949" (Ph.D. diss., University of Akron, 1985), 335–405; Elizabeth Fones-Wolf, *Selling Free Enterprise: The Business Assault on Labor and Liberalism, 1945–60* (Urbana: University of Illinois Press, 1994), 24–25; Elizabeth Fones-Wolf, "Creating a Favorable Business Climate: Corporations and Radio Broadcasting, 1934 to 1954," *Business History Review* 73, no. 2 (summer 1999): 221–55; William L. Bird, Jr., *"Better Living": Advertising, Media, and the New Vocabulary of Business Leadership, 1935–1955* (Evanston, IL: Northwestern University Press, 1999), 53–117; Elizabeth Fones-Wolf and Nathan Godfried, "Regulating Class Conflict on the Air: NBC's Relationship with Business and Organized Labor," in *NBC: America's Network*, ed. Michele Himes (Berkeley: University of California Press, 2007), 61–77; Wendy L. Wall, *Inventing the "American Way": The Politics of Consensus from the New Deal to the Civil Rights Movement* (New York: Oxford University Press, 2008), 49–61.

4. Philip D. Reed, "American Free Enterprise and the Future," *Dun's Review* (July 1940): 5–9, 46–48; H. W. Prentis, Jr., "Preserving the Roots of Liberty," *VSD* 8, no. 9 (15 Feb. 1942): 258–62; F. C. Crawford, "Triangle of Plenty," *Reader's Digest* 42 (Apr. 1943): 74–78. See also Thomas R. Winpenny, "Henning Webb Prentis and the Challenge of the New Deal," *Journal of the Lancaster County Historical Society* 82 (1977): 1–24.

5. C. E. Harrison to Claude Robinson, 28 June 1943, folder Documents Relating to NIIC; "The Public Relations Program of the National Association of Manufacturers" (New York: NAM, 1946), in folder Final Report 1946, both in box 843, Ser. III, NAM Records; Moore, "National Association of Manufacturers," 250–86, 465–70; Andrew A. Workman, "Manufacturing Power: The Organizational Revival of the National Association of Manufacturers, 1941–1945," *Business History Review* 72, no. 2 (summer 1998): 290–91.

6. Fred G. Clark to Pew, 14 Oct. 1941, box 211; Benson to Pew, 21 Oct. 1943, folder H, box 3, Pew Personal Papers; Allan J. Lichtman, *White Protestant Nation: The Rise of the American Conservative Movement* (New York: Atlantic Monthly Press, 2008), 61–129; L. Edward Hicks, *"Sometimes in the Wrong, but Never in Doubt": George S. Benson and the Education of the New Religious Right* (Knoxville: University of Tennessee Press, 1994).

7. Vernon Orval Watts, *Do We Want Free Enterprise?* (Los Angeles: Los Angeles Chamber of Commerce, 1944), iii–iv, 154–55; Carol V. R. George, *God's Salesman: Norman Vincent Peale & the Power of Positive Thinking* (New York: Oxford University Press, 1993), 168–80; Gregory Teddy Eow, "Fighting a New Deal: Intellectual Origins of the Reagan Revolution, 1932–1952" (Ph.D. diss., Rice University, 2007), 110–57, 214–27, 257–63; Kim Phillips-Fein, *Invisible Hands: The Making of the Conservative Movement from the New Deal to Reagan* (New York: W. W. Norton, 2009), 15–19, 61; Jennifer Burns, *Goddess of the Market: Ayn Rand and the American Right* (New York: Oxford University Press, 2009), 101–2.

8. B. C. Forbes, "Americans to Insist upon Squarer Deal for Business," *Forbes* 42 (1 Nov. 1938): 30.

9. Charles R. Hook, "Industry Does Not Want War," *Forbes* 44 (1 July 1939): 15–17; Edwin Laird Cady, "Be Wary of War Orders," *Forbes* 45 (15 Feb. 1940): 14–15; "The Second *Fortune* Forum of Executive Opinion," *Fortune* 22 (Oct. 1940): 75; Moore, "National Association of Manufacturers," 423–24; Roland N. Stromberg, "American Business and the Approach of War, 1935–1941," *Journal of Economic History* 13, no. 1 (winter 1953): 58–78.

10. Richard S. Tedlow, "The National Association of Manufacturers and Public Relations During the New Deal," *Business History Review* 50, no. 1 (spring 1976): 35.

11. Quotation from 15 July 1940 issue of *Sales Management* cited in Stromberg, "American Business and the Approach of War," 74.

12. Merle Thorpe, "They're Whistling Business out of the Doghouse," *Nation's Business* 28 (Aug. 1940): 13.

13. Alfred P. Sloan, Jr., "The Economic Aspects of American Defense," *Proceedings of the Academy of Political Science* 19, no. 2 (Jan. 1941): 130.

14. Richard A. Lauderbaugh, *American Steel Makers and the Coming of the Second World War* (Ann Arbor: University of Michigan Research Press, 1980), 43; *The Papers of Robert A. Taft*, vol. 2: *1939–1944*, ed. Clarence E. Wunderlin (Kent, OH: Kent State University Press, 2001), 75–76.

15. Raoul S. Desvernine, "U.S. Can Prepare Without Scrapping Its Economic System," *Printer's Ink* 192, no. 13 (27 Sept. 1940), 20–21; "The *Fortune* Quarterly Management Poll," *Fortune* 24 (Nov. 1941): 200.

16. Merle Thorpe, "Must We Hitlerize to Fight Hitlerism?," *Nation's Business* 28 (Oct. 1940): 13.

17. Frank W. Fox, *Madison Avenue Goes to War: The Strange Military Career of American Advertising, 1941–45* (Provo, UT: Brigham Young University Press, 1975), 30, 69. On the relationship between geopolitics and domestic political and intellectual developments during this era, see David Ciepley, *Liberalism in the Shadow of Totalitarianism* (Cambridge, MA: Harvard University Press, 2006).

18. Alfred P. Sloan, Jr., "Industrial Statesmanship" [22 May 1940], *VSD* 6 (15 Sept. 1940): 716; F. Donaldson Brown, "Readjustments Required Within Industry Because of the Defense Program," 30 Dec. 1941, copy in box 5, Brown Papers, Hagley.

19. Haake, "A Call to Arms for American Well-Being," 6 Nov. 1941, copy in folder 1940–43, box 235, Pew Personal Papers.

20. Stettinius notes on 27 Dec. 1940, Record Notes 31 Aug. 1940–8 Jan. 1941, box 102, Stettinius Papers; Baruch to Forrestal, 23 Jan. 1941, box 54, Forrestal Papers.

21. "Certain Recommendations in Connection with NAM's Public Information Program in 1941," folder Misc. NIIC Material 1938–40, box 845, Ser. III, NAM Records.

22. Michele Himes, *Radio Voices: American Broadcasting, 1922–1952* (Minneapolis: University of Minnesota Press, 1997), 233.

23. *Defense for America* script, 22 Feb. 1941, box 418, and William V. Lawson to Frank E. Mullen, 8 Oct. 1941, folder 66: *Defense for America*, box 82, both in National Broadcasting Company Records, State Historical Society of Wisconsin; "Fulton Lewis Tours Plants for Manufacturers Assn.," *Variety* (23 Apr. 1941): 34; Fones-Wolf, "Creating a Favorable Business Climate," 232–33; Fones-Wolf and Godfried, "Regulating Class Conflict on the Air," 69; Elizabeth Fones-Wolf, *Waves of Opposition: Labor and the Struggle for Democratic Radio* (Urbana: University of Illinois Press, 2006), 91–97. I thank Liz Fones-Wolf for generously sharing her notes from the NBC papers and the contemporary broadcasting journals.

24. "Radio's War Role on C of C Series," *Broadcasting* (9 Mar. 1942): 43; transcript of *This Nation at War*, NAM-sponsored radio broadcast, 8 Dec. 1942, folder National Association of Manufacturers, carton 13, Kaiser Papers; "Summary of NIIC Activities in 1943," folder Promotional Materials 1943, box 846, Ser. III, NAM Records; *War of Enterprise* script 1, in folder PR Committee Radio Programs—*War of Enterprise* 1944, box 3; William H. McGaughey to Ken Youel, 22 Dec. 1944, in folder Public Relations Committee: GM Corp., box 1, both in drawer 2, cabinet 6, ACWP Records.

25. *Defense for America* script, 22 Mar. 1941, box 418, and *Defense for America* script, 16 Aug. 1941, box 419, both in NBC Papers.

26. Materials in folder *Defense for America* 1942, box 207, Series XV, NAM Records.

27. Fred G. Clark to Pew, 11 Dec. 1941, folder 1941, box 211, Pew Personal Papers.

28. "Promotional Distribution of Industry's War Production," 4 Dec. 1942, folder Industry's War Production, box 844, Ser. III, NAM Records.

29. "Free Enterprise and the Automotive Industry," unboxed folder Public Relations Committee: Free Enterprise, drawer 1; "Government Attitudes Toward Business," 15 Apr. 1942, folder Public Relations Committee: Inter-Office Memos, 1942–1943, box 1, drawer 2, both in cabinet 6, ACWP Records; "Auto Industry's War Report: 'The Stuff Is Rolling Out,'" *Newsweek* (15 June 1942): 42.

30. "The 1942 Public Information Campaign," folder Promotional Material for 1942, box 846, Ser. III, NAM Records.

31. "'Production for Victory' Tour Ends," *NAM Newsletter* (29 May 1942): 5. Wire-service stories include "Baldwin Tank Output 3.5 Times Rate Set by Army," *WSJ*, 8 May 1942; "Speed Liberty Ship Program," *Charlotte Observer*, 9 May 1942; "War Speed-Up in Industry Said Amazing," *Atlanta Constitution*, 29 May 1942; "U.S. Industry Wasn't Fooling, Two-Year Turnout Shows," *Newsweek* (25 May 1942): 42–44.

32. Edgar M. Queeny, *The Spirit of Enterprise* (New York: Charles Scribner's Sons, 1943), 14–15; Sidney M. Shalett, "Giant Plant Pours Aluminum Sheets," *NYT*, 11 May 1942; Shalett, "Magic Deeds Laid to Chemical Plant," *NYT*, 12 May 1942; Shalett, "Hartford Output Up 1,500 Per Cent," *NYT*, 29 May 1942; "'Production for Victory' Tour Ends," 5.

33. "U.S. Industry Goes over the Top," *NAM Newsletter* (23 May 1942): 1.

34. "U.S. Launches 21 Big Ships on Maritime Day," *Life* (8 June 1942): 19–23; "New High in Ship Production," Bethlehem Steel advertisement, *Newsweek* (11 May 1942): 43; "U.S. Industry Wasn't Fooling, Two-Year Turnout Shows," *Newsweek* (25 May 1942): 42–44.

35. Roland Marchand, *Creating the Corporate Soul: The Rise of Public Relations and Corporate Imagery in American Big Business* (Berkeley: University of California Press, 1998), 312–16, 338.

36. "Woods Sees Bright Prospects for Radio and Blue This Fall" and "Dramatic Program Spurs GM Series," both in *Broadcasting* (27 July 1942): 14.

37. "Curtiss-Wright Meets Defense Employee Problems with Pictures," *Business Screen* 3, no. 6 (1941): 16.

38. Bird, *"Better Living,"* 147.

39. Nelson to Forrestal, 8 Sept. 1942, folder Nelson, box 188, entry 116, RG 80, NARA; Fox, *Madison Avenue Goes to War*, 41; Mark H. Leff, "The Politics of Sacrifice on the American Home Front in World War II," *Journal of American History* 77, no. 4 (Mar. 1991): 1307–9; Marchand, *Creating the Corporate Soul*, 320–21.

40. Board of Directors Meeting Minutes, 21 Oct. 1942, 20 Oct. 1943, and 24 Nov. 1943, box 3584; "Boeing Public Relations and Advertising: Review and Proposed Budget for 1952 [*sic*]," copy in unboxed bound volume, Boeing Board of Directors Minutes 1949–51, all in BHA.

41. "Smoke Gets in Their Eyes: All-Out U.S. Production," Philco advertisement, *Time* (11 May 1942): 14.

42. GM ad in *Forbes* 51 (1 Mar. 1943): 18–19.

43. "Lightning Strikes: Look to Lockheed for Leadership," Lockheed advertisement, *Time* (25 May 1942): 65.

44. Cynthia Lee Henthorn, *From Submarines to Suburbs: Selling a Better America, 1939–1959* (Athens: Ohio State University Press, 2006), 74.

45. This political work suited the advertising industry, which, like its private clients, openly endorsed a wartime political project of resisting state regulation. Robert Griffith, "The Selling of America: The Advertising Council and American Politics, 1942–1960," *Business History Review* 57, no. 3 (autumn 1983): 388–412; Gerd Horten, *Radio Goes to War: The Cultural Politics of Propaganda During World War II* (Berkeley: University of California Press, 2002), 92–95; Dawn Spring, *Advertising in the Age of Persuasion: Building Brand America, 1941–1961* (New York: Palgrave Macmillan, 2011), 18–25.

46. James S. Kemper, "American Business Looks Ahead," *VSD* 7, no. 17 (15 June 1941): 539.

47. "Measure Drawn to Rush Defense, Says Roosevelt," *New Orleans Times-Picayune*, 4 June 1941; Scott Hershey, "Press of a Nation Declared Facing Wartime Trials," *New Orleans Times-Picayune*, 17 Apr. 1942; "There's a Great Day Coming!," Ford advertisement, *New Orleans Times-Picayune*, 5 July 1942; "Text of President's Message to Congress, on State of the Union," *NYT*, 8 Jan. 1943.

48. *Production for Victory: Two Years After Pearl Harbor* (New York: NAM, 1943), iv, 63; Tom M. Girdler, "Maximum Production Is Still Ahead," in *Industry and Victory* (New York: NAM, 1944), 26–27; see also Tom M. Girdler with Boyden Sparkes, *Boot Straps: The Autobiography of Tom M. Girdler* (New York: Charles Scribner's Sons, 1943), 2, 392–451.

49. Tedlow, *Keeping the Corporate Image*, 118–20; Fones-Wolf, *Selling Free Enterprise*, 26.

50. "To Whom Credit Is Due—and NOT Due," *Forbes* 49 (15 Mar. 1942): 7; "Big Business U.S. Salvation," *Forbes* (1 June 1942): 9; Samuel Crowther, *Time to Inquire: How Can We Restore the Freedom, Opportunity, and Dignity of the Common Man?* (New York: John Day, 1942), 277–79.

51. James P. Selvage, "Selling the Free Enterprise System," *VSD* 9, no. 5 (15 Dec. 1942): 144–47; George Romney, "It's Your Ship," *VSD* 9, no. 8 (1 Feb. 1943): 242–47; F. C. Crawford, "Jobs, Freedom, Opportunity," *VSD* 9, no. 16 (1 June 1943): 496–500.

52. Ralph W. Carney, "Business Goes to War," *VSD* 10, no. 17 (15 June 1944): 536; undated James F. Lincoln address to Sales Executives Club of New York, copy attached to Lincoln to Romney, 20 Mar. 1945, box 1, drawer 3, cabinet 1, ACWP Records.

53. Norman Lewis, "Wartime Creed for Business Men," *Forbes* (1 Apr. 1942): 13.

54. John L. Collyer, "Three Post-War Goals for America," *Forbes* 54 (15 July 1944): 14–15.

55. Transcript of Batt address to Emergency Aid Society, Philadelphia, 6 Dec. 1942, folder 1942 WPB Addresses, box 4, Batt Papers, TPL.

56. Tedlow, *Keeping the Corporate Image*, 123; Collins, *Business Response to Keynes*, 88–96. By war's end, even some NAM staffers were asking whether their organization might do well to follow the Chamber's lead in this field. See Wall, *Inventing the "American Way,"* 128–31.

57. Eric A. Johnston, *America Unlimited* (Garden City, NY: Doubleday, 1944); idem, "When the Boys Come Marching Home," *Nation's Business* 30 (July 1942): 22.

58. Eric A. Johnston, "America Unlimited," 27 Apr. 1943, in Minutes of the Thirty-First Annual Meeting, April 27–29, 1943, box 17, Ser. I, Chamber Records; Johnston, *America Unlimited*, 102–7.

59. Mark S. Foster, *Henry J. Kaiser: Builder in the Modern American West* (Austin: University of Texas Press, 1989), 96, 128–30; Stephen B. Adams, *Mr. Kaiser Goes to Washington: The Rise of a Government Entrepreneur* (Chapel Hill: University of North Carolina Press, 1997), 109–16.

60. Kaiser speech, "Peace and Free Enterprise," Metropolitan Opera House, New York City / Blue Network, 27 Jan. 1945, folder 1–27–45, carton 262, Kaiser Papers; Foster, *Henry J. Kaiser*, 96, 128–30.

61. Paul Cadman to Kaiser, 11 Nov. 1942, folder Cadman, carton 12; Kaiser speech to *New York Herald Tribune* Forum on Current Problems, 16 Nov. 1942, folder 11–16–42, carton 262, all in Kaiser Papers.

62. Howard L. Freeman to Kaiser, 5 Dec. 1942, folder NAM, carton 13, Kaiser Papers. As Congressman Frank W. Boykin (D-AL) put it to Kaiser in 1943, "I find it impossible to get up any enthusiasm for government in business. I don't know of any conspicuous success that Government has made in business. Like you, I believe in the effectiveness of free enterprise and in its incentives." Boykin to Kaiser, 17 Sept. 1943, folder U.S. Gov't, Navy 1943, carton 153, both in Kaiser Papers.

63. Franklin Miller, Jr. to Kaiser, 4 Dec. 1942, folder NAM, carton 13, Kaiser Papers.

64. Richard H. Pells, *The Liberal Mind in a Conservative Age: American Intellectuals in the 1940s and 1950s* (New York: Harper & Row, 1985), 11; Paul Milkman, *PM: A New Deal in Journalism, 1940–1948* (New Brunswick, NJ: Rutgers University Press, 1997).

65. Pells, *Liberal Mind in a Conservative Age*, 26–32; Alan Brinkley, *The End of Reform: New Deal Liberalism in Recession and War* (New York: Knopf, 1995), 174.

66. I. F. Stone, *A Nonconformist History of Our Times: The War Years, 1939–1945* (Boston: Little, Brown, 1988), 17–23, 42–45, 60–68, 78–87, 116–18; Nathan Robertson, "Defense Dollar-a-Year Men Often Look to Own Dollars," *PM*, 24 Nov. 1940, 5; Robertson, "Plant Expansion for Defense Meets Industry Resistance," *PM*, 25 Nov. 1940, 5; George H. Lyon, "Dollar-a-Year Men Are Running the Big Show," *PM*, 4 Mar. 1941, 10–11; "PM Exposed Standard Oil's Nazi Deal 8 Months Ago," *PM*, 27 Mar. 1942, 6; Stone, "Pooling of Small-Plant Tools Could Boost Output," *PM*, 12 Mar. 1942, 10; Milkman, *PM*, 70–88. On Stone's

career, see Myra MacPherson, *"All Governments Lie": The Life and Times of Rebel Journalist I. F. Stone* (New York: Scribner, 2006).

67. For a valuable digital archive of Pearson's "Washington Merry-Go-Round" columns, see www.aladin0.wrlc.org/gsdl/collect/pearson/pearson.shtml (accessed 5 Dec. 2012).

68. "Investigation of the National Defense Program: Report on Aluminum Investigation," Senate Report 480, Part 1, 77th Cong., 1st Sess., ser. 10545; "Investigation of the National Defense Program: Additional Report," Senate Report 480, Part 5, 77th Cong., 2nd Sess., ser. 10655; "Sweeping Criticism: Truman Blast over Arms Output Hits Everyone Except Congress," *Newsweek* 19 (26 Jan. 1942): 47–48; "Investigation of the National Defense Program: Additional Report [Rubber]," Senate Report 480, Part 7, 77th Cong., 2nd Sess., ser. 10655; Roger Edward Willson, "The Truman Committee" (Ph.D. diss., Harvard University, 1966), 1–27, 197–236; Alonzo L. Hamby, *Man of the People: A Life of Harry S. Truman* (New York: Oxford University Press, 1995), 248–52.

69. Thurman Arnold, "How Monopolies Have Hobbled Defense," *Reader's Digest* 39 (July 1941): 51–55; idem and J. Sterling Livingston, "Antitrust War Policy and Full Production," *Harvard Business Review* 20, no. 3 (spring 1942): 265. On the wartime suspension of many antitrust actions, see Richard Polenberg, *War and Society: The United States, 1941–1945* (Philadelphia; Lippincott, 1972), 77–78; Brinkley, *End of Reform*, 107–22; Wyatt Wells, *Antitrust and the Formation of the Postwar World* (New York: Columbia University Press, 2002), 43–89.

70. "Dollars vs. Defense," *American Federationist* 47 (Oct. 1940): 6; "Editorial: Labor's Defense Risks," *American Federationist* 47 (Oct. 1940): 16; "Defense Profits Are Enormous," *American Federationist* (July 1941): 18–19; "Equality of Sacrifice," *American Federationist* 50 (June 1943): 26; Nathan Robertson, "Business Does Nicely," *American Federationist* 50 (Dec. 1943): 3–5.

71. "Our Readers Write: Workers Back Salary Limit," *American Federationist* 50 (Mar. 1943): 32; George Meany, "Free Enterprise: What It Means to Labor," *American Federationist* 51 (June 1944): 3. It is not clear whether "Janet Kleinsmid" was a real person. I was unable to find a person with this name in the 1940 census, Memphis city directories, or any other source.

72. *War Production* (Washington, DC: CIO, 1942); Brody, "New Deal and World War II," 281–85; Nelson Lichtenstein, *Labor's War at Home: The CIO in World War II* (1982 ed.; Philadelphia: Temple University Press, 2003), 82–109, 171–77; Melvyn Dubofsky, *The State and Labor in Modern America* (Chapel Hill: University of North Carolina Press, 1994), 177; Brinkley, *End of Reform*, 222–24; Leff, "Politics of Sacrifice," 1298–1306.

73. "Profits Jump—Rich Get Richer!," *Labor Action*, 24 Mar. 1941, 1; "Bosses Try to Hide 400% Profit Rise!," *Labor Action*, 28 Sept. 1942, 1; "The Facts on Profits, Salaries and Your Wages," *Labor Action*, 26 July 1943, 1; Cartoon in *Labor Action*, 26 June 1944, 1.

74. Leff, "Politics of Sacrifice," 1305.

75. The first suit was dismissed, but Pullman-Standard appealed in late 1944. The case was finally settled in 1947, when the union was ordered to pay $1 in damages and $209 in court costs. Civil Case File 44C307, U.S. District Court for Northern District of Illinois, Eastern Division: *Pullman Standard Car Manufacturing Co. v. Local Union No. 2928, United Steelworkers of America*, RG 21, NARA-GL.

76. James Caldwell Foster, *The Union Politic: The CIO Political Action Committee* (Columbia: University of Missouri Press, 1975); Steven Fraser, *Labor Will Rule: Sidney Hillman and the Rise of American Labor* (New York: Free Press, 1991); Robert H. Zieger, *The CIO,*

1935–1955 (Chapel Hill: University of North Carolina Press, 1995), 181–86. On related AFL proposals late in the war, see Andrew E. Kersten, *Labor's Home Front: The American Federation of Labor During World War II* (New York: New York University Press, 2006), 189–222.

77. Zieger, *The CIO*, 134–79; Tedlow, *Keeping the Corporate Image*, 134; Bird, *"Better Living,"* 149; Fones-Wolf and Godfried, "Regulating Class Conflict on the Air," 73–74; Fones-Wolf, *Waves of Opposition*, 101–19; Nathan Godfried, *WCFL: Chicago's Voice of Labor, 1926–78* (Urbana: University of Illinois Press, 1997), 210–32. For a piece emphasizing the impressiveness of labor's financial and media resources at war's end, see Victor Riesel, "Labor Is Big Business," *Reader's Digest* 48 (Feb. 1946): 118–20.

78. James T. Sparrow, *Warfare State: World War II Americans and the Age of Big Government* (New York: Oxford University Press, 2012), 166–84.

79. Knudsen addresses to NAM meetings, New York, 13 Dec. 1940, and Chicago, 26 May 1941, folder Speeches 1940–41, box 9, Knudsen Papers.

80. Jesse H. Jones with Edward Angly, *Fifty Billion Dollars: My Thirteen Years with the RFC, 1932–1945* (New York: Macmillan, 1951), 321–49. On Jones, see Jordan A. Schwarz, *The New Dealers: Power Politics in the Age of Roosevelt* (New York: Vintage, 1993), 59–95, 313–15; Steven Fenberg, *Unprecedented Power: Jesse Jones, Capitalism, and the Common Good* (College Station: Texas A&M University Press, 2011).

81. Fenberg, *Unprecedented Power*, 415, 449–50, 468.

82. Donald M. Nelson, "Labor and Production," *American Federationist* 50 (Feb. 1943): 4.

83. Nelson, "Even Greater Production" [3 Mar. 1942 radio address], *VSD* 8, no. 11 (15 Mar. 1942): 323; transcript of Nelson radio address, 10 Mar. 1942, copy in folder Nelson, box 188, e. 116, RG 80; Donald M. Nelson, *Arsenal of Democracy: The Story of American War Production* (New York: Harcourt Brace, 1946), 317.

84. Walter P. Reuther, "Labor's Place in the War Pattern" [1942], in *American Labor Since the New Deal*, ed. Melvyn Dubofsky (Chicago: Quadrangle, 1971), 132–41.

85. William Green, "Labor Faces the Challenge," *VSD* (15 Sept. 1942): 720; "President Green's Keynote and Acceptance Speeches," *American Federationist* 49 (Nov. 1942): 19; William Green, "Labor Backs the Boys," *American Federationist* 51 (Apr. 1944): 4.

86. Robert P. Patterson, "This War Is No Tea Party," *American Federationist* 49 (Oct. 1942): 14–15, 33; James V. Forrestal, "The Navy, Labor and the War," *American Federationist* 49 (Dec. 1942): 17; Lt. Gen. Joseph T. McNarney, "A.F.L.-Built Planes Are Tops," *American Federationist* 50 (Jan. 1943): 10.

87. Levin H. Campbell, Jr., "Watch Them Cut Red Tape," *Nation's Business* 30 (Nov. 1942): 45.

88. Kenneth Crawford, "About the War Against the New Deal and Labor: An Editorial," *PM*, 20 Mar. 1942, 11; "Spring Offensive Against Labor," *American Federationist* 49 (Apr. 1942): 3–7, 29–31;

89. "4,283 Firms Won the Army-Navy 'E,'" *NYT*, 6 Dec. 1945. This number represented roughly 5 percent of the total number of plants with some role in the war program; it covered more than 5 percent of all war workers because many larger plants won the award. Plants could win the award more than once; if they did so, they added white stars to the "E" pennant flying above the plant.

90. "'E' Is for Efficiency," *Nation's Business* 30 (Jan. 1942): 62–63.

91. *Presentation of the Army-Navy "E" Award to the Hamilton Manufacturing Company, Two Rivers, Wisconsin, September 21, 1943*, http://digital.library.wisc.edu/1711.dl/WI.Army NavyE (accessed 29 Oct. 2012); *Presentation of the Army-Navy "E" Award for Production to the Men and Women of Price Brothers Company, April 28, 1944*, http://epfl.mdch.org/cdm/compoundobject/collection/mdww/id/231 (accessed 29 Oct. 2012); Lisa L. Ossian, *The Home Fronts of Iowa, 1939–1945* (Columbia: University of Missouri Press, 2009), 76.

92. Tassava, "Launching a Thousand Ships," 380–81; Harry Camp, "Wartime Industry and Radio: Cleveland Concerns Buy Time to Tell Public About Government Awards," *Broadcasting*, 29 June 1942, p. 30, typescript copy in box 24, James Fly Papers, Rare Book and Manuscript Library, Butler Library, Columbia University. I thank Liz Fones-Wolf for sharing this material with me.

93. Ossian, *Home Fronts of Iowa*, 74–75.

94. Materials in folder Soldiers of Production 1942–43, box 847; "Summary of NIIC Activities in 1943," folder Promotional Materials 1943, box 846; "Companies Which Have Held 'Soldiers of Production' Rallies up to June 12," folder Misc. NIIC Material June–Oct 1944, box 845, all in Ser. III, NAM Records.

95. Junius B. Wood, "Ballyhoo Runs Wild," *Nation's Business* 33 (July 1945): 25–26, 64–68; Robert Mason, *The Republican Party and American Politics from Hoover to Reagan* (New York: Cambridge University Press, 2012), 106.

96. Allan M. Winkler, *The Politics of Propaganda: The Office of War Information, 1942–1945* (New Haven, CT: Yale University Press, 1978), 56–71; John Morton Blum, *V Was for Victory: Politics and American Culture During World War II* (New York: Harcourt Brace, 1976), 16–45; Lawrence R. Samuel, *Pledging Allegiance: American Identity and the Bond Drive of World War II* (Washington, DC: Smithsonian Institution, 1997); William L. Bird, Jr. and Harry R. Rubenstein, *Design for Victory: World War II Posters on the American Home Front* (New York: Princeton Architectural Press, 1998); Horten, *Radio Goes to War*, 41–65, 116–46; Howard Blue, *Words at War: World War II Radio Drama and the Postwar Broadcasting Industry Blacklist* (Lanham, MD: Scarecrow, 2002), esp. 133–34, 249–63; James J. Kimble, *Mobilizing the Home Front: War Bonds and Domestic Propaganda* (College Station: Texas A&M University Press, 2006); Wall, *Inventing the "American Way,"* 110–18; Sparrow, *Warfare State*, 133–59.

97. Thomas Doherty, *Projections of War: Hollywood, American Culture, and World War II* (New York: Columbia University Press, 1993), 70–82, 103–21, 155–56, 242–64; Matthew C. Gunter, *The Capra Touch: A Study of the Director's Hollywood Classics and War Documentaries, 1934–1945* (Jefferson, NC: McFarland, 2012), 124–47; Colin Shindler, *Hollywood Goes to War: Films and American Society, 1939–1952* (London: Routledge and Kegan Paul, 1979), 52–92; Bernard F. Dick, *The Star-Spangled Screen: The American World War II Film* (Lexington: University Press of Kentucky, 1985), 113; Robert L. McLaughlin and Sally E. Perry, *We'll Always Have the Movies: American Cinema During World War II* (Lexington: University Press of Kentucky, 2006), 67–99, 233–38; Jeanine Basinger, *The World War II Combat Film: Anatomy of a Genre* (New York: Columbia University Press, 1986); Lary May, "Making the American Consensus: The Narrative of Conversion and Subversion in World War II Films," in *The War in American Culture: Society and Consciousness During World War II*, ed. Lewis A. Erenberg and Susan E. Hirsch (Chicago: University of Chicago Press, 1996), 71–102.

98. Samuel I. Roseman, ed., *Public Papers and Addresses of Franklin D. Roosevelt*, 1940 vol. (New York: Macmillan, 1941), 337.

99. Samuel I. Roseman, ed., *Public Papers and Addresses of Franklin D. Roosevelt*, 1942 vol. (New York: Harper & Bros., 1950), 113–15, 227–34; Sparrow, *Warfare State*, 3–4.

100. Roosevelt speech of 27 Oct. 1944, quoted in Nelson, *Arsenal of Democracy*, 431; David M. Jordan, *FDR, Dewey, and the Election of 1944* (Bloomington: Indiana University Press, 2011), 253, 287.

101. Samuel I. Roseman, ed., *Public Papers and Addresses of Franklin D. Roosevelt*, 1941 vol. (New York: Harper & Bros., 1950), 195.

102. Samuel I. Roseman, ed., *Public Papers and Addresses of Franklin D. Roosevelt*, 1943 vol. (New York: Harper & Bros., 1950), 181–82.

103. "F. R. Tours Nation, Finds Washington Lags in War Spirit," *Dallas Morning News*, 2 Oct. 1942.

104. "Itinerary of President's Two-Week Tour, with Visits to 29 War Plants and Stations," *NYT*, 3 Oct. 1942.

105. Doris Kearns Goodwin, *No Ordinary Time: Franklin and Eleanor Roosevelt, the Home Front in World War II* (New York: Simon & Schuster, 1994), 360–73; Kenneth S. Davis, *FDR: The War President, 1940–1943* (New York: Random House, 2000), 611–22.

106. Roseman, ed., *Public Papers and Addresses of Franklin D. Roosevelt*, 1942 vol., 384–91; W. H. Lawrence, "An 8,754-mile Tour," *NYT*, 2 Oct. 1942; "F. R. Tours Nation, Finds Washington Lags in War Spirit," *Dallas Morning News*, 2 Oct. 1942; Graham J. White, *FDR and the Press* (Chicago: University of Chicago Press, 1979), 42.

107. Roseman, ed., *Public Papers and Addresses of Franklin D. Roosevelt*, 1942 vol., 420.

108. Ickes Diaries, 45:7063, reel 5.

109. Roseman, ed., *Public Papers and Addresses of Franklin D. Roosevelt*, 1943 vol., 571–75.

110. Richard Polenberg, "The Decline of the New Deal, 1937–1940," in *The New Deal: The National Level*, ed. John Braeman, Robert H. Bremner, and David Brody (Columbus: Ohio State University Press, 1975), 261; David Brody, "The New Deal and World War II," in *The New Deal*, ed. Braeman, Bremner, and Brody, 270–75; Brinkley, *End of Reform*, 143–48.

111. Ickes Diaries, 42:6420–21, reel 5.

112. Julius Hochman, "Labor and the Public," *American Federationist* 50 (Apr. 1943): 20–24.

113. "Big Business Held Halting Progress," *NYT*, 13 Nov. 1943.

114. Byrnes address to American Society of Newspaper Editors, 13 Feb. 1943, folder 8, box 8, Ser. X, Byrnes Papers.

115. Raymond Clapper, *Watching the World* (New York: McGraw Hill, 1944), 295.

116. "War to End 1943: Business Leaders," *Forbes* 49 (1 Jan. 1942): 7.

117. Alan Barth to Ferdinand Kuhn, Jr., 5 Sept. 1941, folder Morgenthau–Editorial Opinion Reports Aug.–Nov. 1941, box 80, PSF-FDR; Harry F. Byrd, "The Failure of Our National Defense Program," *Reader's Digest* 39 (Nov. 1941): 16–25; George H. Gallup, *The Gallup Poll: Public Opinion, 1935–1971*: vol. 1, *1935–1948* (New York: Random House, 1972), 237, 242–43, 271, 284, 313, 330.

118. "Industry's Two Wars," *Forbes* 50 (1 July 1942): 9.

119. Hadley Cantril and John Harding, "The 1942 Elections: A Case History of Political Psychology," *Public Opinion Quarterly* 7, no. 2 (summer 1943): 222–41; Louis L. Bean memo to Hopkins, "The 1942–1943 Political Trend," 4 Feb. 1944, folder Politics 1944, PSF-FDR;

Polenberg, *War and Society*, 189–91; Blum, *V Was for Victory*, 231–234; David M. Kennedy, *Freedom from Fear: The American People in Depression and War* (New York: Oxford University Press, 1999), 782–83.

120. "The U.S.A. Goes Republican," *Life* 13 (16 Nov. 1942): 33–40; Eliot Janeway, "Trials and Errors," *Fortune* 26 (Dec. 1942): 26–32; John Robert Moore, "The Conservative Coalition in the United States Senate, 1942–1945," *Journal of Southern History* 33, no. 3 (Aug. 1967): 368–76; Polenberg, *War and Society*, 193; Ira Katznelson, Kim Geiger, and Daniel Kryder, "Limiting Liberalism: The Southern Veto in Congress, 1933–1950," *Political Science Quarterly* 108, no. 2 (summer 1993): 283–306.

121. *Papers of Robert A. Taft*, 2:366; Blum, *V Was for Victory*, 227–28; Goodwin, *No Ordinary Time*, 384; Meg Jacobs, *Pocketbook Politics: Economic Citizenship in Twentieth-Century America* (Princeton, NJ: Princeton University Press, 2005), 194, 213–17; Lizabeth Cohen, *A Consumer's Republic: The Politics of Mass Consumption in Postwar America* (New York: Alfred A. Knopf, 2003), 66; Joanna Grisinger, *The Unwieldy American State: Administrative Politics Since the New Deal* (New York: Cambridge University Press, 2012), 15, 40–50.

122. Queeny, *Spirit of Enterprise*, 200.

123. "Henderson Resignation Hailed as Congressional Victory," *NAM News* (19 Dec. 1942): 1.

124. Roland Young, *Congressional Politics in the Second World War* (New York: Columbia University Press, 1956), 23.

125. Nancy Beck Young, *Why We Fight: Congress and the Politics of World War II* (Lawrence: University Press of Kansas, 2013), 73–101.

126. Lawrence Sullivan, *Bureaucracy Runs Amuck* (Indianapolis: Bobbs-Merrill, 1944).

127. Robert A. Caro, *The Years of Lyndon Johnson: The Path to Power* (New York: Knopf, 1982), 765–67.

128. Brinkley, *End of Reform*, 92–94.

129. Joseph C. O'Mahoney, "America Is Being Made Over—and We Don't Like It!," *Forbes* 52 (1 Aug. 1943): 12–13, 30; O'Mahoney, "America Is Being Made Over—and We Won't Like It!," *Reader's Digest* 43 (Aug. 1943): 39–43.

130. Weisenburger, "Your Day in the Court of Public Opinion," 3 Dec. 1942, folder Key Documents, box 844, Ser. III, NAM Records.

131. Undated and unsigned memo, "Washington Memorandum on Public Relations Problems, 1943," folder PR Committee: Interoffice Memos, Washington Office, box 1, drawer 2, cabinet 6, ACWP Records.

132. "Proposed Report by Mr. Adams to NIIC Governing Board," 25 Mar. 1943, folder Documents Relating to NIIC, box 843, Ser. III, NAM Records.

133. Frederick C. Crawford, "A Better America Through Freedom of Enterprise," in *A Better America: Industry's Program* (New York: NAM, 1944), 3, 9.

134. Johnston, *America Unlimited*, 179–80; "What's Ahead for American Business? A Symposium," *Forbes* 54 (1 Dec. 1944): 34; David Farber, *Sloan Rules: Alfred P. Sloan and the Triumph of General Motors* (Chicago: University of Chicago Press, 2002), 238.

135. "Detroit Is Dynamite," *Life* 13 (17 Aug. 1942): 15–23; McGaughey to Romney, 15 Aug. 1942, folder Public Relations Committee: Interoffice Memos, 1942–43, box 1, drawer 2, cabinet 6, ACWP Papers.

136. F. C. Crawford to Sorensen, 3 Sept. 1943, folder N, box 131, Accession 38, Ford Records.

137. Workman, "Manufacturing Power," 292; Sparrow, *Warfare State*, 197–99.

138. *Papers of Robert A. Taft*, 2:508; Clapper, *Watching the World*, 180–81; Polenberg, *War and Society*, 213–14; Blum, *V Was for Victory*, 299; Jordan, *FDR, Dewey, and the Election of 1944*, 20.

139. Lilienthal, *TVA Years*, 567.

140. "The Renegotiation Legislative Situation," 3 Jan. 1944, folder Correspondence War Work 1944, box 1, Joseph M. Dodge Papers, Burton Historical Collection, DPL.

141. Truman to George M. Rogers, 4 Nov. 1941, folder National Defense Program—Nov. 1941, box 123, Truman Senatorial File, TPL.

142. "Investigation of the National Defense Program: Interim Report on Steel," Senate Report 10, Part 3, 78th Cong., 1st Sess., ser. 10758 (Washington, DC: GPO, 1943).

143. "Investigation of the National Defense Program: Additional Report, Concerning Faking of Inspections of Steel Plate by Carnegie-Illinois Steel Corporation," Senate Report 10, Part 7, 78th Cong., 1st Sess., ser. 10758; "Investigation of the National Defense Program: Additional Report, Aircraft," Senate Report 10, Part 10, 78th Cong., 1st Sess., ser. 10758; Donald H. Riddle, *The Truman Committee: A Study in Congressional Responsibility* (New Brunswick: Rutgers University Press, 1964), 123–30; Hamby, *Man of the People*, 259; Tedlow, *Keeping the Corporate Image*, 115–16.

144. Truman article in Nov. 1942 issue of *American Magazine*, cited in Grisinger, *Unwieldy American State*, 32.

145. Charles L. Dix to Truman, 14 Dec. 1942, box 120; Frank J. McQuade to Truman, 26 Mar. 1943, box 121; H. D. Kissenger to Truman, 24 Mar. 1943, box 122, all in Truman Senatorial File, TPL.

146. "Investigation of the National Defense Program: Additional Report, Transportation," Senate Report 10, Part 13, 78th Cong., 1st Sess., ser. 10758, pp. 37–38.

147. "Investigation of the National Defense Program: Third Annual Report," Senate Report 10, Part 16, 78th Cong., 2nd Sess., ser. 10839, pp. 3, 16, 44–45; John H. Crider, "Freer Enterprise Urged by Truman," *NYT*, 5 Mar. 1944.

148. Ickes to FDR, 28 Aug. 1941, folder Interior-Ickes 1941, box 55, PSF-FDR; Ickes, draft memoir chapter "Jesse Jones, First Draft" (1949), reel 5, Biographical Memoirs and Sketches, Ickes Papers, LOC. On Ickes, see T. H. Watkins, *Righteous Pilgrim: The Life and Times of Harold L. Ickes, 1874–1952* (New York: Henry Holt, 1990).

149. Ickes Diaries, 52:8499, reel 6; John Morton Blum, ed., *The Price of Vision: The Diary of Henry A. Wallace, 1942–1946* (Boston: Houghton Mifflin, 1973), 361.

150. Chester Bowles, *Promises to Keep: My Years in Public Life, 1941–1969* (New York: Harper & Row, 1971), 89; August W. Giebelhaus, *Business and Government in the Oil Industry: A Case Study of Sun Oil, 1876–1945* (Greenwich, CT: JAI, 1980), 247.

151. Ickes Diaries, 42:6571–72, reel 5; 43:6704, reel 5; 50:8171, 8243, reel 6; 62: unpaginated entry for 17 Feb. 1946, reel 7.

152. Ibid., 44:6904–7; 45:7067–68, both on reel 5; Ickes, draft memoir chapter "Oil Goes to War" [ca. 1950], reel 7, Biographical Memoirs and Sketches, Ickes Papers; Harold L. Ickes, *Fightin' Oil* (New York: Alfred A. Knopf, 1943), viii.

153. Ickes Diaries, 45:7208–9, reel 5; 52:8546–47, reel 6; 61:10081, reel 7.

154. Ralph K. Davies to William R. Boyd, 14 July 1945, and transcript of PIWC meeting, 18 July 1945, both in box 689, entry 15, RG 253.

Chapter 4

1. Lawrence A. Harvey, "Report Based upon an Investigation of the Current Status of the Smaller War Plants in California," [1945], folder Correspondence H, box 23, Julius Krug Papers, LOC. The California survey's findings were consistent with a 1943 U.S. Office of War Information study of 4,500 small manufacturers. Half of these companies had military contracts or subcontracts, the OWI found, but only 14 percent of them wished that they had more war orders. Robert Wood Johnson, *"But, General Johnson—": Episodes in a War Effort* (Princeton, NJ: Princeton University Press, 1944), 59.

2. For a related argument, see Reuel E. Schiller, "Reining in the American State: World War II and the Decline of Expert Administration," in *Total War and the Law: The American Home Front in World War II*, ed. Daniel R. Ernst and Victor Jew (Westport, CT: Praeger, 2002), 185–206.

3. William F. McDermott, "McDermott on Free Enterprise," *Cleveland Plain Dealer*, 18 Feb. 1943.

4. Gross to Cleon T. Knapp, 13 Mar. 1941, box 6, Gross Papers, LOC; "One Unfair Burden on Business," *Forbes* (1 Nov. 1941): 7.

5. Robert B. Lea memo, 12 June 1956 [*sic*], folder 19, box 53, Sperry Records.

6. "Curbing Government Questionnaires," *NAM News* (10 July 1943): 8; Richard H. Keehn and Gene Smiley, "Small Business Reactions to World War II Government Controls," *Essays in Economic and Business History* 8 (1990): 3–16.

7. T. N. Sandifer, "Making Swords from Pen Points," *Nation's Business* 30 (Nov. 1942): 38–40, 93.

8. "Regulation or Strangulation?," *Forbes* 51 (15 June 1943): 9.

9. Alden H. Sypher, "We Can Go No Further," *Nation's Business* 31 (Jan. 1943): 17–18; B. E. Hutchinson to F. Eberstadt, 11 Oct. 1942, folder GM Corp 1942–43, box 1, drawer 3, cabinet 1, ACWP Records; "Government by Bureaucrats," *Charlotte Observer*, 10 Feb. 1944, clipping in folder 6, box 11, Ser. IV, Byrnes Papers.

10. "Resolutions Adopted October 16, 1942 at the Annual Meeting of the Associated Industries of Nebraska," folder 312A, box 5, RG 25, Nebraska State Historical Library, Lincoln; Briggers story in George S. Heyer to Pew, 8 Oct. 1943, folder Politics-Misc., box 110, Pew Personal Papers; L. M. Evans, "Our Lost Freedoms," *VSD* 10, no. 21 (15 Aug. 1944): 659–62. On the travails of smaller grocery stores, see Tracey Deutsch, *Building a Housewife's Paradise: Gender, Politics, and American Grocery Stores in the Twentieth Century* (Chapel Hill: University of North Carolina Press, 2010), 170–71.

11. David Novick, Melvin Anshen, and W. C. Truppner, *Wartime Production Controls* (New York: Columbia University Press, 1949), 118–37; Kenneth H. Hunter and Edward L. Hogan, *War Production Board's Steel Division's Experience with World War II Controls Particularly Under the Controlled Materials Plan* (Washington, DC: U.S. Department of Commerce, 1950), 22–31; Calvin Lee Christman, "Ferdinand Eberstadt and Economic Mobilization for War, 1941–1943" (Ph.D. diss., Ohio State University, 1971), 138; Paul A. C. Koistinen, *Arsenal of World War II: The Political Economy of American Warfare, 1940–1945* (Lawrence: University Press of Kansas, 2004), 180–81, 317–26.

12. Boyce F. Martin, "What Business Learns from War," *Harvard Business Review* 21, no. 3 (spring 1943): 358–68; Christman, "Ferdinand Eberstadt," 160–79.

13. Christman, "Ferdinand Eberstadt," 179–237; Keith E. Eiler, *Mobilizing America: Robert P. Patterson and the War Effort, 1940–1945* (Ithaca, NY: Cornell University Press, 1997), 339–45.

14. Eberstadt and the CMP are hailed in Thomas K. McCraw, *American Business, 1920–2000: How It Worked* (Wheeling, IL: Harlan Davidson, 2000), 80–86. McCraw's sketch draws heavily on the somewhat more circumspect account in Robert Cuff, "Organization Capabilities and U.S. War Production: The Controlled Materials Plan of World War II," *Business and Economic History* 19 (1990): 103–12. The significance of the CMP is questioned in Koistinen, *Arsenal of World War II*, 325–26; and Hugh Rockoff, *America's Economic Way of War: War and the US Economy from the Spanish-American War to the Persian Gulf War* (New York: Cambridge University Press, 2012), 189–90.

15. Col. F. J. Atwood to Col. R. W. Johnson, 19 Aug. 1942, Col. A. B. Quinton, Jr. to Johnson, 15 Aug. 1942, and Brig. Gen. W. P. Boatwright to Johnson, 19 Aug. 1942, folder "Relations with WPB," box 14, RG 156, NARA-GL.

16. WPB *Minutes*, 425; Koistinen, *Arsenal of World War II*, 199, 222.

17. "History of the Army Air Forces Materiel Command, 1926 through 1941 [*sic*]"; Mary L. McMurtrie, "History of the Army Air Forces Materiel Command, 1942," "History of the Army Air Forces Materiel Command, 1943," all on reel A2000, AFHRA; Irving Brinton Holley, Jr., *Buying Aircraft: Matériel Procurement for the Army Air Forces* (Washington, DC: Office of the Chief of Military History, 1964), 466.

18. Levin H. Campbell, Jr., *The Industry-Ordnance Team* (New York: Whittlesey House, 1946), 28–32; Kevin Thornton and Dale Prentiss, *Tanks and Industry: The Detroit Tank Arsenal, 1940–1954* (Warren, MI: U.S. Army Tank-Automotive and Armaments Command, 1995), 43.

19. John T. Flynn, "Cost-Plus and Red Tape Hamper War Production," *Reader's Digest* 41 (Oct. 1942): 110.

20. Annual Inspection, 1 Dec. 1941, Chicago Ordnance District, in box 14; "Industry's Role in Ordnance is Praised by Gen. Hammond," *Chicago Tribune*, 22 July 1943, clipping in folder *Chicago Tribune*, box 2, both in RG 156, NARA-GL; S. A. Zimmerman, "Procurement in the United States Air Force, 1938–1948, vol. 1: Purchasing Phases," reel A2046, AFHRA; Kenneth E. Wierman, "History of the Western Procurement District, 1943," reel 2101, AFHRA; Johnson, *"But, General Johnson—,"* 13; Holley, *Buying Aircraft*, 504–10; Campbell, *Industry-Ordnance Team*, 28–32; Bartholomew H. Sparrow, *From the Outside In: World War II and the American State* (Princeton, NJ: Princeton University Press, 1996), 187.

21. Frederic C. Lane, *Ships for Victory: A History of Shipbuilding Under the U.S. Maritime Commission in World War II* (Baltimore: Johns Hopkins University Press, 1951), 729; Holley, *Buying Aircraft*, 390–97.

22. Sorensen Diary Notes, 1940–44, drafts, folder 1, pp. 791, 815, box 69; Reminiscences of Mr. Anthony Harff, p. 70, box 25; Reminiscences of Mr. L. E. Briggs, pp. 62–63, box 9, Accession 65, Ford Records; B. L. Moeckle (secretary, Ford Motor) to Brig. Gen. F. O. Carroll, 22 June 1944, in "Case History of Ford Engine Plant at River Rouge," reel 2079, AFHRA.

23. WPB *Minutes*, 44; Michael Edelstein, "The Size of the U.S. Armed Forces During World War II: Feasibility and War Planning," *Research in Economic History* 20 (2001): 47–97; Koistinen, *Arsenal of World War II*, 303–7; Jim Lacey, *Keep from All Thoughtful Men: How U.S. Economists Won World War II* (Annapolis, MD: Naval Institute Press, 2011), 40–104.

24. John Morton Blum, ed., *The Price of Vision: The Diary of Henry A. Wallace, 1942–1946* (Boston: Houghton Mifflin, 1973), 119–20; Joel R. Davidson, *The Unsinkable Fleet: The Politics of U.S. Navy Expansion in World War II* (Annapolis, MD: Naval Institute Press, 1996),

51–52; Koistinen, *Arsenal of World War II*, 308–313; Lacey, *Keep from All Thoughtful Men*, 105–16.

25. Krug speech, "Wartime Power Supply," 13 Apr. 1944, folder Midwest Power Conference Speech, box 113, Krug Papers, LOC.

26. Lane, *Ships for Victory*, 174–201; Peter Neushul, "Andrew Jackson Higgins and the Mass Production of World War II Landing Craft," *Louisiana History* 39, no. 2 (1998): 161–63; Stephen B. Adams, *Mr. Kaiser Goes to Washington: The Rise of a Government Entrepreneur* (Chapel Hill: University of North Carolina Press, 1997), 121–22.

27. Harry C. Thompson and Lida Mayo, The *Ordnance Department: Procurement and Supply* (Washington, DC: Office of the Chief of Military History, 1960), 64, 234–38.

28. Charles E. Wilson to Maj. Gen. L. H. Campbell, Jr., 7 Nov. 1942, folder 004.4–1942, box L88, entry 931, RG 156, NARA.

29. Lt. Gen. Jacob L. Devers to Maj. Gen. L. H. Campbell, Jr., 16 Apr. 1943, and Brig. Gen. David G. Barr to Campbell, 20 Apr. 1943, both in box L106, entry 931, RG 156, NARA; R. P. Hunnicutt, *Sherman: A History of the American Medium Tank* (Belmont, CA: Taurus Enterprises, 1978); Nicholas D. Molnar, "The Sherman Paradox: America's Main Battle Tank of WWII in Reality and Postwar Pop Culture, 1940–Present" (M.A. thesis, Rutgers University, 2007).

30. Mortimer Kline to Julius Amberg, 10 June 1942 and A. R. Glancy to Amberg, 19 June 1942, both in folder Guiberson Diesel Engine Co., box 862, entry 154, RG 107; Thompson and Mayo, *Ordnance Department*, 341–43. For more on contract terminations, see Chapter 6.

31. H. H. Gilbert to Brig. Gen. Donald Armstrong, 5 Nov. 1942, box L106, entry 931, RG 156, NARA; H. H. Gilbert to Lt. Col. John Slezak, 30 Sept. 1942 and R. M. Fox to Gen. Christmas, 12 Nov. 1942, both in folder 451.3/33 Medium Tank 1942, box L108, entry 931, RG 156, NARA.

32. C. W. Wright (Pullman-Standard) to Christmas, 30 Mar. 1943, and Del Harder (Fisher) to Christmas, 2 Apr. 1943, both in folder 004.4-Mar.–Apr. 1943, box L88, entry 931, RG 156, NARA.

33. Patterson to Clay, 6 Feb. 1943, and Hugh Fulton memo on ACF, 18 Mar. 1943, both in folder Ordnance-Tanks, box 156, Patterson Papers, LOC; Lubin memo to Hopkins, Byrnes and Baruch, 2 Mar. 1943, folder 4, box 10, Ser. IV, Byrnes Papers.

34. Materials in folder "History of the Quad Cities Tank Arsenal," box 3, RG 156, NARA-GL; "Huge Contract for Tanks Let," *Seattle Daily Times*, 22 Jan. 1942; Karl Keyerleber, "Reconverting Industry After the War," *Cleveland Plain Dealer*, 21 May 1944; "1st Major War Contract Ends," *Seattle Daily Times*, 27 July 1944; "Sales Jump for Apex in '44," *Cleveland Plain Dealer*, 27 Jan. 1945; Thompson and Mayo, *Ordnance Department*, 341–43.

35. Keyerleber, "Reconverting Industry After the War."

36. Allen Drury, *A Senate Journal, 1943–1945* (New York: McGraw Hill, 1963), 82.

37. Maj. Gen. T. J. Hayes to Maj. Gen. J. D. Clay, 15 July 1943, folder 004.4-July–Sept 1943, box L88, entry 931, RG 156, NARA.

38. Thompson and Mayo, *Ordnance Department*, 256–57.

39. Christmas comments in Ordnance Department production planning meeting, 21 Jan. 1942, box L184, entry 936, RG 156, NARA.

40. Pigott to Col. Dean Witte (San Francisco Ordnance District), 6 July 1943, folder 451.3/33 Medium Tank M4 1943, box L108; Christmas memo to OCO-DC, 31 July 1943, folder 004.4-July–Sept. 1943, box L88, both in entry 931, RG 156, NARA.

41. Sorensen to Edsel Ford, 27 Mar. 1943, folder F, box 130; memo on "Termination of Tank Contract," 13 July 1943, folder Letters of Recommendations, box 103, both in Accession 38, Ford Records; Christmas memo to OCO-DC, 28 Sept. 1943, folder 004.4-July–Sept 1943, box L88, entry 931, RG 156, NARA.

42. Transcript of 30 June 1943 Byrnes press conference, box 14, Ser. IV, Byrnes Papers.

43. Minutes of meeting of executive committee on tank tracks, 12 Apr. 1943, folder 4, box 8; "History of the Activities of the Ordnance Department Industry Integration Committee for Tank Tracks," 16 Aug. 1943, box 1, both in RG 156, NARA-GL.

44. Knox to FDR, 9 Sept. 1943; Forrestal to FDR, 21 Sept. 1943, both in folder Navy Dept. 1943, box 7, PSF-FDR; Robert F. Cross, *Shepherds of the Sea: Destroyer Escorts in World War II* (Annapolis, MD: Naval Institute Press, 2010), 67–70; U.S. Navy, *An Administrative History of the Bureau of Ships During World War II: First Draft Narrative* (Washington, DC, [1952]), 2:175 and 4:73–74; Davidson, *Unsinkable Fleet*, 59.

45. Mowry, *Naval and Maritime Shipbuilding Programs*, 10; Peter Neushul, "Science, Technology, and the Arsenal of Democracy: Production Research and Development During World War II" (Ph.D. diss., University of California, Santa Barbara, 1993), 227–31.

46. Robinson memo to Forrestal, 31 July 1942, in U.S. Navy, *Administrative History of the Bureau of Ships*, 2:347–50; Forrestal to Nelson, 17 Jan. 1943, folder Materials—Rubber, Synthetic, box 169, entry 115, RG 80.

47. Bound vol. "Index of Contract Prices, Bureau of Ships," box 221, entry 118, RG 80; William F. Trimble, "Pittsburgh's Dravo Corporation and Naval Shipbuilding in World War II," *American Neptune* 38, no. 4 (Oct. 1978): 282.

48. U.S. Navy, *Administrative History of the Bureau of* Ships, 2:335–52; 3:174; Lane, *Ships for Victory*, 609–12; Trimble, "Pittsburgh's Dravo Corporation," 279–85.

49. Undated Byrnes memo to FDR, ca. 31 Aug. 1943, folder 3, Forrestal to FDR, 21 Sept. 1943, folder 4, both in box 11, Ser. IV, Byrnes Papers; "Index of Contract Prices, Bureau of Ships"; Davidson, *Unsinkable Fleet*, 95–97, 153–56; Thomas Heinrich, "'We Can Build Anything at Navy Yards': Warship Construction in Government Yards and the Political Economy of American Naval Shipbuilding, 1928–1945," *International Journal of Maritime History* 24 (Dec. 2012): 155–80.

50. Among the companies controlled by Western Cartridge was Winchester. In late 1944, Western Cartridge and the Olin Corp. merged, to create Olin Industries.

51. Grant G. Simmons to Carpenter, 4 Aug. 1942, folder 48.1a, box 840, Walter Carpenter Papers, Hagley; "Fight Munitions Lay-Off," *NYT*, 7 Sept. 1944.

52. Campbell, *Industry-Ordnance Team*, 203; Thompson and Mayo, *Ordnance Department*, 218.

53. "CIO Aide Attacks U.S. War Lay-Offs," *NYT*, 28 Feb. 1944; William Sentner to Truman, 29 May 1944, copy in folder 8, box 11, Ser. IV, Byrnes Papers.

54. WPB *Minutes*, 378, 387.

55. "Krug Calls for Doubled Small Arms Bullet Output," *Washington Post*, 25 Nov. 1944, clipping in folder Newspaper Articles, box 113, Krug Papers; "Administration of Cost-Plus-a-Fixed Fee Contracts, for the Operation of Government-Owned, Contractor-Operated Ammunition Plants" (Washington, DC: Office of the Chief of Ordnance, Mar. 1945), copy in folder General Files–General Correspondence (1 of 3), box 4, DPED; Thomas G. Alexander and Leonard J. Arrington, "Utah's Small Arms Ammunition Plant During World War II," *Pacific Historical Review* 34, no. 2 (May 1965): 191–92.

56. Holley, *Buying Aircraft*, 550–54.

57. Mark S. Foster, *Henry J. Kaiser: Builder in the Modern American West* (Austin: University of Texas Press, 1989), 180–84.

58. Joong-Jae Lee, "'We Went to Washington to Raise a Little Hell': Wartime Alternative Unionism of Local 365 of the UAW-CIO and the State, 1939–1945" (Ph.D. diss., New York University, 2000).

59. "Cancels Cutbacks on Wooden Planes," *NYT*, 4 Aug. 1943; "Orders Increase in Superbombers," *NYT*, 11 Aug. 1944; "Higgins Cut Off Again," *New Orleans Times-Picayune*, 11 Aug. 1944.

60. "3,689 NAA Workers Face Layoff Monday," *Dallas Morning News*, 13 Aug. 1944; "What We Did in 1944," *North American Skyline* 6 (Mar.–Apr. 1945): 5; "North American Aviation Inc. Analysis of Performance, 1944 Fiscal Year, Prepared for War Contracts Price Adjustment Board," folder NR1371–07–02, BHA.

61. "Comparison of Sales Forecasts," folder 7, box 53, Sperry Records.

62. "Contractual and Production Problems Encountered in Type K-13 Gun Sight—World War II," folder 13, box 53, Sperry Records.

63. Paul A. C. Koistinen, "The Hammer and the Sword: Labor, the Military, and Industrial Mobilization, 1920–1945" (Ph.D. diss., University of California at Berkeley, 1964), 580. Many histories quote only the first half of the statement, leaving out the reference to high taxes. See, e.g., Richard Polenberg, *War and Society: The United States, 1941–1945* (Philadelphia: J. B. Lippincott, 1972), 12; Richard Overy, *Why the Allies Won* (New York: W. W. Norton, 1995), 198.

64. Joseph J. Thorndike, *Their Fair Share: Taxing the Rich in the Age of FDR* (Washington, DC: Urban Institute Press, 2013), 224–65.

65. CPA, *Industrial Mobilization for War*, 25; Jacob A. Vander Meulen, *The Politics of Aircraft: Building an American Military Industry* (Lawrence: University Press of Kansas, 1991), 202; James F. Nagle, *A History of Government Contracting*, 2nd ed. (Washington, DC: George Washington University, 1999), 401–3.

66. Robert Dallek, *Franklin D. Roosevelt and American Foreign Policy, 1932–1945* (New York: Oxford University Press, 1979), 224; Rockoff, *America's Economic Way of War*, 166.

67. Morgenthau to "Missy" LeHand, 29 June 1940, folder Morgenthau May–June 1940, box 79, PSF-FDR; *Excess Profits Taxation, 1940: Joint Hearings* (Washington, DC: GPO, 1940), 87.

68. *Second Revenue Act of 1940: Hearings Before the Committee on Finance* (Washington, DC: GPO, 1940), 267, 303.

69. P. W. Conrad to Wallace Donham, 24 July 1940, folder P. W. Conrad, box 1, National Defense Course Materials, accession AA940.58, Harvard Business School Archives, Baker Library, Boston.

70. Campbell notes, 11 Oct. 1941, box 13H2, entry 636, RG 156, NARA.

71. J. K. Lasser, "What the New Excess Profits Tax Requires and Permits," *Dun's Review* (Dec. 1940): 18–24; see also Mark R. Wilson, "The Advantages of Obscurity: World War II Tax Carryback Provisions and the Normalization of Corporate Welfare," in *What's Good for Business: Business and American Politics Since World War II*, ed. Kim Phillips-Fein and Julian Zelizer (New York: Oxford University Press, 2012), 20.

72. James T. Sparrow, *Warfare State: World War II Americans and the Age of Big Government* (New York: Oxford University Press, 2012), 62.

73. Michael Stephen Czaplicki, "The Corruption of Hope: Political Scandal, Congressional Investigations, and New Deal Moral Authority, 1932–1952" (Ph.D. diss., University of Chicago, 2010), 272.

74. *The Papers of Robert A. Taft*, vol. 2: *1939–1944*, ed. Clarence E. Wunderlin (Kent, OH: Kent State University Press, 2001), 334.

75. Thorndike, *Their Fair Share*, 228.

76. "New Hope for Business," *Time* (26 Oct. 1942): 88–90; Keith Hutchison, "Everybody's Business: A Tax Victory for Business," *Nation* (31 Oct. 1942): 450–51; Randolph E. Paul, "Corporation Taxes and the Wartime Tax Structure," *Dun's Review* (July 1943): 11–15, 31–36; Herbert Bratter, "Tax Relief When Figures Fail," *Nation's Business* 32 (Aug. 1944): 27, 85–87; Wilson, "Advantages of Obscurity," 26–29.

77. *Excess-Profits Tax Special Amortization House Bill HR 10413* (Washington, DC: Chamber of Commerce of the USA, Finance Dept., 1940), copy in box 15, Ser. II, Chamber Records; *Second Revenue Act of 1940: Hearings Before the Committee on Finance*, 111–14, 232–37, 358–60; *Excess Profits Taxation, 1940: Joint Hearings*, 119–26, 414–15.

78. *Revenue Act of 1942: Hearings Before the Committee on Finance* (Washington, DC: GPO, 1942), 1963–64.

79. E.g., *Lincoln Electric Co. v. Commissioner of Internal Revenue*, 162 F. 2nd 379 (1947); *Eitel-McCullough, Inc. v. Commissioner of Internal Revenue*, 9 T.C. 1132 (1947).

80. Joseph M. Weresch, "A Girl with a Grip of Steel," *Nation's Business* 29 (Aug. 1941): 44–46, 56–57; Carolyn C. Jones, "Vivien Kellems and the Folkways of Taxation," in *Total War and the Law*, ed. Ernst and Jew, 121–48; Olivier Burtin, "'The One-Woman Army': Vivien Kellems and American Conservatism, 1896–1975" (M.A. thesis, Sciences Po, 2011), 49, 61–72; Romain Huret, *American Tax Resisters* (Cambridge, MA: Harvard University Press, 2014), 181–207.

81. Andrew H. Bartels, "The Office of Price Administration and the Legacy of the New Deal," *Public Historian* 5, no. 3 (summer 1983): 5–29; Keehn and Smiley, "Small Business Reactions to World War II Government Controls"; Meg Jacobs, "'How About Some Meat?': The Office of Price Administration, Consumption Politics, and State Building from the Bottom Up, 1941–1946," *Journal of American History* 84, no. 3 (Dec. 1997): 910–41; Deutsch, *Building a Housewife's Paradise*, 157–81; Rockoff, *America's Economic Way of War*, 174–80.

82. Eiler, *Mobilizing America*, 313.

83. Report on meeting of Ordnance District Chiefs, 11 Oct. 1939, box 41, entry 644, RG 156, NARA.

84. "Army Service Forces Manual M601: Pricing in War Contracts," 2 Aug. 1943; "Army Service Forces Manual M609: Company Pricing," 30 Oct. 1944, copies in folder ASF Procurement Conference, Chicago, box 116, Patterson Papers, LOC.

85. Glancy to Brig Gen. H. R. Kutz, 29 Oct. 1942, folder Office of Chief of Ordnance Correspondence, box L73, entry 930, RG 156, NARA.

86. Materials in box 1, entry 3430 (Papers of Brig. Gen. John K. Christmas), RG 200.

87. Sketches of officers' careers may be found in the *Official Army Register* (Washington, DC: Office of the Adjutant General, 1944–45). Army Industrial College graduates are listed by graduating class in the *1995 ICAF Directory* (Washington, DC: Industrial College of the Armed Forces, 1995), 9–17. I thank Scott Gower, of the National Defense University Library, for providing me with this reference.

88. Col. P. Schneeberger to Lt. Col. F. M. Hopkins, 26 July 1941, copy in "Case History of the Expansion of Facilities for the Production of Magnesium Metal," reel 33011, AFHRA.

89. Vander Meulen, *Politics of Aircraft*, 213, 266.

90. H. H. Arnold to Louis Johnson, 22 Mar. 1940, folder Aircraft Expansion—Memoranda to Johnson, box 34, Johnson Papers.

91. P. G. Johnson memo to Boeing Aircraft Co., 29 Mar. 1940, folder 3, box 2357, BHA.

92. "Case History of the Boeing Aircraft Company, Seattle, Washington," reel 2077, AFHRA.

93. Zimmerman, "Procurement in the United States Air Force, 1938–1948, vol. 1."

94. Transcript of telephone call between Symington and Maj. Burnside, 8 Dec. 1941; Symington to Lt. Col. D. C. Swatland, 12 Sept. 1942; Symington to Col. McGrath, 10 Aug 1944; Symington to Gen. K. B. Wolfe, 12 Aug. 1944, all in "Case History of Emerson Electric Manufacturing Co.," reel A2078, AFHRA.

95. Col. John W. N. Schulz to assistant secretary of war, 16 July 1940, folder Smokeless Powder, box 79, Johnson Papers.

96. "Statement Showing Amount of Fixed Fees Paid to Du Pont Company as of September 30, 1941 Under Terms of Contract," folder 5.0, box 830, Walter Carpenter Papers, Hagley.

97. "Reduction of Fees Under U.S. Government Contracts," Finance Committee memo, 21 Apr. 1942, folder Smokeless Powder—Gen'l Correspondence (2 of 2), box 5, DPED.

98. Campbell notes, 16 Jan. 1941, box 13G1, entry 636, RG 156, NARA; F. W. Bradway memo, "Fees and Overhead—Defense Plants," 13 Oct. 1941; E. B. Yancey memo, "U.S. Government Contracts: All Ordnance Plants and Ammonia," 15 Feb. 1943, folder Govt. Contracts (2 of 5); F. W. Bradway memo on explosives plants fees, 28 Apr. 1944, folder Govt. Contracts (5 of 5), all in box 2, DPED.

99. W. Browne Baker memo, 18 May 1943, folder Procurement and Material, box 174, entry 115, RG 80.

100. Summary of negotiations of first 5½ months at Aviation Supply Office, Naval Aircraft Factory, in box 6, Mark E. Andrews Papers, TPL.

101. Morgan Adams, "Summary of Negotiations Completed 1 Jan. 1944 to 31 Mar. 1944," 11 Apr. 1944, folder Contracts, box 165, entry 115, RG 80.

102. Memo on carrier order, 9 Dec. 1944, folder New York Shipbuilding, box 12, Andrews Papers.

103. Board of Contract Control meeting minutes, 17 July 1942, folder 334.8/4, box L3, entry 923; transcript of 1 Feb. 1943 meeting on Ford-Narragansett Machine Co. cancellation negotiations, folder Misc., box L72, entry 930, both in RG 156, NARA.

104. The following overview of renegotiation is based on Mark R. Wilson, "'Taking a Nickel Out of the Cash Register': Statutory Renegotiation of Military Contracts and the Politics of Profit Control in the United States During World War II," *Law and History Review* 28, no. 2 (May 2010): 343–83. That article contains comprehensive citations to the relevant primary and secondary sources. Among the latter are Richards C. Osborn, *The Renegotiation of War Profits* (Urbana: University of Illinois Press, 1948); John Perry Miller, *Pricing of Military Procurements* (New Haven, CT: Yale University Press, 1949).

105. *U.S. v. Bethlehem Steel Corp.*, 315 U.S. 289 (1942); *Investigation of the National Defense Program: Hearings Before the Committee on Naval Affairs, House of Representatives*, 77th Cong., 2nd Sess. (Washington, DC: GPO, 1942), 1:1–112; "Jack Pot," *Newsweek* (6 Apr.

1942): 48–51; Joseph Melia to Ferdinand Kuhn, Jr., 27 Mar. 1942, folder Morgenthau–Editorial Opinion Reports, Mar.–May 1942, box 81, PSF-FDR; Nicholas Parrillo, "'The Government at the Mercy of Its Contractors': How the New Deal Lawyers Reshaped the Common Law to Challenge the Defense Industry in World War II," *Hastings Law Journal* 57 (2005): 93–197.

106. NDAC *Minutes*, 110.

107. Board of Directors minutes, 18 Feb. 1942, in unboxed folder Douglas Board minutes, 1940–45, BHA; Charles Detmer to Forrestal, 27 Mar. 1942, binder "Com Plants," box 162, entry 114, RG 80; "Letter to Secretaries Knox and Stimson from Thomas A. Morgan," 27 Apr. 1942, box 17, Sperry Records.

108. Herbert Merillat to Ferdinand Kuhn, Jr., 26 Sept. 1941 and 3 Oct. 1941, folder Morgenthau–Editorial Opinion Reports, Aug.–Nov. 1941, box 80, PSF-FDR.

109. Wilson, "'Taking a Nickel Out of the Cash Register,'" 352–60.

110. E.g., B. F. Goodrich Co., "A Statement to the Army Price Adjustment Board Ordnance Division," 1942, box M1, B. F. Goodrich Records, University of Akron Special Collections Library; "General Motors Corporation, Report to War Department Price Adjustment Board," Sept. 1943, box 3, F. Donaldson Brown Papers, accession 1334, Hagley; "Boeing's Contribution to the War Effort—1943," unboxed folder 1750/1, BHA; bound report, "North American Aviation Inc. Analysis of Performance, 1944 Fiscal Year, Prepared for War Contracts Price Adjustment Board," folder NR1371–07–02, BHA.

111. "The Trading Post: Small Business and Renegotiation," *Business Week* (13 Feb. 1943): 107.

112. John T. Flynn, "Cost-Plus and Red Tape Hamper War Production," *Reader's Digest* 41 (Oct. 1942): 108–9; "Renegotiate Renegotiation," *Forbes* 52 (15 Nov. 1943): 9; "Dictatorship over United States Industry Under Public Law 528," copy in folder 5, box 2050, Lukens Steel Corp. Records, Hagley; A. B. Echols to Walter Carpenter, 19 May 1943, folder 48.7, box 840, Walter Carpenter Papers; Wilson, "'Taking a Nickel Out of the Cash Register,'" 360–77.

113. Wilson, "'Taking a Nickel Out of the Cash Register,'" 343–73. On Hawley's career, see Carol Pine, *Follow Me: The Life of John B. Hawley* (St. Cloud, MN: North Star, 2007).

114. Truman to J. B. Cronheim, 11 Jan. 1944, folder Renegotiation, box 158, Truman Senatorial File, TPL.

115. Typescript timeline and tables, "Edward G. Budd Manufacturing Company," 23 Aug. 1943, Folder E. G. Budd Manuf. Co., box 153, entry 113, RG 80; Edward G. Budd to Truman, 14 Apr. 1944, box 121, Truman Senatorial File, TPL.

116. *Lord Manufacturing Co. v. United States*, 114 Ct. Cl. 199 (1949); Zimmerman, "Procurement in the United States Air Force, 1938–1948, vol. 1."

117. Minutes of Division Chiefs Conference, 2 Feb. 1945, Folder Staff Meetings, June 1944–Nov. 1945, box 9, RG 156, NARA-GL.

118. Holley, *Buying Aircraft*, 345.

119. Lenore Fine and Jesse A. Remington, *Corps of Engineers: Construction in the United States* (Washington, DC: Office of the Chief of Military History, 1972), 568–69; Holley, *Buying Aircraft*, 411–16.

120. Sparrow, *From the Outside In*, 177; Trimble, "Pittsburgh's Dravo Corporation," 285.

121. Forrestal to James F. Byrnes, 8 Sept. 1943, file Byrnes, box 182, entry 116, RG 80; Robert H. Connery, *The Navy and Industrial Mobilization in World War II* (Princeton, NJ: Princeton University Press, 1951), 218.

122. Sparrow, *From the Outside In*, 179.

123. Lt. Commander H. L. Kempner to Forrestal, 11 Mar. 1944, folder Contracts, box 165, entry 115, RG 80.

124. Morgan Adams to Forrestal, 7 Mar. 1944, folder Contracts, box 165, entry 115, RG 80.

125. Memos of 17 May 1944 and 7 Feb. 1945, folder Dravo Corp—LSTs, box 7, Andrews Papers.

126. Lane, *Ships for Victory*, 119–25; Peter Thompson, "How Much Did the Liberty Shipbuilders Learn? New Evidence for an Old Case Study," *Journal of Political Economy* 109, no. 1 (2001): 116–17.

127. Brig. Gen. A. B. Quinton, Jr., "The Procurement of Army Ordnance," 21 Feb. 1946, AIC/ICAF presentation, AIC/ICAF Archives, NDU; Campbell, *Industry-Ordnance Team*, 413; R. Elberton Smith, *The Army and Economic Mobilization* (Washington, DC: GPO, 1959), 343–50; Connery, *Navy and Industrial Mobilization*, 243–65; Miller, *Pricing of Military Procurements*, 188–201; Holley, *Buying Aircraft*, 441–43.

128. Remarks by J. F. Oates, Jr., in transcript of Detroit Ordnance District "Purchase Policy Meeting," 3 Nov. 1943, folder 1, box 9, RG 156, NARA-GL.

129. Boeing press release, 24 Dec. 1943, unboxed folder 1231/19, BHA; Holley, *Buying Aircraft*, 560; Charles John McCann, "Labor and the Making of the Postwar Order at the Boeing Company" (Ph.D. diss., University of Oregon, 1994), 46, 58.

130. Bound report, "North American Aviation, Inc.: Statement of Performance, 1943 Fiscal Year," folder NR 1371–07–01; Board of Directors Meeting Minutes, 11 Feb. 1944 and 28 July 1944, bound vol. North American Aviation Board Minutes, 1943–45, both in BHA.

131. Vol. "Index of Contract Prices, Bureau of Aeronautics," box 222, entry 118, RG 80.

132. Thompson, "How Much Did the Liberty Shipbuilders Learn?," 106–8.

133. Lane, *Ships for Victory*, 122; U.S. House, Committee on Merchant Marine and Fisheries, *Investigation of Shipyard Profits* (Washington, DC: GPO, 1946), 525.

134. E. S. Duffield memo to file, 6 Dec. 1943, folder Escort Vessels, box 175, entry 115, RG 80.

135. Helen Fuller, "The Rich Get Richer," *New Republic* (20 Sept. 1943): 383.

136. "The Outlook for Corporation Profits," *NAM News* (3 Oct. 1942): 10.

137. F. G. Donner to Maurice Karker, 20 Jan. 1943, folder 33c, box 837, Walter Carpenter Papers.

138. Frederick C. Crawford, *What's Behind the Hue and Cry About Profits* (NAM, 1944), 3–11, copy in box 3, Joseph M. Dodge Papers, Detroit Public Library.

139. " 'Huge War Profits' Mythical," *Forbes* 55 (15 Feb. 1945): 12. See also "War Profits Lean," *Forbes* 54 (1 Oct. 1944): 10; "Fixed Profits," *Nation's Business* 34 (Apr. 1946): 9.

140. Standard & Poor, "Earnings and Dividends During and After the War, Study Number One: General Motors Corporation," copy in folder 33c, box 837, Walter Carpenter Papers.

141. "General Motors Corporation, Report to War Department Price Adjustment Board," Sept. 1943, box 3, F. Donaldson Brown Papers, accession 1334, Hagley; Donaldson Brown to Carpenter, 3 Nov. 1943, folder 33c, box 837, Walter Carpenter Papers.

142. Ralph W. Carney, "Business Goes to War," *VSD* 10, no. 17 (15 June 1944): 535–36.

143. *Historical Statistics of the United States, Colonial Times to 1957* (Washington, DC: U.S. Dept. of Commerce, 1960), 580.

144. In 2012–15, the ratio of after-tax corporate profits to GDP averaged around 10 percent. See data publicized by the St. Louis Fed: https://research.stlouisfed.org (accessed October 2015).

145. For questions about whether the wartime GDP increases translated into any real improvement in the living standards of Americans, see Robert Higgs, "Wartime Prosperity? A Reassessment of the U.S. Economy in the 1940s," *Journal of Economic History* 52, no. 1 (Mar. 1992): 41–60.

146. A similar conclusion is reached by Sparrow, *From the Outside In*, 240–42, and by Fred R. Kaen, "World War II Prime Defence Contractors: Were They Favoured?," *Business History* 53, no. 7 (Dec. 2011): 1046–47.

147. David A. Hounshell and John Kenly Smith, Jr., *Science and Corporate Strategy: Du Pont R&D, 1902–1980* (New York: Cambridge University Press, 1988), 602; Charles W. Cheape, *Strictly Business: Walter Carpenter at Du Pont and General Motors* (Baltimore: Johns Hopkins University Press, 1995), 187, 217, 227.

148. David O. Woodbury, *Battlefronts of Industry: Westinghouse in World War II* (New York: John Wiley, 1948), 331. Many companies in the oil industry, which had performed well in the 1930s and was only semi-mobilized for military production, enjoyed relatively high wartime profits. E.g., Humble Oil, a subsidiary of Standard–New Jersey, saw net earnings grow from $30 million in 1939 to $60 million in 1944. After a stock split in 1943, investors enjoyed an increase in dividends in 1944–45. Henrietta M. Larson and Kenneth Wiggins Porter, *History of Humble Oil & Refining Company* (1959; New York: Arno, 1976), 610, 687.

149. Gene Duffield to Forrestal, 5 Jan. 1944, and tables prepared by Kenneth H. Rockey, 10 Jan. 1944, both in folder Bethlehem Steel, box 152, entry 113, RG 80.

150. Lane, *Ships for Victory*, 810–11; Sparrow, *From the Outside In*, 240–42; "Draft Statement," folder Government Investigations, box 8, Sun Shipbuilding and Dry Dock Co. Records, accession 1718, Hagley.

151. Reynolds Metals Co., annual reports, 1942–44, boxes 37, 39, and 53; Richard S. Reynolds, Sr. to Sen. Lister Hill, 16 Mar. 1942, folder Senator Lister Hill, box 29; Reynolds to Hill, 3 Apr. 1943, folder New Extrusion Plant, box 36; R. S. Reynolds, Sr. to Jesse Jones, 24 Oct. 1944, folder Hugh Fulton, box 50, all in Reynolds Papers.

152. On the improved financial positions of top producers of warships and tanks, see Ralph L. Snow, *Bath Iron Works: The First Hundred Years* (Bath: Maine Maritime Museum, 1987), 317, 335, 415; Herbert Corey, "Baldwin Locomotive Steams Up," *Nation's Business* 33 (Apr. 1945): 88.

153. Raymond L. Hoadley, "Sound Financial Status Braces Industry Readjustment," *Aviation* 45 (June 1946): 42–43.

154. Sparrow, *From the Outside In*, 241; Kaen, "World War II Prime Defence Contractors," 1044–73.

155. George H. Gallup, *The Gallup Poll: Public Opinion, 1935–1971* (New York: Random House, 1972), 1:674.

Chapter 5

1. Roy P. Seymour to Eleanor Roosevelt, 8 Mar. 1945; Eleanor Roosevelt to FDR, 17 Mar. 1945, both in folder 1, box 12, Ser. IV, Byrnes Papers.

2. Christopher L. Tomlins, *The State and the Unions: Labor Relations, Law, and the Organized Labor Movement in America, 1880–1960* (New York: Cambridge University Press, 1985), 157, 188; Howell John Harris, *The Right to Manage: Industrial Relations Policies of American Business in the 1940s* (Madison: University of Wisconsin Press, 1982), 37–40; James T. Patterson, *Grand Expectations: The United States, 1945–1974* (New York: Oxford University Press, 1996), 40–46. Among more recent works covering the World War II period, see Jean-Christian Vinel, *The Employee: A Political History* (Philadelphia: University of Pennsylvania Press, 2013); and Sophia Z. Lee, *The Workplace Constitution from the New Deal to the New Right* (New York: Cambridge University Press, 2014).

3. Nelson Lichtenstein, "Class Politics and the State During World War II," *International Labor and Working Class History* 58 (fall 2000): 261–74; idem, *Labor's War at Home: The CIO in World War II* (1982 ed.; Philadelphia: Temple University Press, 2003); James Atleson, *Labor and the Wartime State: Labor Relations and Law During World War II* (Urbana: University of Illinois Press, 1998); Andrew E. Kersten, *Labor's Home Front: The American Federation of Labor During World War II* (New York: New York University Press, 2009).

4. Robert B. Lea memo, 29 May 1956 [*sic*], folder 8, box 53, Sperry Records; N. P. Wescott, report to Du Pont exec. committee on "Possible Segregation of Military Business," 24 Aug. 1939, folder Munitions Exports and Technical Assistance, box 2, DPED.

5. James A. Hagerty, "Willkie Assails Plant-Seizure Plan as a Step to 'Sovietize' All Industry," *NYT*, 30 Aug. 1940; Hagerty, "Willkie Condemns Plant-Seizing Plan as 'a Cheap Trick,'" *NYT*, 1 Sept. 1940; "Industry Draft Bill Halts Plant Expansion of 'Vast' Scope by Consolidated Aircraft," *NYT*, 3 Sept. 1940.

6. "Upset in Senate Sends Draft Bill Back for Revision," *NYT*, 14 Sept. 1940; "Text of the Selective Service Measure," *NYT*, 15 Sept. 1940; "Patterson Pledges Few Mill Seizures," *NYT*, 19 Sept. 1940.

7. Noel Sargent, "Governmental Labor Policy During World War I," *NAM Labor Relations Bulletin* 35 (Jan. 1941): 9–13; George Wharton Pepper to Pew, 14 Jan. 1941, folder 2, box 84, Pew Presidential Files, Sun Oil Co. Records, Hagley.

8. Andrew Anthony Workman, "Creating the Center: Liberal Intellectuals, the National War Labor Board, and the Stabilization of American Industrial Relations, 1941–1945" (Ph.D. diss., University of North Carolina at Chapel Hill, 1993), 14–15.

9. Edward McGrady memo on defense strikes, ca. 8 Mar. 1941, folder Strikes, box 165, PSF-FDR; Joel Seidman, *American Labor from Defense to Reconversion* (Chicago: University of Chicago Press, 1953), 44; Steven Fraser, *Labor Will Rule: Sidney Hillman and the Rise of American Labor* (New York: Free Press, 1991), 460–64; Charles John McCann, "Labor and the Making of the Postwar Order at the Boeing Company" (Ph.D. diss., University of Oregon, 1994), 173–286; Lichtenstein, *Labor's War at Home*, 46; Paul A. C. Koistinen, *Arsenal of World War II: The Political Economy of American Warfare, 1940–1945* (Lawrence: University Press of Kansas, 2004), 161; Byron Fairchild and Jonathan Grossman, *The Army and Industrial Manpower* (Washington, DC: Office of the Chief of Military History, 1959), 58–66.

10. Stephen Meyer, *"Stalin over Wisconsin": The Making and Unmaking of Militant Unionism, 1900–1950* (New Brunswick, NJ: Rutgers University Press, 1992), 84–103; Lichtenstein, *Labor's War at Home*, 49–50; Richard L. Pifer, *A City at War: Milwaukee Labor During World War II* (Madison: Wisconsin Historical Society Press, 2003), xvii–11, 117–18.

11. Styles Bridges, "This Is Our Enemy," *Forbes* (1 Apr. 1941): 12; Stettinius notes on telephone conversation with Benjamin Fairless, 26 Mar. 1941, folder Calendar Notes 1940–41,

box 89; Stettinius notes, 19 Mar. 1941, in Record Notes, 9 Jan.–3 June 1941, box 102, both in Stettinius Papers.

12. Edward McGrady memo on defense strikes, ca. 8 Mar. 1941, folder Strikes, box 165, PSF-FDR; William W. Dulles to Forrestal, 11 Mar. 1941, folder Allis-Chalmers, box 151, entry 113, RG 80.

13. Eugene S. Duffield, "U.S. Has Authority to 'Draft' Plants, but Officials Don't Want to Employ It," *WSJ*, 3 Apr. 1941; Paul A. C. Koistinen, "The Hammer and the Sword: Labor, the Military, and Industrial Mobilization, 1920–1945" (Ph.D. diss., University of California, Berkeley, 1965), 113; Workman, "Creating the Center," 21–23; Meyer, *Stalin over Wisconsin*," 100–101.

14. Harold L. Ickes, *The Secret Diary of Harold L. Ickes*, vol. 3: *The Lowering Clouds, 1939–1941* (New York: Simon & Schuster, 1954), 454, 472.

15. Patterson memo, 15 Nov. 1940, folder Award of Contracts, box 7, John H. Ohly Papers, TPL; Fairchild and Grossman, *Army and Industrial Manpower*, 37–43; Ickes, *Lowering Clouds*, 289–90, 315; "Henry Ford and His Ways," *Forbes* (15 Feb. 1941): 11.

16. Workman, "Creating the Center," 38.

17. Allan Nevins and Frank Ernest Hill, *Ford: Decline and Rebirth, 1933–1962* (New York: Charles Scribner's Sons, 1963), 159–67.

18. Research Institute of America, "Your Business Now Belongs to Uncle Sam," *Business and Defense Bulletin* (28 May 1941), copy in folder National Defense 1941, box 236, Joseph C. O'Mahoney Papers, American Heritage Center, Laramie, WY.

19. McCann, "Labor and the Making of the Postwar Order at the Boeing Company," 36–38; John S. Olszowka, "From Shop Floor to Fight: Work & Labor in the Aircraft Industry, 1908–1945" (Ph.D. diss., Binghamton University, State University of New York, 2000), 385–405; Jacob Vander Meulen, "West Coast Labor and the Military Aircraft Industry, 1935–1941," *Pacific Northwest Quarterly* 88, no. 2 (spring 1997): 82–92.

20. James R. Prickett, "Communist Conspiracy or Wage Dispute? The 1941 Strike at North American Aviation," *Pacific Historical Review* 50, no. 2 (May 1981): 219; Paul Shroup to Roger Lapham, 5 June 1941, folder North American Aviation I, box 803, entry 177, RG 160; Olszowka, "From Shop Floor to Fight," 360–366; Workman, "Creating the Center," 19–20; Lichtenstein, *Labor's War at Home*, 56–63.

21. Prickett, "Communist Conspiracy or Wage Dispute?," 223–30; Stimson memo, 10 June 1941, folder North American Aviation II, box 803, entry 177, RG 160.

22. Transcripts of Branshaw phone calls, 8–10 June 1941, folder North American Aviation II, box 803, entry 177, RG 160; John H. Ohly, *Industrialists in Olive Drab: The Emergency Operation of Private Industries During World War II* (Washington, DC: Center of Military History, 1999), 19–37.

23. Transcript of telephone conversation between Branshaw, Lt. Col. Edward S. Greenbaum, and Patterson, 13 June 1941, folder North American Aviation Inc. Strike, box 151, Patterson Papers, LOC.

24. Prickett, "Communist Conspiracy or Wage Dispute?," 231–32.

25. "Airplane Strike Resembles Insurrection, Says Jackson," *Seattle Times*, 10 June 1941; Atleson, *Labor and the Wartime State*, 28; Michael Stephen Czaplicki, "The Corruption of Hope: Political Scandal, Congressional Investigations, and New Deal Moral Authority, 1932–1952" (Ph.D. diss., University of Chicago, 2010), 247–48.

26. "Nationalization in U.S. Held Aim," *Seattle Times*, 10 June 1941; "Settling Future Strikes," *NYT*, 12 June 1941.

27. "Navy to Take Over Strike-Bound Kearny Yards Tomorrow," *Atlanta Constitution*, 24 Aug. 1941, 1; David Palmer, "Organizing the Shipyards: Unionization at New York Ship, Federal Ship, and Fore River, 1898–1945" (Ph.D. diss., Brandeis University, 1990), 531–32, 653–54, 678–708; David Winkler, "The Construction and Manning of the U.S.S. *Atlanta*," draft manuscript paper in author's possession.

28. Palmer, "Organizing the Shipyards," 662–64, 766, 892–97, 930; Winkler, "Construction and Manning," 17.

29. Workman, "Creating the Center," 69–74.

30. Walter Johnson and Carol Evans, eds., *The Papers of Adlai E. Stevenson*, vol. 2: *Washington to Springfield, 1941–1948* (Boston: Little, Brown, 1973), 9–12; Palmer, "Organizing the Shipyards," 678–708; Winkler, "Construction and Manning," 23–27.

31. Harold G. Bowen, *Ships, Machinery and Mossbacks: The Autobiography of a Naval Engineer* (Princeton, NJ: Princeton University Press, 1954), 3–144.

32. Stevenson memos to Knox and Forrestal, 16 Aug. 1941 and 4 Sept. 1941, folder Federal Shipbuilding and Dry Dock Co., box 155, entry 113, RG 80.

33. "A Challenge to Sovereignty," *WSJ*, 26 Aug. 1941; "Using the Emergency," *WSJ*, 27 Aug. 1941; "Some Unanswered Questions," *WSJ*, 10 Sept. 1941; "Union Terms Met by Navy at Kearny," *NYT*, 18 Sept. 1941; Foster Hailey, "Kearny Shipyard Hums for Navy," *NYT*, 4 Oct. 1941; "Federal Shipbuilding: Whose Is It?," *Fortune* (Jan. 1942): 138–39; Bowen, *Ships, Machinery and Mossbacks*, 208–22.

34. W. H. Lawrence, "Navy Turns Back Kearny Shipyard," *NYT*, 7 Jan. 1942; "Asks 'All-Out' U.S. Effort," *NYT*, 28 Oct. 1941; Bowen, *Ships, Machinery and Mossbacks*, 217–22.

35. "Fuller Raps U.S. Labor Policy," *WSJ*, 2 Sept. 1941; "The Government Is Cornered," *WSJ*, 8 Nov. 1941.

36. "Findings and Recommendations," NDMB Case #51, 9 Oct. 1941, copy in folder Air Associates, box 777, entry 177, RG 160; "President Asked by Union to Seize Plant at Bendix," *NYT*, 21 July 1941.

37. Ohly memo on "Air Associates Company," 19 Oct. 1941; Ohly to Patterson, 24 Oct. 1941; and summary of Nunn 02:30 phone call to Ohly, all in folder Air Associates, box 777, entry 177, RG 160; Ohly, *Industrialists in Olive Drab*, 40–42.

38. Ohly to Patterson, 3 Dec. 1941, folder Air Associates, box 777, entry 177, RG 160; Ohly, *Industrialists in Olive Drab*, 42–44; "Aircraft Plant Reopens with 2,100 on Guard," *Atlanta Constitution*, 1 Nov. 1941.

39. "Fire the Boss?," *Time* (3 Nov. 1941): 14–15; "No. 3," *Time* (10 Nov. 1941): 20–21; "Coburn Made Head of Air Associates," *NYT*, 27 Nov. 1941; Ohly, *Industrialists in Olive Drab*, 46–51.

40. War Dept. press release, 16 Nov. 1941; Ohly memo, 8 Nov. 1941, folder Air Associates, both in box 777, entry 177, RG 160.

41. "Progress of the Week: Labor Trouble Remains the Most Serious Problem Facing the Defense Program," *WSJ*, 3 Nov. 1941; "By What Authority of Law?," *WSJ*, 21 Nov. 1941; "Some Aspects of the Current Labor Situation," enclosure in Walter D. Fuller to O'Mahoney, 28 Nov. 1941, folder Strikes 1941, box 255, O'Mahoney Papers.

42. "NAM Asks Better Aid from Labor, Government to Speed Defense," *WSJ*, 4 Dec. 1941; "N.A.M. Demands Defense Be Put Under One Head," *NYT*, 5 Dec. 1941; "Industry

Hears Call to Defend Free Enterprise," *NYT*, 6 Dec. 1941; *The Papers of Robert A. Taft*, vol. 2: *1939–1944*, ed. Clarence E. Wunderlin (Kent, OH: Kent State University Press, 2001), 310.

43. "Back to Owners," *Business Week* (3 Jan. 1942): 49–50; Ohly memo to file, 17 Dec. 1941; Ohly to Patterson, 25 Mar. 1942; and Ohly to Amberg, 3 July 1942, all in folder Air Associates, box 777, entry 177, RG 160.

44. *The Termination Report of the National War Labor Board: Industrial Disputes and Wage Stabilization in Wartime, January 12, 1942–December 31, 1945* (Washington, DC: GPO, 1946), 3: 169–73; Workman, "Creating the Center," 150–55; Palmer, "Organizing the Shipyards," 751–57.

45. Workman, "Creating the Center," 156–58.

46. Atleson, *Labor and the Wartime State*, 104–6.

47. Joshua B. Freeman, *In Transit: The Transport Workers Union in New York City, 1933–1966* (New York: Oxford University Press, 1989), 257; Atleson, *Labor and the Wartime State*, 119; Davis testimony in *Investigation of the Seizure of Montgomery Ward & Co.: Hearings Before the Select Committee* (Washington, DC: GPO, 1944), 73; "Americans Want Victory . . . Not the Closed Shop," *NAM Newsletter* (18 Apr. 1942): 10.

48. Roughly 5 million person-days were lost because of strikes in 1942, compared with 23 million person-days in 1941, 13 million in 1943, and 9 million in 1944. Fairchild and Grossman, *Army and Industrial Manpower*, 63.

49. J. Carlyle Sitterson, *Aircraft Production Policies Under the National Defense Advisory Commission and the Office of Production Management, May 1940 to December 1941* (Washington, DC: CPA, 1946), 152–54; Vander Meulen, "West Coast Labor and the Military Aircraft Industry, 1935–1941," 82–89.

50. "The No. 1 Bottleneck Now Is Lack of Ships," *Fortune* 25 (May 1942): 166; *United States v. Savannah Shipyards, Inc.*, 139 F. 2d 953 (1944); Lane, *Ships for Victory*, 155–58, 493–535; Tony Cope, *On the Swing Shift: Building Liberty Ships in Savannah* (Annapolis, MD: Naval Institute Press, 2009), 23–66.

51. U.S. House Committee on Naval Affairs, *Investigation of the Progress of the War Effort*, vol. 4: *Brewster Investigation* (Washington, DC: GPO, 1944); Joong-Jae Lee, "'We Went to Washington to Raise a Little Hell': Wartime Alternative Unionism of Local 365 of the UAW-CIO and the State, 1939–1945" (Ph.D. diss., New York University, 2000), 55–57, 82–92, 119–25.

52. Forrestal to Capt. George C. Westervelt, 23 Apr. 1942, folder Brewster Aero Corp, box 152, entry 113, RG 80; U.S. House Committee on Naval Affairs, *Investigation of the Progress of the War Effort: Hearings Before a Subcommittee Appointed to Investigate Causes of Failures of Production of Brewster Aeronautical Corporation . . .* (Washington, DC: GPO, 1943), 2188.

53. Lee, "'We Went to Washington,'" 213–88.

54. "Triumph's Tribulations," *Fortune* (Mar. 1944): 20, 30, 44; "Convicted Man a Suicide," *NYT*, 6 Apr. 1944, 24; *Decker v. U.S.*, 140 F. 2d 378 (1944); *Decker v. U.S.*, 321 U.S. 792 (1944); *Kann v. U.S.*, 323 U.S. 88 (1944).

55. "Navy Seizes Plant of Remington Rand," *NYT*, 30 Nov. 1943; Bowen, *Ships, Machinery and Mossbacks*, 235–45.

56. Bowen, *Ships, Machinery and Mossbacks*, 252–77.

57. John L. Blackman, Jr., "Navy Policy Toward the Labor Relations of Its War Contractors—Part II," *Military Affairs* 19, no. 1 (spring 1955): 21–31.

58. "F.D.R. Orders Seizure of York Lock Company," *Atlanta Constitution*, 25 Jan. 1944; "York Safe Plant Seized," *NYT*, 1 Feb. 1944.

59. "Featherbedridden McNear," *Time* (18 May 1942): 82–84; Seidman, *American Labor from Defense to Reconversion*, 146.

60. "Head of Railroad, Hit by Strike, Slain," *NYT*, 11 Mar. 1947.

61. "Firm Protests Occupation of Two Plants," *Atlanta Constitution*, 21 Aug. 1942; *To Investigate Executive Agencies: Hearings Before the Special Committee to Investigate Executive Agencies, House of Representatives*, 78th Cong., Part 2 (Washington, DC: GPO, 1944), 1551–624; NWLB, *Termination Report*, 2:700; Ohly, *Industrialists in Olive Drab*, 67–83.

62. "Navy Turns Back Plant in Bayonne," *NYT*, 21 Aug. 1942, 9; Bowen, *Ships, Machinery and Mossbacks*, 223–29.

63. "Witherow Protests Plant Confiscation as Method to Make Labor Behave," *NAM News* (15 Aug. 1942): 10; "W.L.B. Needs a Rule Book," *WSJ*, 20 Aug. 1942.

64. NWLB, *Termination Report*, 1:xv, xxviii. On Taylor and the work of the NWLB, see Ronald W. Schatz, " 'Industrial Peace Through Arbitration': George Taylor and the Genius of the War Labor Board," *Labor: Studies in the Working-Class History of the Americas* 11, no. 4 (2014): 39–62.

65. Forrestal to W. C. Buchanan, 16 Jan. 1942, folder Allis-Chalmers, box 151, entry 113, RG 80; Umstattd testimony, 10 Dec. 1943, in *To Investigate Executive Agencies*, Part 2, 1721–23. Sometimes the threat of seizure worked in favor of the companies. In Dec. 1943, a mid-level NWLB mediator considered a giant Wright Aeronautical plant in New Jersey, where the leaders of a UAW local wanted the company to remove a supervisor whom they regarded as arrogant and disruptive. Deciding against the union, the arbitrator referred to the seizure threat. "When an industry breaks down and the Government takes it over under its war powers," Young B. Smith wrote, "it is the management who is removed. This is because it is management who is responsible for results. This being so, the management should be free to manage." *Wright Aeronautical Corp.*, 1 Lab. Arb. Rep. 79 (1943).

66. Koistinen, "Hammer and the Sword," 118–19; Melvyn Dubofsky and Warren Van Tine, *John L. Lewis: A Biography* (New York: Quadrangle, 1977), 378–413; Workman, "Creating the Center," 60–62, 73–86; Ickes, *Lowering Clouds*, 489, 642–43.

67. Workman, "Creating the Center," 188–89.

68. Polenberg, *War and Society*, 160; Harris, *Right to Manage*, 47.

69. Ickes, draft typescript chapter, "John L. Lewis & Coal Confrontation 1943," Ickes Unpublished Cabinet Memoirs, Biographical Memoirs and Sketches, reel 5, Harold L. Ickes Papers, LOC; Ickes Diaries, 48:7829–34, 7928, reel 6.

70. Ickes Diaries, 49:8034; and 50:8211, 8263, 8275, 8918, 9018, reel 6. Dubofsky and Van Tine, *John L. Lewis*, 438–39; Lichtenstein, *Labor's War at Home*, 159–70; Workman, "Creating the Center," 261–68; T. H. Watkins, *Righteous Pilgrim: The Life and Times of Harold L. Ickes, 1874–1952* (New York: Henry Holt, 1990), 754–59; John William Partin, " 'Assistant President' for the Home Front: James F. Byrnes and World War II" (Ph.D. diss., University of Florida, 1977), 179–82.

71. "The *Fortune* Survey," *Fortune* 25 (Feb. 1942): 98; Ickes Diaries 42:6416, reel 5; Richard Polenberg, *War and Society: The United States, 1941–1945* (Philadelphia; J. B. Lippincott, 1972), 166; Melvyn Dubofsky, *The State & Labor in Modern America* (Chapel Hill: University of North Carolina Press, 1994), 191; Elizabeth Fones-Wolf, *Waves of Opposition: Labor*

and the Struggle for Democratic Radio (Urbana: University of Illinois Press, 2006), 89; James T. Sparrow, *Warfare State: World War II Americans and the Age of Big Government* (New York: Oxford University Press, 2011), 194–96.

72. "Plant Seizure Bill Revived," *NYT*, 30 Mar. 1943, 10; Ohly, *Industrialists in Olive Drab*, 94–99.

73. "Passage of Connally Bill Reflects Public's Wrath over Labor Strife," *NAM News* (26 June 1943): 1; Raymond S. Smethurst, "The War Labor Disputes Act," presentation at Manpower Stabilization Conference of the American Management Association, 28–30 Sept. 1943, in folder World War II Legislation, box 136, Ser. VII, NAM Records.

74. "The Anti-Strike Bill," *NYT*, 14 June 1943, 16.

75. NWLB, *Termination Report*, 1:423, 2:698; Atleson, *Labor and the Wartime State*, 190. This executive order was evidently used first against a union in 1944 and then again in summer 1945 to punish striking workers at Goodyear. It was employed against a company in Mar. 1945, when E. A. Laboratories, a Brooklyn manufacturer of aircraft accessories, had its military contracts canceled. See Ludwig Teller, "Government Seizure in Labor Disputes," 60 *Harvard Law Review* (1947): 1030–31.

76. "Stimson Seizes 7 Textile Plants," *NYT*, 8 Feb. 1944; "Says Textile Strike Curbs Pacific Plans," *NYT*, 12 Feb. 1944; "Textile Strike Ended," *NYT*, 14 Feb. 1944; Fairchild and Grossman, *Army and Industrial Manpower*, 209–18; Ohly, *Industrialists in Olive Drab*, 113–31, 252–53.

77. Various documents in folder Plant Seizure—Western Electric Co., box 807, entry 177, RG 160; Fairchild and Grossman, *Army and Industrial Manpower*, 161–64; Stephen B. Adams and Orville R. Butler, *Manufacturing the Future: A History of Western Electric* (New York: Cambridge University Press, 1999), 144–47.

78. Detailed accounts of the Philadelphia strike and seizure are provided in Louis Ruchames, *Race, Jobs & Politics: The Story of FEPC* (New York: Columbia University Press, 1953), 100–18; and Allan W. Winkler, "The Philadelphia Transit Strike of 1944," *Journal of American History* 59, no. 1 (June 1972): 73–89. On the broader context, see Ruchames, *Race, Jobs & Politics*; Andrew Edmund Kersten, *Race, Jobs, and the War: The FEPC in the Midwest, 1941–1946* (Urbana: University of Illinois Press, 2000); Bruce Nelson, "Organized Labor and the Struggle for Black Equality in Mobile During World War II," *Journal of American History* 80, no. 3 (Dec. 1993): 952–88; George Lipsitz, *Rainbow at Midnight: Labor and Culture in the 1940s* (Urbana: University of Illinois Press, 1994), 74–78; Clarence Lang, *Grassroots at the Gateway: Class Politics & Black Freedom Struggle in St. Louis, 1936–75* (Ann Arbor: University of Michigan Press, 2009), 44–63.

79. The strike was settled with an agreement for an increase in wages and benefits of nine cents an hour for most workers. See Partin, "Assistant President," 183–97; "Rail Executives Endorse Seizure," *NYT*, 28 Dec. 1943; Ohly, *Industrialists in Olive Drab*, 133–40.

80. "'Taking Over,'" *WSJ*, 29 Dec. 1943; also, "Buying Off Strikes," *NYT*, 29 Dec. 1944; Arthur Krock, "In the Nation: How Railway Labor Situation Got That Way," *NYT*, 7 Jan. 1944; "For a Labor Policy," *NYT*, 8 Jan. 1944.

81. "Seizure Called Unnecessary," *NYT*, 29 Dec. 1944; "Willkie Criticizes Railroad Seizure," *NYT*, 9 Jan. 1944.

82. "Brooklyn Plant Is Seized by U.S.," *NYT*, 4 Sept. 1943; "Land Names Aide to Run Shipyard," *NYT*, 5 Sept. 1943; "Shipyard Bows to WLB," *NYT*, 17 Sept. 1943; "WSA Returns Shipyard," *NYT*, 23 Sept. 1943.

83. "Army, Navy Seize Two War Plants; WLB Pay Raise Orders Are Ignored," *NYT*, 15 Apr. 1944.

84. Col. Hebert memo to Ohly, 10 Apr. 1944, folder Ken-Rad Tube & Lamp Corp., box 797, entry 177, RG 160.

85. Miscellaneous materials in folder Ken-Rad Tube & Lamp Corporation, box 797, entry 177, RG 160; *Ken-Rad Tube & Lamp Co.*, 43 NLRB No. 154 (1942); Ohly, *Industrialists in Olive Drab*, 149–70.

86. *Ken-Rad Tube & Lamp Corp. v. Badeau*, 55 F. Supp. 193 (1944); Fred Whitney, *Wartime Experiences of the National Labor Relations Board, 1941–1945* (Urbana: University of Illinois Press, 1949), 84–85.

87. Ohly, *Industrialists in Olive Drab*, 163.

88. Polenberg, *War and Society*, 171–75.

89. The most comprehensive account of the struggle is Nancy Allen Hobor, "The United States vs. Montgomery Ward: A Case Study of Business Opposition to the New Deal, 1933–1945" (Ph.D. diss., University of Chicago, 1973). See also Frank M. Klieler, "The World War II Battles of Montgomery Ward," *Chicago History* 5, no. 1 (1976): 19–27; John Bussa, "Montgomery Ward of the State" (B.A. thesis, University of Tennessee, 2011).

90. Avery to NWLB, 13 Nov. 1942; FDR to Avery, 18 Nov. 1942; Avery to NWLB, 10 Dec. 1942; FDR to Avery, 12 Dec. 1942, all in folder 7, box 25, MWCR; Hobor, "United States vs. Montgomery Ward," 121, 165–72.

91. Thorpe to Avery, 25 Nov. 1942, folder 7, box 16; Moushey to Avery, 8 Mar. 1943, folder 1, box 11; Kett to Avery, 9 Dec. 1942, folder 6, box 6B; Swift to Avery, 11 Dec. 1942, folder 5, box 16; W. R. Yeakel to Avery, 2 Mar. 1943, folder 1, box 17C, all in MWCR.

92. Avery to Garrard Winston, 21 Jan. 1943, folder 3, box 17B; F. W. Jameson to Avery, 29 Dec. 1942, folder 6, box 26, both in MWCR.

93. Copy of Knutson press release, 25 Nov. 1942; McGehee to Avery, 14 Jan. 1943, both in folder 3, box 4, MWCR.

94. Hobor, "United States v. Montgomery Ward," 180–85.

95. Jesse Jones with Edward Angly, *Fifty Billion Dollars: My Thirteen Years with the RFC* (New York: Macmillan, 1951), 478; transcripts of telephone calls between Gen. Davis and Gen. Styer, 18:00 and 18:30; Capt. Martin D. Jacobs memo to Gen. Styer, all 26 Apr. 1944, all in "Montgomery Ward File," box 802, entry 177, RG 160; Hobor, "United States vs. Montgomery Ward," 193.

96. Francis Biddle, *In Brief Authority* (New York: Doubleday, 1962), 314–15; transcript, "Telephone Conversation Between Gen. Styer and Gen. Davis, 15:15," 27 Apr. 1944, "Montgomery Ward File," box 802, entry 177, RG 160.

97. "A National Disgrace," Ithaca [MI] *Herald*, 4 May 1944, folder 1, box 206; Morton to Avery, 1 May 1944, folder 1, box 11, both in MWCR; "Editorial: Avery vs. U.S.," *Life* (8 May 1944): 26–27.

98. "Herewith We Cut Short a Controversy," *New York Sun*, 6 May 1944, clipping in folder 4, box 207; and summary of Cut Bank [MT] *Pioneer Press* editorial in "About the Montgomery Ward Case," Peck Associates *Weekly Bulletin*, 19 May 1944, folder 4, box 12, both in MWCR.

99. "Letters Laud Avery's Spunk, Rap 'Bureaucratic Misrule,'" Washington [DC] *Times-Herald*, 30 Apr. 1944; "Congress Hears from Home," Valparaiso [IN] Vidette *Messenger*, 5

May 1944; George Gallup, "3 to 5 [sic] Against Ward Seizure," *Decatur* [IL] *Review*, 28 May 1944, clippings in folder 4, box 207, MWCR; Hobor, "United States vs. Montgomery Ward," 201–3; George H. Gallup, *The Gallup Poll: Public Opinion, 1935–1971* (New York: Random House, 1972), 1:447.

100. C. N. Bloomfield to O'Mahoney, 3 May 1944, folder Legislation—Montgomery Ward Strike, box 226, O'Mahoney Papers; Thomas Roy Jones [president, NJ State Chamber of Commerce] to Avery, 28 Apr. 1944, folder 2, box 6B; American Association of Small Business resolution, 8 May 1944, copy in folder 3, box 4; J. M. Williams to Avery, 15 May 1944, folder 1, box 17B; Arthur C. Watson to Avery, 27 Apr. 1944, folder 2, box 17A, all in MWCR.

101. Thomas F. Reynolds and Charles O. Gridley, "Sewell Avery Versus the People," *Chicago Sun*, 15 May 1944, reproduced in *Congressional Record*, May 1944, clip in folder 7, box 25, MWCR; Gladstone Williams, "More About Montgomery Ward Case," *Atlanta Constitution*, 5 May 1944.

102. "Rule at Machine-Gun Point," *Los Angeles Times*, 28 Apr. 1944, clipping in folder 2, box 207; "Everything a War Plant?," Rome [GA] *News-Tribune*, 30 Apr. 1944, clipping in folder 7, box 206; Albert W. Hawkes speech of 4 May 1944, folder 4, box 4; "Montgomery Ward Case Threat to Private Business—Senator Wherry," *American Banker* (13 May 1944), clipping in folder 4, box 207, all in MWCR; Westbrook Pegler, "The Ward Case," *Atlanta Constitution*, 29 Apr. 1944; Pegler, "Rebel Avery," *Atlanta Constitution*, 1 May 1944; "Seizure!," *Time* (8 May 1944): 11–13.

103. Ickes Diaries, 53:8866; 54:8907, reel 6; Biddle, *In Brief Authority*, 308; Alan Drury, *A Senate Journal, 1943–1945* (New York: McGraw-Hill, 1963), 154.

104. Roland Young, *Congressional Politics in the Second World War* (New York: Columbia University Press, 1956), 66; *Investigation with Respect to the Seizure by the Government of Property of Montgomery Ward and Company: Report of the Select Committee* (Washington, DC: GPO, 1944); "The Avery Problem," *Time* (19 June 1944): 23.

105. Elliott Roosevelt, ed., *F.D.R.: His Personal Letters, 1928–1945* (New York: Duell, Sloan & Pearce, 1950), 2:1563–64; Ohly, *Industrialists in Olive Drab*, 197–201.

106. Transcript, "Conversation Between Gen. Stryer and Col. Dietz," 28 Dec. 1944, folder Montgomery Ward & Co. Dec. 1944–Jan. 1945, box 800, entry 177, RG 160; "Army Blames Ward Defiance for Army Losses," *Chicago Journal of Commerce* (12 Jan. 1945), clipping in folder 1, box 210, MWCR.

107. Arthur Evans, "War Production Debate Center in Ward Trial," *Chicago Tribune*, 10 Jan. 1945; "Judge Upholds Avery," *Chicago Tribune*, 28 Jan. 1945, both clippings in folder 1, box 210, MWCR; *United States v. Montgomery Ward & Co.*, 58 F. Supp. 408 (1945); Ohly, *Industrialists in Olive Drab*, 208–13.

108. Abramson to Patterson, 10 May 1945, folder Montgomery Ward & Co. May–June 1945, box 800, entry 177, RG 160.

109. John Morton Blum, ed., *The Price of Vision: The Diary of Henry A. Wallace, 1942–1946* (Boston: Houghton Mifflin, 1973), 449; *United States v. Montgomery Ward & Co.*, 150 F. 2d 369 (1945).

110. Ohly running memo on "Montgomery Ward—Miscellaneous Developments—21 Dec. to 8 Jan. [sic]," folder Montgomery Ward & Co., box 800; Maj. Gen. Joseph W. Byron to Commanding General, ASF, 16 Jan. 1945, folder Montgomery Ward 1945, box 799; "Kuhn,

Sachse, and Boland," memo to Ohly, 28 Jan. 1945, folder Montgomery Ward Dec. 1944–Jan. 1945, box 800; John J. McCloy to U.S. Attorney General, 1 Feb. 1945, folder Montgomery Ward 1945, box 799; Lt. Col. Daniel L. Boland to Ohly, 14 May 1945, folder Montgomery Ward 1945, box 799, all in entry 177, RG 160; David Dillman, "Army Turns Back 2 of Ward's Major Units Here," *Chicago Journal of Commerce*, undated clipping; Robert Lewin, "'Army of Occupation' Cuts Its Staff 40 Pct at Wards," *Chicago Daily News*, 7 Mar. 1945, both in folder 2, box 210, MWCR.

111. Lt. Col. Daniel L. Boland to Ohly, 14 May 1945, folder Montgomery Ward 1945, box 799, entry 177; Capt. John P. Chapman to John H. Ohly, 16 July 1945, folder General, box 761, entry 176; Ohly memo to Sec War, 14 Aug. 1945, folder Montgomery Ward 1945, box 799, entry 177, all in RG 160.

112. Robert A. Lovett to Avery, 4 Aug. 1945, folder Montgomery Ward 1945, box 799, entry 177, RG 160; John L. Blackman, Jr., *Presidential Seizure in Labor Disputes* (Cambridge, MA: Harvard University Press, 1967), 43; Ohly, *Industrialists in Olive Drab*, 215–16.

113. "Experiment Querulous," *Time* (29 Oct. 1945): 86.

114. Ohly, *Industrialists in Olive Drab*, 218; "Earnings of Ward Show Rise in Year," *NYT*, 4 Apr. 1946.

115. David Dillman, "Ward Takes Over; Faces Strike Threat," *Chicago Journal of Commerce* (19 Oct. 1945), clipping in folder 2, box 210, MWCR; "CIO Union Asks Boycott," *NYT*, 24 Jan. 1946.

116. Lichtenstein, *Labor's War at Home*, 121–27.

117. "Army Will Operate Big Nickel Plant," *NYT*, 30 Aug. 1944; "President Orders Ten Mines Seized," *NYT*, 1 Sept. 1944; Richard P. Boyden, "The San Francisco Machinists and the National War Labor Board," in *American Labor in the Era of World War II*, ed. Sally M. Miller and Daniel A. Cornford (Westport, CT: Greenwood, 1995), 105–19.

118. Capt. O'Donnell to Gen. Styer, 2 Sept. 1944, folder Cleveland Graphite Bronze Co., box 781; materials in bound vol. "Publicity, Newspaper Clippings . . . etc., re: Cleveland Graphite Bronze Company," box 782; "MESA Calls Out 20,000 in Detroit Interunion Fight," *Cleveland Plain Dealer*, 3 Nov. 1944; "Settle Strike or 25,000 Quit Here, Smith Insists," *Cleveland News*, 4 Nov. 1944, clippings in box 782, all in entry 177, RG 160.

119. George Norris Green, *The Establishment in Texas Politics: The Primitive Years, 1938–1957* (Westport, CT: Greenwood, 1979); Harris, *Right to Manage*, 108.

120. "History of the Army Operation of the Hughes Tool Company, Houston, Texas, 6 Sept. 1944 to 29 Aug. 1945," bound document in box 794, entry 177, RG 160; Michael R. Botson, Jr., *Labor, Civil Rights, and the Hughes Tool Company* (College Station: Texas A&M University Press, 2005), 63–135.

121. Ohly memo to file, 9 Sept. 1944, and R. H. Epperson to Patterson, 13 Sept. 1944, both in folder Hughes Tool Co. July–Nov. 1944, box 794, entry 177, RG 160; *Hughes Tool Co. v. NLRB*, 147 F. 2d 69 (1945); Botson, *Labor, Civil Rights, and the Hughes Tool Company*, 137–41.

122. Henrietta M. Larson and Kenneth Wiggins Porter, *History of Humble Oil & Refining Company* (1959; New York: Arno, 1976), 598–604; Harris, *Right to Manage*, 108–9.

123. "Enjoins WLB in Oil Case," *NYT*, 21 Sept. 1944.

124. *Humble Oil Refining Co. v. Eighth Regional War Labor Board*, 56 F. Supp. 950 (1944); *Eighth Regional War Labor Board v. Humble Oil & Refining Co.*, 145 F. 2d 462 (1944).

125. "Plane 'Gas' Plant Closes," *NYT*, 11 Apr. 1945; "Seizes a Plant of Cities Service," *NYT*, 18 Apr. 1945; "Strike in Refinery Seized by U.S. Ends," *Atlanta Constitution*, 20 Apr. 1945; Blackman, *Presidential Seizure*, 77.

126. Memo by "W. S. S.," 17 Aug. 1945, folder Plant Seizures–General Information, box 2079; miscellaneous materials in box 2081, both in entry 358, RG 253; "Truman Orders Ickes to Seize Two Oil Plants," *Atlanta Constitution*, 7 June 1945; "President Orders Oil Plant Seizure to Assure War 'Gas,'" *NYT*, 2 July 1945; "Truman Signs for Seizure of Texas Plant," *Atlanta Constitution*, 2 July 1945.

127. "Truman Directs Seizure of Factory Vital to War Tires," *NYT*, 21 May 1945; "Plant Seizure," *NYT*, 22 May 1945; Ohly, *Industrialists in Olive Drab*, 176–78.

128. Blackman, *Presidential Seizure*, 42; Ohly, *Industrialists in Olive Drab*, 164–65, 361–62; Timothy J. Minchin, *What Do We Need a Union For? The TWUA in the South, 1945–1955* (Chapel Hill: University of North Carolina Press, 1997), 71–72.

129. "U.S. Seizes Strike-Hit Ga. Fire Bomb Plant," *Atlanta Constitution*, 2 June 1945; "Mill Seizure Is Ordered," *NYT*, 2 June 1945.

130. On the difficulty of pinpointing the legal end of World War II, see Mary L. Dudziak, *War-Time: An Idea, Its History, Its Consequences* (New York: Oxford University Press, 2012).

131. Bound Army Services Forces report, "Chrysler Corporation Strike Manual, 3 Mar. 1945," box 781, entry 177, RG 160, NARA; Lipsitz, *Rainbow at Midnight*, 87–88.

132. Jerry E. Strahan, *Andrew Jackson Higgins and the Boats that Won World War II* (Baton Rouge: Louisiana State University Press, 1994), 272–73.

133. Ickes Diaries, 59:9640, 9703, 9710, reel 7.

134. Blackman, *Presidential Seizure*, 93.

135. Ohly memos to file, 2 July 1945 and 17 July 1945, folder Diamond Alkali Co., box 786, entry 177, RG 160.

136. Summary of Krug telephone call to Adm. Robinson, 2 July 1945, Conference Records, box 47, Krug Papers, LOC; "Navy Takes Over 5 Strikebound Goodyear Plants," *Atlanta Constitution*, 6 July 1945; Keith E. Eiler, *Mobilizing America: Robert P. Patterson and the War Effort, 1940–1945* (Ithaca, NY: Cornell University Press, 1997), 436–38.

137. White House press release, 25 Aug. 1945, folder Plant Seizures–General Information, box 2079, entry 358, RG 253.

138. "Seized Properties Returned by U.S.," *NYT*, 13 Sept. 1945; Larson and Porter, *History of Humble Oil*, 598–604; Harris, *Right to Manage*, 108–9; Botson, *Labor, Civil Rights, and the Hughes Tool Company*, 142–84.

139. Minchin, *What Do We Need a Union For?*, 71–72.

140. Patterson, *Grand Expectations*, 43–44.

141. "'Big Five' Packers Get Back Control," *NYT*, 30 Apr. 1946; Teller, "Government Seizure in Labor Disputes," 1031–48; Larson and Porter, *History of Humble Oil*, 605.

142. For a description of the broader struggle, see Meg Jacobs, *Pocketbook Politics: Economic Citizenship in Twentieth-Century America* (Princeton, NJ: Princeton University Press, 2005), 218–31. On a wartime seizure of a meat packer, see Jonathan Rees, "Caught in the Middle: The Seizure and Occupation of Cudahy Brothers Company, 1944–1945," *Wisconsin Magazine of History* 78, no. 3 (spring 1995): 200–218.

143. Ickes Diaries, 63:unpaginated entry for 2 June 1946, reel 7.

144. Alonzo L. Hamby, *Man of the People: A Life of Harry S. Truman* (New York: Oxford University Press, 1995), 377–79; David McCullough, *Truman* (New York: Simon & Schuster, 1993), 494–506; Patterson, *Grand Expectations*, 47–48.

145. *United States v. United Mine Workers of America*, 330 U.S. 258 (1947); Teller, "Government Seizure in Labor Disputes," 1052–53; Hamby, *Man of the People*, 419–20.

146. Tomlins, *State and the Unions*, 298–99; Harris, *Right to Manage*, 118–27, 150–53; Hamby, *Man of the People*, 424; Elizabeth Tandy Shermer, "Counter-Organizing the Sunbelt: Right-to-Work Campaigns and Anti-Union Conservatism, 1943–1958," *Pacific Historical Review* 78 (2009): 81–118; Kim Phillips-Fein, " 'As Great an Issue as Slavery or Abolition': Economic Populism, the Conservative Movement, and the Right-to-Work Campaigns of 1958," *Journal of Policy History* 23 (2011): 491–516.

147. These new mechanisms were used first in the case of a dispute over wages at a GOCO uranium-processing laboratory in Oak Ridge, Tennessee, in spring 1948. Just after the injunction expired, the AFL-affiliated local representing the lab workers settled with the Carbide & Chemicals Corp., the operator. See "Call Atomic Strike Menace to Nation," *NYT*, 17 Mar. 1948; "Truman Will Seek Atom Labor Code," *NYT*, 19 June 1948.

148. "War Powers Opposed," *NYT*, 2 Mar. 1952; "U.S. Hands Back Railroads to Owners After 21 Months," *NYT*, 24 May 1952; "Seizure Questions," *NYT*, 25 May 1952; Archibald Cox, "Seizure in Emergency Disputes," in *Emergency Disputes and National Policy*, ed. Irving Bernstein, Harold L. Enarson, and R. W. Fleming (New York: Harper & Bros., 1955), 230.

149. NAM Industrial Relations Committee policy statement 13 Mar. 1951, folder Program re. Plant Seizure, box 138, Ser. VII, NAM Records.

150. Hamby, *Man of the People*, 578; Maeva Marcus, *Truman and the Steel Seizure Case: The Limits of Presidential Power* (New York: Columbia University Press, 1977), 6–28; Paul G. Pierpaoli, Jr., *Truman and Korea: The Political Culture of the Early Cold War* (Columbia: University of Missouri Press, 1999), 36–130.

151. "Free Enterprise or One-Man Government," 18 Apr. 1952 memo, folder Program re. Plant Seizure, box 138, Ser. VII, NAM Records; Karen S. Miller, *The Voice of Business: Hill & Knowlton and Postwar Public Relations* (Chapel Hill: University of North Carolina Press, 1999), 91–119.

152. The most comprehensive account of this episode is Marcus, *Truman and the Steel Seizure Case*. But also valuable are Harold L. Enarson, "The Politics of an Emergency Dispute: Steel, 1952," in *Emergency Disputes and National Policy*, ed. Bernstein et al., 46–74; Alan F. Westin, *The Anatomy of a Constitutional Law Case: Youngstown Sheet and Tube Co. v. Sawyer, the Steel Seizure Decision* (New York: Macmillan, 1958); Phillip E. Stebbins, "Truman and the Seizure of Steel: A Failure in Communication," *Historian* 34, no. 1 (Nov. 1971): 1–21; "President Truman and the Steel Seizure Case: A 50-Year Retrospective, Transcript of Proceedings," *Duquesne Law Review* 41 (summer 2003): 686–722; Patricia L. Bellia, "The Story of the Steel Seizure Case," in *Presidential War Power Stories*, ed. Christopher H. Schroeder and Curtis A. Bradley (New York: Thomson Reuters, 2009), 233–85.

153. Westin, *Anatomy of a Constitutional Law Case*, 172–73.

Chapter 6

1. Alfred P. Sloan, Jr., "The Challenge," speech to NAM dinner, 10 Dec. 1943, copy in folder NAM 1943–44, box 2, drawer 3, cabinet 1, ACWP Records; published in pamphlet form as Alfred P. Sloan, Jr., *The Challenge* (New York: NAM, 1944).

2. Business leaders were more optimistic, as a group, than were most government economists. See David Hugh Shepard, "Reconversion, 1939–1946: Images, Plans, Realities" (Ph.D.

diss., University of Wisconsin, 1981), 67, 135; William Steinert Hill, Jr., "The Business Community and National Defense: Corporate Leaders and the Military, 1943–1950" (Ph.D. diss.,
Stanford University, 1980), 112–15; Robert Higgs, "From Central Planning to the Market:
The American Transition, 1945–1947," *Journal of Economic History* 59, no. 3 (Sept. 1999):
615.

3. George William Steinmeyer, "Disposition of Surplus War Property: An Administrative
History, 1944–1949" (Ph.D. diss., University of Oklahoma, 1969), 160.

4. Appendix to Clarence L. Collans statement on contract termination, 27 Apr. 1943, in
Minutes of the Thirty-First Annual Meeting, box 17, Chamber Records; J. Donald Edwards,
"Termination of Ordnance Contracts, 1918" (Jan. 1943), in folder Sec. 17 Contract Settlement
Act Cases, box E-107, entry 671, RG 156, NARA; I. J. Gromfine and J. Donald Edwards,
"Terminations After World War I," *Law and Contemporary Problems* 10, no. 4 (spring 1944):
563–93.

5. Byrnes, "Problems of Mobilization and Reconversion: First Report" (1 Jan. 1945),
folder 12, box 15, Ser. IV, Byrnes Papers.

6. Eugene E. Wilson, "The Economics of Air Power," *VSD* 10, no. 12 (1 Apr. 1944): 383;
"Termination Notes and Data for Use at the Rochester Meeting of District Chiefs," undated
report [1943], folder Shepherd Speeches, box E-120, entry 681, RG 156, NARA; Ickes Diaries,
50:8282–83, reel 6.

7. National Resources Planning Board, *After the War, 1918–1920* (Washington, DC:
GPO, 1943), 6–25; William Hoyt Moore, "Termination of Contracts and Disposal of Surpluses After the First World War," *American Economic Review* (March 1943): 138–44; Steinmeyer, "Disposition of Surplus War Property," 12–16.

8. William Haber, "The Strategy of Reconversion," *American Political Science Review* 38,
no. 6 (Dec. 1944): 1114–24.

9. Lt. Col. Harold Shepherd, "Termination Notes and Data for Use at the Rochester
Meeting of District Chiefs," 19 May 1943, box E-109, entry 671, RG 156, NARA; materials in
Folder History of the Legal Division, box 2, RG 156, NARA-GL; Leon Malman, "Policies and
Procedures for the Termination of War Contracts," *Law and Contemporary Problems* 10, no.
3 (winter 1944): 462–63; Irving Brinton Holley, Jr., *Buying Aircraft: Matériel Procurement for
the Army Air Forces* (Washington, DC: Office of the Chief of Military History, 1964), 449–51.

10. H. P. Isham to Lt. Col. Harold Shepherd, 31 July 1943; Isham to Lt. Col. A. R. Cutter,
14 Aug. 1943; "Termination Procedure for War Contracts," May 1944, all in box E-108,
entry 671, RG 156, NARA; Commander J. H. Stewart, "War Contract Termination from the
Viewpoint of the Navy Department," in *Accounting Problems in War Contract Termination,
Taxes, and Postwar Planning, 1943* (New York: American Institute of Accountants, 1943), 2–5.

11. *War and Post-War Adjustment Policy* (Washington, DC: GPO, 1944), 10, 41–43; John
William Partin, "'Assistant President' for the Home Front: James F. Byrnes and World War
II" (Ph.D. diss., University of Florida, 1977), 311–12.

12. *War and Post-War Adjustment Policy*, 78–90; V. O. Key, Jr., "The Reconversion Phase
of Demobilization," *American Political Science Review* 38, no. 6 (Dec. 1944): 1142–43; press
release, 12 June 1944, folder 9, box 14, Ser. IV, Byrnes Papers.

13. Malman, "Policies and Procedures for the Termination of War Contracts," 504–6;
Gerald D. Nash, *World War II and the West: Reshaping the Economy* (Lincoln: University of
Nebraska Press, 1990), 184. Warren continued to criticize the fast settlements into the late

1940s. But there was never a full-blown scandal. Some critics even suggested that Warren was exaggerating the problem. They observed that the World War II terminations involved contracts with an original value of $64 billion, which had been settled for about $4 billion, or about six cents on the dollar. "Big Frauds Alleged in U.S. Payment of War Contracts," *NYT*, 5 Aug. 1949; Benjamin Ginsberg, "War Contract Settlements" [letter to the editor], *NYT*, 11 Aug. 1949; "Frauds Uncovered in War Contracts," *NYT*, 12 May 1950; Herman Miles Somers, *Presidential Agency, OWMR: The Office of War Mobilization and Reconversion* (Cambridge, MA: Harvard University Press, 1950), 180; Gerald T. White, *Billions for Defense: Government Financing by the Defense Plant Corporation During World War II* (University: University of Alabama Press, 1980), 120–22.

14. James E. Murray, "Contract Settlement Act of 1944," *Law and Contemporary Problems* 10, no. 4 (spring 1944): 683–92; Key, "Reconversion Phase of Demobilization," 1146–47; Edward M. Taylor, "Partial Payments at Termination Now Liberalized," *Dun's Review* (Oct. 1944): 14–15; Capt. J. Harold Stewart, "Negotiated Settlements of Terminated War Contracts," and Capt. N. Loyall McLaren, "Government Pricing Policies," both in *Termination and Taxes and Papers on Other Current Accounting Problems* (New York: American Institute of Accountants, 1944), 20–26, 142.

15. Raymond L. Hoadley, "Cancellation Demands Action—and Quick," *Aviation* 42 (Nov. 1943): 119, 320; "If the War Ends, Where Do We Stand?," *Fortune* 30 (Oct. 1944): 132; Roy A. Foulke, "Let's Tackle the First Post-War Problem Now," *Dun's Review* (May 1943): 7–14, 26–37; "NAM Recommendations for Termination Legislation," *NAM News* (30 Oct. 1943): 4–5; Sen. Arthur H. Vandenberg to B. E. Hutchinson, 12 Nov. 1943, folder Hutchinson, box 1, drawer 3, cabinet 1; B. E. Hutchinson to K. T. Keller and George Romney, 27 Nov. 1943, folder Chrysler Corp, box 2, drawer 2, cabinet 1; George Romney letter "to members of the automotive community," 21 Apr. 1944, box 1, drawer 3, cabinet 2; all in ACWP Records.

16. Gen. A. B. Quinton letter, 22 Jan. 1944, folder Correspondence on Term. Sch., box E-118, e. 681, RG 156, NARA; James F. Byrnes, "Reconversion: A Report to the President," 7 Sept. 1944, copy in folder 10, box 15, Ser. IV, Byrnes Papers; Holley, *Buying Aircraft*, 451–61.

17. U.S. Senate, *Investigation of the National Defense Program, Hearings, Part 31* (Washington, DC: GPO, 1946), 15467–68; CPA-*History*, 903–4.

18. Key, "Reconversion Phase of Demobilization," 1139; Somers, *Presidential Agency*, 196–99.

19. U.S. Senate, *Investigation of the National Defense Program, Hearings, Part 31*, 15445, 15586; Irvin R. Friend, "History of the Air Technical Service Command, 1945," reel A2001, AFHRA.

20. "The Reconversion Controversy," in *Public Administration and Policy Development: A Case Book*, ed. Harold Stein (New York: Harcourt, Brace & World, 1952), 215–83; Barton J. Bernstein, "The Debate on Industrial Reconversion: The Protection of Oligopoly and Military Control of the Economy," *American Journal of Economics and Sociology* 26, no. 2 (Apr. 1967): 159–72; Alan Brinkley, *The End of Reform: New Deal Liberalism in Recession and War* (New York: Alfred A. Knopf, 1995), 235–40; Paul A. C. Koistinen, *Arsenal of World War II: The Political Economy of American Warfare, 1940–1945* (Lawrence: University Press of Kansas, 2004), 446–97.

21. U.S. Senate, *Investigation of the National Defense Program, Hearings, Part 31*, 14869.

22. Barton J. Bernstein, "The Removal of War Production Controls on Business," *Business History Review* 39, no. 2 (summer 1965): 252; George Vincent Sweeting, "Building the

Arsenal of Democracy: The Government's Role in the Expansion of Industrial Capacity, 1940 to 1945" (Ph.D. diss., Columbia University, 1994), 279.

23. "Case History of Boeing Aircraft Company, Renton, WA," reel A2074, AFHRA; U.S. Senate, *Investigation of the National Defense Program, Hearings, Part 31*, 15315–16, 15445, 15584–85.

24. Office of Contract Settlement, "Statistics of War Contract Terminations and Settlements, Jan.–June 1946," vol. 4, box E-120, entry 681, RG 156, NARA; Frederick A. Alling, "History of the Air Materiel Command, 1946" (1951), reel A2001, AFHRA; Industrial College of the Armed Forces, *The Economics of National Security: Reconversion and Partial Mobilization* (Washington, DC: ICAF, 1956), 19.

25. Mark R. Wilson, "The Advantages of Obscurity: World War II Tax Carryback Provisions and the Normalization of Corporate Welfare," in *What's Good for Business: Business and American Politics Since World War II*, ed. Kim Phillips-Fein and Julian E. Zelizer (New York: Oxford University Press, 2012), 16–29.

26. A. H. Sypher, "Post-War Problem No. 1," *Nation's Business* 31 (May 1943): 21–22, 56–58; Allan Spalding, "How to Dodge Your Taxes," *New Republic* 110 (3 Jan. 1944): 13–16; J. Keith Butters, "Tax Revisions for Reconversion Needs," *Harvard Business Review* 22, no. 3 (spring 1944): 299–315.

27. Carl S. Shroup, "The Revenue Act of 1945," *Political Science Quarterly* 60, no. 4 (Dec. 1945): 481–91; Barton J. Bernstein, "Charting a Course Between Inflation and Depression: Secretary of the Treasury Fred Vinson and the Truman Administration's Tax Bill," *Register of the Kentucky Historical Society* 66, no. 1 (1968): 53–64; Stephen A. Bank, *From Sword to Shield: The Transformation of the Corporate Income Tax, 1861 to Present* (New York: Oxford University Press, 2010), 195–210.

28. Higgs, "From Central Planning to the Market," 609–10.

29. Jason E. Taylor, Bharati Basu, and Steven McLean, "Net Exports and the Avoidance of High Unemployment During Reconversion, 1945–1947," *Journal of Economic History* 71, no. 2 (June 2011): 444–54.

30. Charles D. Bright, *The Jet Makers: The Aerospace Industry from 1945 to 1972* (Lawrence: Regents Press of Kansas, 1978), 12; Hill, "Business Community and National Defense," 202; Wilson, "Advantages of Obscurity," 35–36.

31. Louis Kahn, "Don't Let the War Plants Scare You," *Nation's Business* 32 (Apr. 1944): 27, 70; "Management Polls," *Fortune* (Aug. 1944): 252; Sweeting, "Building the Arsenal of Democracy," 288.

32. Shepard, "Reconversion, 1939–1946," 121; Eberstadt to Forrestal, 21 Jan. 1941, box 54, Forrestal Papers.

33. "The Tenth *Fortune* Round Table: On Demobilizing the War Economy," 10, 17–18, insert in *Fortune* 24 (Nov. 1941); "Through the Editor's Specs: After the Ball, What?," *Nation's Business* 29 (Sept. 1941): 7; "It's a Favorable Wind . . . Sail with It" (Chamber of Commerce, 1941), copy in box 15, Ser. II, Chamber Records.

34. *The Papers of Robert A. Taft*, vol. 2, *1939–1944*, ed. Clarence E. Wunderlin (Kent, OH: Kent State University Press, 2001), 310; "Resolutions Adopted at the Thirty-First Annual Meeting, Apr. 29, 1942," folder Board Resolutions, 1942–46, box 1, Chamber Records; *War Program of American Industry and Resolutions* (New York: NAM, 1943), 15–16; James M. Barker, "Surveying the Boundary Lines Between Government and Private Enterprise in the

Field of Business," *American Economic Review* (Mar. 1943): 4–5; "1022 Government-Owned War Plants," *Reader's Digest* 42 (June 1943): 27–28. On oil executives' fears that the war mobilization might lead to nationalization, see Ickes Diaries, 44:6821, reel 5.

35. W. H. Lawrence, "Post-War Program," *NYT*, 11 Mar. 1943; Alvin H. Hansen, "Full Employment After the War," *American Federationist* 51 (July 1944): 12; John Morton Blum, *V Was for Victory: Politics and American Culture During World War II* (New York: Harcourt Brace Jovanovich, 1976), 237–39; Shepard, "Reconversion, 1939–1946," 73–116; Marion Clawson, *New Deal Planning: The National Resources Planning Board* (Baltimore: Johns Hopkins University Press, 1981), esp. 136–43, 181–86.

36. "Post-War Industry: New Deal Style," *NAM News* (13 Mar. 1943): 6; John W. Jeffries, "The 'New' New Deal: FDR and American Liberalism, 1937–1945," *Political Science Quarterly* 105, no. 3 (autumn 1990): 397–418; Brinkley, *End of Reform*, 250–58.

37. Jerome S. Bruner, *Mandate from the People* (New York: Duell, Sloan, and Pearce, 1944), 191–209.

38. Clifford J. Durr, "The Postwar Relationship Between Government and Business," *American Economic Review* (Mar. 1943): 45–53; Colston E. Warne, "What We Can Do with War Plants," *Current History* 7 (July 1944): 24–30; James G. Patton, "The Federal Government's Role in the Postwar Economy," *American Political Science Review* 38, no. 6 (Dec. 1944): 1124–36; White, *Billions for Defense*, 90–91; Brinkley, *End of Reform*, 242–43.

39. Evidently, this idea came to Ickes from a group of New Deal lawyers, in New York, including Abe Fortas and Jerome Frank. A month after Ickes's speech, he had lunch with Bernard Baruch, who scolded him for it. Ickes Diaries, 52:8796–97; 54:8900–8901, reel 6.

40. CIO Department of Research and Education, "With Victory" comic, July 1944, folder Administration: CIO-UAW, box 2, drawer 2, cabinet 1, ACWP Records. For similar claims, see U.S. Senate, *Investigation of the National Defense Program, Hearings, Part 31*, 15180; Nash, *World War II and the West*, 209.

41. "CIO Political Action Committee Program for 1944," press release, 16 June 1944, copy in folder 11, box 13, Ser. IV, Byrnes Papers; "Reuther Challenges 'Our Fear of Abundance,'" *NYT*, 16 Sept. 1945.

42. Virgil Jordan, "Reconversion—to What?," *VSD* 11, no. 9 (15 Feb. 1945): 279–83; Stephen Kemp Bailey, *Congress Makes a Law: The Story Behind the Employment Act of 1946* (New York: Columbia University Press, 1950), 129–49; Robert M. Collins, *The Business Response to Keynes, 1929–1964* (New York: Columbia University Press, 1981), 99–112.

43. "One Fifth of a Nation Government Owned," *Business Week* (19 June 1943): 53; Steinmeyer, "Disposition of Surplus War Property," 27–28.

44. F. C. Crawford, "What Are the Post-War Prospects for Business in this Country?," *Dun's Review* (Sept. 1943): 7–8; undated James F. Lincoln address to Sales Executives Club of New York, copy attached to Lincoln to Romney, 20 Mar. 1945, box 1, drawer 3, cabinet 1, ACWP Records; "Industry Wants to Know," *Forbes* 52 (1 Oct. 1943): 9; "Remarks of Alfred P. Sloan, Jr. at meeting of NIIC program committee, Apr. 29, 1943," folder Documents Relating to NIIC, box 843, Ser. III, NAM Records.

45. Leslie E. Neville, "A Sermon in a Swan Song," *Aviation* (May 1943): 109; Harry Woodhead, "Our Planes and Our Peace," *Aviation* (Aug. 1943): 122; Frederick B. Retschler (United Aircraft Corp.) to Forrestal, 8 Sept. 1943, folder Aircraft-General, box 163, e. 115, RG 80; Eugene E. Wilson, "The Economics of Air Power," *VSD* 10, no. 12 (1 Apr. 1944): 383.

46. Lynn L. Bollinger, Tom Lilley, and Albert E. Lombard, Jr., "Preserving American Air Power," *Harvard Business Review* 23, no. 3 (spring 1945): 391.

47. *War and Post-War Adjustment Policy*, 1, 23–24; Brinkley, *End of Reform*, 243–45.

48. Steinmeyer, "Disposition of Surplus War Property," 46–49, 79–103; Partin, "Assistant President," 315; Sweeting, "Building the Arsenal of Democracy," 298; minutes of meeting on 29 June 1944, folder Meetings of Surplus War Property Policy Board, box 1, entry 12, RG 270.

49. Frederick J. Dobney, "The Evolution of a Reconversion Policy: World War II and Surplus Property Disposal," *Historian* 36, no. 3 (May 1974): 515; White, *Billions for Defense*, 95–96; Sweeting, "Building the Arsenal of Democracy," 299–300.

50. Aaron L. Friedberg, *In the Shadow of the Garrison State: America's Antistatism and Its Cold War Grand Strategy* (Princeton, NJ: Princeton University Press, 2000), 49.

51. "The War Inventory," *Fortune* 30 (Sept. 1944): 107.

52. "Surplus Property: Must a Great Chance to Broaden Economic Freedom Go by Political Default?," *Life* (18 Dec. 1944): 20.

53. Ibid.

54. Robert S. Allen, "Arsenal of Monopoly," *New Republic* (21 Apr. 1947): 18–21; Gregory Hooks, *Forging the Military-Industrial Complex: World War II's Battle of the Potomac* (Urbana: University of Illinois Press, 1991), 156.

55. "The War Inventory," *Fortune* 30 (Sept. 1944): 108, 248; James R. Chiles, "How the Great War on War Surplus Got Won—or Lost," *Smithsonian* 26, no. 9 (Dec. 1995): 52–60.

56. SPA, *White Elephants with Wings* (Washington, DC: GPO, 1945); WAA, *Buyers of Surplus Aircraft* (Washington, DC: GPO, 1946); Friend, "History of the Air Technical Service Command, 1945," p. 113, reel A2001, AFHRA; Alling, "History of the Air Materiel Command, 1946," 96–119.

57. James Allan Cook, *The Marketing of Surplus War Property* (Washington, DC: Public Affairs Press, 1948), 48; Joseph A. Pratt and Christopher J. Castaneda, *Builders: Herman and George R. Brown* (College Station: Texas A&M University Press, 1999), 99–101; Nicholas A. Veronico, A. Kevin Grantham, and Scott Thompson, *Military Aircraft Boneyards* (Osceola, WI: MBI, 2000).

58. *An Administrative History of the Bureau of Ships During World War II* (Washington, DC: Navy Dept., 1952), 4:329, 392; Jonathan M. Weisgall, *Operation Crossroads: The Atomic Tests at Bikini Atoll* (Annapolis, MD: Naval Institute Press, 1994); James P. Delgado, *Ghost Fleet: The Sunken Ships of Bikini Atoll* (Honolulu: University of Hawaii Press, 1996).

59. "Merchant Marine I: The Postwar Fleet," *Fortune* 30 (Nov. 1944): 105–10.

60. Daniel Marx, Jr., "The Merchant Ship Sales Act of 1946," *Journal of Business of the University of Chicago* 21, no. 1 (Jan. 1948): 12–28; John G. B. Hutchins, "United States Merchant Marine Policy and Surplus Ships," *Journal of Political Economy* 59, no. 2 (Apr. 1951): 117–25; "The Sale of the Tankers," in *Public Administration and Policy Development*, ed. Stein, 445–532; Peter Elphick, *Liberty: The Ships That Won the War* (Annapolis, MD: Naval Institute Press, 2001), 401–46.

61. Moore, "Termination of Contracts and Disposal of Surpluses After the First World War," 146; Steinmeyer, "Disposition of Surplus War Property," iv, 12–16, 27, 118; Sweeting, "Building the Arsenal of Democracy," 373.

62. "The Road to Tokyo and Beyond: Third Report to the President, the Senate and the House of Representatives," copy in folder 14, box 15, Ser. IV, Byrnes Papers; "Selling the

Surplus Plant," *War Progress Report* 256 (11 Aug. 1945) in folder War Progress Reports, box 208, entry 118, RG 80.

63. U.S. Senate, *Aluminum Plant Disposal: Joint Hearings* (Washington, DC: GPO, 1945), 3–4.

64. SPA, *Government-Owned Pipe Lines* (Washington, DC: GPO, 1946), 28.

65. WAA, *Quarterly Progress Report: Second Quarter, 1949* (Washington, DC: GPO, 1949), 3; Steinmeyer, "Disposition of Surplus War Property," 166–84, 271; Sweeting, "Building the Arsenal of Democracy," 373.

66. John D. Sumner, "The Disposition of Surplus War Property," *American Economic Review* 34, no. 1 (Sept. 1944): 463; White, *Billions for Defense*, 94–129.

67. Steinmeyer, "Disposition of Surplus War Property," 274–75; White, *Billions for Defense*, 105–6, 173; Mark S. Foster, *Henry J. Kaiser: Builder in the Modern American West* (Austin: University of Texas Press, 1989), 142–62; Sweeting, "Building the Arsenal of Democracy," 404–5, 478; Richard Macias, "'We All Had a Cause': Kansas City's Bomber Plant, 1941–1945," *Kansas History* 28, no. 4 (winter 2005–6): 260.

68. Steinmeyer, "Disposition of Surplus War Property," 57.

69. SPA, *Government-Owned Pipe Lines*; Jesse Jones with Edward Angly, *Fifty Billion Dollars: My Thirteen Years with the RFC* (New York: Macmillan, 1951), 343–44; Steinmeyer, "Disposition of Surplus War Property," 249–54; White, *Billions for Defense*, 109. On the involvement of Brown & Root in the pipeline deal, see Pratt and Castaneda, *Builders*, 101–31.

70. White, *Billions for Defense*, 106.

71. Steinmeyer, "Disposition of Surplus War Property," 243–44; Sweeting, "Building the Arsenal of Democracy," 478.

72. Many were badly polluted; costly cleanups continue into the twenty-first century. On the most extreme case, see John M. Findlay and Bruce Hevly, *Atomic Frontier Days: Hanford and the American West* (Seattle: University of Washington Press, 2011).

73. Steinmeyer, "Disposition of Surplus War Property," 279–80; White, *Billions for Defense*, 123–28; Louis Cain and George Neumann, "Planning for Peace: The Surplus Property Act of 1944," *Journal of Economic History* 41, no. 1 (Mar. 1981): 132–33; Sweeting, "Building the Arsenal of Democracy," 389–400, 432–33; Robert Lewis, "World War II Manufacturing and the Postwar Southern Economy," *Journal of Southern History* 73, no. 4 (Nov. 2007): 837–66.

74. U.S. Senate, *Aluminum Plant Disposal: Joint Hearings*, 6–12.

75. U.S. Senate, *Investigation of the National Defense Program, Hearings, Part 31*, 15185–210.

76. For a detailed, firsthand account, see [Harold Stein], "The Disposal of the Aluminum Plants," in *Public Administration and Policy Development*, ed. Stein, 313–61.

77. Richard S. Reynolds to M. M. Caskie, 2 Nov. 1944, folder TVA, box 46, and Richard S. Reynolds to RFC, 28 Nov. 1945, folder Surplus Plants, box 54, both in Reynolds Papers; U.S. Senate, *Investigation of the National Defense Program, Hearings, Part 31*, 15157–72; "Aluminum Reborn," *Fortune* 33 (May 1946): 104–5; Sweeting, "Building the Arsenal of Democracy," 404, 478.

78. Kaiser to Symington, 9 Aug. 1945, in folder Aluminum 1941 [*sic*], carton 6, Kaiser Papers; Cook, *Marketing of Surplus War Property*, 35; Richard S. Reynolds to Hugh Fulton, 9 Dec. 1946, folder Fulton, box 56, Reynolds Papers; Charles M. Wiltse, *Aluminum Policies of*

the War Production Board and Predecessor Agencies, May 1940 to November 1945 (Washington, DC: CPA, 1946), 319–20; Sweeting, "Building the Arsenal of Democracy," 404.

79. U.S. Senate, *Investigation of the National Defense Program, Hearings, Part 31*, 15232–33; [Stein], "Disposal of the Aluminum Plants," 318; "Aluminum Reborn," *Fortune* 33 (May 1946): 212. A comparable de-concentration was achieved in the synthetic ammonia business, in which a prewar duopoly (consisting of Du Pont and Allied Chemical) became a multi-firm industry, thanks in part to the disposal of GOCO plant. See Cain and Neumann, "Planning for Peace," 132.

80. White, *Billions for Defense*, 106–7; Foster, *Henry J. Kaiser*, 196–210.

81. U.S. Senate, *Aluminum Plant Disposal: Joint Hearings*, 18–25; White, *Billions for Defense*, 106–7; George David Smith, *From Monopoly to Competition: The Transformations of Alcoa, 1888–1986* (New York: Cambridge University Press, 1988), 250–90. In the case of magnesium, a comparable industry, postwar demand was negligible. See Mark R. Wilson, "Making 'Goop' Out of Lemons: The Permanente Metals Corporation, Magnesium Incendiary Bombs, and the Struggle for Profits During World War II," *Enterprise & Society* 12 (Mar. 2011): 10–45.

82. "If the War Ends, Where Do We Stand?," *Fortune* 30 (Oct. 1944): 132; "Steel in the West," *Fortune* 31 (Feb. 1945): 130–33, 258–61; Steinmeyer, "Disposition of Surplus War Property," 130.

83. Allen, "Arsenal of Monopoly"; Craig Loal Whetter, "'This Strange Enterprise': Geneva Steel and the American West" (M.A. thesis, University of Utah, 2011).

84. The best account of the Geneva plant sale is in Steinmeyer, "Disposition of Surplus War Property," 204–24. On Kaiser's interest, see Kaiser to Symington, 25 Sept. 1945, and copy of Nov. 1945 Kaiser testimony before Senate Military Affairs Committee, both in folder U.S. Gov't, Navy 1945, carton 153, Kaiser Papers.

85. "Steel in the West," *Fortune* 31 (Feb. 1945): 130–33, 258–61; Kenneth Warren, *The American Steel Industry, 1850–1970: A Geographical Interpretation* (Oxford: Clarendon, 1973), 263–77; Foster, *Henry J. Kaiser*, 98–106.

86. White, *Billions for Defense*, 108–9; Vernon Herbert and Attilio Bisio, *Synthetic Rubber: A Project That Had to Succeed* (Westport, CT: Greenwood, 1985), 143, 163–65.

87. WAA, *Synthetic Rubber Plants and Facilities: First Supplementary Report* (Washington, DC: GPO, 1946); idem, *Synthetic Rubber Plants and Facilities: Second Supplementary and Final Report* (Washington, DC: GPO, 1946); Robert Solo, "The Sale of the Synthetic Rubber Plants," *Journal of Industrial Economics* 2, no 1 (Nov. 1953): 32–43.

88. Hill to Krug, 9 Jan. 1948, folder National Securities Resources Board, box 91, Krug Papers, LOC; *Report with Respect to the Development of a Program for Disposal of the Government-Owned Rubber-Producing Facilities* (Washington, DC: RFC, 1949); Solo, "Sale of the Synthetic Rubber Plants"; Stanley E. Boyle, "Government Promotion of Monopoly Power: An Examination of the Sale of the Synthetic Rubber Industry," *Journal of Industrial Economics* 9, no. 2 (Apr. 1961): 151–69; Herbert and Bisio, *Synthetic Rubber*, 138–41, 166–67.

89. "Synthetic Rubber: All Aboard!," *Fortune* 48 (July 1953): 71–72; "Profit $10,000,000 on Rubber Plants," *NYT*, 14 June 1955; White, *Billions for Defense*, 109; Herbert and Bisio, *Synthetic Rubber*, 171–90.

90. Boyle, "Government Promotion of Monopoly Power"; Charles F. Phillips, Jr., "Market Performance in the Synthetic Rubber Industry," *Journal of Industrial Economics* 9, no. 2 (Apr. 1961): 132–50; Herbert and Bisio, *Synthetic Rubber*, 195–208.

91. John E. Bryan, "General Tire's O'Neil Hails Rubber Industry Solid Front," *Cleveland Plain Dealer*, 25 Mar. 1954; "Sale of Rubber Plants," *Dallas Morning News*, 10 Jan. 1955; "Rubber: A Plan for Freedom," *Time* (16 Mar. 1953): 97–98; "Government: End of a Monopoly," *Time* (27 Dec. 1954): 61.

92. My emphasis on this transformation departs from the central concerns of much of the literature on the subject. According to many of the most strident critics of the MIC, the most striking thing about the nation's giant Cold War defense sector was the way in which it came to entangle all sorts of public and private actors, who came to seem indistinguishable. See, e.g., Joseph D. Phillips, "Economic Effects of the Cold War," in *Corporations and the Cold War*, ed. David Horowitz (New York: Monthly Review, 1969), 190; David F. Noble, *Forces of Production: A Social History of Industrial Automation* (New York: Knopf, 1984), 10–20; Stuart W. Leslie, *The Cold War and American Science: The Military-Industrial-Academic Complex at MIT and Stanford* (New York: Columbia University Press, 1993); Margaret Pugh O'Mara, *Cities of Knowledge: Cold War Science and the Search for the Next Silicon Valley* (Princeton, NJ: Princeton University Press, 2005); James Ledbetter, *Unwarranted Influence: Dwight D. Eisenhower and the Military-Industrial Complex* (New Haven, CT: Yale University Press, 2011), 147–51; Paul A. C. Koistinen, *State of War: The Political Economy of American Warfare, 1945–2011* (Lawrence: University Press of Kansas, 2012), 113–67. A different view of the early Cold War MIC has been developed by a handful of historians and political scientists who have called attention to the ways in which it was shaped—and constrained—by what the political scientist Aaron Friedberg has called America's antistatist "traditional political culture." See Paul G. Pierpaoli, Jr., *Truman and Korea: The Political Culture of the Early Cold War* (Columbia: University of Missouri Press, 1999), 4; Michael J. Hogan, *A Cross of Iron: Harry S. Truman and the Origins of the National Security State, 1945–1954* (New York: Cambridge University Press, 1998), esp. 1–22, 234; Friedberg, *In the Shadow of the Garrison State*. For a slightly earlier exploration of similar themes, see Robert Cuff, "American Mobilization for War, 1917–1945: Political Culture Versus Bureaucratic Administration," in *Mobilization for Total War: The Canadian, American, and British Experience, 1914–1918, 1939–1945*, ed. N. F. Dreiszinger (Waterloo, Ont.: Wilfrid Laurier University Press, 1981), 71–86. My emphasis is closer to that of scholars who have pointed to the rise of a "contract state," or a "hollowed-out state," in which the public sector shed much of its in-house industrial and regulatory capacities. See H. L. Nieberg, *In the Name of Science* (Chicago: Quadrangle, 1966); Walter Adams, "The Military-Industrial Complex and the New Industrial State," *American Economic Review* 58, no. 2 (May 1968): 652–65; Walter A. McDougall, *The Heavens and the Earth: A Political History of the Space Age* (New York: Basic, 1985), 440; Alex Roland, *The Military-Industrial Complex* (Washington, DC: American Historical Association, 2001), 9; Christopher D. McKenna, *The World's Newest Profession: Management Consulting in the Twentieth Century* (New York: Cambridge University Press, 2006),106.

93. U.S. Senate, *Investigation of the National Defense Program, Hearings, Part 31*, 15390; Michael S. Sherry, *Preparing for the Next War: American Plans for Postwar Defense, 1941–1945* (New Haven, CT: Yale University Press, 1977), 102–19; Philip Shiman, *Forging the Sword: Defense Production During the Cold War* (Washington, DC: U.S. Air Force Combat Command, 1997), 55.

94. Edward A. Kolodziej, *The Uncommon Defense and Congress, 1945–1963* (Columbus: Ohio State University Press, 1966), 64–123; John Lewis Gaddis, *Strategies of Containment: A*

Critical Appraisal of Postwar American National Security Policy (New York: Oxford University Press, 1982), 89–95; Melvyn P. Leffler, *A Preponderance of Power: National Security, the Truman Administration, and the Cold War* (Stanford, CA: Stanford University Press, 1992), 220–29, 304–9, 356–60; Hogan, *Cross of Iron*, 69–118, 186–90, 284–314.

95. Iwan W. Morgan, *Eisenhower Versus "The Spenders": The Eisenhower Administration, the Democrats and the Budget, 1953–60* (New York: St. Martin's, 1990), 76–131; Hogan, *Cross of Iron*, 384–418; Friedberg, *In the Shadow of the Garrison State*, 124–39; Gerard Clarfield, *Security with Solvency: Dwight D. Eisenhower and the Shaping of the American Military Establishment* (Westport, CT: Praeger, 1999), 147–58; David L. Snead, *The Gaither Committee, Eisenhower, and the Cold War* (Columbus: Ohio State University Press, 1999).

96. H. E. Bowman to Board of Directors, 22 Oct. 1946, folder 2, Box 2357; board minutes for 4 Dec. 1946, unboxed binder Boeing Board Minutes, 1946–47; Boeing Airplane Co., Report to Stockholders: Year Ended December 31, 1946, all in BHA; Bright, *Jet Makers*, 135–36; Bartholomew H. Sparrow, *From the Outside In: World War II and the American State* (Princeton, NJ: Princeton University Press, 1996), 244–45.

97. SPA, *Aircraft Plants and Facilities* (Washington, DC: GPO, 1946), 20–21.

98. Douglas board minutes for 17 Oct. 1945, in Douglas Board Minutes, 1940–45, BHA; Cook, *Marketing of Surplus War Property*, 35; Shiman, *Forging the Sword*, 40.

99. Transcript of telephone conversation between William M. Allen and Brig. Gen. R. W. Rawlings, 10 June 1946; Col. William D. Eckert memo, 13 Sept. 1946, both in "Case History of Boeing Aircraft Company, Renton, WA," reel A2074, AFHRA.

100. Donald J. Mrozek, "The Truman Administration and the Enlistment of the Aviation Industry in Postwar Defense," *Business History Review* 48, no. 1 (spring 1974): 73–94; Hill, "Business Community and National Defense," 207–38; Hogan, *Cross of Iron*, 103–13; Karen S. Miller, *The Voice of Business: Hill & Knowlton and Postwar Public Relations* (Chapel Hill: University of North Carolina Press, 1999), 31–44.

101. Alling, "History of the Air Materiel Command, 1946," 130; Gary E. Weir, *Forged in War: The Naval-Industrial Complex and American Submarine Construction, 1940–1961* (Washington, DC: Naval Historical Center, 1993), 151; Sparrow, *From the Outside In*, 171; White, *Billions for Defense*, 103–4; Sweeting, "Building the Arsenal of Democracy," 314–40; *Administrative History of the Bureau of Ships*, 4:463–70; Joel R. Davidson, *The Unsinkable Fleet: The Politics of U.S. Navy Expansion in World War II* (Annapolis, MD: Naval Institute Press, 1996), 181.

102. Steinmeyer, "Disposition of Surplus War Property," 196–97, 255–68; White, *Billions for Defense*, 111–12; Shiman, *Forging the Sword*, 44–45.

103. Weir, *Forged in War*, 91–97.

104. Pierpaoli, Jr., *Truman and Korea*, 177–90; Hill, "Business Community and National Defense," 369–72; Elliott V. Converse III, *Rearming for the Cold War, 1945–1960* (Washington, DC: Office of the Secretary of Defense, 2012), 281–82; Friedberg, *In the Shadow of the Garrison State*, 212–21.

105. Donald M. Pattillo, *Pushing the Envelope: The American Aircraft Industry* (Ann Arbor: University of Michigan Press, 1998), 194.

106. Friedberg, *In the Shadow of the Garrison State*, 287; Shiman, *Forging the Sword*, 49; White, *Billions for Defense*, 138–41; Judith Stein, *Running Steel, Running America: Race, Economic Policy, and the Decline of Liberalism* (Chapel Hill: University of North Carolina Press,

1998), 14; Glen Ross Asner, "The Cold War and American Industrial Research" (Ph.D. diss., Carnegie Mellon University, 2006), 174–203; Bank, *From Sword to Shield*, 213–26.

107. Hooks, *Forging the Military-Industrial Complex*, 159, 243; Gregory Hooks and Raymond A. Jussaume, Jr., "Warmaking and the Transformation of the State: Japan and the U.S. in World War II," in *Total War and 'Modernization,'* ed. Yasushi Yamanouchi, J. Victor Koshmann, and Ryuichi Narita (Ithaca, NY: Cornell University Press, 1998), 86–87; Shiman, *Forging the Sword*, 49–53, 69.

108. Meg Jacobs, *Pocketbook Politics: Economic Citizenship in Twentieth-Century America* (Princeton, NJ: Princeton University Press, 2005), 220–31; Jonathan Bell, *The Liberal State on Trial: The Cold War and American Politics in the Truman Years* (New York: Columbia University Press, 2004), 28–30.

109. Sen. Claude Pepper, "The Battle for Democracy at Home and Abroad," transcript of speech delivered in Hollywood, CA, 2 Sept. 1946, folder 11, box 2, series 203B, Claude Pepper Papers, Claude Pepper Library, Florida State University, Tallahassee.

110. George H. Gallup, *The Gallup Poll: Public Opinion, 1935–1971*: vol. 1, *1935–1948* (New York: Random House, 1972), 731.

111. Herman E. Krooss, *Executive Opinion: What Business Leaders Said and Thought on Economic Issues, 1920s–1960s* (Garden City, NY: Doubleday, 1970), 213–16; Elizabeth A. Fones-Wolf, *Selling Free Enterprise: The Business Assault on Labor and Liberalism, 1945–60* (Urbana: University of Illinois Press, 1995); Sanford M. Jacoby, *Modern Manors: Welfare Capitalism Since the New Deal* (Princeton, NJ: Princeton University Press, 1997), 232–35; Hogan, *Cross of Iron*, 426–44; Wendy L. Wall, *Inventing the "American Way": The Politics of Consensus from the New Deal to the Civil Rights Movement* (New York: Oxford University Press, 2008), 201–40; Kim Phillips-Fein, *Invisible Hands: The Making of the Conservative Movement from the New Deal to Reagan* (New York: W. W. Norton, 2009); Kevin M. Kruse, *One Nation Under God: How Corporate America Invented Christian America* (New York: Basic Books, 2015).

112. White, *Billions for Defense*, 135–37; Alonzo L. Hamby, *Man of the People: A Life of Harry S. Truman* (New York: Oxford University Press, 1995), 456–500; Alonzo L. Hamby, "The Vital Center, the Fair Deal, and the Quest for a Liberal Political Economy," *American Historical Review* 77, no. 3 (Jun. 1972): 660–65; Jacobs, *Pocketbook Politics*, 242–43. For a recent account of Truman's electoral victory that emphasizes the lack of support for his domestic policies, see Andrew E. Busch, *Truman's Triumphs: The 1948 Election and the Making of Postwar America* (Lawrence: University Press of Kansas, 2012), 203–4.

113. Bell, *Liberal State on Trial*, 73, 145–46, 198–205, 257.

114. Gary Dean Best, *The Life of Herbert Hoover: Keeper of the Torch, 1933–1964* (New York: Palgrave Macmillan, 2013), 271–72, 294.

115. Ronald C. Moe, *The Hoover Commissions Revisited* (Boulder, CO: Westview, 1982), 24–39; William E. Pemberton, "Struggle for the New Deal: Truman and the Hoover Commission," *Presidential Studies Quarterly* 16, no. 3 (summer 1986): 511–27.

116. *The Hoover Commission Report on Organization of the Executive Branch* (New York: McGraw Hill, [1949]), 402–12; Frank Gervasi, *Big Government: The Meaning and Purpose of the Hoover Commission Report* (New York: Whittlesey House, 1949), 142–55; Peri E. Arnold, "The First Hoover Commission and the Managerial Presidency," *Journal of Politics* 38, no. 1 (Feb. 1976): 46–70; Moe, *Hoover Commissions Revisited*, 48–51; McKenna, *World's Newest*

Profession, 87–93; Joanna L. Grisinger, *The Unwieldy American State: Administrative Politics Since the New Deal* (New York: Cambridge University Press, 2012), 192–93; Best, *Life of Herbert Hoover*, 334–39.

117. "How the RFC Got That Way," *Fortune* 43 (Apr. 1951): 81–82; "The Slow Death of RFC," *Fortune* 47 (Apr. 1953): 119, 252; Andrew J. Dunar, The *Truman Scandals and the Politics of Morality* (Columbia: University of Missouri Press,1984); Hamby, *Man of the People*, 503–4, 585–86; Grisinger, *Unwieldy American State*, 137–38.

118. Hamby, *Man of the People*, 576–79.

119. Bert G. Hickman, *The Korean War and United States Economic Activity, 1950–1952* (New York: National Bureau of Economic Research, 1955), 9; Morgan, *Eisenhower Versus "The Spenders,"* 57; Hogan, *Cross of Iron*, 350–55; Charles K. Hyde, *Riding the Roller Coaster: A History of the Chrysler Corporation* (Detroit: Wayne State University Press, 2003), 167–68; Colleen Doody, *Detroit's Cold War: The Origins of Postwar Conservatism* (Urbana: University of Illinois Press, 2013), 103–5.

120. Krooss, *Executive Opinion*, 248–63; Robert Griffith, "Dwight D. Eisenhower and the Corporate Commonwealth," *American Historical Review* 87, no. 1 (February 1982): 87–122; Chester J. Pach, Jr., and Elmo Richardson, *The Presidency of Dwight D. Eisenhower*, rev. ed. (Lawrence: University Press of Kansas, 1991), 57; Morgan, *Eisenhower Versus "The Spenders,"* 16–17; M. Stephen Weatherford, "Presidential Leadership and Ideological Consistency: Were There 'Two Eisenhowers' in Economic Policy?," *Studies in American Political Development* 16 (fall 2002): 111–37; James T. Patterson, *Grand Expectations: The United States, 1945–1974* (New York: Oxford University Press, 1996), 270–71; Alex Roland, "The Grim Paraphernalia: Eisenhower and the Garrison State," in *Forging the Shield: Eisenhower and National Security for the 21st Century*, ed. Dennis E. Showalter (Chicago: Imprint, 2005), 18–19; Steven Wagner, *Eisenhower Republicanism: Pursuing the Middle Way* (DeKalb: Northern Illinois University Press, 2006), 13.

121. Moe, *Hoover Commissions Revisited*, 82–90, 105–7.

122. Best, *Life of Herbert Hoover*, 393.

123. Neil MacNeil and Harold W. Metz, *The Hoover Report, 1953–1955: What It Means to You as Citizen and Taxpayer* (New York: Macmillan, 1956), 3–4, 154–55.

124. Ibid., 100–101.

125. Commission on Organization of the Executive Branch of the Government, *Subcommittee Report on Business Enterprises of the Department of Defense* (Washington, DC: GPO, 1955), 34–59; MacNeil and Metz, *Hoover Report, 1953–1955*, 158–61, 304; Moe, *Hoover Commissions Revisited*, 97.

126. MacNeil and Metz, *Hoover Report, 1953–1955*, 156.

127. Alvin Shuster, "U.S. Reduces Role as Business Rival," *NYT*, 13 June 1955; MacNeil and Metz, *Hoover Report, 1953–1955*, 173; Roger W. Lotchin, *Fortress California, 1910–1961: From Warfare to Welfare* (New York: Oxford University Press, 1992), 240–41; McKenna, *World's Newest Profession*, 81–82.

128. Charles C. Alexander, *Holding the Line: The Eisenhower Era, 1952–1961* (Bloomington: Indiana University Press, 1975), 161–63; Phyllis Komarek de Luna, *Public Versus Private Power During the Truman Administration: A Study of Fair Deal Liberalism* (New York: Peter Lang, 1997); Wyatt Wells, "Public Power in the Eisenhower Administration," *Journal of Policy History* 20, no. 2 (2008): 227–62; Grisinger, *Unwieldy American State*, 199–200.

129. Harold Orlans, *Contracting for Atoms* (Washington, DC: Brookings Institution, 1967); Richard G. Hewlett and Jack M. Holl, *Atoms for Peace and War, 1953–1961* (Berkeley: University of California Press, 1989), 7–11, 127–39, 406–15; Brian Balogh, *Chain Reaction: Expert Debate and Public Participation in American Commercial Nuclear Power, 1945–1975* (New York: Cambridge University Press, 1991), 69–133.

130. White, *Billions for Defense*, 142; Wilson quoted in Commission on Organization of the Executive Branch of the Government, *Subcommittee Report on Business Enterprises of the Department of Defense*, 69.

131. Boeing *Annual Report*, 1958.

132. U.S. Senate, *Investigation of the National Defense Program, Hearings, Part 31*, 15394.

133. James William Spurlock, "The Bell Telephone Laboratories and the Military-Industrial Complex: The Jewett-Buckley Years, 1925–1951" (Ph.D. diss., George Washington University, 2007), 343–48.

134. Norman Polmar and Thomas B. Allen, *Rickover* (New York: Simon & Schuster, 1982), 146–47; Weir, *Forged in War*, 117, 162–95.

135. Weir, *Forged in War*, 164, 198–225; Thomas P. Hughes, *American Genesis: A Century of Innovation and Technological Enthusiasm, 1870–1970* (New York: Viking, 1989), 433; Francis Duncan, *Rickover: The Struggle for Excellence* (Annapolis, MD: Naval Institute Press, 2001), 114; Shiman, *Forging the Sword*, 61–62.

136. Mark D. Mandeles, *The Development of the B-52 and Jet Propulsion: A Case Study in Organizational Innovation* (Maxwell, AL: Air University Press, 1998); Stephen B. Johnson, *The United States Air Force and the Culture of Innovation, 1945–1965* (Washington, DC: Air Force History and Museums Program, 2002), 36–39; Martin J. Collins, *Cold War Laboratory: RAND, the Air Force, and the American State, 1945–1950* (Washington, DC: Smithsonian Institution Press, 2002), 52–53.

137. Bright, *Jet Makers*, 67; Johnson, *USAF and the Culture of Innovation*, 50–55; Shiman, *Forging the Sword*, 56–60; Converse, *Rearming for the Cold War*, 233–41.

138. Harry B. Yoshpe and Charles F. Franke, *Production for Defense* (Washington, DC: Industrial College for the Armed Forces, 1968), 20; Morgan, *Eisenhower Versus "The Spenders,"* 131; I. N. Fisher and G. R. Hall, *Defense Profit Policy in the United States and the United Kingdom* (Santa Monica, CA: RAND, 1968), 4.

139. Michael H. Armacost, *The Politics of Weapons Innovation: The Thor-Jupiter Controversy* (New York: Columbia University Press, 1969); Jacob Neufeld, *The Development of Ballistic Missiles in the United States Air Force, 1945–1960* (Washington, DC: Office of Air Force History, 1990), 150; Friedberg, *In the Shadow of the Garrison State*, 272–77; Joan Lisa Bromberg, *NASA and the Space Industry* (Baltimore: Johns Hopkins University Press, 1999), 28–29; Converse, *Rearming for the Cold War*, 592–93, 623–30.

140. Thomas P. Hughes, *Rescuing Prometheus* (New York: Pantheon, 1998), 69–139; Johnson, *USAF and the Culture of Innovation*, 59–116; Converse, *Rearming for the Cold War*, 457–521; Neil Sheehan, *A Fiery Peace in a Cold War: Bernard Schriever and the Ultimate Weapon* (New York: Random House, 2009).

141. John C. Lonnquest and David F. Winkler, *To Defend and Deter: The Legacy of the United States Cold War Missile Program* (Washington, DC: DoD Legacy Resource Management Program Cold War Project, 1996), 67–73. On the Navy's missile program, see Harvey M. Sapolsky, *The Polaris System Development: Bureaucratic and Programmatic Success in Government* (Cambridge, MA: Harvard University Press, 1972).

142. Glenn E. Bugos, *Engineering the F-4 Phantom II: Parts into Systems* (Annapolis, MD: Naval Institute Press, 1996); Converse, *Rearming for the Cold War*, 573–75; Friedberg, *In the Shadow of the Garrison State*, 269–80; Johnson, *USAF and the Culture of Innovation*, 34.

143. Robert J. Gordon, "$45 Billion of U.S. Private Investment Has Been Mislaid," *American Economic Review* 59, no. 3 (Jun. 1969): 231; McDougall, *Heavens and the Earth*, 362–88; Howard E. McCurdy, *Inside NASA: High Technology and Organizational Change in the U.S. Space Program* (Baltimore: Johns Hopkins University Press, 1993), 134–41; Bromberg, *NASA and the Space Industry*, 41, 187–88; McKenna, *World's Newest Profession*, 101–6.

144. Kolodziej, *Uncommon Defense and Congress*, 405–8; Robert M. Collins, *More: The Politics of Economic Growth in Postwar America* (New York: Oxford University Press, 2000), 56–57.

145. Bright, *Jet Makers*, 70–72; Walter S. Poole, *Adapting to Flexible Response, 1960–1968* (Washington, DC: Historical Office of the Office of the Secretary of Defense, 2013). On the discomfort that the winner-take-all orders created for shipbuilders, see Ralph L. Snow, *Bath Iron Works: The First Hundred Years* (Bath: Maine Maritime Museum, 1987), 478–84.

146. William L. Baldwin, *The Structure of the Defense Market, 1955–1964* (Durham, NC: Duke University Press, 1967), 182–86.

147. "Shipyards: Who Gets the Ax?," *Newsweek* (23 Nov. 1964): 82; "The Pentagon's Big Cutback of Bases," *Newsweek* (30 Nov. 1964): 73–74; "The Nation: Defense," *Time* (27 Nov. 1964): 29–30; Bright, *Jet Makers*, 66; Friedberg, *In the Shadow of the Garrison State*, 291.

148. Edward C. Ezell, "The Search for a Lightweight Rifle: The M14 and M16 Rifles" (Ph.D. diss., Case Western Reserve University, 1969); Thomas L. McNaugher, *The M16 Controversies: Military Organizations and Weapons Acquisition* (New York: Praeger, 1984); Friedberg, *In the Shadow of the Garrison State*, 277–80; Shiman, *Forging the Sword*, 70–72; Poole, *Adapting to Flexible Response*, 133–41.

149. James M. Knox, "Private Enterprise in Shipbuilding," *Harvard Business Review* 24, no. 1 (autumn 1945): 83–84; James W. Culliton et al., *The Use and Disposition of Ships at the End of World War II* (Washington, DC: GPO, 1945), 203–5.

150. James W. Culliton, "Economics and Shipbuilding," in *The Shipbuilding Business in the United States of America*, ed. F. G. Fassett (New York: Society of Naval Architects and Marine Engineers, 1948), 1:8; Rear Admiral F. G. Crisp, "Navy Yards," in *Shipbuilding Business in the United States*, 2:224.

151. "Transfer of Navy-Yard Work Asked," *Seattle Daily Times*, 25 Sept. 1961; Shiman, *Forging the Sword*, 69–70.

152. Arthur Andersen & Co., *Report on Survey and Analysis of Differences Between U.S. Navy Shipbuilding Costs at Naval and Private Shipyards* (Chicago, 1962); U.S. Bureau of Ships, *Analysis of Arthur Andersen and Company, Shipbuilding Cost Study* (Washington, DC, 1962); "Big and Urgent Navy Business in Brooklyn," *Fortune* 66 (Nov. 1962): 133–38; "More Work for Private Shipyards," *Forbes* 94 (1 Dec. 1964): 30.

153. Victor Risel, "Navy Yard Costs High," *New Orleans Times-Picayune*, 7 Jan. 1964.

154. "Big and Urgent Navy Business in Brooklyn," *Fortune* 66 (Nov. 1962): 138.

155. "More Work for Private Shipyards," *Forbes* 94 (1 Dec. 1964): 30; Norman Friedman, *U.S. Submarines Since 1945: An Illustrated Design History* (Annapolis, MD: Naval Institute Press, 1994), 237–39; Frederick R. Black, *Charlestown Navy Yard, 1890–1973* (Boston: National Park Service, 1988), 2:802–11; Fritz Peter Hamer, "A Southern City Enters the Twentieth Century: Charleston, Its Navy Yard, and World War II, 1940–1948" (Ph.D. diss., University of South Carolina, 1998), 259–63.

156. "Hurrah for McNamara's Ax," *Life* (4 Dec. 1964): 4.

157. Friedberg, *In the Shadow of the Garrison State*, 256–64.

158. Yoshpe and Franke, *Production for Defense*, 45; Jonathan Soffer, "The National Association of Manufacturers and the Militarization of American Conservatism," *Business History Review* 75 (winter 2001): 795–96; Hugh Rockoff, *America's Economic Way of War: War and the US Economy from the Spanish-American War to the Persian Gulf War* (New York: Cambridge University Press, 2012), 288–89; "Contract Renegotiation: It Destroys Incentive to Cut Defense Costs," *Time* (14 July 1958): 76; Sanford Watzman, "Little Watchdog of the Dollar Warriors," *Nation* 206 (4 Mar. 1968): 297–300; Meredith H. Lair, *Armed with Abundance: Consumerism & Soldiering in the Vietnam War* (Chapel Hill: University of North Carolina Press, 2011).

159. Draft, chapter 3 of proposed Ickes book on planning (1946), reel 7, Biographical Memoirs and Sketches, Ickes Papers, LOC.

160. Nieberg, *In the Name of Science*, 184–243; Adams, "Military-Industrial Complex and the New Industrial State," 655.

161. Bromberg, *NASA and the Space Industry*, 66.

162. Eugene Gholz, "The Curtiss-Wright Corporation and Cold War–Era Defense Procurement: A Challenge to Military-Industrial Complex Theory," *Journal of Cold War Studies* 2, no. 1 (winter 2000): 35–75; Mark R. Wilson. "Economy and National Defense," in *The Encyclopedia of Military Science*, ed. G. Kurt Piehler and M. Houston Johnson V (Los Angeles: SAGE, 2013), 503–9.

163. Friedberg, *In the Shadow of the Garrison State*, 287–95, 342–43.

164. Hill, "Business Community and National Defense," 425–37; Soffer, "National Association of Manufacturers and the Militarization of American Conservatism," 775–805.

Conclusion

1. P. W. Singer, *Corporate Warriors: The Rise of the Privatized Military Industry* (Ithaca, NY: Cornell University Press, 2003); Deborah D. Avant, *The Market for Force: The Consequences of Privatizing Security* (New York: Cambridge University Press, 2005); Philip L. Shiman, "Defense Acquisition in an Uncertain World: The Post–Cold War Era, 1990–2000," in *Providing the Means of War: Perspectives in Defense Acquisition, 1945–2000*, ed. Shannon A. Brown (Washington, DC: U.S. Army Center of Military History, 2005), 283–315; Beth Bailey, *America's Army: Making the All-Volunteer Force* (Cambridge, MA: Harvard University Press, 2009); Allison Stanger, *One Nation Under Contract: The Outsourcing of American Power and the Future of Foreign Policy* (New Haven, CT: Yale University Press, 2009); Laura A. Dickinson, *Outsourcing War & Peace: Preserving Public Values in a World of Privatized Foreign Affairs* (New Haven, CT: Yale University Press, 2011); Jennifer Mittelstadt, *The Rise of the Military Welfare State* (Cambridge, MA: Harvard University Press, 2015).

2. On "left-liberals" in U.S. history, see Doug Rossinow, "Partners for Progress? Liberals and Radicals in the Long Twentieth Century," in *Making Sense of American Liberalism*, ed. Jonathan Bell and Timothy Stanley (Urbana: University of Illinois Press, 2012), 1–37.

3. Among the most sophisticated works in this now massive literature are Lisa McGirr, *Suburban Warriors: The Origins of the New American Right* (Princeton, NJ: Princeton University Press, 2001); Steven P. Miller, *Billy Graham and the Rise of the Republican South* (Philadelphia: University of Pennsylvania Press, 2009); Jennifer Burns, *Goddess of the Market: Ayn Rand and the American Right* (New York: Oxford University Press, 2009); Darren Dochuk,

From Bible Belt to Sunbelt: Plain Folk Religion, Grassroots Politics, and the Rise of Evangelical Conservatism (New York: W. W. Norton, 2011); and Angus Burgin, *The Great Persuasion: Reinventing Free Markets Since the Depression* (Cambridge, MA: Harvard University Press, 2012). Among the many other works that focus on the post-1945 period are George H. Nash, *The Conservative Intellectual Movement in America: Since 1945* (New York: Basic Books, 1976); Donald T. Critchlow, *The Conservative Ascendancy: How the GOP Right Made Political History* (Cambridge, MA: Harvard University Press, 2007). For more citations, see the notes to the Introduction and to Chapters 3 and 6.

4. Here, albeit with more emphasis on the World War II years, I concur with the arguments of works such as Elizabeth A. Fones-Wolf, *Selling Free Enterprise: The Business Assault on Labor and Liberalism, 1945–60* (Urbana: University of Illinois Press, 1995); Kim Phillips-Fein, *Invisible Hands: The Making of the Conservative Movement from the New Deal to Reagan* (New York: W. W. Norton, 2009); Kevin M. Kruse, *One Nation Under God: How Corporate America Invented Christian America* (New York: Basic Books, 2015).

5. David J. Vogel, *Fluctuating Fortunes: The Political Power of Business in America* (New York: Basic Books, 1989); Benjamin C. Waterhouse, *Lobbying America: The Politics of Business from Nixon to NAFTA* (Princeton, NJ: Princeton University Press, 2013). On 1970s role of John M. Olin, former leader of an important World War II ammunition-making contractor, see Alice O'Connor, "Financing the Counterrevolution," in *Rightward Bound: Making America Conservative in the 1970s*, ed. Bruce J. Schulman and Julian E. Zelizer (Cambridge, MA: Harvard University Press, 2008), 148–68.

6. Mary O. Furner, "From 'State Interference' to the 'Return of the Market': The Rhetoric of Economic Regulation from the Old Gilded Age to the New," in *Government and Markets: Toward a New Theory of Regulation*, ed. Edward J. Balleisen and David A. Moss (New York: Cambridge University Press, 2012), 141; see also Suzanne Mettler, *The Submerged State: How Invisible Government Policies Undermine American Democracy* (Chicago: University of Chicago Press, 2011).

7. Vernon Herbert and Attilio Bisio, *Synthetic Rubber: The Project That Had to Succeed* (Westport, CT: Greenwood, 1985), 223–24; consider also the implications of James T. Sparrow, *Warfare State: World War II Americans and the Age of Big Government* (New York: Oxford University Press, 2012).

8. For one recent set of essays on this issue, see Jody Freeman and Martha Minow, eds., *Government by Contract: Outsourcing and American Democracy* (Cambridge, MA: Harvard University Press, 2009).

9. Gerald T. White, *Billions for Defense: Government Financing by the Defense Plant Corporation During World War II* (University: University of Alabama Press, 1980), 146–51.

10. For a suggestive history of declining public capacities in an area in which the national security and health-care spheres overlap, see Kendall Hoyt, *Long Shot: Vaccines for National Defense* (Cambridge, MA: Harvard University Press, 2012).

Index

defense spending, 61, 266–67, 272. *See also* munitions
Democratic Party, 8, 35, 130, 227
destroyer escorts (DEs), 153–55, 179
destroyers, 2, 15, 52–53, 176, 179, 200
Desvernine, Raoul E., 31, 97–98
Detroit Tank Arsenal, 71–72, 122, 150–52. *See also* Chrysler Corporation
Douglas, Donald, 57–58, 168
Douglas Aircraft Company, 50, 55, 72; as B-17 producer, 89; conflicts with AAF, 166, 168; as leading contractor, 65, 182; and voluntary price reductions, 171
Dow Chemical Company, 76, 166, 182, 260
Dravo Corporation, 155, 176–77
Du Pont, Pierre S., 18, 30–31
Du Pont de Nemours, E. I., & Company, 120; concerns about seizure, 194; considers ending munitions work, 47; as leading contractor, 64–66, 69–70, 80, 182; and plutonium, 80–81, 169; pressured to lower prices, 168–69; and profits, 184–87; struggles with Nye Committee, 36–37; and taxes, 163; and World War I, 16–20
Durr, Clifford J., 73, 251

Eastman Kodak Company, 64, 81, 171, 182, 184
Eberstadt, Ferdinand, 143–44, 250
Echols, Oliver P., 166, 267
economic concentration, 64, 82–90, 255, 261. *See also* antitrust
Eisenhower, Dwight D., 43, 266, 273
Electric Boat Company, 15, 41, 52, 155; as leader of nuclear submarine program, 276–77; as operator of GOCO yard at Groton, 66, 268–69; public relations efforts by, 103
electricity and electric utilities, 26–29, 79, 149. *See also* Tennessee Valley Authority
Emergency Fleet Corporation, 12, 15, 21. *See also* ships and shipbuilding industry
Emerson Electric Company, 86, 168
Excess Profits Tax (EPT), 20, 35–38, 161–64, 172–73. *See also* taxes and tax policy
explosives and explosives industry: expansion for World War II, 69–70, 80; government investment in, 62, 64; in World War I, 8, 15–18, 25–26. *See also* Atlas Powder; Du Pont de Nemours, E. I., & Company; Hercules Powder Co.; Tennessee Valley Authority

Feasibility Dispute, 147–49
Federal Shipbuilding and Dry Dock Company, 52, 65, 191, 200–207. *See also* United States Steel Corporation
Federal Trade Commission (FTC), 10, 26
films, 101, 105, 121
Fleet, Reuben H., 194, 209
Flynn, John T., 37–38, 145
Forbes, B. C., 96, 107, 126
Ford, Henry, 26, 198
Ford Motor Company: advertising, 106; as aircraft engine manufacturer, 74; experience with on-site inspectors and auditors, 146–47; as leading contractor, 64–65, 182; struggles with strikes and unions, 197–98; and tank program, 150–52. *See also* Willow Run
Forrestal, James V., 61, 210, 250; defends unions, 118; and renegotiation, 174–75; and shipbuilding cutbacks, 154; threatens seizure, 214
France, 36, 55–56, 194, 253
Fuller, Walter D., 203–4, 206, 250

Gaffney Manufacturing Company, 234, 236
Gary, Elbert H., 9, 46
General Accounting Office (GAO), 146–47, 245
General Electric Company (GE), 54, 65, 87, 182–84, 276
General Motors Corporation (GM), 2, 87; advertising and public relations, 103, 105; Allison Division of, 58, 65; Buick Division of, 74; Chevrolet Division of, 65, 74; as leading contractor, 64–66, 182; profits, 180, 184–87; reconversion, 247; and surplus war plant, 259–60; and tank program, 65, 72, 150–52; taxes, 163; voluntary price reductions by, 171
GFE. *See* government-furnished equipment
Gibbs & Cox, 53–54
Girdler, Tom, 97, 106, 209
Glenn L. Martin Company. *See* Martin, Glenn L., Company
Goodyear Tire and Rubber Company, 80, 235

labor unions, 11, 22–23, 119, 190–240. *See also* American Federation of Labor; Congress of Industrial Organizations; strikes; *names of specific unions*
Land, Emory S. ("Jerry"), 41, 68–69, 80, 219
landing vessels and landing craft, 2, 154–55
Lend-Lease, 61
Lewis, John L., 214–16
Liberty League, 31
Liberty ships, 68–69, 80, 149, 177, 179, 258. *See also* ships and shipbuilding industry
licensing arrangements, 74, 85–86, 320 n.120
Lilienthal, David E., 9, 28, 130–31
Lincoln, James F., 108, 174, 252
Little Steel Formula, 214–15
lobbying, 41–42, 83, 267–68, 282, 287
Lockheed Aircraft Corporation, 55–56, 58; advertising, 105; as B-17 producer, 89; financial performance of, 58; as leading contractor, 65, 182; and paperwork, 141; subcontracting by, 84

M4 ("Sherman") medium tanks, 72, 150–52
machine tools, 62, 104, 268, 315 n.73
magnesium and magnesium industry, 62, 64, 76, 79
maintenance of membership, 192, 199–222, 232–36
Manhattan Project. *See* atomic bomb program
Mare Island Naval Shipyard, 64, 122
Maritime Commission. *See* U.S. Maritime Commission
Martin, Glenn L., 57–58
Martin, Glenn L., Company, 55, 72, 81; conflict with military officers, 166; as leading contractor, 65, 182
Materiel Command (AAF), 4, 88–89, 145–47, 168, 276–77. *See also* Army Air Forces
McAdoo, William Gibbs, 7, 12–13, 19, 21–22, 25
McNamara, Robert S., 279–84
meatpacking industry, 10, 236–37
merchant marine and merchant ships. *See* ships and shipbuilding industry; U.S. Maritime Commission
MIC. *See* military-industrial complex
midsize manufacturing firms, 49, 85–88, 173–75. *See also* small business

military-industrial complex (MIC), 265–85, 359 n.92
missiles, 277–78
monopsony, 166–67
Monsanto Chemical Corporation, 80, 103, 221
Montgomery Ward and Company, 191, 193, 220–31. *See also* Avery, Sewell L.
Morgan, J. P., 12, 19, 26
munitions: debates over, in 1930s, 34–35; output, 76, 244; spending on, by category, 309 n.3. *See also* Nye Committee; *specific categories of weapons*
Muscle Shoals (Alabama). *See* Tennessee Valley Authority

National Aeronautics and Space Administration (NASA), 278–79
National Association of Manufacturers (NAM): concerns about war plant, 251; opposition to government competition, 23–24; opposition to New Deal, 31; opposition to maintenance of membership, 208; opposition to seizures, 206, 213, 238–39; and paperwork, 141; on profits, 179–80; on taxes, 161–62; wartime public relations efforts, 94–108, 120, 127–30
National Council of American Shipbuilders, 41–42
National Defense Advisory Commission (NDAC), 60
National Defense Mediation Board (NDMB), 197–207
National Labor Relations Act of 1935. *See* Wagner Act
National Labor Relations Board (NLRB), 190, 204, 231
National Resources Planning Board (NRPB), 251–52
National War Labor Board (NWLB): and coal industry, 214–15; and Hughes Tool case, 231–32; and Humble Oil case, 232–33; and Ken-Rad case, 219–20; and Montgomery Ward case, 221–22; and threat of coercion, 213; in World War I, 11; in World War II, 207–8, 212. *See also* maintenance of membership
Naval Aircraft Factory, 16, 41
Naval Research Laboratory, 16, 276

Acknowledgments

My research and writing of this book, which took place over the course of about a decade, was helped along by dozens of people and institutions. I was fortunate to receive grant support from my home institution, the University of North Carolina at Charlotte, via its faculty research grants and small grants programs, as well as a Frances Lumsden Gwynn Award, made possible by the generosity of Ruth Shaw. I could not have completed the book without the grants and fellowships I received from the John M. Olin Institute for Strategic Studies at Harvard University; the Harry S. Truman Library Institute; the Hagley Museum and Library; and the National Endowment for the Humanities. (Any views, findings, conclusions, or recommendations expressed in this book do not necessarily reflect those of the National Endowment for the Humanities.)

The research for this book was conducted in many libraries and archives across the United States. I am grateful to all of the people who help to maintain and staff those facilities. In particular, I thank Marcie T. Green and Sylvester Jackson at the Air Force Historical Research Agency; Ginny Kilander, Shaun Hayes, and Shannon Maier at the American Heritage Center in Laramie, Wyoming; Janet Caldwell at the Bedford (Ohio) Historical Society; Linda Skolarus, John Bowen, and Terry Hoover at the Benson Ford Research Center in Dearborn, Michigan; Mike Lombardi and Tom Lubbesmeyer at the Boeing Historical Archives in Bellevue, Washington; James Cross at the Special Collections Library, Clemson University; Barbara Thompson and Mark Bowden at the Detroit Public Library; Katie McCormick and Robert Rubero at the Claude Pepper Library, Florida State University; Marge McNinch, Lucas Clawson, Carol Lockman, and Roger Horowitz at the Hagley Museum and Library; the staff at the Library of Congress Manuscripts Division, in Washington, D.C., and at National Archives II in College Park, Maryland; Scott Forsythe at the Great Lakes division of the National Archives, in Chicago; Scott Gower at the National

Defense University Library; Matt Piersol at the Nebraska State Historical Society Library; John Miller and Craig Holbert at the Special Collections department of the libraries of the University of Akron; David Kessler at the Bancroft Library, University of California, Berkeley; Margaret Hrabe and Greg Johnson at the Albert and Shirley Small Special Collections Library, at the University of Virginia; and Mary Virginia Currie at the Virginia Historical Society. Thanks also to Ann Davis, head of the interlibrary loan office at Atkins Library at UNC Charlotte.

During the whole time that I worked on this book, I had the good fortune to be a part of the history department at the University of North Carolina at Charlotte. For their generous support and encouragement of my work, I thank the dean of my college, Nancy Gutierrez, and my department chairs: John Smail, Dan Dupre, and Jurgen Buchenau. I thank all of my colleagues for their support. For their thoughtful suggestions for improving early draft material that made its way into this book, I owe special thanks to Jurgen Buchenau, Karen Cox, Jerry Dávila, Dan Dupre, Maren Ehlers, Karen Flint, David Goldfield, Cheryl Hicks, Jim Hogue, David Johnson, Jill Massino, Shep McKinley, Gregory Mixon, Heather Perry, Ritika Prasad, Steve Sabol, John Smail, John David Smith, Peter Thorsheim, and Jim Walsh.

Over the past several years, I have been fortunate to be able to talk about the book-in-progress with dozens of students and professional colleagues, who offered me valuable criticism and encouragement. I thank the audiences at presentations I made at workshops, seminars, and lectures, including those at Charles University and the American Center in Prague, Czech Republic; the École des Hautes Études en Sciences Sociales, in Paris; Florida State University; the Heidelberg Center for American Studies in Heidelberg, Germany; the History of the Military, War and Society Seminar at the National Humanities Center in North Carolina; Lyon 2 University in France; the Olin Institute for Strategic Studies at Harvard; the Organization of American Historians; the Policy History Conference; Rutgers University; the Society for Military History; Temple University; the University of Georgia; the University of Paris–Diderot; the University of Texas, Austin; and the University of Washington. For their encouragement and valuable suggestions, I thank especially Beth Bailey, Steve Bank, Nicolas Barreyre, Michael Bernstein, Steve Berry, Dirk Bönker, Elliott Converse, Agnès Delahaye, Jason Doom, Mary Dudziak, Dan Ernst, Maria Fanis, David Farber, Robert Ferguson, Alex Field, Liz Fones-Wolf, Patrick Fridenson, Walter

Friedman, Jason Gart, Eugene Gholz, Terry Gough, Joanna Grisinger, Thomas Heinrich, Romain Huret, Beth Kier, Dick Kohn, Felicia Kornbluh, Kryštof Kozák, Ron Krebs, Dan Kryder, Jim Lacey, Lorenz Lüthi, Laura McEnaney, Chuck McShane, Ajay Mehrotra, Stephen Mihm, Polly Myers, Kurt Piehler, Alex Roland, Sebastian Rosato, Steve Rosen, Mick Rowlinson, Phil Scranton, David Sicilia, Ben Smith, Jim Sparrow, Paul Starr, Christopher Tassava, Dominic Tierney, Monica Duffy Toft, Gyorgy Toth, Gail Triner, Steve Usselman, Jean-Christian Vinel, Dan Wadhwani, Jessica Wang, and Eugene White. Another historian who encouraged and inspired me was the late Tom McCraw, who knew a good deal about the subject of this book and warned me not to mess it up. Tom, I did my best.

As I was finishing the manuscript, I had the good fortune to spend a year teaching, and learning, at the Heidelberg Center for American Studies, in Heidelberg, Germany. I am thankful to everyone at HCA, including Detlef Junker, Wilfried Mausbach, John Turner, Tobias Endler, Anthony Santoro, and—most especially, for all their warm friendship and generosity—Anja Schüler and Manfred Berg.

Some colleagues, friends, and family members did me the great favor of reading and commenting on rough drafts of chapters. For this hard work, which helped point the way to important revisions, I owe special thanks to Ed Balleisen, Kate Epstein, Jeff Fear, Shane Hamilton, Richard John, Anne Kornhauser, Rowena Olegario, Kim Phillips-Fein, Gail Radford, Hugh Rockoff, Ellie Shermer, Bat Sparrow, Ben Waterhouse, Diane Wilson, and Gary Wilson.

A few hardy souls agreed to read one or more lengthy drafts of the entire manuscript. Their suggestions for revision were essential, as was their encouragement. So thank you, thank you, to the book's main editors: Andrew Cohen, Christine Haynes, Bob Lockhart, Mark Rose, and Jason Scott Smith.

During the time that it took for me to research and write this book, my wife Christine Haynes and I were busy raising our two sons, Oliver and Simon. Now they are old enough to ask to be thanked for their support. Well, boys, thank you. It has been an honor to be with you and love you, as you have grown up, from infants into accomplished young men.

I dedicate this book to Christine, who did much more than make it possible for me to complete it. Thank you, Christine, for your companionship, and for all you've done to lead us into so many adventures, foreign and domestic, over the last couple of decades. You make everything more beautiful and exciting—past, present, and future.

www.ingramcontent.com/pod-product-compliance
Ingram Content Group UK Ltd.
Pitfield, Milton Keynes, MK11 3LW, UK
UKHW042108180325
456433UK00002B/43